Nursing and the Law

Second Edition

Sue Dill Calloway

PROFESSIONAL
EDUCATION SYSTEMS, INC.
®

This publication is designed to provide general information to the reader. The procedures and advice reflect currently accepted practice. However, they cannot be considered absolute and universal recommendation. Nursing law is constantly changing. This publication should not be utilized as a substitute for professional service in specific situations. If legal advice or other expert assistance is required, the service of a professional should be sought. Each state has its own set of special laws known as statutes. At the time of this printing, Professional Education Systems, Inc., has statute manuals available for almost all states. The statute manuals are sold separately and are meant to supplement this text.

For information on the state statute manuals and other PESI manuals, audiotapes and videotapes, please contact Customer Relations at the above toll-free number.

ISBN 0-941161-23-4

*Portions of Chapters 8 and 9 of this book are taken from **Nursing Ethics and the Law**, copyright 1986 by Professional Education Systems, Inc.*

All previously published material included in this book is reprinted with permission.

AUTHOR

SUE DILL CALLOWAY has been employed in the nursing profession for more than 13 years and is an emergency room nurse at Mercy Hospital in Columbus, Ohio. She is also an attorney, and has legal experience in medical malpractice defense for physicians, nurses and other health professionals.
Ms. Calloway received her A.D.N. from Central Ohio Technical College. Her B.A., B.S.N. and J.D. degrees are from Capital University in Columbus, Ohio. She is past president of the Central Ohio Emergency Nurses Association (ENA) and is counsel for the state ENA. She is a member of the American Nurses' Association, Ohio Nurses' Association, The American Association of Nurse Attorneys, and the Ohio State and Columbus bar associations. She serves as chairperson of the Risk Management Committee and is a member of the Health Care Law and Doctor-Lawyer committees of the Columbus Bar Association.

Ms. Calloway has given numerous presentations locally and nationally to nurses, physicians and attorneys on legal issues for health professionals. She has authored numerous articles and books, including *Nursing and the Law* (Professional Education Systems, Inc., 1986 and 1987) and *Nursing Ethics and the Law* (Professional Education Systems, Inc., 1986). She has also appeared in and written the scripts for two videotapes on malpractice issues, and serves as a medical-legal consultant.

This book is dedicated to my best friend and husband, Ralph E. Dill, and to my parents, Rodney and Geraldine Hobbs. Their support and encouragement were greatly appreciated.

TABLE OF CONTENTS

PREFACE

Approximately one year ago, Butch Severson, Paul Greve and Kathy Mangru Mentink approached me about writing a book for nurses on nursing law. I have always been concerned that nurses are inadequately prepared in legal issues. I recalled my first day as a graduate nurse from an associate degree program. I questioned an order, and the physician responded by saying, "If anything happens, I'll take the responsibility." I realized then that I did not have the necessary legal educational preparation. The truth was that if I gave the wrong dose of medication, not only was I personally responsible, but so was my employer hospital! It was at this time that I decided to do something about it. I decided to be a nurse attorney and work to educate nurses about nursing law.

I worked full time and all the overtime I could get for the next four years. I worked as a nurse while working on my B.A. and B.S.N. degrees. After that I went to law school, during which time I worked weekends at the hospital and part time for the law firm of Porter, Wright, Morris and Arthur. Upon graduation from law school, I spent many hours lecturing and writing articles for nurses on legal issues.

Several years ago, I joined an association of nurse attorneys. I discovered many other nurse attorneys who had also made the commitment to educating nurses on nursing law issues. Professional Education Systems, Inc., has made a firm commitment to this purpose and has already sponsored nursing law programs in nearly all states. These programs have been well received. Because nursing law is constantly changing, it has been decided that these programs should be updated on a yearly basis. This book has been sold nationwide and has been used as a textbook for many nursing law seminars. Several schools of nursing have just informed me that this is going to be used as their course book.

This book focuses on the legal aspects of general nursing practice. Nursing issues dealing with the ethical aspects are covered in the book entitled *Nursing Ethics and the Law* and will not be provided here. *Nursing Ethics and the Law* discusses the following subjects: principles of ethical decision making, the President's Commission on Ethical and Legal Problems, treating critically ill patients, setting boundaries for nutritional support, living wills, durable power of attorney, No Code Blue orders and withholding treatment, organ transplantation, hospice — legal and nursing issues, caring for patients with AIDS, issues in reproduction, abortion, sterilization, in vitro fertilization, surrogate motherhood, patient bill of rights, children and the elderly, bioethics committees, legal issues in defective newborns, nursing policy and procedures, and clinical research and the law.

CHAPTER ONE

LEGAL ASPECTS OF NURSING PRACTICE

Introduction
Tort Reform
Sources and Types of Law

INTRODUCTION

Nursing is an ancient and honorable profession. The role and function of the nurse has drastically changed throughout time. The nurse is no longer a hand-maiden of the physician.

Slightly over one hundred years ago, the nurse's professional responsibilities were defined in the following "job description":

> In addition to caring for your 50 patients, each bedside nurse will follow these regulations:
> 1. Daily sweep and mop the floors of your ward, dust the patients' furniture and windowsills.
> 2. Maintain an even temperature in your ward by bringing in a scuttle of coal for the day's business.
> 3. Light is important to observe the patient's condition. Therefore, each day fill the kerosene lamps, clean chimneys and trim wicks. Wash the windows once a week.
> 4. The nurse's notes are important in aiding the physician's work. Make your pens carefully. You may whittle nibs to your individual taste.
> 5. Each nurse on day duty will report to duty every day at 7 a.m. and leave at 8 p.m., except on the Sabbath, on which you will be off from 12 noon to 2 p.m.
> 6. Graduate nurses in good standing with the director of nurses will be given an evening off each week for courting purposes, or two evenings a week if they go to church regularly.
> 7. Each nurse should lay aside from each pay a goodly sum of her earnings for her benefits during her declining years so that she will not be a burden. For example, if you earn $30 a month, you should set aside $15.
> 8. Any nurse who smokes, uses liquor in any form, gets her hair done at a beauty shop, or frequents dance halls will give the director of nurses good reason to suspect her worth, intentions, and integrity.
> 9. The nurse who performs her labors and serves her patients and doctors faithfully and without fail for a period of five years will be given an increase by the hospital administration of five cents a day, providing there are no hospital debts that are outstanding.

The modern-day nurse has a recognized professional duty to actively participate in the decision-making process. Today, nurses perform a wide variety of highly skilled and specialized services and, consequently, are exposed to greater liability risks. With more responsibility comes more accountability. An increasing number of lawsuits are being filed against nurses and their employers.

A recent article in a trial lawyers' association magazine advocated that nurses, as well as the physician and the hospital, should be included in the lawsuit. The patient's attorney frequently sues everyone involved in the patient's care. This is what is called the "deep pocket theory." The attorney believes there will be more parties available to contribute to a verdict or settlement if there are several defendants.

In recent years there have been significant changes in the law caused by the changes in nursing and hospital standards. Historically, hospitals contributed little more to patient care than bed and board. Circumstances have changed dramatically; hospitals now provide not only food and lodging, but also a host of support functions.

In the early 1900s, all states had accepted the doctrine of charitable immunity. This doctrine made hospitals, churches and schools immune from prosecution. If a patient were harmed by the negligence of another, the doctrine prevented the patient from suing to recover damages. Most states have revoked the charitable immunity doctrine, resulting in an increased number of suits against hospitals and nurses.

Laws have been passed that create more causes of action for the patient. Infliction of emotional distress, loss of consortium, wrongful death statutes and longer statutes of limitation are a few of the laws which have been passed in some states, resulting in greater liability risks for nurses.

Beginning in 1880, many states protected their physicians with what came to be called the "locality rule." Physicians and nurses who practiced in small towns did not want to be held to the standards of the large city physicians. Physicians and nurses in one state did not want to be held to the standards of physicians or nurses in another state. The rule primarily affected physicians since at that time nurses were rarely sued.

The locality rule required that the plaintiff prove a deviation from the standard of care in the defendant doctor's community. This led to the so-called "conspiracy of silence": Physicians were reluctant to testify against another fellow physician in their community.

The locality rule has been abolished or altered in most states. This has had a direct impact upon nursing liability exposure. Expert testimony is generally required to prove negligence on the part of the nurse; and with the increased specialization of nurses come arguments for application of similar rules.

New legal theories bring not only an increased number of lawsuits against nurses, physicians and hospitals, but also higher verdicts against those defendants. These factors resulted in what has been commonly called "the malpractice crisis" of the mid-1970s. Many practitioners were unable to obtain malpractice insurance, and for those who could obtain coverage, it was very expensive. Many say that this crisis is reoccurring. In response to this, many states have recently passed tort reform bills. These will be discussed later.

Several good things emerged from the crisis of the 1970s. Health care risk management developed. The focus was directed toward preventive law in medicine. It is this author's objective to aid that process. Nurses can prevent unnecessary suits by gaining an awareness of law and legal requirements.

When sued by a patient, the nurse, doctor or employer is called the *defendant*. The patient is referred to as the *plaintiff*. This is easy to remember because both *patient* and *plaintiff* begin with the letter *p*.

Nurses rendering professional services to an ill or injured patient are under a legal duty to exercise due care in the performance of such services. The nurse also owes a duty to the employer and to the physician whom he or she assists.

Professional nurses are liable for any harm to patients that is due to negligence. Nurses are held to a standard of care expected of reasonably competent nurses. The standard of care will be discussed later.

The concept of malpractice goes back as far as the fourteenth century. In 1375, a patient sought treatment for an injured hand from Dr. John Swanlord. The patient was upset about the unsatisfactory healing of his arm. He sued the surgeon, but the court ruled in the doctor's favor.

The word *malpractice* seems to have come into the English language about 1671. A London practitioner used the word to discredit a number of physicians who were teaching in London's Royal College of Physicians. A decision handed down by the Courts of King's Bench in 1697 also employed the term and gave it legal direction.

William Blackstone's "Commentaries on the Laws of England," published in 1768, utilized the word *malpractice*. The word has been used ever since. Historically, the term *malpractice* referred only to the negligence of a physician.

The terms *negligence* and *malpractice* are used interchangeably in this book. However, it is important for the nurse to realize that a few states make a slight distinction between them.

Many courts have considered the question of whether the nurse is a member of a profession and thus capable of committing malpractice. If not, any actions which fall below the standard of care are simply negligent. The states are split on this decision.

In *Richardson v. Doe*, the Ohio court stated that the term *malpractice* is sometimes used loosely to refer to the negligence of a member of any professional group.[1] However, legally and technically, it is still subject to the limited common-law definition. At common law, only physicians commit malpractice. If a nurse falls below the standard of care, he/she is simply negligent.

Malpractice was defined in this case as the failure by a member of the medical profession to provide care with that degree of skill exercised by members of the same profession. The court said that a nurse is skilled and well trained; however, it said a nurse's responsibilities differ from a physician's because the physician has to exercise independent judgment.

On the other hand, a New York court stated that nurses are classified as professional persons.[2] Nurses are frequently called upon to use their expert skills. The court said, "Nurses are better grouped with physicians than maids and cooks."[3]

It is less than an optimal situation in those states where the nurses are simply negligent. The majority of these states remain reluctant to subject nurses to the special provisions relating to malpractice actions. The result is an increased liability risk not only to the nurse and employer, but also to the physician.

In the performance of his/her professional duties, a nurse is required to exercise ordinary or reasonable care to see that no harm comes to his/her patient.[4] In the *Oldis* case, the court said,

> Every defendant in whose custody the plaintiff was placed for any period was bound to exercise ordinary care to see that no unnecessary harm came to him and each would be liable for failure in this regard. Any defendant who negligently injured him, and any defendant charged with his care who so neglected him as to allow injury to occur, would be liable.[5]

TORT REFORM — THE CHANGING LAW WHICH IMPACTS ON NURSES AND THEIR EMPLOYERS

The January 1986 edition of *Medical Liability Advisory Service* reported that the American Hospital Association (A.H.A.) was studying the malpractice crisis of 1985.[6] The A.H.A. even formed a special task force to study the effectiveness of both tort reform and proposed federal legislation.

Federal legislation, namely HR 3084, proposes a method to settle claims outside the court system. At the state level, thirty-seven legislatures examined professional liability tort reform bills during 1985.

During 1985, three states were able to pass comprehensive tort reform legislation. These included New York, Florida and Illinois. Twenty-one states were able to pass at least one liability-related bill. Additionally, there were ten states that formed a committee to study the problem. The May 30, 1986, edition of *Hospital Week* indicated that during 1986, twelve states had already passed tort reform legislation.[7] These included Wisconsin, Colorado, Connecticut, Kansas, Maine, Minnesota, Missouri, South Dakota, Utah, Washington, West Virginia and Wyoming.

A summary of some of tort reform bills that have been introduced or passed include the following:

1. *Collateral Source Rule.* This rule would allow the jury to be informed of any other benefits paid or available to a plaintiff from other sources before the jury makes a damage award. Currently, many states forbid that this information even be mentioned during a civil suit. For example, an employee was working in a lumberyard when a car negligently struck him. He collected worker's compensation benefits and his $10,000 hospital bill was paid by Blue Cross. He sued the driver of the automobile. The driver was found negligent and had to pay him $10,000 for hospital bills even though he did not have to pay this amount out of his pocket.

The opponents of this bill express concerns that such a bill would punish the prudent victim who purchases health or disability insurance and that the wrongdoer would benefit. However, it is generally agreed that the prudent victim purchases the insurance to protect himself/herself against many different losses. Many of those losses would not give rise to a claim for recovery by a third person. For example, a person slips walking out the front porch of his/her house. The party would not have a claim against another person.

The effect of this bill is to assure that a jury does not incorrectly assume that a particular claimant is entirely without resources. It would reduce the tendency of a jury to award duplicate damages for expenses already awarded. Tennessee,[8] California,[9] Florida,[10] Iowa,[11] Nebraska[12] and Arizona[13] are among some of the states which have recently abolished the collateral source rule.

2. *Comparative Negligence Reform — Joint and Several Liability.* This bill would ensure that juries are made aware that there are or may be other persons responsible for plaintiff's injuries. The jury would also be informed if the plaintiff had settled with those parties prior to trial.

This is geared at eliminating the prejudice to the nonsettling defendant which presently prevails when a plaintiff settles 90 to 95 percent of his injury claim against other parties. The plaintiff then proceeds against the remaining defendant in hopes of recovering more money against a defendant that has little or no liability. Frequently, in a professional liability action, the plaintiff will sue as many parties as necessary. For example, in the *Parker v. King* case, the plaintiff sued both the physician and the hospital, alleging that his knee surgery was negligently performed.[14] The plaintiff had a arthrotomy and meniscectomy of the right knee. In the case at bar, the court granted the summary judgment motions. However, had the physician made a settlement with the plaintiff, then the hospital would have been left holding the bag. The laws of many states do not allow the jury to be informed that there is any person who may be liable for the injury and that the plaintiff has previously settled with that party.

Opponents of such bills contend that this would be contrary to the philosophy of the underlying tort system that the plaintiff be made whole. The purpose of the tort system is to put the plaintiff back in the same or similar position, not a better position. The plaintiff may have recovered all the damages from the settling defendant and then be allowed to proceed against those who have no share in the fault causing the injury. The plaintiff does so comfortable and safe in the knowledge that the jury will not know that the plaintiff has recovered all his/her damages against other sources.

The president's task force report of 1986 recommended that "[j]oint and several liability, which has made it easier for plaintiffs to obtain compensation from defendants only found to be minimally at fault," be eliminated.

Similar statutes have already been passed in at least four other states: Washington (ESSB 4630, March 6, 1986), Utah (SB 674, March 18, 1986), Missouri (SB 663, February 3, 1986) and Wyoming (SB 17, March 14, 1986).

3. *Periodic Payment of Judgments Act.* Many states are adopting the Uniform Periodic Payment of Judgment Act. This would allow either party to an action who has sustained losses in excess of $100,000 to be paid by installments instead of one lump sum. This is done upon the election of either party and only with the approval of the court. This would apply to actions involving nurses and hospitals.

A provision is made for adequate security. The inflation rate and market factors are also taken into account. Similar statutes regarding medical malpractice cases have been passed in California,[15] Florida,[16] New York, Washington (ESSB 4630, passed March 6, 1986), Utah (SB 155, passed March 18, 1986) and Missouri (SB 663, passed February 3, 1986).

4. *Product Liability Reform.* The law of product liability impacts on the nursing profession. It affects the machinery available in the nurse's profession and the medications prescribed to the patients. Recently, the most effective IUD, the Copper 7, was taken off the market. This had a direct impact on the health care industry. Many drugs, such as Zomax, are taken off the market because of the law of product liability. Many states have had laws that allow juries to apply a test involving hindsight to determine whether a product is unreasonably dangerous or defective.

Most other states have not used a negligence standard in determining liability, but rather a "strict liability" standard. Many of the bills introduced or passed by the various states are attempting to restore a balance of fairness in product liability actions. Most bills would establish a common-law standard of foreseeability as of the date of manufacture or sale.

This type of bill would make it clear that a manufacturer would not be liable if a product were mishandled or abused. Many of the bills create a rebuttable presumption in favor of the manufacturer if the product is substantially altered.

Presently, in many states, anyone may come into the courtroom and point out how the accident may have been prevented. Literally all accidents could have been prevented if the facts were known in advance. This standard eliminates the question of foreseeability, which has also been important to the tort system. If one additional screw or a different design might have prevented the accident, the jury is free to conclude that the product was defective.

Most of the bills redefine the terms *defective* and *unreasonably* by providing express examples of when and under what circumstances the manufacturer would be liable. The manufacturer will be held liable only when the injury is produced because of a defect that existed at the time of manufacture. The manufacturer will also be liable if the manufacturer knew or should have known the product was unreasonably dangerous and if the actual use or misuse was foreseeable.

5. *Evidence Reform — Remarriage.* This bill would also allow the judge or jury to be apprised of the fact the spouse in a wrongful death case is remarried. It would also be admissible that the spouse has a means of support with the remarriage. Many states do not allow this information to be presented to the jury.

6. *Limitation of Pain and Suffering Award.* Many states have recently passed laws limiting the amount that could be recovered for pain and suffering. This does not effect the plaintiff's award for other damages such as medical bills, time lost from work and other incidental expenses. Massachusetts, New York and Maryland have recently enacted such bills.[17] Maryland limited pain and suffering awards to $350,000.

Assistant Attorney General Richard K. Willard, head of a presidential task force on the current liability crisis, recommends that noneconomic damages be limited to a fair and reasonable amount, with $100,000 being a reasonable limitation.

7. *Imposition of Costs on One Who Files a Frivolous Suit.* Many states are passing laws which impose legal costs on someone who files a "frivolous" suit for liability damages. New York has recently passed a law by which the judge can impose up to $10,000 in legal costs on anyone filing a frivolous suit.[18] New York law also provides that a settlement for loss of earnings must be reduced by the amount of taxes that the victim would have paid if the money had been earned yearly in wages.

8. *Limitation of Attorney's Fees.* The presidential task force on the current liability crisis recommended that attorney's fees be limited.[19] The task force noted that attorney's fees are sometimes as high as 50 percent of an award. A sliding scale should be adopted giving attorneys 25 percent of the first $100,000 of an award; 20 percent of the next $100,000; and 10 percent of the remainder.

Illinois and New York have recently limited what is known as the "contingency fee."[20]

9. *Punitive Damages.* Many of the bills and laws differ with respect to punitive damages. Ohio recently proposed a bill stating that punitive damages cannot be awarded *except* upon proof beyond a reasonable doubt.[21] If punitive damages are appropriate, then

(1) the amount is determined by the judge, not the jury;

(2) the amount may not exceed compensatory damages awarded in the same case;

(3) attorney's fees may not be calculated on the basis of the punitive damage award; and

(4) the punitive damages are paid into the general revenue fund of the state of Ohio.

The proponents of the bill state that the purpose of the civil justice system is to compensate, not to punish. Punitive damages are for punishment and do not belong in the civil system.

Opponents of the bill state that punitive damages are rare, according to an American Bar Association study. Proponents state that the study did not account for the many cases that were filed alleging punitive damages. Many of the cases resulted in punitive damages because of the threat of damages. Illinois, among a number of other states, has already passed a law abolishing punitive damages.[22]

HOSPITALS RESPOND TO MALPRACTICE PROBLEM

The January 1986 edition of *Medical Liability Advisory Service* featured an article on how hospitals are responding to the malpractice problem. The American Hospital Association said that hospitals are attempting to identify and remove those individuals or procedures that put the patient at risk in order to minimize their potential for involvement in a malpractice action.

It is interesting to note the American Hospital Association (A.H.A.) report indicated that approximately 5 to 15 percent of the nation's practicing physicians suffer from an impairment of some kind (see the section on reporting incompetence of health care practitioners). The AMA now maintains a computer data base on physician credentials and licensing. The computer also contains information about when a state notifies a physician that his or her license has been revoked.

The A.H.A. has been working with several governmental agencies to investigate the purchase of fraudulent medical degrees. Even though most physicians are independent contractors, some courts have held the hospital liable for not checking out the references of their staff physicians and employees.

The A.H.A. has also indicated that the best way to minimize risks to patients is to develop a risk management program. (See the section on risk management.) In 1983, the A.H.A. did a survey that showed that 75 percent of the hospitals that responded had at least a risk management department or one individual who was assigned to that job description. Another method of minimizing risks to patients was the development in 1984 of peer review organizations (PROs). These peer review organizations monitor the quality and appropriateness of care delivered to Medicare patients. (See also the section on peer review.)

SOURCES AND TYPES OF LAW

Sources of Law

Legislation (Statutes), Common Law (Cases) and the Executive Branch
The law helps us define our personal and professional relationships, and assists us in knowing what it is we are to do. The law as it exists today has developed

from many sources. American law developed from the English system of law. In the United States we have both common law and statutory law.

The United States employs a tripartite governmental system, and its three separate powers are the legislative, judicial and executive branches. The primary purpose of the legislative branch is the enactment of statutes. A statute is the written will of the legislature and constitutes the law of the state or the federal government. Each state has statutes that directly affect nurses. The Nurse Practice Act is an example of a statute enacted by the legislature. Statutory law is written in state codes. It is very important for all nurses to know the statutory laws in their states. Copies of the pertinent statutes in your state have been included in a separate book. (At the time of publication of this book, statute books published by Professional Education Systems, Inc. were available for all but seven states.)

The judicial branch is another part of the tripartite system. Judges review statutes and apply them to the facts of each case. Judge-made law is also called common law. Common-law decisions are another way in which standards of legal conduct are created. Case law can differ from state to state.

One important function of common law is to settle or resolve the dispute. Common-law decisions which affect nursing practice also help to establish a precedent for other nurses to follow. Common-law decisions assist the nurse in determining how the court would rule in any case of similar facts. *Stare decisis* is the common-law principle which prohibits the courts from changing the legal rules unless the previous judicial opinions become meaningless.

Each state has its own nurse practice act which is written by the legislature. Assume a nurse is sued by a patient who alleges that the nurse was negligent in doing a pap and pelvic exam. The patient also alleges that the nurse could not do a pap and pelvic exam under the nurse practice act in her state. The judge is called upon to interpret the laws made by the legislature. If the judge decides that the nurse practice act is broad enough to cover doing pap and pelvic exams, then common law is established. In this way, other nurses would rely on the court's decision to know what activities can and cannot be done.

The Constitution of the United States describes the interplay between the legislative and judicial branches. The Constitution is called the "law of the land." Each state can make its own laws unless it directly affects federal law. If the state's law is contradictory, the federal law prevails. There are few federal laws that affect nurses. Nurses who are in the military service are affected by the Federal Tort Claims Act. The release of medical records of a patient treated for drug or alcohol problems is regulated by federal law. Federal law is the same in all states; state law is different from state to state.

Types of Law

Criminal, Tort, Contract, Constitutional and Administrative Law

Civil law and criminal law are two classifications of law. A crime is an act in violation of the penal law, which imposes a criminal penalty. A *crime* is an offense against the state and is a violation and a breach against society. A *civil* case is an infringement against an individual's rights. Murder and theft are two examples of crime. If a nurse intentionally kills a patient, the nurse may be prosecuted by the government for a crime.

When an individual's rights are violated, the aggrieved person may seek restitution by filing a civil or tort action. If the nurse errs and the patient is damaged, the patient may file a malpractice or negligence suit against the nurse. Civil law resolves disharmony between individual members of society. The proper forum in which to litigate disputes when the parties cannot agree is the courtroom. This is to protect the members of society from taking the law into their own hands and creating undue violence. Malpractice suits which are filed against nurses are civil cases.

Besides criminal and tort law, there are also contract law, constitutional law and administrative law. *Contract law* is private law and involves an agreement between two or more parties. To have a binding, valid contract there must generally be an offer, acceptance and consideration (something of value like money). It involves a bargained-for exchange. Some nurses have a union contract which dictates their performance. Some nurses or employers obtain an oral or written contract prior to employment which sets out the nurse's compensation, work schedules and job description. There has been a trend for both nurses and their employers to insist on a contract so that later on there are no misunderstandings.

Constitutional law is a type of public law that is based on our rights and responsibilities under the federal and state constitutions. The United States and state supreme courts interpret constitutional law. One constitutional right which most nurses are familiar with is the "right to privacy." The United States Supreme Court has recognized that each individual has a right to privacy. This right flowed from the penumbra of rights in the amendments to the Constitution. It is this legal basis that has been relied on to allow a competent patient to forego life-sustaining treatment.[23] In one case, a man was allowed to refuse amputation surgery which was necessary to prevent the spread of a gangrenous infection.

It was 1973 when the Supreme Court decided the landmark case of *Roe v. Wade*.[24] The Court found that the right to privacy is broad enough to encompass a woman's decision as to whether to terminate her pregnancy. The right to an abortion was premised on another famous case which had been decided earlier, in 1965. The Court in *Griswold v. Connecticut* found the unwritten constitutional right to privacy in the shadow of the specific guarantees of the Bill of Rights.[25] The Court recognized a right of individual privacy in the area of personal conduct involving the purchase of contraceptives. It has only been in the past two decades that the law has begun to recognize the individual's right to privacy and has provided more choices regarding procreation.

Besides the patient's right to life and right to self-determination in refusing treatments, the right to privacy also includes the right to die when treatment would only prolong death. In *Satz v. Perlmutter*, the court of appeals upheld the right of a 73-year-old competent man to have his life-sustaining respirator removed.[26]

The patient had an incurable disease which had progressed to the point that he was unable to breathe without the respirator. There was no cure, and his illness had progressed to the point where he was barely able to speak. The patient was alert and wanted the respirator removed because of the pain and suffering. In fact, on one occasion he even attempted to disconnect it himself.

The court found that since his condition was terminal, the continuation of the life support system was only a temporary postponement of death. The court allowed the respirator to be removed pursuant to his request.

Religious freedom is also based on the right of privacy. Sometimes this area can affect the nursing care rendered. These situations arise when a patient refuses blood transfusions, stating they are contrary to the tenets of his/her religion. This belief is generally held by Jehovah's Witnesses and the Christian Scientists. The court may uphold such decisions in the absence of countervailing interests.[27] Generally, a countervailing interest is present if the patient is pregnant or a minor. It is virtually certain that courts will order blood for pregnant mothers[28] and children[29] [30] if either are at risk.[31]

The decisions of courts faced with the question of whether to order blood transfusions for adults vary depending on the facts of each case. One of the first cases to decide this issue was in 1964 in the District of Columbia.[32] The patient had a 7-month-old child at home. The court ordered the transfusion because the mother had a responsibility to the community to care for her infant. The same reasoning was used in a recent New York case.[33]

If the patient could show that his/her minor children would be cared for, many courts have upheld the right to refuse blood.[34] In one case, a 34-year-old man had been admitted to a D.C. hospital.[35] He was admitted with injuries and internal bleeding. The wife said her husband wanted to refuse blood even if he had to die. The wife and other immediate family members could care for the two children. The family business could continue to furnish them with their material needs. The court could find no compelling state interest to overrule the patient's decision based on his religious conviction.

Administrative law is a type of public law that concerns administrative agencies and boards. These are legislated by Congress or the state legislature. Often, the state board of nursing is an administrative agency. The board of nursing is then responsible for formation of the nurse practice act. In some states, many of the statutes affecting nursing practice are found in the administrative code.

REFERENCES

1. *Richardson v. Doe*, 176 Ohio St. 370 (1964).
2. *Volk v. City of New York*, 19 N.Y.S.2d 53 (1940).
3. *See also Grogan v. Garrison*, 27 Ohio St. 50, 63 (1875).
4. *Ybarra v. Spangard*, 25 Cal. 2d 486 (1944).
5. *Oldis v. La Societe Francaise de Bienfaisance Mutuelle*, 130 Cal. App. 2d 461, 279 P.2d 184 (1955).
6. 11 *Medical Liability Advisory Service*, No. 1, at 1 (January 1986).
7. American Hospital Association, *22 Hospital Week*, No. 22 (May 30, 1986).
8. *Baker v. Vanderbilt University*, 616 F. Supp. 330 (D.C. Tenn. 1985).
9. *Fein v. Permanente Medical Group*, 695 P.2d 665 (Cal. 1985).
10. *Pinelles v. Cedars of Lebanon Hospital*, 293 N.W.2d 550 (Iowa 1980).
11. *Rudolph v. Iowa Methodist Medical Center*, 293 N.W.2d 550 (Iowa 1980).
12. *Prendergast v. Nelson*, 256 N.W.2d 657 (Neb. 1977).
13. *Eastin v. Broomfield*, 570 P.2d 744 (Ariz. 1977).
14. *Parker v. King*, 402 So. 2d 877 (Ala. 1981).
15. *American Bank and Trust Co. v. Community Hospital of Los Gatos-Saratoga*, 683 P.2d 670 (Cal. 1984).
16. *Florida Patient's Compensation Fund v. Von Stetina*, 474 So. 2d 783 (Fla. 1985).
17. 11 *Medical Liability Advisory Service*, No 7, at 10 (July 1986).
18. *Id.* at 3.
19. *Id.* at 1.
20. *Id.* at 2.
21. Ohio Senate Bill 338, House Bill 895.
22. *Medical Liability Advisory Service, supra* note 6, at 2.
23. *In re Quakenbush*, 156 N.J. Super. 282 (1978).
24. *Roe v. Wade*, 410 U.S. 113 (1973).
25. *Griswold v. Connecticut*, 381 U.S. 479 (1965).
26. *Satz v. Perlmutter*, 379 So. 2d 359 (Fla. 1980).
27. *Holmes v. Silver Cross Hospital*, 340 F. Supp. 125 (D.C. Ill. 1972); *New Jersey v. Perricone*, 37 N.J. 463 (1965); *Sampson v. Taylor*, 29 N.Y.2d 900, 328 N.Y.S.2d 686 (1972); *John F. Kennedy Hospital v. Heston*, 58 N.J. 576 (1971).
28. *Muhlenberg Hospital v. Patterson*, 320 A.2d 518 (N.J. Super. 1974).
29. *In the Interest of Ivey*, 319 So. 2d 53 (Fla. App. 1975).
30. *Muhlenberg, supra* note 28.
31. *Crouse Irving Memorial Hospital v. Paddock*, 485 N.Y.S.2d 443 (1985).
32. *Application of the President and Directors of Georgetown College, Inc.*, 331 F.2d 1000 (D.C. Cir. 1964).
33. *In the Matter of the Application of Winthrop University Hospital*, 490 N.Y.S.2d 996 (1985).
34. *Id*; *St. Mary's Hospital v. Ramsey*, 465 So. 2d 666 (Fla. App. 4 Dist. 1985).
35. *In re Osborne*, 294 A.2d 372 (D.C. 1972).

CHAPTER TWO

OVERVIEW
OF PROFESSIONAL NEGLIGENCE

Nursing Negligence and the Nursing Standard of Care
Four Elements of Nursing Negligence/Malpractice
Intentional Torts
Types of Evidence
The Necessity of Expert Testimony

NURSING NEGLIGENCE AND THE
NURSING STANDARD OF CARE

When a nurse has been sued, one of the first questions frequently asked is, "How do I know if what I did was legally sufficient?" The answer is always the same: if the acceptable nursing standard of care has been satisfied, there is generally no negligence on the part of the nurse. Additionally, the plaintiff has the burden of proving that the nurse was negligent. The plaintiff must prove each and every one of the four elements of negligence. (The four elements of negligence will be discussed in the next section.)

This is the reason that it is important for every nurse to have an understanding of what constitutes the nursing standard of care. Negligence cannot be fully understood unless the nurse understands the relationship between negligence and the standard of care. Not too many years ago, nurses were rarely sued, and, when they were, there were no clear guidelines by which to judge the nurse's performance. This is not true today.

Negligence is defined as conduct that falls below the standard of care established by law for the protection of others against unreasonable risk or harm. Nursing negligence is carelessness which causes harm to the patient. Nursing negligence was recently defined by the Michigan courts as "failure to apply that degree of skill and learning in treating and nursing patients which is customarily applied in treating or caring for the sick or wounded."[1]

This case involved a certified registered nurse anesthetist (CRNA). The patient was having disc surgery, for a blockage in the L3, L4 area. During the surgery, the patient suffered a cardiac arrest. The court made it clear that the plaintiff had the burden of showing that the nurse's actions were negligent.

The standard of care is the yardstick by which nursing performance is measured. Standards of nursing care set minimum criteria for nursing performance. The standard of care is established when an ordinary, prudent nurse would have performed *in the same or similar manner*. The law of negligence presupposes some uniform standard of behavior by which the defendant nurse's conduct can be measured. The nursing standard of care calls for adequately documenting patient care. It dictates that I.V.s be started appropriately and dressing changes be performed in a certain manner. Minimal standards for a medical nurse would include the development of a nursing care plan based on the nursing process. The nursing process includes what is generally taught in nursing schools: assessment, planning, intervention and evaluation.

A nurse owes a duty to the patient to possess the degree of learning and skill ordinarily possessed by nurses in good standing and to exercise that degree of care ordinarily exercised by other members of the profession acting in similar circumstances.[2] To avoid being negligent, a nurse must act as a reasonable nurse would act under like circumstances. If another nurse would have done the procedure or administered similar care, the standard of care has been satisfied.

Health care providers, because they possess skill and knowledge uncommon to laypeople, must act in a manner consistent with that superior knowledge. In addition, the conduct of health care professionals is judged by professional standards determined by members of the profession. In other words, in order to prove that a nurse acted negligently, a nurse or physician would have to testify that the nurse deviated from the standard of care. The exception to this rule is the situation where the alleged negligence is a matter of common knowledge. For example, a layperson would know, without being told by a physician, that removal of the wrong leg is negligent. Giving hydrochloric acid instead of Alka Seltzer is another example.

Often the defendant nurse's attorney will have the case reviewed by a physician or nurse who can testify for the nurse at trial. The reviewing nurse or physician is then known as an expert witness. The expert witness is allowed to testify because of the expert's special training, experience, skill and knowledge. Having an expert testify in the defendant nurse's behalf is one way to establish that the required standard of care has been met.

Twenty years ago, there were few clear-cut guidelines by which to judge the nurse's performance. Today, there are formidable numbers of written standards available on national, state and local levels. For example, at the national level, the Joint Commission on the Accreditation of Hospitals (JCAH), the American Osteopathic Association (A.O.A.) and the American Nurses' Association (A.N.A.) have established standards of nursing practice. The A.N.A.'s "Standards of Nursing Practice" dictate that the nurse should obtain a history from the patient and document the information in an ongoing fashion. This is found in the first standard, which discusses the collection and recording of data about the health status of the client. Furthermore, the nurse is to formulate a nursing diagnosis based on the information received from the health status data. A plan of nursing care should be made which includes goals derived from the nursing diagnosis.

Many specialty organizations have adopted specific guidelines. For example, the Emergency Nurses' Association has promulgated national standards for emergency room nurses. There are also national standards on critical care nursing. The Association of Operating Room Nurses has standards on recommended practices for perioperative nursing. (See the Standards for Nursing in the appendix.)

At the state level, there are the nurse practice acts. Nurse practice acts are the authority by which nurses can practice. They dictate the duties and functions that nurses can perform. Many states, like Ohio, are in the process of revising their nurse practice acts. The state legislature may also empower the state nursing board to promulgate nursing standards. All state nursing associations promulgate standards and position statements for nurses on a variety of subjects. For example, the Ohio Nurses' Association has a standard of the "Registered Nurse's Role in Performing Emergency Endotracheal Intubation" and "Restraining Patients in the Nonpsychiatric Setting." Most state nursing associations have a practice committee. Many will specifically address concerns of nurses about nursing issues.

At the local level, employer policy and procedure manuals set forth even more specific standards. It is important for the nurse to be aware of all the employer's written policies, procedures and standards. A nurse who follows an employer's policy can use the policy to demonstrate that he or she has met the standard of care. On the other hand, if a nurse violates the employer's own policy and patient injury occurs, the nurse may be found to be negligent. This area will be discussed in detail later.

Additional standards can be ascertained from nursing texts and nursing articles. One nurse even showed that the standard of care had been satisfied by having her nursing instructor testify that she was trained in a procedure in a certain manner.

The standard of practice can be evidenced by showing custom. Custom is an unwritten policy which is demonstrative of the usual and acceptable way of nursing practice. The standard of practice is also evidenced by case law. For example, a judge in a case rules that it is acceptable nursing practice for a nurse to give a tetanus toxoid injection in the vastus lateralis. If another nurse is sued for similar conduct, she can use this case to show she is not negligent.

The standard of care works in this way. A patient cuts his foot on a rusty nail and comes to the emergency room for treatment. The triage nurse notes, "The patient stepped on a one-half inch rusty nail while barefoot in his garage one-half hour prior to admission. Right pedal pulse 2+. Puncture wound noted bottom right great toe." The patient is taken into the emergency room. Another nurse charts, "Betadine soak x 20 minutes." The physician orders a tetanus shot, which the nurse administers I.M. in the right deltoid. The physician prescribes the antibiotic Keflex and warm soaks for twenty minutes, four times a day. The patient is instructed in writing on the signs and symptoms of infection. He is given written instructions which states he is to follow up with his family physician if any problems arise.

Suppose the patient goes home and does not bother to fill his prescription. A week later, he is admitted with an infection and eventually has his toe and part of his foot amputated. Upon discharge from the hospital, he sues the nurse, hospital and physician for negligence.

Under the facts given, the nurse can demonstrate in a number of ways that the standard of care has been satisfied and that there is no evidence of negligence. *First*, the nurse followed hospital policy that states that all wounds should be soaked for twenty minutes in Betadine. *Second*, the nurse can demonstrate that this treatment regimen was pursuant to the training and education obtained in nursing school. Nursing texts and articles can be used to demonstrate that the care was consistent with acceptable standards. Another nurse from a similar setting can be employed to review the defendant nurse's conduct and offer a written report. These are some of the ways a nurse can demonstrate that the requisite standard of care has been met.

THE FOUR ELEMENTS OF NURSING NEGLIGENCE

The Negligence Standard

The plaintiff must show that the nurse deviated from the acceptable standard of care in order to prove negligence. Generally, nursing negligence is based on fault. Nurses are not insurers of patients and will not be held liable for injuries simply because a complication or untoward result occurred.

Negligence has previously been defined as conduct which falls below the standard of care established by law for the protection of others and thus involves an unreasonable risk of harm to the patient. Negligence refers to conduct as opposed to state of mind. The unintentional tort of negligence differs from an intentional tort, which requires a specific state of mind. To prove negligence, the patient does not have to show that the nurse intended to do something incorrectly. It is a situtation where a mistake was made by the nurse, like administering the wrong I.V. or medication.

In order for the plaintiff to prevail, the jury must find that the nurse did something that fell below the standard of care. As previously mentioned, the mere fact that the patient suffered a complication or an unfavorable result does *not* necessarily mean that there was negligence. Furthermore, the jury or judge must find that the nurse's violation of the standard of care directly caused the plaintiff's injury. In fact, the jury or judge must find that the plaintiff has proved each and *every* one of the four elements of negligence. If there is anything that a nurse should remember from this book, it is this fact. The nurse may make the worst mistake in his or her career, but if it does not cause the injury nor any damage, there is no liability. Many times when nurses or physicians have made mistakes, they are willing to "throw in the towel." It is hoped they will now have an understanding of the legal requirements for professional liability.

The four elements necessary to prove legal liability are duty, breach of duty, proximate or direct cause, and harm or injury (damages).

Duty

This first element has two components: a duty to act and a duty to do so in an acceptable way. A duty arises for the nurse when the plaintiff becomes a patient in the hospital and is assigned to that nurse's unit.[3] The office nurse has a duty to any of the patients of his/her employer physician.[4] A nursing supervisor has a duty to all the patients in the hospital or other health care center. Agreement by the nurse with regard to this duty may be expressed or implied. The duty to act according to the accepted standard of care arises when the nurse-patient relationship is formed.

In most states, the nurse is under no duty to provide emergency care to an accident victim observed during off hours. However, once the nurse assumes to care for the accident victim, the nurse must do so properly. If the nurse abruptly leaves, an abandonment action may result. This is why every state has enacted a "Good Samaritan" law. The Good Samaritan law is aimed at encouraging nurses and other persons to render emergency care. The Good Samaritan law is different in all fifty states. It is the law of the state the nurse is in that is effective. For example, a nurse is licensed by the Ohio Industrial Commission as a rehabilitative nurse. Several of her clients are located in Pennsylvania. Once she has crossed over the Pennsylvania border, it is the Pennsylvania Good Samaritan statute that applies.

In the 1985 case of *Lindsey v. Miami Development Corporation*, the court discussed the element of duty.[5] The plaintiff filed a wrongful death action alleging a negligent failure to render emergency care. The defendant was the lessee of some rental property. The decedent was attending a political fund raiser. She was observed sitting on the edge of the balcony with her feet dangling when she saw defendant Castile. She indicated she wanted to come down. Castile told her to go around and come down the steps. The decedent refused and commented that she was coming down. She jumped from the balcony, striking her head. A blood sample later taken from Mrs. Lindsey revealed she had a blood alcohol level of 0.23 percent.

There was evidence that an ambulance was called immediately. Another person testified that Castile waited a few minutes before calling an ambulance. The lower court had granted the defendant's summary judgment, and the plaintiff appealed.

The court noted that it is axiomatic for the plaintiff to prove duty, breach of duty, proximate cause and damages. "A duty in negligence cases may be defined as an obligation to which the law will give recognition and effect, to conform to a particular standard of conduct toward another."[6]

The court's role in determining whether a duty exists has been defined as follows:

> **The Existence of a Duty.** In other words, whether, upon the facts in evidence, such a relation exists between the parties that the community will impose a legal obligation upon one for the benefit of others — or, more simply, whether the interest of the plaintiff which has suffered invasion was entitled to legal protection at the hands of the defendant. This is entirely a question of law, to be determined by reference to the body of statutes, rules, principles and precedents which make up the law; and it must be determined only by the court . . . . A decision by the court that, upon any versions of the facts, there is not duty, must necessarily result in judgment for the defendant. A decision that if certain facts are found to be true, a duty exists, leaves open the other questions now under consideration [concerning the existence of negligence].[7]

The court noted the common-law rule that a stranger owes no duty to render aid to another in peril. This is true as long as there is no special relationship between the parties. The court noted the tendency to extend the duty to any employer when his/her employee is injured. If the nurse invites someone onto his/her premises or into his/her home, the court noted there may be a duty to render emergency care.[8] Not only would a nurse owe a duty to the patients he/she has been assigned, but also to their family members.

The Good Samaritan laws affect the standard of care in emergency situations. Most of the statutes provide that the nurse who renders emergency care will not be liable for negligence. However, most of the statutes do not provide this immunity when the nurse's actions have been "grossly negligent." The difference between negligence and gross negligence is one of degree. Acts that are willful or malicious or in total disregard of human life constitute gross negligence. For example, suppose a nurse witnesses a hit-and-run accident. The child is lying on the sidewalk bleeding profusely. The nurse stops the arterial bleeding. The nurse then pulls the child into the street, where the child is struck by a semi. This is the type of obvious malfeasance that the drafters of most statutes did not want to be covered by the Good Samaritan law. The ramifications of the Good Samaritan laws will be discussed later.

Nurses are under a duty to eliminate risks to the patient that they know about or should have known about. The nurse is responsible for making the premises safe. A nurse who spills a glass of water should remedy the situation immediately to prevent anyone from slipping on the water. Nurses are under a duty to maintain a safe environment by spotting errors and eliminating existing or potential problems.

In *Levine v. Hartford Accident and Indemnity Co.*, Mrs. Levine, a hospital visitor, slipped on the floor while walking toward the elevator.[9] She fractured her hip in the fall and contended that she slipped in a "pool of water." She indicated that she felt a "damp condition" when she was lying on the floor.

At the trial, the hospital produced several witnessess to show that a great amount of care was used to keep the floors safe. Floors were damp-mopped every day and inspected twice daily.

Mrs. Levine's son was present and testified that he did not see any wet spot. The nursing supervisor also witnessed the accident and testified that there was no water present. Another visitor was standing in the hall and witnessed Mrs. Levine walking very rapidly when her ankle "gave out."

Mrs. Levine won in the trial court. The hospital appealed. The appeals court held that the hospital was not negligent because there was no evidence of any water. The appeals court held that the staff had not breached their duty to keep the premises in a safe condition. Had there been evidence of water, the court may have held differently.

In the *D'Antoni* case, a 62-year-old patient was admitted to Sara Mayo Hospital.[10] Her admitting diagnosis was cirrhosis, tonoclonic jerking, epileptic and psychomotor seizures. The physician ordered that side rails be placed and maintained on her bed at all times.

The nurse gave the patient an I.M. injection of Sodium Luminal. After administering this injection, she left the side rail down. The patient was found a half-hour later on the floor. The patient sustained a fracture dislocation of the left ulna, an impacted fracture of the left radius and an intertrochanteric fracture of the left femur.

The hospital nurse was found liable. The nurse was under a *duty* to follow the physician's orders. The nurse failed to follow the physician's order that the side rail be maintained on the bed at all times. The nurse was also under a *duty* to comply with hospital policy. The hospital had a policy requiring that side rails be up at night for all patients who are over sixty or receiving any medication which could cause drowsiness. The nurse violated this duty, which resulted in injury to the patient.

Many nurses have heard of the case of *Lunsford v. Board of Nurse Examiners for the State of Texas*.[11] Martha Lunsford, an R.N. whose license was suspended, tried to convince an appeals court that she violated *no duty* by refusing treatment to a man who came in with chest pain because he had not yet become her patient. The man was sent to another hospital some twenty-four miles away, but he died en route. Nurse Lunsford told the female companion to speed to the next hospital using the emergency flashers. She was advised to use the C.B. radio to call for aid en route. Finally, she was asked if she knew CPR since she may need to use it.

The court said that a nurse situated such as Nurse Lunsford had a *duty* to evaluate the medical status of the ailing person seeking professional care and to institute appropriate nursing care to stabilize a patient's condition and to prevent further complication. This was true even though she was instructed to transfer the patient by the emergency room physician.

Breach of Duty

A failure to conform to the required standard of care is a breach of duty. When the nurse fails to meet the appropriate standard of care, she is breaching her legal duty to the patient.[12] What constitutes the acceptable standard of care has been discussed previously. A nurse breaches her duty to the patient when she breaches that standard of care.

Whether a nurse breached her duty to the patient and fell below the standard was discussed in the famous *Norton* case, which involved the entry of an ambiguous order on the patient's chart.[13] The physician wrote, "Lanoxin 3.0 cc's now." He did not indicate whether the Lanoxin was to be given P.O. or I.M. The nurse was only familiar with the injectable form of Lanoxin and was unaware that the elixir form was far less potent. She asked two physicians in the ward if she should really give Lanoxin 3.0 cc.'s. One physician commented, "If that's what he ordered, it's probably what he wanted."

The nurse gave the 3-month-old child 3.0 cc.'s I.M. instead of P.O. The child died as a result of the dose. The nurse was negligent for failing to clarify the order with the attending physician. The court felt that an ordinary, prudent nurse would have verified a questionable order with the attending physician. The nurse could have also checked with the pharmacy, the *Physician's Desk Reference* or the pediatric nurse on duty. Because the nurse deviated from the standard of practice under the circumstances, she was negligent. Nurses are under a legal duty to always administer the right medication at the right time and by the right route.

The court also held that Dr. Statler, the prescribing physician, was also negligent for failing to denote the intended route of administration. The court said that "Dr. Statler was under a duty to specify the route, considering that the drug is prepared in two forms in which both dosages are measured in cubic centimeters. In dealing with modern drugs it is the duty of the prescribing physician who has full knowledge of the drug and its effect upon the human system."

In cases where there is a clear deviation from the acceptable nursing assessment or treatment, there is little difficulty in determining whether the standard of care was met. In the *Weinstein* case, the nurse was held liable for negligence in the administration of an anesthetic.[14] The patient had a general anesthetic. Before the surgery, the CRNA (certified registered nurse anesthetist) failed to find out if the patient had been N.P.O. Nitrous oxide was given (without the oxygen). This alone would be sufficient to cause death. During the surgery the nurse did not check the mask either. Expert testimony revealed that it is customary to check the mask to observe for signs of gastric contents to prevent aspiration. The report of the microscopic examination of the brain indicated that there was congestion of the white matter of the brain. The patient was found to have been asphyxiated because her trachea was occluded by vomitus.

There are a variety of ways a breach of the nurse's duty can occur. As previously discussed, a nurse is under a duty to administer the right medication to the right patient, in the right dose, at the right time, and in the right route. This is one of the first and most basic things that we are taught as student nurses. It is interesting to note that many nursing errors are made because the nurse forgot "the basics." Getting "back to the basics" could prevent a number of nursing errors from occurring.

In the *Habuda* case, Paula Habuda was admitted to Rex Hospital with a diagnosis of acute lumbosacral sprain.[15] Her physician ordered that a laxative be given of milk of magnesia and cascara.

The laxative was prepared and given to her by a student nurse in her final year at the Rex Hospital School of Nursing. Student nurses are held to the same standard as nurses. The laxative prepared by the student nurse contained a quantity of pHisoHex in it. One of the characteristics of pHisoHex is that it foams when shaken. Milk of magnesia does not foam when shaken. The patient drank the solution, and the student nurse was found negligent.

Proximate Cause

Proximate cause is the most difficult element for most practitioners to grasp. Once the plaintiff has demonstrated that the nurse owed a duty to the patient and that the nurse's action fell below the standard of care, proximate cause must be proven. This element requires that there be a reasonably close connection between the defendant's conduct and the resultant injury. This, in simplistic terms, means that the patient must show that whatever the health care provider did wrong caused the patient's injury.

In the *Kilbane* case, the hospital, physicians and nurses were sued after one of the mental patients was burned by the unshielded steam radiator in her room.[16] The court held that the hospital fell below the standard of care but that it did not directly cause the injury.

The jury found that the hospital had breached the standard of care by having an outmoded hospital facility in that the unshielded radiators could result in burns to the mentally ill persons. The nurses were criticized for not making more frequent observations. However, the jury could have found that the injury might have occurred at any moment that she was not under observation, just as she could have been burned by the unshielded radiators.

The *Gregg* case is also illustrative of the necessity for proving the proximate cause element.[17] The plaintiff came to the emergency room on August 1, complaining of substernal chest pain accompanied by nausea and vomiting. The emergency room physician took an EKG, started an I.V., and admitted him to the intensive care unit as a possible heart attack victim.

Dr. Ruesch, a family practitioner, was the plaintiff's attending physician. He ordered a consultation with the cardiologist, Dr. Forte. Dr. Forte founds the tracing to be normal. He thought the pains were caused by esophagitis or pericarditis.

He felt it was unlikely that he had sustained a myocardial infarction. Dr. Forte ordered daily EKGs and did not see the plaintiff decedent again.

After reading the second EKG, Dr. Ruesch moved the plaintiff from I.C.U. After reading the third EKG on August 3, he ordered additional tests and an x-ray which showed a hiatus hernia. An appointment was made with Dr. Forte for treadmill testing, angiography or any tests Dr. Forte felt were necessary. The plaintiff was then discharged.

The plaintiff's August 2 and 3 tracings were mailed by the hospital to Dr. Forte's office in Tucson. They arrived on August 7 and were read by Dr. Forte that day. Though there were some changes in the tracings, Dr. Forte did not believe the changes were medically significant, and he called his report into the hospital for transcription into the plaintiff's chart.

On August 8 and 9, Gregg again experienced severe chest pains, and on August 9 he collapsed at home and was pronounced dead on arrival at the hospital. The autopsy report indicated that Gregg had suffered from extensive heart disease and concluded that he died of a massive myocardial infarction.

The plaintiff argued that the hospital was independently negligent for its failure to establish appropriate rules and regulations concerning the care and treatment of suspected cardiac patients. In opposing the motion for summary judgment, appellant relied on the affidavit of Dr. Abraham J. Kauver. He had extensive experience in the field in the enactment of hospital rules, regulations and protocol. It was his opinion that the care given by the hospital was substandard because it had failed to adopt regulations or protocol which would have required daily and/or immediate transmission, reading and reporting by cardiologists of electrocardiograms on patients presenting signs and symptoms of acute coronary artery disease and requiring the transmission of the opinions of such cardiologists to the treating physician on a daily basis.

Dr. Kauver further believed that the conduct of the hospital was substandard by not providing regulations and protocol for the referral of patients presenting signs or symptoms of acute coronary disease to other facilities and/or to specialists properly skilled and trained to deal with such problems.

Dr. Kauver did not state anywhere in his affidavit that the failure of the hospital to adopt there rules, regulations and protocol was the proximate cause of Gregg's death. Ordinarily, expert medical testimony is required to establish proximate cause and make out a *prima facie* case of medical malpractice unless a causal relationship is readily apparent to the trier of fact.

The record showed that the plaintiff was in fact referred to a cardiologist and that the cardiologist read Gregg's x-rays two days prior to the time Gregg died. The record showed that even if the hospital did have rules, regulations and protocol requiring immediate reading and the immediate rendering of an opinion to the attending physician, *nothing different would have occurred* since Dr. Forte did not believe there were any significant abnormalities in the EKGs. Furthermore, Dr. Gordon Ewy, a cardiologist, reviewed the records in this case and testified in his deposition that in his opinion he had no reason to believe, based upon his review of the matter, that any delay which occurred in transmitting the EKG reports to Dr. Forte caused or resulted in the patient's death. This lack of medical testimony on the issue of causation rules out the imposition of liability on independent negligence.

These cases exemplify the principle that mere proof of the nurse's negligence or malpractice does not entitle the patient to recover damages from the negligent nurse or hospital. The plaintiff patient must prove by the greater weight of the evidence that the wrongful conduct was a proximate or direct cause of the injury.

Problems of proving proximate cause also arise in situtations where an injury could have been caused by more than one act. In such cases, the jury must decide which act caused the injury and who the responsible party was. Most states have comparative negligence so that the jury can apportion the amount of damage if there are two or more persons who negligently caused the injury.

For example, in a recent unreported Ohio case, a 7-year-old child was riding her bike. She fell going around a corner and the bicycle pedal protruded into her knee. The little girl was brought to the emergency room by squad.

The emergency squad indicated that there was "gushing blood" at the scene, suggesting an arterial bleed. With application of pressure, the squad was able to stop the bleeding. The emergency room nurse did not read the squad report. The patient eventually had an above-the-knee amputation. She sued, through her parents, alleging negligence on the part of the emergency room nurse and the emergency room physician. The jury decided that both the nurse's and the physician's negligence caused the injury. The nurse was cited for failure to read the emergency squad record. The jury found that emergency room nurses were under a legal duty to obtain a complete and concise history on all their E.R. patients, including a review of the squad sheet.

The E.R. physician was negligent for failure to recognize arterial damage. Had he recognized arterial bleeding by conducting a full exam, he could have consulted a vascular surgeon. This would have resulted in saving the little girl's leg.

Therefore, the jury felt that the negligence of both the nurse and the physician proximately resulted in the patient losing her leg. They assessed her damages at $750,000. The nurse was adjudicated to be 50 percent negligent and responsible for $375,000 of the verdict. The physician was 50 percent negligent and responsible for the remaining $375,000. The law on comparative negligence will also be discussed later.

In the *Bugden* case, a physician ordered the nurse to give some Novocaine.[18] The nurse mistakenly drew up Adrenalin, which was injected into the patient. The patient expired and his wife sued the nurse for negligently killing her husband. The jury found that the administration of the wrong medication killed the patient. His death was directly and proximately cau'sed by the nurse's failure to read the bottle. Therefore, the plaintiff should prevail and recover damages.

In the *Palmer* case, the plaintiff went to surgery.[19] Postoperatively, the patient developed gangrenous sores on her heels. She alleged this was due to the surgical straps being applied too tightly to her feet and ankles by the nurse. Her feet were strapped to suspend them above the operating table during a forty-five minute operation. The straps were not loosened or checked at any time during the surgery. The court held that the evidence presented an issue for the jury to decide if the nurse was responsible for proximately causing the injury.

The *Lenger* case is illustrative of the proximate cause element.[20] On August

10, Dr. Rainone performed a colon resection on Mr. Lenger to remove a cancerous growth in the middle aspect of the transverse colon. Mr. Lenger was on bedrest. He had an I.V. running and a nasogastric tube in place.

Dr. Rainone gave explicit instructions that Mr. Lenger was not to be fed by mouth. A N.P.O. sign also appeared above his head.

On August 12, Pauline Jones was on duty, as a licensed practical nurse. A morning tray was brought up for Mr. Lenger by the dietary department. The patient protested when the nurse attempted to feed him breakfast. He asked her to call his doctor but she refused.

At lunch time this procedure was repeated. The chicken and dressing she fed the patient clogged up his nasogastric tube. He refused the evening meal.

The patient received no more food by mouth until ordered by Dr. Rainone on August 16. On August 20, the patient became ill and was taken to surgery. Dr. Rainone discovered that the two ends of the colon had come apart where the colon resection had been sutured. There were gas and fecal matter present in the abdominal cavity.

The case went to trial, and the primary question was whether the feeding four days prior was the cause of the harm. The plaintiff failed to prove that the feeding proximately caused the injury, and the court found in favor of the nurse.

Damages

The plaintiff must prove actual damage. The patient must show that the act or omission damaged him in some way. Damages are legally defined as a pecuniary compensation which may be recovered in the courts by one who has suffered loss, detriment or injury to his person, property or rights through the act, omission or negligence of another. In tort actions, there are three main categories of damages: nominal, compensatory, and punitive.

Nominal damages are small sums of money awarded by the court because there has been a technical invasion of one's legal rights. It may be a dollar or two dollars. This type of damage is awarded when the person has no substantial loss or injury to be compensated, but the standard of care has been violated. For example, a patient tells the nurse he is severely allergic to aspirin. When the patient experiences a headache, the nurse accidentally administers aspirin. The patient suffers no untoward effect. The mistake is not discovered until one week later, at which time the patient is informed. He then sues the nurse for professional negligence. The jury awards him $5. This award is known as nominal damage.

Compensatory damages are meant to compensate the patient for actual loss sustained from the negligently inflicted injury. Most awards in malpractice actions are for compensatory damages. The theory of compensatory damages is to put the injured patient in as good a position as he or she was in before the loss or injury. The law is concerned with making a plaintiff "whole again," not providing him/her with a means to profit by the defendant's act.

An example of compensatory damages is illustrated by the *Richardson v. Doe* case.[21] In this case, the mother delivered a baby, and the delivery was uneventful. Approximately two hours after delivery, the mother started to bleed heavily. The two O.B. nurses discussed and evaluated the situation and decided to notify the physician. There was a full moon out, and the O.B. department was very busy. The nurses forgot to notify the physician until six hours later.

The obstetrician came in and immediately performed a D. and C. By the time she arrived, the patient required two units of packed cells. The patient got hepatitis from the blood and upon her release filed suit.

The court first found that the nurses had a legal duty to provide good care because they had been assigned to the patient. The court then went on to the second element. The court found that the nurses had breached the acceptable standard of care. The nurses should have timely notified the physician of the patient's hemorrhagic condition.

The court then went to the third element. The nurses' failure to timely notify the physician directly and proximately caused the patient to lose blood, which directly caused her to have a transfusion, which directly caused the hepatitis. The only issue left was, "What are the damages?"

The plaintiff wanted her hospital bill for the extra time compensated. She lost four weeks of work which were attributable to this injury. Her husband had to pay a babysitter for the first four weeks in which the plaintiff had planned to care for the infant. The plaintiff also wanted compensation for her pain and suffering. The husband also sued, requesting compensation of his loss of consortium claim. Loss of consortium is an action filed by the spouse of an injured party for the loss of conjugal relations because of the spouse's injury.

The third type of damages are called *punitive damages*. Punitive damages are sometimes called exemplary damages because they are meant to serve as an example to other defendants not to do an intentional act. Punitive damages are for aggravated, wanton and willful acts and are awarded in addition to nominal or compensatory damages.

As a matter of law, punitive damages are not awarded in a simple negligence action. Punitive damages may be awarded when the health care provider has done an intentional act that is willful, wanton, malicious or outrageous.

INTENTIONAL TORTS

As you will recall, negligence refers to conduct as opposed to state of mind. Intentional torts, on the other hand, require a specific state of mind, usually an intention to do the wrongful act. The most important aspect is that, depending on the language of the insurance contract and the public policy of the state, intentional acts may not be covered by one's liability insurance. For example, under Ohio law, an insurer does not have to provide coverage for intentional acts. If a policy specifically states that intentional acts are covered, then the courts have enforced this as a contract.

Punitive damages may be awarded for intentional acts. Punitive damages have already been discussed previously in this section discussing damages. Evidence of the nurse's net worth may be considered by the finder of fact in determining the appropriate amount of punitive damages. As previously mentioned, punitive damages are meant to punish the defendant when his/her conduct is determined to be wanton, willful, malicious or outrageous. A $100 award from a nurse who only has a net worth of $200 is a substantial burden. However, a $100 award from a millionaire does not represent the same burden. Therefore, the court looks at the defendant's net worth to see how much it would take to "hurt" that defendant. Many states, like Ohio, have established that this financial information is not required before a punitive damage award has been granted to a prevailing party.[22]

A recent Ohio case established that concealment of an act of negligence does not render malicious the negligent act.[23] Malice deals with the manner in which the act is performed. In this case, a 9-year-old had developed a malignant brain tumor. Surgery resulted in removal of only approximately 80 percent of the tumor mass, so radiation therapy was prescribed. Due to a miscalculation by the physicist who calibrated the radiation equipment, the radiation was considerably in excess of that which was prescribed.

The plaintiff alleged that she lost her hair, sustained stunted growth, and a speech impediment, and became a quadriplegic as a result of the radium overdose. The court found that punitive damages could not be awarded under the circumstances of this case. As soon as the error was discovered, the hospital notified the public of the error.

The plaintiff argued that the great danger posed by overradiation is of such a nature as to be intentional, reckless, wanton and willful. She argued fraud on the part of the hospital because it reported to the patient's mother that she had received less than 10 percent excess radiation. The court disagreed with this, and said an act of mere negligence does not in itself demonstrate the degree of intention and deliberation necessary to raise a question of punitive damages.

In order to prove that conduct was willful or wanton, there must be circumstances of aggravation or outrage (such as spite, malice, or a fraudulent or evil motive on the part of the defendant), or a conscious and deliberate disregard of the interests of others.

Many states require that in order for punitive damages to be awarded, nominal damages must first be awarded.[24] The purpose of punitive damages is to punish the guilty party for the wicked, corrupt, and malicious motive and design which prompted the wrongful act.[25]

The intent element may be satisfied in several ways. The person may actually *intend* the act or have knowledge to a substantial certainty that a result will follow from his or her actions.

Obviously, a nurse can slander, strike or otherwise intentionally harm as readily as the next person. Items such as assault, battery, slander, wrongful commitment, false imprisonment, defamation and invasion of privacy are examples of intentional acts.

Assault and Battery

Most nurses are familiar with the terms "assault" and "battery" in the criminal context. However, they may be used to describe torts as well. Nurses have been held liable for committing assault and battery against patients.

Though assault and battery are frequently mentioned together, they are two separate entities. Assault is an act that puts another in apprehension of being touched in a manner which is offensive or provoking.[26] It is unlawfully placing an individual in apprehension of immediate bodily harm without consent.[27] Contact, or actual touching, is not an element of assault. The credible threat of harm is enough.

Battery is unlawful touching of another without consent. Everyone has a right to freedom from physical abuse. When one intentionally and willfully strikes another without justification, a battery has been committed. When this occurs, the law provides the injured person with the right to recover damages.

A nurse cannot attend to any patients without touching them. This touching is usually with consent and is not therefore an assault and battery. However, if the nurse exceeds the bounds of the consent, problems may occur.

Consent can only be given by those who are competent to give it. Minors or intoxicated, sedated or mentally incompetent patients may not be competent to give consent. Nurses *can*, however, defend themselves when necessary. Courts will usually determine whether the actions taken by the nurse were justified under the circumstances. For example, assume the nurse is working in the emergency room with an intoxicated patient. The patient strikes at the nurse as she starts to unwrap his dressing. The nurse is justified in using such force as reasonably necessary to protect herself.

In the *Burton* case, a physician attempted to remove the sutures from the healed laceration of a 4-year-old's toe.[28] The child began to cry and wiggle on the cart. The mother was attempting to hold the child down. The physician repeatedly slapped the child on the leg and buttocks. The parents took the child to another physician to have the sutures removed. They then sued Dr. Leftwich, their first doctor, for assault and battery.

In the suit against him, Dr. Leftwich tried to defend himself by claiming the slaps were for the child's own safety. He maintained that he needed to keep the child immobilized to prevent any accidental damage from the scissors. The child had bruises on her legs for three weeks. The court felt the physician had used excessive force and was therefore guilty of assault and battery.

In the *Mattocks* case, a 23-month-old infant fell and suffered a laceration of her tongue.[29] A medical student was in the process of suturing this less-than-accessible area when the infant bit the medical student's finger. The infant had a firm grasp on the medical student's left middle finger and would not release her hold. The child bit hard enough to touch the bone and to cause blood to spurt from the finger.

Panic-stricken, the medical student tried to free his hand. He shouted at the child. Twice he tried to extricate his finger by placing a tongue depressor in her mouth. Finally, he slapped the child, and this resulted in the release of the medical student's fingers. The child's parents sued for assault and battery.

The court found that the medical student's actions were justified. He struck the child only once, and only hard enough to allow for the release of his finger. The amount of force used was justified under the circumstances.

In the *Sarlat* case, a patient in Brooklyn State Hospital had a habit of tapping his foot.[30] The attendant on duty was annoyed by the patient's tapping. The attendant struck the patient, fracturing his mandible. The patient sued for assault and battery and recovered.

Nurses have been successful at suing their patients for assault and battery, especially when the patients were alert, oriented and fully cognizant. The courts that have denied recovery have done so on the theory that the nurse assumes the risk of such harm.

For example, in the *Burrows* case, the nurse sued her former patient for assault and battery.[31] She was a private duty nurse in a Hawaiian hospital when she was hit on the head with a lamp by a patient suffering alcoholic delirium tremens. The court held that in accepting employment the nurse does not assume the risk of injury. She could sue the patient for assault and battery as long as she could not have prevented the injury, the court said.

Many attorneys for patients favor bringing an action for assault and battery in addition to a claim for negligence. This is an attempt to avoid procurement of an expert witness by the other side. Others will proceed on a negligence-only theory.

Assault and battery are intentional acts — acts for which most insurance policies do not provide coverage. Therefore, if a judgment is obtained for assault and battery, the insurance company will not have to pay, and the individual is personally responsible for the judgment. Since the insurance company has a deeper pocket, most attorneys elect to proceed on a negligence theory.

False Imprisonment

False imprisonment is the intentional and unjustifiable detention of a person against his/her will. The detention can be by physical restraint, barriers or even threats of harm. For example, locking a patient in her room unjustifiably may result in liability for false imprisonment, as may any attempt to restrain a competent adult.

False imprisonment is an intentional tort, and arises frequently in conjunction with assault and battery claims. There are three elements for false imprisonment: willful detention of the individual, detention without consent, and action by the person detaining the individual without the authority of law.[32]

Many false imprisonment cases allege wrongful confinement of a patient to a mental institution. However, cases are not as frequent as they once were, due to recent changes in the law.

In the *Whitree* case, a patient recovered damages for false imprisonment after being unjustly confined in a state mental hospital for twelve years.[33] In *Big Town Nursing Homes, Inc.*, an alcoholic patient voluntarily admitted himself.[34] He later attempted to leave and was forcibly restrained. Employees at the nursing home locked away his suitcase and clothes, and restricted his use of the phone and his right to see visitors. They locked him in his room and tied him to a chair to prevent him from leaving. He sued for false imprisonment and obtained a $13,000 judgment.

Patients who want to sign out against medical advice (A.M.A.) can present a problem. Patients who are alert, oriented, competent and not under legal commitment should be permitted to sign out A.M.A. However, it is not always easy for the nurse to determine the patient's competency. Generally, patients may be detained in the hospital if there is danger that they may jeopardize their lives or the lives of others. (See the section in Chapter 7 on advising patients who want to sign out A.M.A.)

Nurses should never detain a patient for failure to pay a bill. It is reasonable and permissible for the nurse to have the patient stop momentarily at the business office to check on the status of his/her bill. However, it is impermissible to retain the patient for hours, days or weeks because the patient either disputes or is unable to pay the medical bill.

In the *Gadsden General Hospital* case, a patient was detained for eleven hours for failure to pay her hospital bill.[35] There was evidence that the nurse threatened to tie her to the bed if she did not keep quiet. The patient was locked in her room. Her detention ended when the hospital administrator received a writ of *habeas corpus* seeking her release. The patient sued for false imprisonment and the court ruled in her favor, awarding $1,500.

In the *Bailie* case, a mother came to the hospital to pick up her child who had been discharged from the hospital.[36] The nurse sent the mother to the business office. It took the mother about thirty minutes to arrange payment for the child's bill. The mother sued, alleging that the child had been unlawfully detained for thirty minutes. The court disagreed, finding that there was no false imprisonment. There was no threat that the child would not be able to leave the hospital. This exemplified that a hospital or nursing home can delay a patient's discharge until the paperwork is complete. This is true as long as the delay is reasonable.

The law regarding false imprisonment is one of reasonableness. There are many cases which have ruled against the patient who sues for false imprisonment. For example, in the *Pounders v. Trinity Court Nursing Home* case, a 75-year-old disabled widow sued after spending two months in a nursing home.[37] She previously resided with her niece who no longer wanted her to live with her. When the niece arranged for her to move to the nursing home, she did not object. She only complained on one occasion and to a nurse's aide. She failed to report the complaint to anyone in authority.

Mrs. Pounders was released to the home of another niece with the assistance of an attorney. She sued for false imprisonment and lost. She was unable to prove she had been detained.

The nurse is also faced with the difficult decision of when to use restraints. This is discussed in the section on restraints in Chapter 8.

Defamation

Defamation is injury to a person's reputation or character through oral or written communications to a third person. Defamation is an intentional act which can result in an award of money damages. Oral defamation is called slander, and written defamation is called libel.

First, the defamatory statement must be communicated or overheard by a third person to be actionable. Statements or comments made, no matter how vindictive, are not actionable if exchanged only between two parties. Second, most states hold that the statement must be false. Third, there must be no legally recognized privilege protecting the statement.

There are generally two defenses to a defamation action: truth and privilege.

In most states, if the disclosure is true, the patient will not win the defamation suit.

When persons with a legal interest or duty communicate with one another, information which is otherwise defamatory is recognized as a qualified privilege.[38] If the information is true and disclosed with good intentions, no liability results. "When the public interest is being served, such as protection of the community from highly contagious disease, it is proper to inform those persons with a public interest in the relevant information."[39]

Courts recognize the importance of allowing nursing supervisors the freedom to discuss a nurse's performance with other members in administration. This is one example of a communication which would be protected by a qualified privilege.

Statements which are otherwise defamatory, when made in testimony, pleadings, or other papers in a judicial proceeding, are absolutely privileged. Of course, these must be material to the inquiry being made.

If a hospital or health institution discloses certain information from a patient's medical record, there may be liability for damages. This is true absent a court order or statutory authority to release the information.

It is possible for the hospital or health institution to assert a qualified privilege when disclosure is made to those who have a legitimate interest in the information. The interest of the community in serving justice would create a moral duty of the hospital to comply with such requests by an employer, insurance company or other party in litigation.[40]

One case is illustrative of this point. The court held that a qualified privilege attached to the response by an employer concerning a former employee with respect to an inquiry made by a prospective employer.[41] In another case, the nurse left employment with the city health department and applied for another nursing position.[42] Her prospective employer contacted the director of the health department for references. The nurse was not pleased with the director's response regarding her nursing abilities. She sued, alleging that the statements were defamatory.

The court ruled that a qualified privilege attached and that the statements were made without malice; therefore, there was no liability.

Most prospective employers and nurse managers obtain a release form to check on a nurse's references. This prevents the matter from going to court and having the judge decide if a qualified privilege attaches. Hospitals and employers have a legal duty to make sure the nurses they employ are qualified and licensed. This is why many employers check to make sure the dates and places of employment are verified.

In the *Judge* case, a private duty nurse named Helen Judge was performing nursing services at Rockford Memorial Hospital.[43] She was intermittently employed by the patients and their families. During the time the nurse was on duty, a number of narcotics came up missing. During a three-month period, the director of nursing received notice of three narcotic losses from the pharmacist. Each reported the loss of one 30 cc. vial of Demerol.

An investigation revealed about twenty-two instances where Nurse Judge failed to properly chart the administration of narcotics on the medication record. Mrs. Judge was called into the nursing office but gave no reasons for the discrepancies in her charting.

Mrs. Erdemer called the Nurses Professional Registry and requested that Mrs.

Judge no longer be assigned to Rockford Hospital. The grievance committee at the Registry asked that a letter be sent.

Mrs. Erdemer then wrote a letter detailing what had occurred. In her letter, she mentioned that she spoke with Nurse Judge, who offered no explanation for the charting discrepancies.

Nurse Judge sued for defamation. The court found that a qualified privilege existed and denied recovery. The director of nurses had a duty to make the communication in the interest and protection of the community.

In the *Merritt v. Detroit Memorial Hospital* case, a routine urinalysis of a ward clerk revealed the presence of morphine sulfate.[44] The ward clerk had not been prescribed the medication by any physician.

A hearing was held to review the evidence and the employee was discharged. She filed suit, alleging defamation for comments made during the hearing. The court found that a qualified privilege existed.

Statements made by nurses to their supervisors are protected by this qualified privilege, even if they are in error, as long as they were made in good faith.

There is no formula to the application of the qualified privilege. It is generally one that is justified in the medical record. A qualified privilege is based on a legal or moral duty of common decency.

The nurse should be cautious in his/her personal statements, especially those regarding patients and their families, co-workers, supervisors and physicians. A loose tongue can land the nurse in court. Any remark about a person's reputation and good name that tends to diminish his/her value and esteem and arouse adverse feelings may be defamatory if communicated to a third person.

In Maine, a nurse recovered for harsh and derogatory remarks that were made by a physician to the hospital administrator.[45] These comments were made intentionally to cause a disruption between the hospital administrator and the nurse.

Nurse Farrell was a staff nurse at Gary Memorial Hospital. One day she was openly critical of the physician's postoperative care of a patient. Nurse Farrell was dismissed for unprofessional conduct.

The hospital subsequently rehired the nurse on the condition that she would never make similar communications. When the physician found out the nurse had been rehired, he called the administrator and said, "I want to ask you why you would stoop so low as to hire that creep, that malignant son of a bitch, back to work for you in the hospital."

The physician added that he felt she was unfit to take care of patients. He indicated that he intended to prove this and would continue to make an issue out of the nurse being rehired.

The nurse sued the physician for defamation. The court awarded her $5,000.

Invasion of Privacy

Patients necessarily surrender a certain amount of privacy whenever they enter a hospital. However, an unwarranted exploitation of one's personality or private affairs is an invasion of privacy. To be actionable, the invasion must be of a nature to cause outrage, mental suffering, shame or humiliation to a person of ordinary sensibilities.

Hospitals, physicians and nurses may become liable for invasion of privacy if they disclose certain information contained in patients' medical records. Generally, disclosures of information to private individuals, such as attorneys, insurance companies or family members, is not a violation of the right of privacy.

Situations like this arise in the taking of photographs which are published without the patient's permission. Patients with unusual conditions or operations are especially attractive to photographers or medical writers. To protect against this, most hospitals or employers have their own consent forms which the patient signs if any pictures are taken.

In the *Berthiaume* case, the patient was suffering from cancer of the larynx.[46] He had undergone two surgeries for the cancer. The patient and his wife both told Dr. Pratt, the otolarynologist, not to take any pictures.

Shortly before the patient died, Dr. Pratt went in, raised the patient's head, placed two towels underneath, and took Mr. Berthiaume's picture. The wife sued, and the court found that the unauthorized photography was an invasion of the patient's privacy.

In *Clayman*, the patient refused to allow the doctor to take any pictures of her because of facial disfigurement, but the physician took her picture when she was semicomatose.[47] The patient and her husband sued to have the pictures returned.

The physician said he was privileged to take photographs of his private patients without their consent because they were a part of the medical record. The Pennsylvania court disagreed, and ordered the physician to return the film to the plaintiff.

In one case, the parents of a deceased child sued after the unauthorized picture of their son appeared in the newspaper.[48] Their son had been born with his heart on the outside of his body.

In the *Molein* case, the doctor erroneously told Mrs. Molein that she had syphilis.[49] Mrs. Molein became upset and suspicious that her husband had engaged in extramarital sexual activities. This produced marital discord which resulted in divorce. The California Supreme Court allowed recovery for the mental anguish caused secondary to a misdiagnosis.

The next area is the release of information to the news media. If the publication is of public or general interest, it is not prohibited.

"In the ordinary situation hospitals may release information of legitimate news value for immediate publication by news agencies without fear of a suit for invasion of the right of privacy."[50] Hospital policy concerning this matter should be formulated to protect the patient's interests. Generally only the name and a general statement of the patient's condition is given unless specific consent from the patient is obtained.

TYPES OF EVIDENCE IN NURSING LIABILITY ACTIONS

There are three types of evidence that the plaintiff can present to demonstrate that the nurse fell below the standard of care: direct, circumstantial and *res ipsa loquitur. Direct evidence* is an observation. For example, assume a patient is allergic to penicillin. The nurse erroneously administers the patient an I.V. piggyback of penicillin instead of Keflin. The penicillin is charted on the patient's record. This record would be direct evidence.

Circumstantial evidence also may be used to show that the nurse deviated from the standard of care. For example, in the *D'Antoni* case discussed earlier, it could be inferred that the patient fell because she was found lying on the floor. Since no one witnessed the incident, the plaintiff used circumstantial evidence to create this inference.

The third type of evidence is called *res ipsa loquitur. Res ipsa loquitur* is a Latin term meaning "the thing speaks for itself." In negligence actions, the doctrine is invoked when the plaintiff has no direct evidence, but the injury itself leads to the inference it would not have occurred absent a negligent act. The important thing to know about this doctrine is that the plaintiff need not prove the four elements of negligence. The burden shifts to the defendant nurse to prove she was not negligent.

Res ipsa loquitur is rarely applied to nursing negligence actions and is considered an exception to the rule.[51] It is used only in cases where the plaintiffs would be severely disadvantaged in proving their cases. This theory was derived from the 1863 English case of *Byrne v. Boadle.* A person was walking down the street past a shop when a flour barrel rolled out of the second floor window and struck a passerby. The court realized the problems the plaintiff would have in trying to prove the four elements of negligence. The court carved out an exception to the rule because this was an act which did not ordinarily happen in the absence of negligence. The court also noted that the barrel was in the exclusive control of the shop owner and that there was not evidence of any negligence on the part of the passerby. These three elements remain the key elements even today.

Courts remain reluctant to apply the *res ipsa loquitur* doctrine except in cases where the negligence is obvious. The retention of foreign objects, sponges, instruments and needles is one area where the doctrine has been applied.

The 1985 case of *Powell v. Mullins* is an example of how this doctrine is applied.[52] The plaintiff was a diabetic, and her baby had grown too large to be delivered. She entered the hosptial to have a Caesarean delivery. An eighteen-inch square surgical lap sponge was left inside the abdomen. While performing the Caesarean surgical procedure, which lasted over two hours, the defendant used two rolled-up eighteen-inch square lap sponges, placing them inside plaintiff's abdomen on either side of the uterus. Twenty-eight other sponges were used during the procedure to soak up blood, but only the two eighteen-inch square lap sponges were actually placed inside the plaintiff's abdomen. Despite the defendant's own search of the operative field in preparing to close the incision, as well as two reports given by a nurse that the sponge count was correct, one of the eighteen-inch square lap sponges was left inside the plaintiff. Approximately four days after her surgery, the plaintiff began to complain of pain and swelling on one side. X-rays were taken, revealing the presence of the sponge in plaintiff's abdomen. Five days after the Caesarean section, the plaintiff underwent a second surgical procedure to remove the sponge.

During the trial, the judge directed a verdict in favor of the doctor, hospital and nurses because the plaintiff did not have an expert. The plaintiff appealed, saying that this was a *res ipsa loquitur* case and an expert was not needed.

The court noted the general rule that expert testimony is generally needed to sustain a malpractice case. The court noted that the key to preventing retained surgical sponges is to routinely inspect the operative field and recognize the fallibility of sponge counts. The court noted a 1980 case which found that intraoperative x-rays cannot be justified on cost basis.[53]

The court held that a failure to remove sponges, needles and instruments during surgery constituted prima facie evidence of negligence. The court found the type of harm so strong an inference of negligence that expert testimony was not required to establish the standard of care. The court also said the responsibility to remove sponges was that of the doctor and not that of the nurses assisting him.

In the 1985 case of *Sullivan v. Methodist Hospital of Texas*, the court said the doctrine of *res ipsa loquitur* is applicable to the cases where surgical sponges or instruments are left in during surgery.[54] In the case, a sponge was left in the abdomen following a Caesarean section.

In 1985, Texas passed a comprehensive tort reform bill. This law severely restricted the use of the *res ipsa loquitur* doctrine. *Res ipsa loquitur* could only be applied to health care liability claims if it had been applied by the appellate courts of the state.

The court noted that at common law, *res ipsa loquitur* permitted a finding of negligence by the jury in only limited instance, without expert testimony. The three factors necessary for application of *res ipsa loquitur* are (1) that the nature of the event is such that it would not ordinarily happen absent negligence, (2) that the defendant had sole management and control of the instrumentality causing the injury, and (3) that the plaintiff had not contributed to his own injury.

The court further explained the following:

> The doctrine of *res ipsa loquitur* springs from the very practical process of drawing logical conclusions from circumstantial evidence. Its purpose is to permit one who suffers injury from something under the control of another which ordinarily would not cause the injury except for the other's negligence, to present his grievance to the court or jury on the basis of the reasonable inferences to be drawn from such facts, even though he may be unable to present direct evidence of the other's negligence.[55]

The *res ipsa loquitur* doctrine has also been applied to instances where an anesthetized patient received an injury to a remote part of the body or when the patient was burned during surgery. In *Starnes v. Charlotte-Mecklenburg Hospital Authority*, an action was brought against the anesthetist, surgeon, hospital and nurses.[56] The plaintiff was burned during surgery. The issue was whether it was negligent to provide a hot water bottle to heat the infant patient during surgery instead of a thermal blanket.

In summary, it is important for all nurses to observe patients — especially patients who are asleep, debilitated, very young or anesthetized. Surgical nurses should chart the positions of any equipment and straps used during surgery. They should make sure there is proper grounding and that electrical equipment is working appropriately. *Res ipsa loquitur* does not establish that the nurse is negligent. Rather, it shifts the burden of proof from the plaintiff to the nurse. Generally, the plaintiff has the burden of proof in showing that the nurse was negligent. In this rare exception, it is now up to the nurse to prove he/she was not negligent.

THE NECESSITY OF EXPERT TESTIMONY

Expert testimony is generally required to prove negligence on the part of the nurse. This means that a nurse or physician who is competent in the health practitioner's field must testify that the nurse deviated from the acceptable standard of care. The exception to this rule is the situation where the alleged negligence is a matter of common knowledge. For example, a layperson would know, without being told by a nurse, that there is negligence when a patient who goes for a breast biopsy gets her gallbladder removed erroneously. Removal of the wrong kidney is also something that would not require expert testimony to establish negligence.

The other exception, involving *res ipsa loquitur*, has already been discussed. However, it is worth noting that several states have retained the requirement of expert testimony despite the application of *res ipsa loquitur*.[57]

The 1986 case of *Kanter v. Metropolitan Medical Center* is a good illustration of the necessity for expert testimony.[58] It also shows how courts consider local, state and national nursing standards in nursing malpractice actions.

The plaintiff, age 31, with borderline intellectual function and acting-out behavior, was admitted to the locked psychiatric ward for evaluation. She told the nurse she wanted to take a tub bath. The nurse ran the bath, helped her wash her hair, scrubbed her back, and sat and visited with her while she finished her bath. She told the nurse that she wanted to be left alone to relax in the tub for a short time. The nurse left to help another patient and upon returning found the plaintiff lying in the tub with her face in the water. The plaintiff died as a result of drowning.

The defendants filed a motion for summary judgment because the plaintiff failed to produce an expert to testify that the nurse fell below the acceptable standard of care. The court granted the motion and the plaintiff appealed.

The court found that professional judgment is required by psychiatric nurses in determining the proper amount of supervision to provide a mental patient. The jury cannot be allowed to speculate as to what duty a trained nurse has, for this must be provided by expert testimony. In a psychiatric ward, the potential tendencies of patients suffering from mental illness are not so easily determined by one without special training. There was nothing in the record to show that this patient was suicidal.

Therefore, the appeals court approved the granting of the defendant's motion for summary judgment.

In selecting or opposing an expert witness, it is important to know whether the nurse's or physician's actions are to be judged by a community or a nationwide standard. It all started in 1880, when many states started to protect their physicians with what came to be called the "locality rule." (During this time, hospitals were not sued because they were protected by the charitable immunity doctrine.) Physicians who practiced in small towns did not want to be held to the standard of physicians practicing in large cities.

As discussed in Chapter 1, the "locality rule" required that the plaintiff would have to prove a deviation from the standard of care in the defendant doctor's community. This led to the so-called "conspiracy of silence." Physicians were reluctant to testify against another physician in their community. This hindered a plaintiff from obtaining necessary medical testimony.

In recent years, becaused of enhanced communication and travel, the distinction between the quality of care in rural and urban facilities has narrowed. Today, the locality rule has been limited or abolished in many states.

One author recently summed up the situation as follows:

> "In regard to the nonspecialist, six states have the same-locality rule, and eighteen have the similar-localities rule. Twenty-three jurisdictions have a similar-circumstances standard, one specifically imposes a national standard, three have a 'guess-what' rule, two appear to exclude locality as a consideration, and one state has the standard of the profession in general." In all but the same-locality rule states, the end result may be a national rule.[59]

It is important to note that many jurisdictions continue to judge hospitals by community standards only.[60] The rest utilize primarily a nationwide standard. This means the care by an emergency room nurse in California should be similar to the care rendered by an emergency room nurse in Ohio. Being certified in your area does not hold you to a higher standard. A certified emergency room nurse is held to the same standard as those nurses who are uncertified. Certification tends to increase your credibility with the jury.

The recent case of *Wade v. John Archbold Memorial Hospital* exemplified the principle espoused in the nationwide standard rule.[61] The court said the location or size of a hospital does not alter a hospital's duty to provide competent people to render patient care.

The plaintiff underwent surgery to repair a fractured right femur. After surgery she was given physical therapy which resulted in a refracture of the femur. She alleged negligence on the part of the physical therapist for initiating treatment prematurely.

The hospital was located in Georgia. The plaintiff attempted to introduce at trial an Alabama orthopedic surgeon who was going to testify regarding the standard of care for a physical therapist. The hospital sought to exclude him as an expert because he had never worked in a small Georgia hospital.

The trial court agreed and the plaintiff appealed. The court of appeals agreed with the trial court and ruled that the standard of care was to be determined by the locality rule. However, the Supreme Court reversed.

The Supreme Court discussed the rationale underlying the locality rule. The court said that the plaintiff was not questioning the adequacy of the facilities but rather the professional judgment of one of its employees.

On February 27, 1986, the Illinois Appeals Court decided the *Hansbrough v. Kosyak* case.[62] This case allowed an expert practicing in a large city to comment on standards in a smaller community.

In this case, the plaintiff sued after alleged complications from a subcutaneous mastectomy with Silastic implants. The plaintiff's expert was a board-certified plastic surgeon who was professor and chief of plastic and reconstructive surgery.

The plaintiff's expert testified that such a procedure should not be performed by a surgeon, but only those physicians trained in plastic and reconstructive surgery. The plaintiff's expert also testified that the hospital was negligent by allowing the doctor to perform the surgery.

The court said that a physician is qualified to testify as long as there are certain minimum standards of care that are uniform.

One case recently held that an ocular plastic surgeon was not competent to testify against a general plastic surgeon.[63] The plaintiff had blepharoplastic surgery with a resultant ptosis.

A Colorado appellate court recently held that an internist was not qualified to testify about the standard of care for surgeons.[64] The trial court's decision that refused to permit the internist to testify as to proper indications for surgery was upheld.

The appellant stated that to qualify a witness as an expert on the standard of care, the party offering the witness must establish the witness's knowlege of and familiarity with the standard of care governing the defendant's specialty. The witness must demonstrate more than a casual familiarity with the standards of practice of the defendant's speciality.

Although the internist claimed to have acquired a knowledge and familiarity with the indications for surgery of Denver area surgeons, attended meetings and read literature, he could only identify two meetings of relevance and could not recall any specific substantive discussions with surgeons. He expressly denied any expertise in surgery or having studied the standards of practice in the Denver area. This is why the appellate court held the internist was not qualified to testify about the standard of care for surgeons.

The next issue is who will be allowed to testify against a nurse. The decisions vary from state to state and are dependent on the facts of the case. In the *Hiatt v. Groce* case, the court held that when a patient is in need of a physician, the nurse has a duty to timely notify the physician.[65] The nurse failed to notify the doctor when the plaintiff was about to deliver. The court allowed the physician to testify about the adequacy of the nurse's care.

In purely nursing issues, a nurse should be the only specialist qualified to render a professional opinion as to the standard of care. The American Association of Nurse Attorneys has issued a position statement to this effect. The association also maintains a list of nurse attorneys who are willing to review a case and render an expert opinion.

In *Fein v. Permanente Medical Group*, a patient in a medical clinic complained of chest pain.[66] The plaintiff sued alleging that the family nurse practitioner failed to diagnose his myocardial infarction. The trial court instructed the jury that the standard of care of a nurse practitioner is that of a physician or surgeon. That decision was subsequently appealed. The appeals court agreed with the lower court.

In summary, expert testimony is generally required to prove negligence on the part of the nurse. The only exception is where the negligence is so obvious that it is not outside the understanding of a layperson. The other exception to the rule is the *res ipsa loquitur* doctrine. Expert testimony is needed to show whether the acceptable standard of care has been met. Without standards of care, nursing couldn't claim to be a profession. Most states have a nationwide standard of care.

It is always important to make sure an expert is qualified to render such an opinion. Physicians and nurses who are not qualified by nature of their practice should not be permitted by the court to testify.

REFERENCES

1. *Whitney v. Day*, 100 Mich. App. 707, 300 N.W.2d 380 (1980).
2. *Frayo v. Hartland Hospital*, 99 Cal. App. 3d 331, 160 Cal. Rptr. 246 (1979); *Valentin v. La Societe Francaise de Bienfaisance Mutuelle de Los Angeles*, 76 Cal. App. 2d 1, 172 P.2d 359 (1946); *Lovie v. Chinese Hospital Association*, 249 Cal. App. 2d 774, 57 Cal. Rptr. 906 (1967).
3. *McKenna v. Cedars of Lebanon Hospital*, 93 Cal. App. 3d 282, 155 Cal. Rptr. 631 (1979).
4. *Colby v. Schwartz*, 78 Cal. App. 3d 855, 144 Cal. Rptr. 624 (1978).
5. *Lindsey v. Miami Development Corporation*, 689 S.W.2d 856 (Tenn. 1985).
6. *Prosser and Keeton on Torts* 356 (5th ed. 1984).
7. *Id.* at 236.
8. *Estate of John Starling v. Fisherman's Pier, Inc.*, 401 So. 2d 1136 (Fla. App. 1981); *Hovermale v. Berkeley Springs Moose Lodge No. 1483*, 271 S.E.2d 335 (W. Va. 1980); *Grimes v. Hettinger*, 566 S.W.2d 769 (Ky. App. 1978).
9. *Levine v. Hartford Accident & Indemnity Co.*, 149 So. 2d 433 (1963).
10. *D'Antoni v. Sara Mayo Hospital*, 144 So. 2d 643 (1962).
11. *Lunsford v. Board of Nurse Examiners for the State of Texas*, 648 S.W.2d 391 (Tex. App. 3 Dist. 1983).
12. *Southeastern Kentucky Baptist Hospital Inc. v. Bruce*, 539 S.W.2d 286 (Ky. 1976).
13. *Norton v. Argonaut Insurance Co.*, 144 So. 2d 249 (La. Ct. App. 1962).
14. *Weinstein v. Prostkoff*, 23 Misc. 2d 376, 191 N.Y.S.2d 310, *rev'd*, 213 N.Y.S.2d 571 (1959).
15. *Habuda v. Trustees of Rex Hospital, Inc.*, 164 S.E.2d 17 (1968).
16. *Kilbane v. Ramsey County*, 193 N.W.2d 301 (Minn. 1971).
17. *Gregg v. National Medical Health Care Services*, 145 Ariz. 51, 700 P.2d 925 (1985).
18. *Bugden v. Horbour View Hospital (Nov. Sc.)*, 2 D.L.R. 338 (1947).
19. *Palmer v. Clarksdale Hospital*, 93 Cal. App. 2d 43, 208 P.2d 445 (1949).
20. *Lenger v. Physician's General Hospital Inc.*, 438 S.W.2d 408 (1969).
21. *Richardson v. Doe*, 176 Ohio St. 370 (1964).
22. *Detling v. Chockley*, 70 Ohio St. 185 (1949).
23. *Rouse v. Riverside Methodist Hospital*, 9 Ohio App. 3d 206 (1983).
24. *Richard v. Hunter*, 151 Ohio St. 185 (1949).
25. Morris, Clarence, "Punitive Damages in Personal Injury Cases," 21 *Ohio St. L.J.* 216. *See also Simpson v. McCeffrey*, 13 Ohio 508, 522 (1844) and *Detling v. Chockley*, *supra* note 22.
26. *Black's Law Dictionary* 105 (5th ed. 1978).
27. Prosser, W., *Handbook of the Law of Torts*, 34-38, (4th ed. 1971).
28. *Burton v. Leftwich*, 123 So. 2d 766 (La. Ct. App. 1960).
29. *Mattocks v. Bell*, 194 A.2d 307 (D.C. 1963).
30. *Sarlat v. State of New York*, 52 Misc. 2d 275, N.Y.S.2d 293 (1966).
31. *Burrows v. Hawaiian Trust Co.*, 417 P.2d 816 (Hawaii 1966).

32. Prosser, *supra* note 27, at 43.

33. *Whitree v. State*, 290 N.Y.S.2d 486 (1968).

34. *Big Town Nursing Homes, Inc. v. Reserve Insurance Co.*, 492 F.2d 523 (5th Cir. 1974).

35. *Gadsden General Hospital v. Hamilton*, 212 Ala. 531, 103 So. 553 (1925).

36. *Bailie v. Miami Valley Hospital*, 221 N.E.2d 217 (Ct. Common Pleas, Ohio 1966).

37. *Pounders v. Trinity Court Nursing Home, Inc.*, 576 S.W.2d 934 (Ark. 1979).

38. Springer, Eric, *Automated Medical Records and the Law* 88 (1971).

39. *Doane v. Grew*, 220 Mass. 171, 107 N.E. 620 (1915).

40. Appendix, *Report of the Secretary's Commission on Medical Malpractice, Access to Medical Records*, App. 178-80 (Dept. of H.E.W., Jan. 11, 1973).

41. *Doane v. Grew, supra* note 39.

42. *Wynn v. Cole*, 91 Mich. App. 517, 284 N.W.2d 144 (1979).

43. *Judge v. Rockford Memorial Hospital*, 150 N.E.2d 202 (Ill. App. 1958).

44. *Merritt v. Detroit Memorial Hospital*, 265 N.W.2d 124 (Mich. App. 1978).

45. *Farrell v. Kramer*, 193 A.2d 560 (Me. 1963).

46. *Estate of Berthiaume v. Pratt*, 365 A.2d 792 (Me. 1976).

47. *Clayman v. Bernstein*, 38 P.A., D.C. 543 (1940).

48. *Bazemore v. Savannah Hospital*, 171 Ga. 257, 155 S.E. 194 (1930).

49. *Molein v. Kaiser Foundation Hospitals*, 167 Cal. Rptr. 831 (Cal. 1980).

50. Alsobrook, H., *Problems in Hospital Law* 177 (1979).

51. *Hale v. Venuto*, 137 Cal. App. 3d 910, 187 Cal. Rptr. 357 (1982); *South Miami Hospital v. Sanchez*, 386 So. 2d 39 (Fla. App. 1980); *Stewart v. City of New Orleans*, 418 So. 2d 1389 (La. App. 1982); *Estate of Neal v. Friendship Manor Nursing Home*, 318 N.W.2d 594 (Mich. App. 1982); *Tice v. Hall*, 303 S.E.2d 832 (N.C. App. 1983).

52. *Powell v. Mullins*, 479 So. 2d 1119 (Ala. 1985).

53. *Zills v. Brown*, 382 So. 2d 528 (Ala. 1980).

54. *Sullivan v. Methodist Hospitals of Dallas*, 699 S.W.2d 265 (Tex. App. 13 Dist. 1985).

55. *Zills, supra* note 53.

56. *Starnes v. Charlotte-Mecklenburg Hospital Authority*, 28 N.C. App. 418, 221 S.E.2d 733 (1976).

57. *Hunter v. Benchimol*, 123 Ariz. 516, 601 P.2d 279 (1979); *Thomas v. St. Francis Hospital, Inc.*, 447 A.2d 435 (Del. 1982); *Medina v. Figuered*, 3 Hawaii App. 186, 647 P.2d 292 (1982); *Marquis v. Battersby*, 443 N.E.2d 1202 (Ind. App. 1982); *Crowley v. O'Neil*, 4 Kan. App. 2d 491, 609 P.2d 198 (1980); *Buckelew v. Grossbard*, 87 N.J. 512, 435 A.2d 1150 (1981); *Van Zee v. Sioux Valley Hospital*, 315 N.W.2d 489 (S.D. 1982); *Froh v. Milwaukee Medical Clinic, S.C.*, 85 Wis. 2d 308, 270 N.W.2d 83 (1978).

58. *Kanter v. Metropolitan Medical Center*, 384 N.W.2d 914 (Minn. App. 1986).

59. Hume, Edward, 12 *The Locality Rule, Legal Aspects of Medical Practice* 6 (April 1984).

60. *Lloyd Noland Foundation, Inc. v. Harris*, 295 Ala. 65, 322 So. 2d 709 (1975); *Mellies v. National Heritage, Inc.*, 6 Kan. App. 2d 910 (1981); *Hemingway*

v. Ochsner Clinic, 722 F.2d 1220 (5th Cir.), *cert. denied*, 105 S. Ct. 114, *reh'g denied*, 105 S. Ct. 350 (1985); *Voss v. United States*, 423 F. Supp. 751 (E.D. Mo. 1976); *Horton v. Niagara Falls Memorial Center*, 51 A.D.2d 152, 380 N.Y.S.2d 116 (1976); *Brown v. University Nursing Home, Inc.*, 496 S.W.2d 503 (Tenn. App. 1972).

61. *Wade v. John D. Archbold Memorial Hospital*, 311 S.E.2d 836 (Ga. 1984).
62. *Hansbrough v. Kosyak*, 490 N.E.2d 181 (Ill. App. 4 Dist. 1986).
63. *Burton v. Youngblood*, 711 P.2d 245 (Utah 1985).
64. *Connelly v. Kortz*, 689 P.2d 728 (Colo. App. 1984).
65. *Hiatt v. Groce*, 215 Kan. 14, 523 P.2d 320 (1974).
66. *Fein v. Permanente Medical Group*, 175 Cal. Rptr. 177 (Cal. Ct. App. 1981).

CHAPTER THREE

TYPES OF LIABILITY

Respondeat Superior and Vicarious Liability
Independent Contractor Exception
Strict Liability — Liability for Blood Transfusions
Corporate Liability
Apparent Authority — Ostensible Agency Theory
The Borrowed-Servant Doctrine
Captain-of-the-Ship Doctrine

RESPONDEAT SUPERIOR AND VICARIOUS LIABILITY

Vicarious liability and *respondeat superior* are two terms with which every nurse should be familiar. Vicarious liability is an indirect legal responsibility where an employer is responsible for the acts of its employees. For example, the employer is responsible for the acts of the nurses, interns and residents performing within the scope of their employment. The legal effect is to permit the injured patient to obtain financial recovery against someone else. This is true as long as the plaintiff establishes an employee-employer relationship. The plaintiff can elect to sue the nurse, the nurse's employer or both because of this legal doctrine. Many nurses incorrectly believe that they are insulated from liability because they work for a physician or a hospital.

Respondeat superior is a Latin term meaning "let the master answer." *Respondeat superior* is a form of vicarious liability or imputed negligence. The employer is, arguably, in the best position to supervise and direct the nurses in the scope of their employment. The essential factor in deciding this question is the "right to control" or supervise the details of performing the services. For example, if the hospital-employed nurse errs, the hospital is judged legally responsible. However, just because the hospital must make a settlement, the nurse may still be personally liable for his/her own negligence.

It is a general principle of law that every person is responsible for his/her own acts of negligence. If the employer pays a claim because of the negligence of the nurse, the employer or its insurance company has the legal right to sue the nurse for reimbursement. Although hospitals and physicians generally elect not to seek indemnification, it is always their legal right to do so. This is why it is important for the nurse to have his/her own professional liability policy.

Respondeat superior is based, in part, on the traditional social policy which places the risk of losses caused by negligent conduct of employees upon employers as a cost of doing business. The employer, by prices, rates or liability insurance, is better able to absorb the costs and distribute them to the public. This means the employer may have to buy more professional liability insurance. To make a profit, the costs to patients will have to be increased. This way, the cost for the employer's liability insurance will be borne by all the patients. Recently, an article stated that $4 of every patient's office visit charge goes to pay for the physician's liability policy.

Usually, the plaintiff will try to sue as many people as possible. Today, nurses are performing a wider variety of highly skilled and specialized services, and thus are being exposed to greater liability risks. A recent article in a national magazine of a trial lawyers' association advocated to its members that the nurse should be included in the lawsuit, as well as the hosptial and the physician. This is what attorneys call the "deep pocket theory." The more defendants (hospital, doctors and nurses) named in the action, the more parties that will be available to contribute to a verdict or settlement. As previously mentioned, the doctrine of *respondeat superior* does not absolve the employee of responsibility for negligent conduct. It merely allows the patient to sue the employer, and increases the likelihood of satisfaction by one better able to pay.

For example, in the *Porter* case, a newborn baby was in need of a blood transfusion.[1] The nursery nurse strapped the baby down in the incubator. One of her feet rested against a bare light bulb which was used to warm the incubator. The baby suffered severe burns to her foot and part of her foot had to be amputated. The hospital was liable for the negligence of its nurse employees.

A hospital is not an insurer of the safety of patients within the hospital. The hospital is only liable in damages to the patient for injuries that have resulted from acts of negligence by one of its employees.[2] This is liability by imputed negligence.

The employer can also become liable to the patient for having employed or retained a nurse known to be incompetent.[3] Of course, the nurse must have proximately caused damage or injury to the patient.[4]

It is important to note that the employee must be within the scope of his/her employment to involve the doctrine of *respondeat superior*. There are many factors used to ascertain if the employee is acting within his/her job description. One important element to consider is the employer's and the patient's expectations. The usual or established circumstances are weighed, as are the place and purpose of the act.

For example, in the *Sheran* case, a nurse's aide was backing out of her driveway to come to work when she struck a motorcycle and injured the driver severely.[5] The motorcyclist argued that the nurse's employer was liable for her negligent act under the doctrine of *respondeat superior*. The court rejected this argument, saying that her travel to and from work was not within the scope of her employment.

It is important to note that employer liability arising from negligent acts by employees must be distinguished from hospital corporate liability. Employer liability, through the doctrine of *respondeat superior*, has already been discussed above. Hospital corporate liability is imposed upon the hospital corporation itself for failure to meet a duty recognized by law as a duty of that corporation.

INDEPENDENT CONTRACTOR EXCEPTION

There are several exceptions to the doctrine of *respondeat superior*. First of all, employers are not responsible for independent contractors (self-employed persons). The law defines an independent contractor as a person contracting with another to do something, but not controlled by, nor subject to, the "right to control" with respect to one's physical conduct in the performance of the work.[6]

Most private duty nurses employed by nursing pools are independent contractors. For example, a nurse from the Medical Personnel Pool had been retained to take care of Patient X. The hot water bags that she filled caused several second-degree burns to the patient's left leg. The hospital probably would not be responsible for this patient's injuries. The hospital would have no right to control or direct the private duty nurse since she is not employed by the hospital.

Generally, doctors who have been granted staff privileges are considered to be independent contractors. This is because, generally, the hospital or other health care institution has not had the right to control the physician's practice in a detailed manner. Therefore, the hospital would not be liable for the physician's act of negligence unless the physician was an employee. This is also true as long as the hospital or health care institution used reasonable care in selecting independent contractors.[7] Hospitals have been found negligent when they have granted privileges to incompetent physicians.[8]

Besides private duty nurses and staff physicians, there are a number of nurse practitioners who are independent contractors. Some states have passed laws granting nurse practitioners privileges to practice as independent contractors. These nurse practitioners work directly for patients and bill the patients or third-party insurers.

STRICT LIABILITY — BLOOD TRANSFUSIONS

Strict liability means liability without fault. It is generally only alleged when the patient sustains injury as a result of a blood transfusion or because of faulty equipment.

When the nurse provides a unit of blood for a patient, are the charges for a service, or for the sale of a product? Early cases often held that charging for blood caused the transfusion to become a "sale" of a product. It was a sale to which the implied warranties of fitness and merchantability applied. This meant that the nurse or hospital could be liable for any reaction to the blood even if the best care was given.

As a result, forty-seven states have passed laws classifying the provision of blood as a service and not a sale. Now if the plaintiff wants to succeed in a lawsuit, he/she must show that the reaction was due to the negligence of a nurse or lab technician.

One hospital was negligent in procuring blood from a blood bank when it knew or should have known the blood bank was operating below the minimum standard of care.[9] The plaintiff contracted hepatitis after receiving a blood transfusion.

Another plaintiff sued after contracting hepatitis, claiming that she did not give an informed consent.[10] The court dismissed this argument, indicating there are national limits on the doctor's duty to inform his/her patient of the possible risks.

There have been a number of cases where liability has resulted because the hospital personnel were negligent in either typing or labeling blood.[11]

It is interesting to note that most of the blood contaminated by hepatitis comes from paid donors. Most are due to the non-A, non-B hepatitis virus which cannot be detected. Many states have now enacted "blood labeling acts" which require that the blood be identified as being from either a paid or volunteer donor. The Food and Drug Administration has also adopted this requirement in 21 C.F.R. Section 606.120(2).

Recently, many of the patients who have contracted AIDS through blood transfusions have tried to argue breach of implied warranties and strict liability. Most of these have been unsuccessful because of the statutes passed in the forty-seven states dictating that the provision of blood is a service.

In *Johnstone v. San Francisco Medical Society*, the court dismissed a strict liability claim after the patient contracted AIDS through a blood transfusion.[12] The plaintiff incorrectly argued that in 1985 the HTLV screening test made AIDS

100 percent detectable in donor blood. At that time, the Food and Drug Administration licensed tests to detect the antibodies to the HTLV-III virus, which causes AIDS. However, the tests were not 100 percent reliable.

CORPORATE LIABILITY

In recent years, there has been a significant change in the role of hospitals and health care institutions in patient care. With the dramatic change, a new theory has emerged — the theory of hospital corporate liability. Hospital corporate liability is liability imposed on the hospital corporation because it has failed to meet some duty which is recognized by law.

A hospital no longer is just a place that contributes little more than bed and board. Hospitals now provide a whole array of support functions, including the institution of general policies and procedures to ensure patient care and safety. Hospitals provide nursing care and laboratory services, along with a number of hospital-owned diagnostic and therapeutic services. Hospital operations are now a growing complex system. Detailed state licensing requirements, along with the JCAH (Joint Commission on Accreditation of Hospitals) and A.O.A. (American Osteopathic Association) standards, have developed to promulgate this new theory.

The principle of hospital liability began to develop in the early 1960s. The theory of corporate liability is still considered to be in its early stages. This theory is expected to significantly expand hospital liability.

The landmark case that recognized corporate liability was the *Darling* case.[13] In the *Darling* case, a young athlete with a broken leg was treated in the emergency room by the physician on call. A cast was applied. The patient was then admitted to the orthopedic floor. Obvious danger signals and progressive worsening of the patient's circulation occurred over the next two weeks. On at least one occasion, one of the nurses contacted the physician about the patient's circulation checks. However, she was not persistent and did not bring the problem to the attention of her nursing supervisor. The leg became gangrenous and the young athlete's lower leg was amputated.

The Illinois Supreme Court held that the hospital was negligent, first, for failing to provide a sufficient number of trained nurses and for being understaffed. Second, the hospital staff failed to review the treatment rendered by the attending physician. The hospital failed to require the appropriate consultation on examination by hospital staff physicians.

The court felt that the hospital, as a corporate entity, was in the best position to have prevented this injury. The case was based, in part, on the hospital's failure to follow its own rules and regulations as well as standards in the field. Additional information concerning the hospital's responsibility to follow its own rules and regulations will be discussed later.

The law recognizes the hospital corporation as a "person." As such, the hospital has to meet its legal duty. The hospital has a number of duties and responsibilities which it owes to the patient. (See Appendices C and D.)

There are five basic obligations which have been commonly relied upon to support a claim founded on the corporate liability of a hospital. First, the hospital is under a legal duty to maintain proper medical equipment, supplies, medication and food for the patient.[14] Second, the hospital has a duty to exercise reasonable care to provide safe physical premises for the patient. This means that the buildings and grounds should be adequately maintained.[15] Third, the hospital should adopt internal policies and procedures which are reasonably calculated to protect the safety and interest of patients.[16] Fourth, there is a duty to exercise reasonable care in the selection and retention of hospital employees and in the granting of staff privileges.[17] This includes allowing physicians to practice who are later judged incompetent.[18] Fifth, there is a duty to take reasonable steps in ensuring that adequate patient care is being given.[19]

APPARENT AUTHORITY OR OSTENSIBLE AGENCY THEORY

Even in states which have not adopted the corporate liability doctrine, some courts have found hospitals liable for the negligent acts of independent contractors under an apparent authority or ostensible agency theory.[20] Under this theory, the hospital is estopped from denying liability for the negligent acts of its physicians.

This theory is most frequently applied to emergency room physicians. The patient comes to the hospital's emergency room and is not given a choice of which emergency room physician he/she would like to see. To many patients, it appears that the physician is employed by the hospital. As a result of the apparent authority doctrine, many emergency rooms are trying to negate this appearance by clearly posting a sign stating that the emergency room physician is not employed by the hospital. In addition, many hospitals require the patient to sign a statement acknowledging this fact, and billing is frequently done separately by the emergency room group.

BORROWED-SERVANT DOCTRINE

Many nurses have heard of the borrowed-servant doctrine. A borrowed servant is an employee who is temporarily under the control of another. This doctrine states that a person who "borrows" the use of another's employee is legally responsible for that employee's action. It is not used as often as it once was because of the erosion of the charitable immunity doctrine.

The borrowed-servant doctrine was frequently used in cases involving operating room nurses. The hospital-employed nurse commits a negligent act while under the direction or control of the operating-room surgeon. The physician's liability is vicarious, meaning even though the physician did not commit the negligent act, he/she directed the nurse to do it. The physician is responsible because he/she was in control.

This does not mean that the nurse is not also legally liable. For example, the physician writes a medication order. The nurse administers the medication as a borrowed servant. The dosage administered is twice the normal amount and the patient is injured. The nurse, physician and hospital may be held separately and jointly liable.

Several courts have held that the nurse can serve two masters at the same time.[21] Some courts have distinguished between administrative and medical acts, the hospital being responsible for administrative acts and the physician for medical acts. Medical acts are those the nurse is directed to do for the patient, like applying direct pressure to a bleeding artery. Administrative acts are those which the hospital can control, like care of equipment and preparation of the surgery room. In the *Hart* case, the court said that an accurate accounting of scalpel blades is of mutual interest to both the hospital and the physician.[22]

CAPTAIN-OF-THE-SHIP DOCTRINE

The captain-of-the-ship doctrine is an historical doctrine of liability which should be mentioned. It is a doctrine in which the physician, as "captain," is held liable for the actions of all members of the health care team. It is an expansion of the borrowed-servant doctrine. This doctrine has, for the most part, been discarded by many states. It implied that the surgeon was the captain of the operating room. As such, the surgeon was responsible for the negligent acts of the nurse. This was based on the notion that the surgeon had the right to control. There remain, however, a few states that still hold that the surgeon, by manner of custom and practice, is in complete charge of the surgery.[23]

The reason why many states have abandoned the doctrine is the recognition that the surgeon does not supervise every aspect of the nurse's duties. The nurse will still be responsible for negligently following physician's orders, violations of the hospital's internal policies and procedures, and his/her independent acts of negligence.

REFERENCES

1.   *Porter v. Patterson*, 107 Ga. App. 64, 129 S.E.2d 70 (1962).
2.   *McDonald v. Foster Memorial Hospital*, 170 Cal. App. 2d 85, 338 P.2d 607 (1959); *Gray v. Carter*, 100 Cal. App. 2d 642, 224 P.2d 28 (1950).
3.   *Bing v. Thunig*, 2 N.Y.2d 656, 163 N.Y.S.2d 3 (1957).
4.   *Helms v. Williams*, 4 N.C. App. 396, 166 S.E.2d 852 (1969).
5.   *Sheran v. Band E. Convalescent Home*, 122 Cal. Rptr. 505 (Cal. App. 1975).
6.   *Restatement of Agency* Sec. 2(3) (1933).
7.   *Mooney v. Stainless, Inc.*, 338 F.2d 127 (6th Cir. 1964), *cert. denied*, 381 U.S. 925 (1965).
8.   *Pedroza v. Bryant*, 677 P.2d 166 (Wash. 1984).
9.   *Hoder v. Sayet*, 196 So. 2d 205 (Fla. App. 1967).
10. *Moore v. Underwood Memorial Hospital*, 371 A.2d 105 (N.J. Super. 1977).
11. *Parker v. Port Huron Hospital*, 105 N.W.2d 1 (Mich. 1960); *Walker v. Humana Medical Corp.*, 415 So. 2d 1107 (Ala. Civ. App. 1982); *Renslow v. Mennonite Hospital*, 367 N.E.2d 1250 (Ill. 1977); and *Guthrie v. Bio Medical Laboratories, Inc.*, 442 So. 2d 92 (Ala. 1983).
12. *Johnstone v. San Francisco Medical Society*, No. 826, 447, March 26, 1985.
13. *Darling v. Charleston Community Memorial Hospital*, 33 Ill. 2d 326, 211 N.E.2d 253 (1965), *cert. denied*, 383 U.S. 246 (1966).
14. *See* 54 A.L.R.3d 258 (1973); *Silverhart v. Mount Zion Hospital*, 20 Cal. App. 2d 1022, 98 Cal. Rptr. 187 (1971); *Shivers v. Good Shepherd Hospital, Inc.*, 427 S.W.2d 104 (Tex. Civ. App. 1968); *Mauran v. Mary Fletcher Hospital*, 318 F. Supp. 297 (D. Vt. 1970); *Starnes v. Charlotte-Mecklenburg Hospital Authority*, 28 N.C. App. 418, 221 S.E.2d 733 (1976).
15. *Smith v. Travelers Insurance Co.*, 287 So. 2d 576 (La. 1973); *Carrasco v. Bankoff*, 33 Cal. Rptr. 673 (Cal. 1963).
16. *Kapuschinsky v. U.S.*, 248 F. Supp. 732 (D.S.C. 1966); *Bornmann v. Great Southwest General Hospital, Inc.*, 453 F.2d 616 (5th Cir. 1971); *Johnson v. Grant Hospital*, 32 Ohio St. 2d 169, 291 N.E.2d 440 (1972); *See* 60 A.L.R.3d 380 (1974).
17. *Hipp v. Hospital Authority of City of Marietta, Georgia*, 121 S.E.2d 273 (Ga. 1961); *Corleto v. Shore Memorial Hospital*, 138 N.J. Super. 302, 350 A.2d 534 (1975); *Purcell v. Zimbelman*, 18 Ariz. App. 75, 500 P.2d 335 (1972).
18. *Purcell, supra* note 17; *Kitto v. Gilbert*, 39 Colo. App. 374, 570 P.2d 544 (1977); *Joiner v. Mitchell County Hospital Authority*, 125 Ga. App. 1, 186 S.E.2d 307 (1972); *Ferguson v. Gonyaw*, 64 Mich. App. 685, 236 N.W.2d 543 (1976).
19. *Purcell, supra* note 17; *Lundahl v. Rockford Memorial Hosptial Association*, 93 Ill. App. 2d 461, 235 N.E.2d 671 (1968); *Gridley v. Johnson*, 476 S.W.2d 475 (Mo. 1972); *Tucson Medical Center, Inc. v. Misevch*, 113 Ariz. 34, 545 P.2d 958 (1976).
20. *Schagrin v. Wilmington Medical Center, Inc.*, 304 A.2d 61 (Del. Super. 1973); *Mehlman v. Powell*, 281 Md. 269, 378 A.2d 1121 (1977); *Lundberg v. Bay View Hospital*, 175 Ohio St. 199, 191 N.E.2d 821 (1963); *Braun v.*

Ryeyna, 473 N.Y.S.2d 627 (App. Div. 1984); *Capan v. Divine Providence Hospital*, 287 Pa. Super. Ct. 364, 430 A.2d 647 (1980).

21. *Grubb v. Albert Einstein Medical Center*, 255 Pa. Super. Ct. 381, 387 A.2d 480 (1978); *Synnot v. Midway Hospital*, 287 Minn. 270, 178 N.W.2d 211 (1970); *Mossey v. Mueller*, 163 Wis. 2d 715, 218 N.W.2d 514 (1974).

22. *City of Somerset v. Hart*, 549 S.W.2d 814 (Ky. 1977).

23. *Crumley v. Memorial Hospital, Inc.*, 509 F. Supp. 531 (E.D. Tenn. 1978) *aff'd*, 647 F.2d 164 (6th Cir. 1981); *Kitto v. Gilbert, supra* note 18; *University Hospital Building, Inc. v. Gooding*, 419 So. 2d 1111 (Fla. App. 1982); *Beck v. Lovell*, 361 So. 2d 245 (La. App. 1978); *Schneider v. Albert Einstein Medical Center*, 257 Pa. Super. Ct. 348, 390 A.2d 1271 (1978).

CHAPTER FOUR

DEFENSES TO
NURSING NEGLIGENCE ALLEGATIONS

Statute of Limitations
Contributory Negligence
Comparative Negligence
Assumption of Risk
Good Samaritan Statute

There are certain defenses that will negate liability even if the plaintiff has proven each of the four elements of negligence. (See Chapter 2.) The defenses include the statute of limitations, comparative negligence, contributory negligence, assumption of risk, the Good Samaritan statute, charitable immunity and sovereign immunity.

STATUTE OF LIMITATIONS

The statute of limitations sets forth the time period during which a plaintiff must bring a lawsuit. All states have statutes of limitations, which are generally set by the legislature of each state and interpreted by the courts.

The statutes of limitations for physicians and hospitals are generally specified in each state's medical malpractice act. In some states nurses are covered under the medical malpractice act, while in other states they are covered by a personal injury statute. Many states shortened their statutes of limitations during the malpractice crisis of the mid-1970s. The statute of limitations is generally one, two or three years.

The statute of limitations is necessary to ensure that information sufficient for bringing a lawsuit exists. It prevents the bringing of state claims which can occur as time passes, evidence vanishes, memories fade and witnesses become difficult to locate.

It is important to determine when the statute of limitations begins to run. Some courts, especially in earlier decisions, have held that the time begins to run on the day the patient's injury occurs. This is called the "occurrence rule." For example, a patient had an appendectomy on January 4, 1984. The state has a two-year statute of limitations which begins to run on the day the injury occurs. On January 26, 1987, more than three years later, the patient discovers that a lap sponge had been left in. The court may hold that the time limit for bringing the suit has expired.

A few states still use the "termination-of-treatment rule." Under this rule, the time period for bringing the suit begins to run from the date of the last treatment.

The recent trend has been to use the "discovery rule." The statute starts to run when the patient discovers, or in the exercise of reasonable care should have discovered, the alleged negligence. For example, a patient had surgery on January 4, 1984, and discovers on January 26, 1987, more than three years later, a retained sponge. The statute of limitations requires all claims to be brought within a year from discovery. Thus, since the patient discovered the sponge on January 26, 1987, she must bring suit before the one-year limit ends on January 26, 1988. Many of the states that use the discovery rule have a "cap" or maximum time period within which the negligent act can be discovered.

CONTRIBUTORY NEGLIGENCE

Under this doctrine, if the plaintiff in a negligence lawsuit has contributed to the damage in any way, no matter how minute, he or she is guilty of contributory negligence and will be unable to recover any damages. In many states it was felt that contributory negligence was a harsh principle, and a comparative negligence doctrine has been adopted.

The doctrine of contributory negligence had its roots in the 1809 English case of *Butterfield v. Forrester*.[1] The plaintiff was riding his horse at a fast pace when he ran into an obstruction which had been left in the road by the defendant. The court denied the plaintiff recovery because of his own independent act of negligence. This case became the principle authority for the rule that a plaintiff could not recover if his neligence contributed to the cause of the accident or injury.

The courts started to chew away at the contributory negligence doctrine in the late 1950s and early 1960s. States started modifying the doctrine and apportioning damages much like is done under the doctrine of comparative negligence. Many times courts created fictions and bent over backward to establish an absence of contributory negligence. The "last clear chance" doctrine was also invented at this time. The doctrine differed in its application in each state but generally applied to the situation in which the defendant discovered the plaintiff in a perilous position and had reasonable time to avoid the accident, but failed to do so. Some states applied the last-clear-chance doctrine only to those cases in which the defendant should have but did not discover the plaintiff.

COMPARATIVE NEGLIGENCE

As previously addressed, because of the harsh effect of the contributory negligence doctrine, barring the plaintiff from recovery even if he or she was only minutely negligent, the legislatures and courts have adopted the doctine of comparative negligence. Comparative negligence allows the negligence of the plaintiff to be weighed with that of the defendant. It is a doctrine that allows the comparison of fault.

The comparative negligence systems do not operate in the same manner in each state. For example, Alaska,[2] Arizona,[3] California,[4] Florida,[5] Illinois,[6] Kentucky,[7] Louisiana,[8] Michigan,[9] Mississippi,[10] Missouri,[11] New Mexico,[12] New York,[13] Rhode Island[14] and Washington[15] apply the "pure" comparative negligence doctrine. Under this system, the plaintiff may recover even if his or her negligence was greater than the defendant's. However, the damage award will be reduced in proportion to the amount of the plaintiff's negligence.

For example, a physician negligently failed to review two of the culture and sensitivity reports which indicated the plaintiff's infection was resistant to penicillin. As a result, the plaintiff's staph infection was inappropriately treated for two weeks, and this contributed to osteomyelitis. However, the plaintiff failed to get his prescription for Keflex filled as directed. He also failed to keep his appointment to be evaluated seven days after discharge. The jury found damages in the amount of $100,000, and found plaintiff to be 60 percent negligent. Under a pure comparative negligence principle, the plaintiff collected $40,000, which is 40 percent of $100,000.

There are threee major types of "modified" comparative negligence. They are the equal-division system, the slight-gross system and the 50 percent system.

The equal-division rule (formerly the admiralty rule) is a system where the damages are divided equally regardless of the degree of negligence.[16] States like

Nebraska[17] and South Dakota[18] use the slight-gross system. If the plaintiff's negligence is slight and the defendant's is gross in comparison, the plaintiff can still recover. However, the amount recoverable is proportional to the amount of fault attributable to plaintiff.

The 50 percent or Wisconsin system is commonly adopted.[19] Some states, like Arkansas, Colorado, Georgia, Idaho, Kansas, Maine, North Dakota, Utah, West Virginia and Wyoming, also refer to this as the "49 percent rule."[20] The plaintiff's claim is not barred as long as his contributory negligence is less than that of the defendant. If the plaintiff's negligence is equal to or greater than that of the defendant, the common-law contributory negligence principle applies and the plaintiff collects nothing. For example, in the prior example where the plaintiff suffered osteomyelitis and was found to be 60 percent negligent, he would receive nothing because his percentage of negligence was greater than the physician's.

A variant of the Wisconsin system was first adopted in 1969 in New Hampshire.[21] Many states, like Connecticut, Delaware, Hawaii, Indiana, Iowa, Massachusetts, Minnesota, Montana, Nevada, New Jersey, Ohio, Oklahoma, Oregon, Pennsylvania, Texas and Vermont, have adopted this variant.[22] In 1971, Wisconsin changed to the New Hampshire variant.[23]

ASSUMPTION OF RISK

Assumption of risk is a legal doctrine which does not allow a plaintiff to win a lawsuit when a known or understood risk was ignored. The introduction of comparative negligence into the legal system has required courts to determine whether the assumption of risk should continue as an absolute defense.

In the *Munson* case, a patient crawled over the foot of her hospital bed, fell and fractured her hip.[24] The court held that the patient had been warned of the danger and therefore had assumed the risk.

In the *Memorial Hospital* case, the plaintiff was burned when he activated the bed pan flusher hot water knob instead of the toilet flusher knob in his room.[25] He had not been warned of the proximity of the two knobs, even though there were two prior accidents. He had been medicated with Thorazine prior to the incident and suffered from multiple sclerosis. The court held that the plaintiff did not assume the risk and was free of contributory negligence.

In *Brockman*, a patient had his ears irrigated on several occasions after they became plugged with wax.[26] He came to the office one day and asked the nurse to wash out his ear. He was informed that the physician was out and he could not be treated unless the physician examined him and ordered the irrigation. He insisted the nurse perform the irrigation, which she did reluctantly. During the procedure, both eardrums ruptured. The court held the patient had assumed the risk.

GOOD SAMARITAN STATUTE

Generally, there is no duty to render care to one who is outside of the nurse's employment situation. Good Samaritan statutes were passed to encourage health care workers to render emergency care at the scene of an accident or illness. These statutes protect health care providers from civil liability for acts of negligence. The Good Samaritan statute has been discussed previously under the section on duty in Chapter 2.

REFERENCES

1. *Butterfield v. Forrester*, 11 East 60, 103 Eng. Rep. 926 (1809).
2. *Kaatz v. State*, 540 P.2d 1037 (Alaska 1975).
3. Ariz. Rev. Stat. Ann., Section 12-2505.
4. *Nga Li v. Yellow Cab Co. of California*, 13 Cal. 2d 804, 119 Cal. Rptr. 858, 532 P.2d 1226 (1975).
5. *Hoffman v. Jones*, 280 So. 2d 431 (Fla. 1973).
6. *Alvis v. Ribar*, 85 Ill. 2d 1, 52 Ill. Dec. 23, 421 N.E.2d 886 (1981).
7. *Hilen v. Hays*, 673 S.W.2d 713 (Ky. 1984).
8. La. Civ. Code Ann. art. 2323.
9. *Placek v. City of Sterling Heights*, 405 Mich. 638, 275 N.W.2d 511 (1979).
10. Miss. Code Ann. Section 1454.
11. *Gustafson v. Benda*, 661 S.W.2d 11 (Mo. 1983).
12. *Scott v. Rizzo*, 96 N.M. 682, 634 P.2d 1234 (1981).
13. N.Y. Civ. Prac. L. & R. Section 1411.
14. R.I. Gen. Laws Section 9-20-4.
15. Wash. Rev. Code Ann. Section 4.22.005.
16. *The Schooner Catharine v. Dickinson*, 58 U.S. 233 (1854).
17. Neb. Rev. Stat. Section 25-1151.
18. S.D. Codified Laws Ann. Section 20-9-2.
19. Wis. Stat. Ann. Section 895.045, before 1971 amendment.
20. Ark. Stat. Ann. Section 27-1765; Colo. Rev. Stat. Section 13-21-111; *Christian v. Macon Ry. & Light Co.*, 120 Ga. 314, 47 S.E. 923 (1904); Idaho Code Section 6-801; Kan. Stat. Ann. Section 60-2582(a); Me. Rev. Stat. Ann. tit. 14, Section 156; N.D. Cent. Code Section 9-10-07; Utah Code Ann. Section 78-27-37; *Bradley v. Appalachian Power Co.*, 163 W. Va. 332, 256 S.E.2d 879 (1979); Wyo. Stat. Section 1-1-109.
21. N.H. Rev. Stat. Ann. Section 507:7-2. *See* Orcutt and Ross, "Comparative Negligence in New Hampshire," 12 *N.H.B.J.* 6 (1969).
22. Conn. Gen. Stat. Ann. Section 52-572h; Del. Code Ann. Section 10-8132; Haw. Rev. Stat. Section 663-31; Ind. Code Section 34-4-33-4; Iowa Code Ann. Section 668-3; Mass. Gen. Laws Ann. Section 604.01, Subd. 1; Mont. Code Ann. Section 27-1-702; Nev. Rev. Stat. Section 41.141; N.J. Stat. Ann. Section 2A:15-5-1; Ohio Rev. Code Ann. Section 2315.19; Okla. Stat. Ann. tit. 23, Section 13; Or. Rev. Stat. Section 18.470; Pa. Cons. Stat. Ann. tit. 42, Section 7102; Tex. Rev. Civ. Stat. Ann. art. 2212a (Vernon); Vt. Stat. Ann. tit. 12, Section 1036.
23. Wis. Law 1971, ch. 47, amending Wis. Stat. Ann. Section 895.045.
24. *Munson v. Bishop Clarkson Memorial Hosp.*, 186 N.W.2d 492 (Neb. 1971). *See also DeBlanc v. Southern Baptist Hospital*, 207 So. 2d 868 (La. 1968).
25. *Memorial Hospital of South Bend Inc. v. Scott*, 300 N.E.2d 50 (Ind. 1973).
26. *Brockman v. Harpole*, 444 P.2d 25 (Or. 1968).

CHAPTER FIVE

INSURANCE CONSIDERATIONS

Introduction
Insurability of Nurse Midwives
Considerations when Deciding Whether to Purchase a Policy
Understanding an Insurance Policy

INTRODUCTION

Whether the nurse should purchase his/her own policy of insurance is a personal choice. Imagine the following: You come home extremely tired after working a double shift. You immediately fall asleep and drift into rapid eye movement, where dreaming occurs. You dream that you are sitting at home and hear a knock at the door. The man at the door asks you if you are Nurse Jones. As you reply in the affirmative, he hands you a complaint informing you that you have been sued.

You remember Mr. Smith well. After working an almost double shift, you were tired. When Mr. Smith asked for something for a headache, you accidently gave him two aspirin instead of the Tylenol that was ordered. Mr. Smith's chart and medication record clearly indicated that he was allergic to aspirin. He suffered an anaphylactic reaction requiring emergency treatment and three additional weeks in the hospital. He also suffered some permanent brain damage from the cerebral anoxia that occurred when he arrested.

You are now concerned about all of your tangible assets. You are now wondering what to do when you suddenly awake from the nightmare. You now decide to look into whether you should have your own personal professional liability insurance policy.

Following is a list of nine reasons why a nurse should consider purchasing her own policy. It also gives a reason why one nurse was sorry she ever purchased a policy. If you decide to purchase your own policy, it is very important to shop around and get the best insurance policy for your money. You will also find a short discussion on understanding an insurance policy so you can decide which one to buy, how much insurance to purchase and whether you should select an occurrence or claims-made policy.

INSURABILITY OF NURSE MIDWIVES

If you are a nurse midwife, you don't have the privilege of picking and choosing an insurance company like other nurses do. The crisis for nurse midwives recently hit when the major provider of liability insurance for nurse midwives refused to renew their policies. Other underwriters of professional liability insurance, including the A.N.A.'s provider, moved to exclude nurse midwives as well.

The American College of Nurse Midwives is attempting to alleviate the crisis by forming its own self-insurance program. Some states are attempting to deal with the problem by passing tort legislation to limit malpractice awards and control the amount of liability insurance. (See the section on tort reform.)

In March 1986, nurse midwives asked Congress to amend the 1981 Risk Retention Act, to address the unavailability of reinsurance and to make occurrence-type policies available.

During the Senate hearings, Karen Ehrnman, a spokeswoman for the American College of Nurse Midwives (ACNM), explained that 1,400 certified nurse midwives had their policies with Mutual Fire, Marine and Inland Insurance Company. They were notified in May 1984 that their policies would not be renewed on July 1, 1985. The insurance company indicated that the cancellation was not due to the members' professional performance. Rather, the policies were cancelled because of the general conditions in the insurance industry.

If Congress would amend the Risk Retention Act, then ACNM could establish its own insurance company. This was done by many state medical associations in the late 1970s during the medical malpractice crisis.

New insurance companies cannot generally obtain reinsurance. Therefore, ACNM asked Congress to legislate a plan for federally based reinsurance. It also asked that Congress make occurrence policies available since new companies have to write claims-made policies.

CONSIDERATIONS WHEN DECIDING WHETHER TO PURCHASE A POLICY

Insurance is a financial arrangement where one party agrees to compensate another for a loss which results from an occurrence of a specified event. An insurance policy is a legal contract establishing the rights and duties of the policy owner (you) and the insurer (the insurance company). There are a number of reasons why every nurse should consider carrying his/her own policy:

1. *Increasing Number of Suits Are Being Filed Against Nurses*
   The majority of malpractice suits filed are against hospitals or physicians. However, lately an increasing number of lawsuits have been filed against nurses. A recent article in a national magazine of a trial lawyers' association advocated to its members that the nurse be included in a lawsuit as well as the hospital or physician. The patient's attorney frequently names everyone involved in the patient's care. The attorney feels that the more defendants (hospital, doctors and nurses) named in the action, the more parties available to contribute to a verdict or settlement.

2. *Nurses are Responsible for Their Own Acts of Negligence*
   As pointed out in the discussion of vicarious liability and *respondeat superior* in Chapter 3, the nurse is never completely insulated from liability for acts performed within the scope of employment. While the hospital which employs the nurse may pay a claim resulting from that nurse's negligence, the hospital also has the legal right to indemnification. A professional liability policy will protect the nurse in the event the hospital chooses to invoke this right and sue the nurse for reimbursement.

3. *Protection of the Nurse's Best Interests*
   Many nurses have been advised by their employers that they do not need their own policies. This may not be in the best interest of the nurse. If you own a professional liability policy and are presented with a malpractice claim, your insurance carrier will provide you with an attorney to represent you in the case. This will ensure that your best interests are being looked after during each step of the proceedings. You will also have someone to call or meet

with if you have any questions. You will also be able to call to inquire on the status of the case and can be involved in the decision-making process.

4. *Nurses Are Being Exposed to Greater Risks*

Today, nurses are performing a wider variety of highly skilled and specialized services and, thus, are being exposed to greater liability risks. With more responsibility comes more accountability. As a practicing professional in the health care field, you may want to make sure that you have adequate professional protection to carry out your duties with confidence.

5. *Aggregate Coverage Limitations*

In professional liability coverage, most policies provide a certain amount of financial protection for each individual occurrence and another larger amount for all occurrences which take place during a policy year. If you are relying solely on your employer's policy for your own protection and the claim exceeds that policy's limits, you may be held liable for the unpaid claim balance. If you carry your own policy, you are guaranteed the coverage limits available in your policy, no matter how much the hospital's or physician's policy must pay.

6. *An Act Outside the Nurse's Job Description*

The nurse also should have her own policy in the event her employer decides not to defend her. As previously mentioned, the hospital or physician can only be vicariously liable under *respondeat superior* if the nurse was acting within the scope of her employment. If the hospital or physician decides that the nurse's actions were outside her job description, they may decide not to defend her. Without a policy, you would be on your own. Not only would you have to pay your own defense costs, which can be very expensive, but you also would risk the loss of your personal assets.

7. *Liability Exposure Outside the Hospital or Office*

Many of the nursing professional liability policies cover the nurse outside his/her place of employment. Many plans cover the nurse for acts or omissions as a member of a professional nursing board or committee. Most policies only require that you notify them of your position on a professional board or committee. A nurse who gives the neighbor's child an allergy shot or decides to remove a friend's sutures is not covered under the hospital's or employer's policy. The nurse who volunteers her professional services at a camp or ball game also needs her own personal policy.

8. *Affordable Rates*

Most insurance companies offer individual policies at surprisingly reasonable rates. Most policy premiums range from $35 to $75 a year. A nurse should buy as much coverage as she can afford. The nurse should carry at least $200,000/$600,000 of coverage. In today's consumer-oriented society, it may be even more appropriate to carry limits of $1,000,000/$1,000,000. The amount of coverage you should carry is dependent upon the particular professional situation in which you work and the risk of exposure your nursing duties provide. Also note that your premium payment qualifies as a business deduction for tax purposes.

9. *Nurses Are Personally Liable for a Rendered Judgment*

Individuals can be personally liable for any judgment rendered. This means that if you do not have professional liability insurance protection when a claim is presented against you, the court has a legal right to satisfy the judgment by claiming your personal assets. Many states have a law that stipulates that if a claimant cannot receive a financial judgment due to lack of personal assets, that claimant may renew the claim against you every five years. So, if you do not have adequate assets today, they can attempt recovery every five years until the claim is satisfied.

It cannot be overemphasized that a nurse should examine a policy before purchasing it. In the case of *American Nurses' Association v. Passaic General Hosp.*, a dispute arose as to how much the hospital's insurer would pay and how much the nurse's insurer would pay. The nurse and hospital were sued by a plaintiff who alleged he had received inadequate nursing care while in the recovery room after surgery. The claim settled out of court for $375,000.

The hospital was self-insured for the first $100,000. This means that it had to pay the first $100,000 of any settlement or judgment and that the insurance company, INA, would pay the rest up to $500,000 per claim. The policy covered all of its employees. Therefore, the hospital would have to indemnify its employee on its own up to $100,000.

The nurse had her own policy through the American Nurses' Association from the National Union Fire Insurance Company. Her policy had what is known as an *excess clause*. This clause said that it would pay only the excess of any amount *not* paid by other insurance covering the claim.

The hospital wanted the nurse's policy to pay the first $100,000 and to split the difference. However, since the nurse's policy said it was "excess," her insurer disagreed, and said that the hospital had to pay the first $100,000.

The court held that this question had never arisen before in New Jersey. Courts in other states had decided the issue both ways. The court decided that the hospital should pay the first $100,000, and the remaining amount was to be split. The court ruled this way because the hospital's policy required the hospital to provide indemnification for its employees. (A few hospitals have even stated this in their bylaws.)

Although the resolution of this case concerned the nurse, it would appear to be less stressful knowing that there are two insurers who would pay the amount than being in a situation where a nurse has no insurance. The nurse should not be overly concerned with such a situation. Let the two insurers fight it out in court. All the insured nurse needs to know is that she's covered either way!

In summary, the importance of professional liability insurance for nurses cannot be overstated. For your own peace of mind, you may want to make sure that you have adequate coverage to meet your particular needs from an insurance entity you can trust, one that will be there to ensure that your best interests as a professional are met.

UNDERSTANDING AN INSURANCE POLICY

The amount of coverage varies from policy to policy. For this reason, the nurse should review coverage afforded *before* purchasing a policy. The nurse can usually obtain a sample policy by just requesting one. For example, some policies only provide professional coverage, while others provide professional, personal and medical payment coverage. The information below explains each section of the nursing policy and advises the nurse what to look for.

Insuring Agreement

Section I

This section usually is listed first in the policy. The insuring agreements broadly define coverages in the insurance policy. For example, in most professional liability policies, these agreements cover claims arising from the insured's negligence. They also promise to defend any liability suit brought against the insured if the coverages apply. This section usually starts out by saying,

> The company agrees to pay on behalf of the insured all sums which the insured shall become legally obligated to pay as damages because of (a) injury arising out of malpractice, error, omission, or mistake in rendering or failing to render nursing services, or (b) injury arising out of acts or omissions of the insured, as a member of a formal accreditation board or committee of a hospital or professional society in the practice of the insured's professional occupation as stated in the Declarations.

The insuring agreement may have different coverage sections. Besides the coverage section for malpractice as discussed above, many professional policies now have a coverage section for personal liability and medical payments.

Defense and Settlement

Section II

A major benefit of having a professional liability policy is that the company will pay for the defense costs. The insurance company shall have the right and duty to "defend any suit against the insured seeking damages which are payable under the term of this policy, even if any of the allegations of the suit are groundless, false, or fraudulent." It is customary for the insurance company to retain the right to select the defense counsel. If the nurse or physician obtains legal services on his/her own, he/she generally is personally responsible for the bill.

The language of the policy determines whether it is a consent policy. Some companies reserve the right to settle without the consent of the insured, while others provide that the company will not settle a claim without written consent. Because of the professional implications, the latter provision affords a greater safeguard for the rights of the insured nurse or physician.

Many policies also will pay all costs taxed against the insured in any suit defended by the company. Any interest on the amount of judgment after entry of a judgment is often covered before the company has paid or tendered the judgment amount, as long as the amount does not exceed the limit of the company's liability (the amount of the policy limits).

71

Definitions

Section III

All policies have a section entitled "Definitions." Since a term's actual definition may differ from its ordinary meaning, the professional should read the definition when its meaning is at issue.

1. Exclusions

Exclusions reduce the broad coverage provided in the insuring agreement. It is often said that what the insurer gave in the insuring agreement, it hath taken away in the exclusions. Insuring agreements are modified for many reasons. Elimination of duplicate coverage, management of physical and moral hazard, elimination of unnecessary coverage, and elimination of an uninsurable exposure are some of the reasons for modification of the insuring agreement. Exclusions lower the price of the insurance.

Most policies do not apply to injury for which the insured may be held liable as a proprietor, superintendent, officer, director or shareholder of any hospital, sanitarium, clinic with bed and board facilities, nursing home, laboratory or other business enterprise.

Liability from worker compensation, unemployment disability, watercraft, automobile injury, nuclear damage and airplane injuries are typically excluded from most professional liability policies.

2. Declarations

The declarations are descriptive material relating to subjects covered, persons injured, premiums charged and policy limits. The declarations for a malpractice policy generally list the policyholder's name and address and agent's name.

The policy period is listed and includes the dates and times that the policy will be effective and in force. It is common for professional liability policies to commence at 12:01 a.m. standard time. Most are issued for one-, two- or three-year periods.

This section also deals with the dollar amount of the different coverages. Each coverage section has a limit of liability. The limit of liability is the maximum amount of money the company will pay. There are two different dollar amounts. For example, the professional buys a policy with limits of $200,000/$600,000. The first amount, $200,000, is the limit per each individual claim. Say, for example, the nurse accidentally gives an injection of Narcan, instead of Epi., to a patient in anaphylactic shock. The patient dies as a result of the negligence and an award is rendered against the nurse for $225,000. Since the policy limit is $200,000, the company will pay only $200,000. Therefore, the nurse is personally responsible for $25,000.

The second amount, $600,000, is an aggregate or yearly amount. This is the most the company will pay in one year. For example, the professional has three separate suits in which the following judgments were rendered against her: $225,000, $200,000, and $250,000. These judgments total $675,000. However, the company will pay only the total amount of their aggregate liability, $600,000. This means the professional has a personal exposure of $75,000.

The declarations also will indicate if the policy is a "claims made" or "occurrence" policy. The occurrence policy covers the alleged malpractice incident which occurs within the policy period, regardless of when such events are actually reported. For example, the professional has an occurrence policy effective from January 5, 1982 to January 5, 1983. She cancels her occurrence policy on January 6, 1983. On September 1, 1984, she is sued for the care rendered in the emergency room on January 3, 1983. The plaintiff is alleging that the death of her son was caused by the nurse's failure to relate to the doctor that the child's mother had removed two ticks. The child died of Rocky Mountain spotted fever. Luckily, January 3, 1983, fell within the time period in which the nurse had an occurrence policy so she is covered. Most policies are of this type.

A claims-made policy is different from an occurrence policy. In a claims-made policy, the company is responsible only for claims reported during that policy period. For example, suppose the same nurse discussed above has a claims-made policy which was effective from January 5, 1982, to January 5, 1983. After January 5, 1983, it is too late to report any claim. If the nurse is sued on September 1, 1984, there is no coverage, since the claim was not reported during the policy period.

Finally, the declarations page would list any additional coverages or endorsements. Endorsements are simply written language that is used to modify or change the policy so that it can be complete.

3. Conditions

The conditions are the ground rules of the transaction. They control the insurer's liability for covered losses by imposing obligations on the policy owner and the insurer. Typically, conditions discuss the policy owner's duties and obligations after a loss, other insurance, subrogation, assignment, cancellation, and assistance and cooperation.

The insured is responsible for notifying the company whenever a suit or claim is made against him/her. The policy may require that this notice be written and given as soon as practicable. The notice should identify the insured and contain information with respect to time, place and circumstances to enable the insurer to understand the basis and nature of the claim. Every demand, notice, summons or other process received by the insured should be forwarded.

This notice is important because the insurance company must secure defense counsel to answer the legal paper. When the nurse or physician has been served with a summons and complaint, a legal answer must be filed with the court within a set period of time. Failure to timely file this answer could result in a default judgment against the practitioner. If the practitioner has caused this failure, then the insurance company may deny liability. This "cooperation clause" requires the assistance and cooperation of the insured in the resolution of any claim or suit as a condition of the contract for insurance.

Most policies have an "other insurance" clause which states that if the insured has other insurance which would apply, the company shall not be liable for an amount greater than its proportional share. This clause is activated by the practitioner who buys two policies at the same time. It limits the total payments to the amount of the loss. The pro rata liability clause or the limit of liability rule are two provisions for figuring out what amount of the judgment each of the two companies will pay.

The conditions section of a policy also contains the "cancellation" clause. The policy usually can be cancelled by the practitioner by surrendering his/her policy to the company. The policy may be cancelled by the company by mailing written notice to the insured, at the address shown in the policy, at least 30 days in advance.

The assignment clause simply indicates that the practitioner cannot transfer or assign his/her interest to another. Many policies provide that if the insured should die or be rendered incompetent, the policy would terminate. However, the insured's legal representatives would be covered as far as any previously incurred liability.

Subrogation, also discussed in the conditions section, occurs after a claim is paid, the insurer steps into the insured's position and takes all the rights he/she had. It is important that the insured do nothing to endanger these rights.

CHAPTER SIX

LEGAL ASPECTS OF MEDICAL RECORDS

Charting with a Jury in Mind
Charting Pointers for the Office Nurse
Incident Reports
Patient Education and Discharge Instructions
Patient Access to Medical Records
Peer Review

CHARTING WITH A JURY IN MIND

Charting is a means of documenting the nursing care rendered. The patient's medical chart is a legal record. Good, concise charting can be the nurse's best defense in a malpractice suit. Concise, complete and accurate documentation can determine a suit's outcome.

Recently, one court warned hospitals and nurses that the availablity and accuracy of documents are not mere technicalities, but if absent can result in liability.[1] After the plaintiff had given birth to her fifth child, she asked to be sterilized. Pursuant to her request, a Pomeroy tubal ligation was done. Several years later, she suffered a ruptured ectopic pregnancy, which almost resulted in her death.

The plaintiff sued the hospital, alleging negligent sterilization. The hospital could not produce the medical records. Without the records, she could not prove her case. The appeals court stated that the fact a record is missing raises a presumption that the surgery was negligently performed. To be presumed negligent is a very difficult problem.

The Joint Commission on Accreditation of Hospitals (JCAH) has a section which addresses the maintenance of medical records. The JCAH *Accreditation Manual for Hospitals*, Section 9.1, states the following:

> The hospital maintains medical records that are *documented accurately* and in a timely manner, are readily accessible, and permit prompt retrieval of information, including statistical data.[2]

The JCAH requires the medical record to be sufficiently detailed and organized so that the practitioner who is responsible for the patient can provide continuing care. The record should demonstrate what the patient's condition was and mention the diagnostic and therapeutic procedures performed and the patient's response to treatment.

The American Nurses' Association (A.N.A.) has included standards for documentation in its Standards of Nursing Practice. According to Standard 1, documentation must be systematic and continuous. The data should be recorded, communicated and accessible. The nursing diagnosis should be derived from the health status data that is collected by the nurse through interviews, examination and observation.

Recently, a case was dismissed based on a nurse's documentation. A 16-year-old girl was involved in an auto accident and sustained a 4-centimeter laceration over the anterior portion of the distal tibia, which subsequently became infected. The patient and her mother testified that the cut was not cleansed with an antiseptic prior to suturing. The nurse had charted that the area was soaked in Betadine for twenty minutes. The physician also had charted that the wound was cleansed with Betadine and saline. Merely stating, without documentation, that all wounds were cleansed with an antiseptic would have made the defense unnecessarily difficult. Many times, problems arise when the basic things are not charted. In this instance, the case was dismissed because of the excellent documentation.

In 1981, the Kentucky Supreme Court decided the case of *Rogers v. Kasdan*.[3] The patient was involved in an auto accident and admitted to the hospital. She died seven days later from brain damage. The court ruled against the doctor and hospital nurses based on the medical records. The emergency room records were incomplete, the I and O sheet was incorrectly tallied, and the records contained a number of discrepancies. Several records were illegible, and others contained incomplete notations. This case demonstrates the legal importance of good charting. Nursing notes can be used as evidence of the quality or lack of quality of nursing care.

The medical record was the determinative factor in another recent case.[4] After delivery of her fourth child, the plaintiff continuously hemorrhaged, and died three hours later. The nurse's notes indicated that the vital signs were poorly monitored. The nurse also failed to contact the obstetrician to inform him of the plaintiff's condition.

Common Charting Errors

As the above cases illustrate, charting errors, inadequacies and omissions undermine the credibility of nursing care. Good charting employs common sense and good nursing practice. Good charting is not difficult if the nurse can remember the basics and avoid common charting mistakes.

Charting helps the nurse to formulate an initial assessment of the patient. For example, an 18-year-old is brought in on a stretcher after being involved in an automobile accident. The paramedic informs the nurse that the patient has a frontal hematoma and was unconscious for several minutes after the arrival of the squad. An examination of the right wrist shows an obvious Colles' fracture. The patient has a 7-centimeter laceration over the anterior part of the middle section of the left femur. The nurse's assessment and charting helps him/her to determine the priority of care for the patient's problems.

The nurse then documents the patient's injuries, vital signs, and neurological and circulation checks. By doing this, the nurse demonstrates his/her accountability. An evaluation of the emergency room record helps other members of the health team to spot any changes in the patient's status. Therefore, good documentation has helped not only in the care of the patient, but also in protecting the nurse from a malpractice suit.

1. Write Legibly

Illegible writing causes problems in defending any malpractice suit. Often malpractice suits are filed unnecessarily because the plaintiff's attorney cannot read the nurse's or physician's writing. The plaintiff's reviewing physician may not be able to read the notes either.

A number of practitioners have been embarrassed in court after admitting that they could not read their own writing. If the court cannot decipher the notes, it may doubt the credibility of the writer.

The nurse should write clearly and neatly. If the writing is difficult to read, print. This will help with patient care as well as prevent any unnecessary malpractice suits from being filed against the nurse.

2. Record the Date and Time

The nurse should make sure that the correct date appears on every page of the nursing notes. The time of each entry should be recorded.

Block charting has caused many documentation problems for defense attorneys and risk managers. There is always a danger of omitting pertinent information. It also makes it difficult to figure out the time sequence of events, which is often an issue in many cases. It is for these reasons that block charting has been discouraged.

3. Document Safeguards Used to Protect Patient

Patient falls are one of the most common causes of liability against nurses, hospitals and nursing homes. Nurses should document when the use of side rails is applied. For example, one nurse recently charted the following: "10:30 p.m. Call cord within reach. All 4 side rails were raised and bed is in its usual low position. Patient appears to be sleeping. Posey vest on." The night nurse came on duty shortly after. Upon making her initial rounds, she discovered the patient on the floor. Since the safeguards used to protect the patient were documented, the jury found in favor of the hospital and the nurse.

4. Documenting Restraints

The appropriate use of restraints is discussed at length in Chapter 8. If restraints are used, the nurse should describe the type used (soft wrist restraints, Posey vest, glove restraints, leather restraints, sheet restraints, et al.). The nurse should also describe the patient's current mental status and behavior. It is especially important to document circulation checks and the period during which the restraints are used. A restraint that is too tight can interfere with adequate blood flow and can result in ischemia and loss of limb.

The nurse should also be aware of his/her employer's policy on the use of restraints if one exists. Many hospitals and health care institutions will release a leather or soft arm restraint every two hours while the patient is awake. (Leather restraints are checked at fifteen-minute intervals by some institutions but not actually loosened at two-hour intervals unless the patient's condition warrants it.)

5. Chart All Nursing Actions

The nurse should chart everything that has been done for the patient in addition to a pertinent history. Below is an example that documents the nursing actions taken when a patient came into the emergency room for a drug overdose.

Nursing Notes

1300	Patient arrived per Squad 15 with an I.V. 1000 cc. D_5W in right antecubital with a 20-gauge Angiocath. Squad stated mother related to them the patient took 20 Valium 5 mg. tablets one hour P.T.A. Mother accompanied 18-year-old daughter. PERLA. Upon arrival, Pt. was A+0 to time, place, and person. 110/60, 98-84-18.
1303	Dr. Emergency examined. #18 nasogastric tube inserted in right naris without difficulty. I.V. rate increased to 250 cc. per hour. Nasogastric tube irrigated with 1000 cc. NaCl until clear. Liquid was initially clear

with small pieces of what appeared to be undigested pill particles. Patient states took pills after losing job. Pt. connected to monitor. Monitor shows normal sinus rhythm with rate of 80. (Attach copy of the monitor strip.)

1306   CBC, SMA6, and blood for drug screen drawn. Patient voided 120 cc. clear yellow urine. Sample of urine, blood, and gastric specimen also sent for drug screen. 112/64-88-18.

1313   Portable chest x-ray taken. ABG's right femoral artery drawn. Pt. remains alert. S. Calloway, R.N.

All I.V. sites, Foley insertions, nasogastric insertions and dressing appearances should be documented. The records should be detailed enough so that in two years, if the nurse is sued, he/she will be able to tell every nursing procedure that was performed and when it was performed.

It is often the basic things that are not charted that get the nurse into trouble. There was a recent case in which the plaintiff was treated in a nursing home for two weeks before being transferred to the hospital. The patient died in the hospital due to sepsis. The family filed suit, claiming that the plaintiff was given inadequate nursing care at the nursing home. The family alleged that as a result of not changing the plaintiff's position, she developed decubitus. They claimed that the decubitus became infected, which caused her septicemia.

The nurses' notes reflected only that a decubitus existed. Upon admission and thereafter, the nurses should have charted more specifically, such as, "Pt. admitted from home. 2.0 x 2.0 cm. decubitus present on coccyx area. A 3.0 x 3.0 cm. decubitus productive of a small amt. of yellow purulent drainage noted rt. iliac crest."

The nurse's documentation should also reflect the nursing process. Documentation of the assessment, care plan, actual care rendered and evaluation of the plan's effectiveness should be charted.

Nurses often complain that they just don't have enough time to do complete charting. This excuse doesn't hold up in court. If the nurse recalls something that was not charted, she is still allowed to testify. However, it is very difficult to convince a jury that a busy nurse, who has seen many patients during the interval between the event and the trial or deposition, actually remembers a particular detail. The court is left to weigh the nurse's word against the patient's in the absence of a writing. Frequently the plaintiff prevails on important issues which are not documented.

The nurse should also remember to document not only all nursing acts taken in response to the patient's problem, but also all responses to medication and treatment. This has been coined by some as "outcome-oriented charting." The patient complains of a frontal headache at 9:00 a.m. At 9:05, the nurse administers two aspirin. At 9:30, the nurse charts that "patient states headache is 100 percent relieved by aspirin."

6. *Using Flow Charts*

Flow sheets are often helpful in ensuring that all nursing actions have been documented. Even though flow charts are helpful, they are usually supplemented with some type of narrative charting.

Floor nurses have often used work sheets prepared during report to document the care rendered when making their rounds. The times and results can be inserted later. This helps the nurse who waits until the end of the shift to chart to avoid missing any important facts. Example:

202A Jones, Mrs. Appendectomy 9/26 I.V.
1000cc D₅W @ 125cc/hr.
_____ checked at_____
Drsg._____ Binder _____
TED thigh-high hose _____ Cough & deep breathe _____
Dinner _____ Medications_____
Dr. _____ Visited _____Act.-walk in hall x1
Foley draining _____

Every time the nurse enters the room to check the I.V., he/she should quickly jot down the time on the flow sheet. If the institution does not use flow sheets, he/she can simply jot it down on a work sheet. This assists the nurse when he/she does charts to avoid skipping any pertinent information.

7. Avoid Generalizations and Vague Expressions

The nurse's notes should be specific. Phrases like "ate fair" or "having a good day" are useless. I recently reviewed a chart that stated that the patient was having a "good day." She was a 64-year-old diabetic patient who was on bedrest. The patient also had metastatic cancer which was terminal. The next chart I reviewed, which was written by the same nurse, also stated that the patient was having a "good day." This patient was an ambulatory 22-year-old female who was recovering from appendicitis and receiving intravenous antibiotics. The difference between these patients is not reflected by the notation that each was "having a good day." Several years later, if the nurse is sued, she may be asked to define what she meant by "having a good day." If she is unable to provide an appropriate answer, her credibility with the jury will be affected.

Nurses also should not be afraid to quote the patient when it is relevant. Symptoms may also be documented by using the patient's own words. Also, the nurse should never use a medical term unless he/she knows exactly what it means. Below are a few examples to illustrate this point:

Subjective	Objective
Pt. ate fair	Pt. ate ½ of his reg. tray and drank 360 cc.'s.
Good day	Pt. has denied any complaints and required no medication. Has been ambulating in halls last 1 hour with visitor. Pt. states she is anxiously planning discharge in a.m.

B.S. normal	Bowel sounds are present in all 4 quadrants. Abd. soft. No guarding. No rebound tenderness. Denies any abd. pain.
B.S. normal	Breath sounds on auscultations are clear bilaterally.
Drsg. changed — wound OK	Old drsg. removed per Dr. Old's order. No drainage present. Area cleansed with Betadine. Incision line well approximated, without redness, and appears to be healing well.
Vd. q.s.	Pt. up to bedside commode and voided 350 cc.'s clear yellow urine.
Circ. check OK	Pedal pulse present 2+/4+ bilaterally. Toes blanch well and warm to touch. Moves all toes well. Denies any pain.

8. Record All Pertinent Information

The practitioner should chart all pertinent health histories, drug information, present medication and allergies. This is especially important to prevent administering drugs which would interfere with any medication the patient is currently taking. For example, in one case, the patient was taking eight aspirin a day for her arthritis as recommended by her family physician. The patient came to the emergency room complaining of right calf tenderness. A diagnosis of phlebitis was made, and the patient was placed on Heparin. The patient was asked if she was taking any medicine and she replied no. She was not specifically asked about over-the-counter medications. The patient had the aspirin in her purse and continued to take them. She then started having gross hematuria.

Failure to note the patient's drug allergies has also caused a number of problems. In one case, the patient told the nurse that she was severely allergic to aspirin. The nurse, however, forgot to chart it. When the intern gave the patient the aspirin-containing drug Darvon 65, the patient had a severe anaphylactic reaction.

The patient's medical history should also be recorded. Diseases such as diabetes, glaucoma and hypertension are important items to document.

9. Omissions and Documentation During a Code

Nursing notes should contain *all* the facts that another nurse would consider important in assessing the patient's needs. Again, the general proposition is that if it isn't charted, it wasn't done. One common area of omission is code situations.

Most states now recognize a cause of action for wrongful death if the nurse's action proximately resulted in the patient's death. Wrongful death actions differ from nursing malpractice actions. Nursing malpractice actions are commenced in order to compensate patients for their lost wages, hospital costs and other medical bills. In most states, the spouse can also sue for loss of consortium. This is to compensate the spouse for loss of advice, guidance, companionship, sex, attention and assistance which is caused by the negligence of another.

A wrongful death action, on the other hand, commences at the time of the decedent's death and is meant to compensate the spouse, children and next of kin. Recently, there has been a trend in many states to greatly expand the potential for recovery in wrongful death actions. Ohio is one such state. Section 2125.02 of the *Ohio Revised Code Annotated* now permits that compensatory damages may be awarded in an action for wrongful death and may include the following:

1) Loss of support from the reasonably expected earning capacity of the decedent;

2) Loss of services of the decedent;

3) Loss of society of the decedent, including loss of companionship, consortium, care, assistance, attention, protection, advice, guidance, counsel, instruction, training and education suffered not only by the surviving spouse, but also the minor children, parents or next of kin;

4) Loss of prospective inheritance to the decedent's heirs at law at the time of his/her death; and

5) The mental anguish incurred by the surviving spouse, minors, parents or next of kin.

The expanded wrongful death actions make it even more important to document well the nursing care rendered during a code. Good, concise charting during this critical time can be the nurse's best defense in a malpractice suit. Because many wrongful death actions have resulted in large verdict awards, a plaintiff may be persuaded to file suit where a death has occurred even if liability is not clearly established. This makes it of paramount importance to have concise, complete and accurate documentation. Often documentation during a code is the poorest instead of the most optimal.

It would be of great assistance if each hospital could appoint an R.N. to the code team whose only responsibility would be documentation. The nurse would not push medicines or start I.V.'s or perform CPR. Rather, this nurse's responsibility would be to document everything that is being done for the patient.

A number of cases of nursing liability have resulted from failure to resuscitate patients promptly and properly. All nurses who work in hospitals or health institutions should be adequately trained in CPR. They should receive in-service instruction and complete a return demonstration on a yearly basis. Any patient who does not have a "No Code Blue" order in place should be promptly resuscitated. This should be documented by the recording nurse.

The recording nurse should be familiar with the hospital's policy on documentation during codes, if there is one. It would be helpful if the recording nurse could write on the nursing note or code sheet the names of all staff members who have responded to the code. The nurse then should proceed to describe and chart everything that is being done for the patient. A short and pertinent history is also helpful. For example, the nurse may chart that "this is a 46-year-old white male who was jogging approximately two minutes ago and collapsed. Patient was approximately two blocks from the hospital and was brought to the E.R. by a good Samaritan. No history available. No identification. Patient slightly cyanotic and diaphoretic upon arrival, with a shallow respiratory rate of eight. Monitor applied. Patient went into cardiopulmonary arrest as placed on cart."

10. Incident Reports

If an incident occurs, the nurse should record the facts of the occurrence, what action was taken, the results of the medical evaluation and any tests that were done. The nurse should *not* write in the nursing notes that an incident report has been filled out. (See the section on incident reports.)

11. Improper Abbreviations

Only commonly accepted abbreviations should be used. Most hospitals have a list of approved abbreviations. Creative but unapproved abbreviations can cause problems not only legally, but for co-workers who are trying to decipher the records. I recently reviewed a chart which read as follows: "Pt. complains of H.A. x 1 hr. No. N-V-D-V. BP 110/80, 90-20. Grip Strong P=RL; PMH-H.A. 1979, P.E.-1982, appy. 1984 NKDA's. Takes tyl., antibiotic o.d."

Can you interpret these abbreviations? The patient came in complaining of a frontal headache which started one hour prior to admission. The patient denied any nausea, vomiting, diarrhea or vertigo. The patient's grip was equally strong bilaterally. Her pupils were also equal and reactive to light. Her past medical history included a heart attack in 1979, a pulmonary embolus in 1982 and an appendectomy in January of 1984. The patient had no known drug allergies, and the only medication she took was Tylox. Does the "o.d." mean that the patient was using an antibiotic eyedrop to the right eye? The patient was actually taking one tablet of tetracycline for her acne. ("O.d." meant once a day to the recording nurse.)

12. Correct Spelling

If you are unaware of the correct spelling of a word, consult the dictionary. In one case, a nurse charted that "the patient vominited x 1-appears to contain much flim." The plaintiff's attorney projected a copy of these notes on a screen before the jury, and undoubtedly the nurse's credibility was damaged as a result of the spelling errors.

13. Document Only the Procedures You Have Performed

A nurse should document only the care and treatment he/she has rendered. It is never good practice to document for someone else, absent a code situation or another valid reason.

14. Charting on the Wrong File

If the nurse erroneously charts on the wrong file, he/she should simply draw a line through it, mark "error," sign his/her initials, and make the correct notation above the error. If more room is needed, he/she can simply chart it at the bottom and mark it as a late entry. Nurses should always chart in ink. Erasures should never be made, nor should errors be obliterated. Also, correction fluid should never be used.

15. Signing the Chart Properly

Notes should be signed with the nurse's first initial, last name and title, and the signature should always be on the right side of the page. Many nurses draw a line through any blank space to prevent others from adding information to their nursing notes. The nurse should not skip lines between entries.

If the nurse does not have enough room on the last line written to sign his/her name, he/she can draw a line from the last word to the end of that line. The nurse can then skip to the next line, draw a line through it up to the point where his/her signature should begin, and sign his/her name. The nurse should never write in the margins.

16. Patient Noncompliance

Discharge instructions and patient noncompliance should always be documented. This is discussed in more detail under the section in this chapter on discharge instructions.

Summary

Remember that the chart is a legal record. Well-documented nursing notes are the nurse's most effective way to bolster his/her defense and to demonstrate that he/she has met the standard of care. Good nursing records also facilitate better patient care.

CHARTING POINTERS FOR THE OFFICE NURSE

An accurate record of the exam and treatments rendered will provide a solid foundation in case a lawsuit is filed by an office patient. Failure to maintain complete, accurate and current records can have a severe and adverse effect on the nurse and his/her employer-physician in a malpractice action.

The first pointer concerns the *return visit date*. After the patient is examined, the date on which the patient is advised to have a follow-up appointment should be documented. This practice will protect against the patient's claim that he/she was not told to return.

Second, chart all *cancelled and failed appointments*. Patients are often damaged as a result of their failure to follow the prescribed medical advice. A documented pattern of missed appointments is very helpful in the nurse's and employer-physician's defense if the patient later sues. A documented record can help absolve the nurse or her employer of any liability due to the patient's negligence.

Third, document *all phone conversations*. The chart should reflect the substance of any conversation in which advice is given or a drug refill is prescribed. Nurses and physicians alike should be cautious about giving any advice or treatment over the telephone without seeing the patient. An increasingly large number of malpractice suits center around disputes about the contents of a telephone call. If advice is given, document the date, time and substance of the conversation.

This includes the symptoms complained of and those denied by the patient.

The fourth pointer deals with *prescriptions and refills*. All prescriptions that are issued should be recorded along with their dosage and amount. A number of cases have alleged improper or excessive sedation by prescribed drugs.

Fifth, check to be sure that the patient is not *allergic* to the drug prescribed. The physician writing the prescription should elicit this information. If the nurse delivers the prescription to the patient, he/she should verify that the patient is not allergic to the medication.

Sixth, *document all follow-up instructions*. Many patients are unable to recall many facts about the follow-up instructions they were given. A patient who has just been treated with sutures for a severe laceration may not recall the suture removal and care instructions. It is often helpful to tell a friend or family member and to provide the patient with a written copy of the instructions.

Seventh, *make the records legible*. Illegible records make it impossible to evaluate the standard of care. Some medical records can't even be deciphered by the person who wrote them.

Eighth, *correctly change any error in charting*. Draw a line through the error and mark it as such. The correct notation can then be made.

Ninth, *if you witness the consent form being signed*, document this in the office record. When the nurse signs the consent, he/she is only certifying that he/she saw the patient signing the document. A copy of the consent form should be retained for the office file.

Tenth, hospitals or other health care institutions often send the attending physician a copy of the emergency room record, discharge summary, lab report, pathology report and other such documents. These are usually placed in the physician's box or mailed. After the physician reviews these, he/she sometimes gives them to the nurse so they can be placed in the patient's office record. *The nurse should question any abnormality*.

There have recently been a number of suits filed for failure to notify patients of pertinent information contained in office records. For example, if the emergency room physician looks at an x-ray of a patient's wrist and reads it as normal, and then the radiologist interprets it the next day and reads it as a fracture, or if test results concerning a patient's potassium level come back and read 2.0, there is a duty to promptly notify the patient.

INCIDENT REPORTS

An incident report has been designated by the American College of Surgeons as an account of "an unfavorable deviation of expectation involving patient care which may be the result of medical management."[2] An incident is a deviation from the routine operation of the hospital or health care facility.

Incident reporting is a vital element of risk management. Incident reports help the risk manager to identify potential areas of liability so that changes can be made to prevent similar instances from occurring in the future. For example, an emergency room waiting area had recently been remodeled and new chairs were installed. The nurse observed that as one of the patients sat down, a chair collapsed. The nurse completed an incident report. The next day, the same incident occurred, and she completed another incident report. Luckily, neither patient was injured. The hospital's risk manager investigated and discovered that the chairs were improperly assembled at the factory. The chairs were immediately replaced to prevent any future injury.

The second purpose of the incident report is to alert the risk manager, hospital attorney or professional liability carrier of a potential claim. The nurse who discovers the incident can be contacted to assist in obtaining additional evidence and preserving it. The risk manager or attorney can then conduct an investigation while the facts are still fresh in everyone's memory. For example, a patient in a local hospital was recently having an arthroscopy. The knife broke inside the patient's knee and could not be retrieved. The operating room nurse completed an incident report, which alerted the risk manager to quickly confiscate the remainder of the blade and preserve it as evidence. A lawsuit ensued. The risk manager had the metal analyzed, and it was found to be substandard. The suit against the hospital was then dropped.

The Joint Commission on Accreditation of Hospitals (JCAH) requires the establishment of an incident reporting system.[6] Chapter 15, Section 15.3.1.3, entitled "Plant, Technology and Safety Management," requires the reporting of all accidents, injuries and safety hazards, and states that the procedure for investigating and evaluating each report and all follow-up actions must be documented.

An incident report is an important adminstrative tool.[7] It is an internal device used to study and report the causes of accidents or incidents in the institution. The data is compiled and evaluated by the administrator, risk manager or hospital attorney, and then used to pinpoint problem areas and assist in the reduction of accidents. An incident report should be made soon after the accident or incident, while the information is fresh in the minds of those who report it. It can be especially valuable in legal actions, as it allows the hospital or institution to gather necessary information in case a lawsuit is ever filed. It also assists in keeping a patient profile to identify any individual who is a habitual complainer or has frequent accidents. One local hospital recently discovered that one of its patients, a 34-year-old female, had fallen in her room three times during the past five years. Each time, the patient claimed to have slipped in water or a liquid in the bathroom.

For years the American Hospital Association has been urging hospitals to establish reporting systems.[8] Any incident which is not consistent with the routine operation of the hospital or the routine care of the patient should be documented. The incident report covers both incident and accident situations; for this reason, many hospitals now call this form an "accident or incident report." The American Hospital Association suggests that the routine practice and evaluation of incident reports can provide important information which will lead to effective preventive measures. This is why most hospitals and health care institutions ask nurses to report events even if they do not cause patient injury. For example, if the pharmacy sends up the wrong I.V. for a patient and the nurse catches the error and does not administer the I.V., most hospitals would request that this information be put in an incident report.

Every facility should have a written policy on incident reporting, which should be reviewed by all new employees during orientation. The staff should be adequately instructed on the proper procedure for filling out the incident report. It should be a factual report and void of admissions of guilt or negligence. The incident report should be carefully worded to avoid any implication of blame or retribution. Shifting the blame through express statements is dangerous.

The incident report is to facilitate the flow of communication and to objectively document treatment, diagnosis and observation. This purpose is *not* served when the nurse writes an entry like, "I walked into Mrs. Jones' room upon making my initial morning rounds. I noted the I.V. hanging was heparin instead of D_5W. I verified the order and discontinued the heparin. It was probably started by that incompetent night nurse, J. Doe, who is one of these days going to kill somebody."

Most incident reports do, however, contain the following information:

1. The patient's name and room number.

2. Any witnesses to the incident.

3. The exact place or room where the incident occurred.

4. The exact position where the incident occurred. (I recently reviewed an incident report that stated that the patient fell in her room. The plaintiff later tried to say that she fell in the bathroom. The recording nurse did not recall, and the position of the fall was critical to the case.)

5. Whether the incident involved a patient, employee, visitor or none of the above.

6. The sex of the individual, if applicable.

7. The age of the individual, if applicable.

8. The marital status of the individual, if applicable.

9. The exact time and date when the incident took place.

10. The shift during which the incident occurred.

11. The hospital number if the injury involved a patient.

12. If the injury involved a visitor, the name of the patient being visited.

13. If the incident involved a patient, his/her prior condition (normal, senile, sedated, unconscious or other).

14. If the incident involved a patient fall, whether he/she received any prior medication.

15. A short, factual, carefully worded narrative which is descriptive of the incident and void of any admissions of guilt.

16. The name, title and department of the person preparing the report.

17. The patient's vital signs before and after the incident, if applicable.

18. An entry as to whether the supervisor has been notified and, if applicable, his/her signature.

19. An entry indicating whether the physician was notified. If so, the name of the physician and the time notified. Most health care institutions require the

physician's signature and statement if the incident directly involved a patient accident or incident.

20.   The result of laboratory or x-ray exams and their results.

21.   The treatment prescribed, if applicable.

Most hospitals or employers feel that the practioner should *not* state in the medical record that an incident report has been completed, because the plaintiff cannot subpoena into court a document which he/she does not know exists. However, the nurse should still document his/her clinical observation in the nurse notes.

Most states hold that the incident report is not discoverable. (This means that the plaintiff's attorney cannot obtain a copy of the incident report and attempt to introduce it as evidence in the courtroom.) However, because there is still a concern by defense lawyers and risk managers that the incident report could be discoverable and the patient may be able to secure a copy, it is important for this report to be nonjudgmental and complete. It is always better for the nurse to write the report assuming it will be viewed by others, possibly an adversary, than to assume it is confidential and inaccessible.

Many states have held that incident reports are immune from discovery either under the attorney-client privilege or the attorney work-product rule. To be protected under this rule, the incident report must have been made in anticipation of litigation or in preparation for trial or arbitration.

One recent author suggested the following to protect a hospital's incident reports:

1.   Treat incident reports as confidential documents and clearly mark each page as such.

2.   Strictly limit the number of copies made and the distribution of the reports in the institution.

3.   Do *not* place a copy of the report in the patient's medical records.

4.   Limit the content of the report to facts; do not include conclusions or assignments of blame.

5.   Address the report to the hospital's attorney or claims manager by name.

6.   Train hospital personnel to complete incident reports with the same care used in completing medical records.[9]

One appellate court in Ohio ruled that a particular hospital incident report was discoverable only because it was placed in the patient's medical records.[10] Generally, if an incident report is requested by the plaintiff's attorney, the hospital's attorney will refuse to provide it. As previously mentioned, this denial is usually made on the theory that the incident report is a confidential communication protected by the attorney-client privilege and work-product immunity. If the court agrees, the incident report is not admissible evidence. This means the plaintiff's attorney cannot obtain a copy of the report, read it or use it as evidence at trial.

In the *Bernardi v. Community Hospital Association* case, an incident report was made regarding a patient's footdrop, and copies of the incident report were forwarded to the hospital administrator and the nursing director.[11] A copy was also placed in the patient's medical records and the court ruled the incident report was admissible. Again, incident reports should never be made a part of the patient's medical records.

Since the incident report is generally not part of the hospital records, the facts should be charted objectively. For example, the nurse walks in and finds Mr. Jones on the floor. The nurse should chart, "Patient found lying on floor, parallel to and approximately 12 inches from bed. Bed in low position with side rails up. No obvious injury. Did not strike head. R.O.M. well. P.E.R.L.A. Denies any injury. Patient returned to bed. Supervisor and medical resident notified. Patient alert and oriented to me, place, and person. Call cord within reach."

In summary, most hospitals and health care facilities have policies and procedures for the use of incident reports. Incident reports should be carefully worded to avoid any implication of blame and retribution, and the nurse should stick to the facts and avoid making assumptions in the report. An account of what happened should be obtained from the patient whenever possible. The facts should be checked and signed by a corroborating party. The nurse should *not* document in the nursing notes that an incident report has been completed.

The incident report is a valuable document because it is recorded when recollections are still fresh. It also is a powerful administrative tool that can lead to corrective, preventive measures by the hospital. Hospitals and health care facilities should set and follow the guidelines discussed above to ensure that the incident reports are nondiscoverable.

PATIENT EDUCATION AND DISCHARGE INSTRUCTIONS

Instructions are usually given to the patient or his/her caregiver once the patient has been treated and the decisions for discharge have been made. With the implication of DRGs (diagnostic-related groups), patients are spending less time in the hospital. This has increased the nurse's role in providing patient education and discharge instructions.

The nurse's responsibility to provide patient education and discharge instructions stems from many sources. First of all, the JCAH requires the nurse to document the nursing process (assessment, planning, intervention and evaluation) for each patient's hospitalization from admission through discharge.[12] The JCAH *Accreditation Manual for Hospitals* specifically states the following:

> Patient education and patient/family knowledge of self-care are given special consideration in the nursing plan. The instructions and counseling given to the patient are consistent with that of the responsible medical practitioner.[13]

Furthermore, the nurse's plan of care should, when appropriate, document both family education and discharge planning. Evidence of all discharge instructions should be documented in the patient's medical record.

In addition to JCAH requirements, the nursing practice standards published by the American Nurses' Association are broad enough to encompass patient education and the providing of discharge instructions. Standard III states that the plan of nursing care includes goals derived from the nursing diagnosis. Standard IV sets out that the plan of nursing care includes priorities and the prescribed measures to achieve the goals derived from the nursing diagnosis. The interpretive statement accompanying these standards indicates that "teaching-learning principles should be incorporated into the plan of care."[14]

The A.N.A. Statement of Function also identifies teaching as one of the nurse's professional activities. It states, in part, that professional nursing is "the direction and education to secure physical and mental care."[15] It is always considered good nursing practice, for instance, to instruct those patients who are going home with Foley catheters on proper catheter care. Likewise, patients who are sent home with dressings should be properly instructed on sterile dressing changes. Courts have viewed and are likely to continue to view patient teaching as a health care provider's legal duty.

An illustration is the *Kyslinger v. United States* case, in which the hospital staff sent a hemodialysis patient home with an artificial kidney.[16] The patient died at home. The wife filed suit, alleging that the hospital staff had failed to teach her husband how to properly use and maintain a home dialysis unit. The hospital and nurses eventually won the suit after proving that appropriate education was provided.

Most hospitals, to avoid liability for premature discharge, have a policy that requires that a physicial examination be performed by the physician prior to discharge. Other hospitals at least require that a review of the medical record be made prior to discharge. The recent case of *Polischeck* illustrates this well.[17] The plaintiff decedent came to the hospital's emergency room and had symptoms of a subarachnoid hemorrhage. The hospital had a policy under which patients were first seen by a physician's assistant. In this case, the physician's assistant discharged the plaintiff after deciding that the prerequisite symptoms of a subarachnoid hemorrhage were not present. The plaintiff, who was never examined by a physician, went home and was later found dead. The hospital was found liable for deviating from acceptable hospital practice.

Normally, a hospital will not be held liable if the physician has examined the patient and decided that he/she can be discharged. The question of medical readiness is one for a physician to determine. However, this general rule is not without exception. First of all, if the nurse knew or should have know that discharge was contraindicated, liability can result. Any nurse who is concerned that a patient is not ready for discharge should communicate this to the physician. If the nurse has any concerns after consulting with the physician, he/she should relate this to his/her immediate supervisor.

When there are changes or deterioration in a patient's condition that occur after the discharge order has been written, the nurse should postpone the discharge and contact the physician as soon as possible. For example, a patient is admitted overnight for observation after being struck in the head. The physician comes in the next day and writes an order that the patient be discharged. During the physician's discussion with the patient, he complains of some aching in the neck. The doctor orders that a cervical x-ray be done before discharge. Before the patient is actually discharged, the radiologist calls up to the patient's floor and indicates there is a possible cervical fracture. This change must be communicated to the physician prior to discharge. Otherwise, the nurse and the hospital face a liability exposure.

A potential new source of liability is premature discharge by a hospital's utilization review committee. Utilization review committees were established to deal with the appropriate allocation of scarce medical resources, and their importance has increased with the institution of DRGs. These committees have the responsibility of terminating unwarranted hospital stays.

What does the nurse do if the patient refuses to leave? The nurse should first find the reason for the patient's refusal, and contact the patient's physician about the problem. If the patient still refuses to leave, the nurse should contact his/her supervisor. The nurse's supervisor will probably contact the hospital attorney, who will then aid the hospital in having the patient physically removed from the premises. To do this, the hospital attorney may request an injunction or an order of eviction.

North Carolina has a law that makes such a refusal by a patient a criminal offense.[18] Even in states without such a statute, it is still trespassing. In the *Lucy Webb* case, the court said that a hospital has a duty to reserve its rooms for persons who are in actual need of medical care and treatment.[19]

Nurses should be cautious when discharging patients to make sure that they have suitable transportation. It would be hazardous, for instance, to dismiss an intoxicated patient who states that he/she is going to walk one mile to his/her house. Many hospitals have policies stating that they will pay for a cab and add it to the patient's bill.

If the nurse is apprised of the fact that the patient has nowhere to go, he/she has no choice but to keep the patient until transfer to an appropriate facility can be arranged.[20] This situation can be disruptive to the hospital staff.

At the time of discharge, written instructions may prove to be helpful to both the patient and the staff. However, common sense should be used. Intelligent use of discharge sheets is more important than the ritual of handing the patient a paper. The written discharge instructions should be in duplicate, and the patient should sign the bottom of the instructions sheet. There should also be a sentence at the end stating the following:

> I hereby acknowledge that I have read the above discharge instructions, that they have been explained to me, and that I have had the opportunity to ask any questions and that all questions have been answered to my satisfaction. I hereby acknowledge that this is my signature and that I have been provided a copy of my discharge instructions.

Documentation that the patient received a copy of the discharge instructions should be charted in the nursing notes.

Many lawsuits have resulted from the failure to provide discharge instructions. For example, a 12-year-old boy was struck in the head during a fight at school.[21] He was taken to the emergency room, where he was examined and x-rayed. The patient was pale and lethargic. Plans were made to admit the child. After examination and consultation with the pediatrician, the decision to discharge the patient was made.

An instruction sheet for head injuries was ordered but never received. The child went home and returned later that evening with acute epidural hematoma. The child is now a quadriplegic. The jury awarded $4,000,000 against the school district, hospital and physician.

This case illustrates the importance of written discharge instructions. Patients are often anxious when leaving the hospital and have difficulty remembering their instructions. Having written sheets which are closely reviewed by the nurse will assist in alleviating this problem. Written instructions will aid patients and will also help to protect the hospital in the event it is sued.

Bernard v. Gravois is probably the earliest case where a court acknowledged the nurse's role in instruction and education.[22] The mother alleged that the nurse was negligent in instruction on the application of a heating pad to her child's neck in order to localize pus. The child sustained a burn. The court ruled in the nurse's favor after establishing that proper instructions were given.

In *Kaiser*, a patient had treatment for a nasal condition.[23] He received the drug Pyribenzamine. The patient was given no discharge instructions or warning of drowsiness, a side effect of the drug. He took his first pill and went to work. He was a bus driver, and as he was driving, he lost consciousness and struck a telephone pole. Instructing the patient about the medication's side effects could have prevented this.

In a similar case, a physician was found liable for failure to provide discharge instructions regarding the side effects of a medication.[24] The patient was prescribed Quaaludes and received no warning about drowsiness. The Quaaludes had a detrimental effect on the patient's ability to drive his car, and he collided with another car. The court of appeals held that there was sufficient evidence to state a cause of action for negligence against the physician, based upon his failure to provide warning.

In another case, the issue was whether discharge instructions had been given to a patient with a head injury.[25] The patient had been struck on the head with a bat and stabbed in the right shoulder. He was treated and released that night. The next morning, his mother found him dead. The nurse specifically recalled giving the patient's mother discharge instructions. In fact, the court gave great weight to the fact the nurse refused to send the patient home in a cab as requested by the mother so that the mother could be given discharge instructions.

In summary, the nurse's obligation for patient teaching is well recognized today. Courts have accepted for more than forty years that instruction and education are nursing functions. The nurse can be liable if proper instructions are not given and patient injury results.[26] Adequate written discharge instructions should be given, the patient should sign them, and a copy should be placed in the patient's medical records.

PATIENT ACCESS TO MEDICAL RECORDS

The law concerning the patient's access to medical records has changed dramatically over the past twenty years. As is set out in some states' regulations, the hospital or institution owns and physically possesses the medical records and is responsible for their use. The hospital generally has the right to restrict the removal of the records from the premises.

In a malpractice case, the patient, along with the person against whom liability is asserted, may have an interest in the information contained in the records. In some states the patient has a legal right to review his or her own records.[27] The following are among the states that allow this by statute: Alaska,[28] Ohio,[29] Idaho,[30] Illinois,[31] Indiana,[32] Louisiana,[33] Maine,[34] Massachusetts,[35] Minnesota,[36] Nevada,[37] New Jersey,[38] New York,[39] Oklahoma,[40] Pennsylvania,[41] Tennessee,[42] Utah,[43] and Virginia.[44]

However, in many states, the hospital can refuse the patient the right to review these records unless he/she has a substantial reason or the consent of his/her physician.[45] For example, California's law specifically allows the patient's attorney to obtain a copy of the records with proper authorization.[46] In Hawaii, the patient can obtain a copy of his/her medical records unless, in the opinion of the health care provider, it would be detrimental to the patient's care.[47] Psychiatric or psychological records may be withheld in Maryland if the attending physician feels the disclosure would be "medically contraindicated."[48]

Generally, if a hospital allows a patient or authorized third parties to review the patient's record, there is no problem. However, if the hospital denies access to an authorized agent of the patient or if the hospital releases the record to an unauthorized person, problems may arise.

Denial of access to medical records to the patient has recently been the subject of judicial scrutiny, and injunctions have been ordered to compel hospitals to disclose information which is legitimately needed by others. In some cases, courts have awarded not only actual damages, but also punitive damages to patients denied access.

Maryland law states that a hospital or related institution shall comply within a reasonable amount of time to a patient's written request for medical records.[49] If the facility refuses to disclose a medical record within a reasonable amount of time, the facility may be liable for actual damages, and possibly punitive damages.

Ohio's new law on access to medical records also states that the patient should be provided with a copy of his/her medical records within a reasonable time after discharge and the signing of a written request.[50] If the hospital fails to furnish a finalized medical record, the patient may bring a civil action to enforce his/her right of access to that record.

Information from medical records may also be disclosed to other persons and agencies. Third parties who have recognized interests include those covered by hospital insurance programs, governmental medical research agencies, health departments and in-house staff committees.

One case discussed this issue in particular: Could a hospital deny access to a person who had an authorization from the patient and a legitimate interest in the record? The court held that access could not be denied. It did, however, place a qualifier on situations in which the doctor certified under oath that release of the records would be detrimental to the patient's health.

In most cases, if the patient is refused access to his/her records, he/she will get a subpoena; if the hospital receives such a court order, it must generally produce the medical records. Many hospitals realize that refusal to the patient will result in this legal process, so they generally grant such requests initially. Whether the medical records are introduced into trial is dependent on the rules of evidence of the particular state.

If a hospital is sued, it may also use the medical records. Physicians, nurses and other health personnel can consult the records in gathering statistical information. The records may also be used for purposes of research and education. However, this must not interfere with the patient's right to confidentiality.

It is advisable to require an authorization form which is written, signed and dated by the patient before the release of records, whether it is to the patient or his/her attorney. Many states require such written authorization by statute. A few states require that the release form not only be signed, but notarized. For example, Utah's law states that whenever an attorney is authorized to obtain a copy of the records, the health care facility must produce them if a written authorization signed and acknowledged by the patient before a notary public is presented.[51]

Federal law dictates that if any record concerning drugs or alcohol is released, the release form must be dated within sixty days of receipt.[52] This is to prevent the utilization of outdated release forms. Many states, like Ohio, also require that all release forms be dated within sixty days.[53] The nurse should be aware of his/her institution's policy on the release of records. Most policies specify the date the release must be signed in order to be effective. If the nurse is confused, he/she should contact the medical records administrator.

The hospital or other health care institution can require that the record be examined only during reasonable business hours and upon reasonable notice. This is necessary to prevent interference with the orderly operation of the medical records department.

The institution may also charge a reasonable fee for the release of records. Tennessee law states the records may be released upon payment of a reasonable charge.[54] This implies that payment could be required before the release of the record. New York law states that hospitals and physicians must be reimbursed for the expense of providing copies of medical records or x-rays to the patient.[55]

In summary, it appears that earlier court decisions held the hospital had physical and absolute ownership of records.[56] The fee charged the patient was only for professional services and nothing else. However, more recent decisions demonstrate a change in judicial thinking.[57] The hospital may have the possession and ownership of the medical record, but the patient has a right to the information contained therein. This includes an absolute right to have a copy of this record.[58] In the event of the patient's death, the privilege is extended to the next of kin.[59] Attorneys, agents and subsequent physicians have also been held to have the right to examine medical records.[60] Only recently has there been this distinction made between the hospital's ownership of medical records and the patient's ownership of the information therein.

PEER REVIEW

PSRO and PRO

In 1972 Congress created the Professional Standards Review Organization (PSRO). The purpose of the PSRO was to promote the effective, efficient and economical delivery of health care services.[61] It was created to promote the quality of care and cost efficiency in health care institutions receiving Medicare, Medicard, and maternal and child health financing.

Local physicians were employed to review the care provided and to make sure it met the acceptable standard of care. It was established that the PSRO could delegate its responsibilities to peer review committees.[62]

There was a concern that the PSROs were not cost effective. In 1982 the PSROs were phased out and Peer Review Organizations (PROs) were established. Medical services rendered by a health care institution must be necessary and reasonable as determined by the PRO. The PRO is required for institutions with Medicare services only. If an institution does not heed PRO criteria it can either permanently or temporarily be excluded from Medicare reimbursement.

Peer Review Committees

The trend has been to impose a duty on the hospital to monitor the quality of care rendered to its patients. In fact, all fifty states have passed laws regarding the establishment of peer review committees.[63]

Even without a statute, JCAH-accredited institutions are required to have certain review committees. These committees are formed to review functions relating to tissue specimens, pharmaceutical and therapeutic policies and practices, medical records, blood utilization and antibiotics, among other services.[64]

In recent years, the activities of hospital review committees have been the center of legal controversy. Peer review committee statutes were drafted with the idea that they would improve the quality of care rendered to patients. To ensure this purpose, the state statutes provided immunity clauses. It was felt that the immunity provisions were necessary. Without the frank, uninhibited exchange among committee members and witnesses, the statutes' purpose would not be reached. Witnesses and committee members would not feel free to discuss information concerning colleagues if the information could be used in court against them.

The only problem has been that this "area of law is in its infancy, undeveloped and often unpredictable."[65] John Horty, in his book on hospital law, succinctly points out that even though the courts and legislatures have attempted to provide immunity and confidentiality, this has been done in a piecemeal fashion.

Confidentiality is crucial to every peer review committee. "A peer review committee needs confidentiality in order to challenge and argue a colleague's credentials while maintaining an atmosphere of professional cordiality in the hospital."[66]

The courts are called upon to interpret the peer review laws enacted by the legislatures in all fifty states and the District of Columbia. The courts attempt to maintain a balance between plaintiffs' rights and the statutory purpose of peer review: to protect the public.

It is for these reasons that hospitals must comply with the formalities of state law concerning peer review committees. Hospital policies should be well drafted and consistent with state law. Furthermore, any investigations should be initiated only under the auspices of committees defined by such policies.

All committee reports should be marked as such and should also be marked confidential. Some committees stamp in red ink at the top of each page, "Confidential: Protected from Discovery by Applicable State Statute." Many defense attorneys are not aware that the material is protected from discovery. Clearly marking confidential reports will aid in preventing the release of sensitive, confidential and privileged material.

The law books are full of cases where hospitals have been forced to turn over reports because these guidelines were not strictly followed. In the *Baldwin v. McGrath* case, an ad hoc committee investigated an incident involving a physician.[67] Problems arose because the committee was not created by formal procedure; the hospital's Joint Conference Committee never got around to establishing a peer review committee.

The physician who was being investigated brought suit against the hospital. The physician demanded copies of the committee records and the hospital refused. The court ruled that the records were not given protection from discovery because the committee was not authorized to engage in peer review. The court also found the ad hoc committee was never formally created. This and many other cases stress the importance of strict adherence to state statutes.[68]

There are a multitude of cases that uphold the protection of committee documents when the hospital has an authorized policy which conforms to the state's law on peer review. In the *Weiner* case, the plaintiff was erroneously diagnosed as having cancer of the lung.[69] A thoracotomy and lobectomy of the right upper bronchus were performed, and the pathologist found no evidence of cancer.

A committee investigation was done to find out what steps could be taken to prevent this from happening again. The plaintiff wanted to obtain a copy of the investigative study report or "complication report." However, a state statute protected members of a medical committee engaged in reviewing actions of that medical committee, and the court concluded that the complication report was not discoverable.

In summary, the following should be remembered about peer review committees:

1. Peer review committees have been the center of a continuing legal controversy.

2. Immunity and confidentiality is crucial to every peer review committee in a hospital.

3. The hospital and any member of a peer review committee should be familiar with the JCAH guidelines.

4. The hospital should have a policy on peer review.

5. The hospital should be familiar with its state statute on peer review.

6. The hospital policy should specifically adhere to the formalities dictated by state law.

7. The peer review committee members should adhere closely to the hospital's policy.

8. Committee members should be advised to avoid statements or actions of malice, since this is an exception to the immunity and confidentiality of the committee.

9. All committee reports should be stamped in red, at the top of the page, that they are confidential and nondiscoverable under state law.

REFERENCES

1. *Valcin v. Public Health Trust of Dade County*, 3rd District, Case No. 81-2131 (Fla., June 5, 1984).
2. Joint Commission on Accreditation of Hospitals, *Accreditation Manual for Hospitals* 87 (1986).
3. *Rogers v. Kasdan*, 612 S.W.2d 133 (Ky. 1981).
4. *Maslonka v. Hermann*, 414 A.2d 1350 (N.J. Super. Ct. 1980).
5. The American College of Surgeons, *Patient Safety Manual* 57 (1979).
6. Joint Commission on Accreditation of Hospitals, *supra* note 2.
7. *See* "Hospital Accident Reports; Admissibility and Privilege," *Dick. L. Rev.* 493 (1975).
8. *See* Huffman, E., *Medical Records Management* (6th ed. 1972).
9. *Hospital Law Manual* 76 (Aspen Systems Corporation 1983).
10. *Rees v. Doctors Hospital*, No. CA-5226 (Ohio App., Stark County, Feb. 6, 1980).
11. *Bernardi v. Community Hospital Association*, 443 P.2d 708 (Colo. 1968). *See also D.I. Chadbourne, Inc. v. Superior Court of San Francisco*, 60 Cal. 2d 723, 388 P.2d 700 (Cal. S. Ct. 1964); *Nazareth Literary and Benevolent Institution v. Stephenson*, 503 S.W.2d 177 (Ky. 1973); *Payless Drug Stores, Inc. v. Superior Court of Alameda County*, 54 Cal. App. 3d 988; *Sligar v. Tucker*, 267 So. 2d 54 (Fla. App. 1972).
12. Joint Commission on Accreditation of Hospitals, *supra* note 2, at 134.
13. *Id.*
14. American Nurses' Association, *Standards of Nursing Practice* (1973).
15. Lesnik, J., and Anderson, B.E., *Nursing Practice and the Law* 260 (2d ed., J.B. Lippincott Co., Philadelphia, 1962). *See also* Creighton, Helen, "Patient Teaching," *Nursing Management* 16:12-18 (Jan. 1985).
16. *Kyslinger v. United States*, 406 F. Supp. 800 (W.D. Pa. 1975).
17. *Polischeck v. United States*, 535 F. Supp. 1261 (E.D. Pa. 1982).
18. N.C. Gen. Stat. Sections 131-137 (1965).
19. *Lucy Webb Hayes National Training School v. Geoghegan*, 281 F. Supp. 116 (D.C. 1967).
20. *See* Horty, John F., *Hospital Law* 1 (1978).
21. *Niles v. City of San Rafael School District*, No. 624337 (Cal. Super. Ct., San Francisco County, Feb. 5, 1973).
22. *Bernard v. Gravois*, 20 So. 2d 181 (La. App. 1 Cir. 1944).
23. *Kaiser v. Suburban Transportation System*, 398 P.2d 14, *amended*, 401 P.2d 351 (Wash. S. Ct. 1965).
24. *Gooden v. Tips*, 651 S.W.2d 364 (Ct. App. Tex. 1983).
25. *Crawford v. Earl K. Long Memorial Hospital, et al.*, 431 So. 2d 40 (La. App. 1 Cir. 1983).
26. *Bernard v. Gravois*, *supra* note 22.
27. Fleisher, "Ownership of Hospital Records," 4 *Ill. Continuing Legal Education* 73 (1966).
28. Alaska Stat. Section 18.23.065.
29. Ohio Rev. Code Ann. 3701.74 (1985).

30. Idaho Code Section 39-1392d.
31. Ill. Rev. Stat. ch. 51, para. 71.
32. Ind. Code Ann. Section 34-3-15.5-4.
33. La. Rev. Stat. Ann. Section 41:2014.1.
34. Me. Rev. Stat. Ann. tit. 22, Section 1711.
35. Mass. Gen. Laws Ann. ch. 111, Sections 70, 70E.
36. Minn. Stat. Ann. Section 144.335.
37. Nev. Rev. Stat. Section 629.061.
38. N.J. Stat. Ann. Section 2A:82-42.
39. New York Pub. Health Law Section 17.
40. Okla. Stat. Ann. tit. 76, Sections 19-20.
41. 28 Pa. Code Sections 115.29, 103.22(b)(15).
42. Tenn. Code Ann. Sections 53-1322, 68-11-304.
43. Utah Code Ann. Section 78-25-25.
44. Va. Code Ann. Section 8.01-413.
45. Galanter, "Patient Rights," 37 *Health L. Newsletter* 3 (1974).
46. Cal. Evid. Code Section 1158 (1968, amended 1978).
47. Hawaii Rev. Stat. Section 622-57 (1976).
48. Annotated Code of Maryland Sections 4-302(b)(1) to (d)(2).
49. *Id.*
50. Ohio Rev. Code Ann. Section 3701.74 (1985).
51. Utah Code Ann. 78-25-25.
52. 42 C.F.R. Section 2.
53. Ohio Rev. Code Ann. Section 3701.74 (1985).
54. Tenn. Code Ann. Section 68-11-304.
55. New York Pub. Health Law Section 17.
56. Department of Health, Education, and Welfare, *Report of the Secretary's Commission on Medical Malpractice, Access to Medical Records* 178-80 (Jan. 11, 1973); *McGarry v. J.A. Mercier Co.*, 272 Mich. 501, 262 N.W. 296 (1935).
57. Fleisher, *supra* note 27.
58. Galanter, *supra* note 45; *Pyramid Life Insurance Co. v. Gleason Hospital, Inc.*, 360 P.2d 858 (Kan. 1961).
59. *Emmett v. State of Michigan*, 187 N.E.2d 429 (Mich. 1971), *affirming* 180 N.E.2d 308 (Mich. 1970).
60. *Bush v. Kallen*, 302 A.2d 142 (N.J. Super. App. Div. 1973).
61. 42 U.S.C. Section 1320(c).
62. 42 C.F.R. Sections 460-473.
63. Ariz. Rev. Stat. Ann. Section 36-445; Iowa Code Ann. Section 135 c.25; Mich. Comp. Laws Ann. Secton 333.21513(d); Minn. Stat. Ann. Section 145.61; Neb. Rev. Stat. Section 71-2046; Or. Rev. Stat. Section 441.055(3)(d); R.I. Gen. Laws Section 23-17-24.
64. Joint Commission on Accreditation of Hospitals, *supra* note 2, at 84-88. *See also* Smith, James, *Hospital Liability*, Section 15.02(3), (Law Journal Seminars Press, New York, 1985).
65. Horty, *supra* note 20.
66. *Id.*

67. *Baldwin v. McGrath*, 8 Pa. D. & C.3d 341 (York County 1978).
68. *See also Young v. King*, 344 A.2d 792 (N.J. Super. 1975); *Matchett v. Superior Court*, 115 Cal. Rptr. 317 (Cal. App. 1974).
69. *Weiner v. Memorial Hospital for Cancer and Allied Diseases*, 453 N.Y.2d 142 (Sup. Ct. 1982).

ADDITIONAL REFERENCES

PEER REVIEW STATUTES

1. Ala. Code Sections 34.24-58.
2. Alaska Stat. Section 18.23.010 *et seq.*
3. Ariz. Rev. Stat. Ann. Sections 36-441, 36-445 *et seq.*
4. Ark. Stat. Ann. Sections 71-5101, 82-3201 *et seq.* and 82-359.
5. Cal. Civ. Code Sections 43.7, 43.8; Cal. Evidence Code Section 1157; Cal. Bus. and Prof. Code Section 2124.7.
6. Colo. Rev. Stat. Sections 12-43.5-101 *et seq.*, 13-21-110, and 13-90-107.
7. Conn. Gen. Stat. Ann. Sections 38-19a *et seq.*, and 52-557e.
8. Del. Code Ann. tit. 24, Sections 1768 and 1191.
9. D.C. Law No. 32-501 *et seq.*
10. Fla. Stat. Ann. Section 768.40.
11. Ga. Code Ann. Sections 88-3201 *et seq.*, and 84-7601 *et seq.*
12. Haw. Rev. Stat. Sections 624-25.5 and 663-1.7.
13. Idaho Code Section 39-1392 *et seq.*
14. Ill. Rev. Stat. ch. 51, para. 101 *et seq.*; ch. 111, para. 4406; ch. 111½, para. 4141 *et seq.*
15. Ind. Code Section 34-4-12.6-1 *et seq.*
16. Iowa Code Ann. Sections 135.40 *et seq.*, and 147.135.
17. Kan. Stat. Ann. Sections 65-436, 65-442 and 65-4909.
18. Ky. Rev. Stat. Ann. Section 331.337.
19. La. Rev. Stat. Ann. Sections 37:1733-34 and 44:7.
20. Me. Rev. Stat. Ann. tit. 32, Sections 2596, 2599, 3293 and 3296.
21. Md. Code Ann. Section 14-601 *et seq.*
22. Mass. Gen. Laws Ann. ch. 231, Section 85N.
23. Mich. Comp. Laws Ann. Section 331.531 *et seq.*
24. Minn. Stat. Ann. Section 145.61 *et seq.*
25. Miss. Code Ann. Section 41-63-1 *et seq.*
26. Mo. Rev. Stat. Section 537.035.
27. Mont. Code Ann. Sections 37-2-201 and 50-16-20 *et seq.*
28. Neb. Rev. Stat. Sections 71-2046 *et seq.*, 25-12,121 and 71-147.01.
29. Nev. Rev. Stat. Sections 49.265 and 630.364 *et seq.*
30. N.H. Rev. Stat. Ann. Sections 329:26 *et seq.* and 507:8-c.
31. N.J. Stat. Ann. Section 2A:84A-22.8 *et seq.*
32. N.M. Stat. Ann. Section 41-9-1 *et seq.*
33. N.Y. Educ. Law Section 6527(3)(5).
34. N.C. Gen. Stat. Section 131-168 *et seq.*
35. N.D. Cent. Code Sections 23-01-02.1 and 31-08-01.

36. Ohio Rev. Code Ann. Section 2305.24 *et seq.*
37. Okla. Stat. Ann. tit. 76, Section 16.
38. Or. Rev. Stat. Section 41.675.
39. Pa. Stat. Ann. tit. 40, Section 1301.103; tit. 62, Section 444.2; tit. 63, Section 425.1 *et seq.*
40. R.I. Gen. Laws Section 5-37.1-1 *et seq.*
41. S.C. Code Ann. Section 40-71-10, -20.
42. S.D. Codified Laws Ann. Section 36-4-25.
43. Tenn. Code Ann. Section 62-623.
44. Tex. Rev. Civ. Stat. Ann. art. 4447d (Vernon 1971).
45. Utah Code Ann. Sections 26-25-1 *et seq.* and 58-12-25.
46. Vt. Stat. Ann. tit. 26, Section 1441 *et seq.*
47. Va. Code Ann. Section 8.01-581.13 *et seq.*
48. Wash. Rev. Code Section 4.24.240 *et seq.*
49. W.Va. Code Section 30-3C-1 *et seq.*
50. Wis. Stat. Section 146.37 *et seq.*
51. Wyo. Stat. Sections 35-2-601 *et seq.* and 35-17-101.
52. *See also* 42 U.S.C. Section 1320c-15 *et seq.*

CHAPTER SEVEN

HOW TO DECREASE THE CHANCES
OF BEING SUED

Good "P.R."
Risk Management
Verbal Orders
Telephone Orders
Advising Patients Who Sign out A.M.A.
Confidentiality

GOOD "P.R."

I am frequently asked by nurses and physicians, "If there is one piece of advice you could give us to keep us out of the courtroom, what would it be?" My answer is always the same: "Good P.R." A good personal relationship with patients is one of the best ways to prevent malpractice suits. Patients frequently sue when they are mad.

If a complication or side effect occurs and no one sits down with the patient to discuss this during his or her hospitalization, it is not uncommon for the patient to seek the services of an attorney. On the other hand, patients who have had a good interpersonal relationship with their nurses and physicians are less likely to sue. In the appendix is an article on primary nursing and its effect on liability. Primary nursing tends to reduce the number of lawsuits not only because it decreases the amount of errors, but also because of the better interpersonal relationship between the patient and the nurse.

A good illustration is the time I had a physician turn in a claim because he was concerned that a suit would be filed. The physician had been the patient's family physician for about ten years. He was generally described by his patients as being a conscientious, kind and considerate physician. The patient had undergone gallbladder surgery. He progressed well after surgery and there were no known complications.

Approximately six months later, the physician was doing an I.V.P. for the patient for an independent problem. Upon reviewing the I.V.P. film, the physician noticed a large retained instrument. The physician went directly up to the patient's room and said, "Joe, I have to take you back to surgery tomorrow. I just discovered I left in my best hemostats. You know they cost $50 and I have to get them back."

Neither the hospital nor the physician billed the patient for expenses arising from the removal of the retained instrument. The patient never filed suit and I've always suspected it was due to the good "P.R." between the physician and the patient.

The nurse should always listen to a patient's complaint and make every effort to investigate. In one case, the patient complained of burning on three different occasions shortly after a plaster splint had been applied to her right lower leg. The nurse did not heed the patient's request to remove the splint, and the patient suffered second degree burns to the back of her leg as a result of the overheated plaster. The first time the patient complained, the nurse told her it was "only normal to experience warmth from the plaster." The patient called the nurse back two minutes later and pleaded with her to remove the splint, if not but for a second. The nurse reiterated that she could not do that and stated she was very busy caring for sick patients and didn't wish to be disturbed unless it was important. Several minutes later, the patient started to unwrap the Ace wrap which held the splint in place. The nurse walked by and attempted to hold the patient's hand to prevent her from unwrapping it any further. The patient was so upset about the nurse's treatment that she immediately went out to find an attorney in order to initiate a lawsuit.

This illustrates well that the patient who is treated in a rude and inconsiderate manner is more likely to sue if something goes wrong. Any evidence of disrespectful treatment by the nurse can be very damaging in the eyes of a jury.

RISK MANAGEMENT

It is surprising that many nurses have never heard of risk management. Risk management will become more familiar as the JCAH strives for inclusion of a section on this topic in its 1988 *Accreditation Manual for Hospitals*. On July 25, 1986, the JCAH distributed its proposed standards, along with background material, to approximately 2,000 hospitals for field review.

A multitude of risk-management techniques have been integrated throughout this book. Following policies, appropriate drafting of procedures, making incident reports, and optimal documentation are all measures to reduce the exposure and risk of loss. Good "P.R." and good communication with patients, subordinates and peers are also good risk-management strategies.

Risk management occupies an important place in management because the minimizing of adverse and accident losses by an organization is essential to its survival. Risk management is the process of planning, organizing, leading and controlling the activities of the organization in order to minimize the adverse effects of accidental losses on that organization at reasonable cost.

Risk management can also be defined in terms of making decisions regarding potential accidental losses. Risk management, as a decision-making process, can be described as follows:[1]

(1) identifying exposures to accidental loss which may interfere with an organization's basic objectives;

(2) examining feasible alternative risk-management techniques for dealing with these exposures;

(3) selecting the apparently best risk-management techniques;

(4) implementing the chosen risk-management techniques; and

(5) monitoring the results of the chosen techniques to assure that the risk-management program remains effective.

The duties of the risk manager vary from institution to institution. Most risk managers are responsible for more than purchasing the institution's insurance and preventing fire loss. They are responsible for identifying loss exposures of property, net income, liability and personnel, and for performing appropriate analyses.

The JCAH Board of Commissioners has suggested that formal risk-management standards are necessary to strengthen and assure active and appropriate practitioner involvement in risk-management activities. Clinical expertise should be used to identify major areas of clinical risk, develop criteria for identifying cases with unacceptable risk, design programs to reduce clinical risk, correct clinical risk, and correct clinical problems identified by the risk manager, the board has said. In addition, formal standards would serve to ensure formal administrative linkages and relevant communication between risk management and quality assurance personnel.

Malpractice Prevention: Hospitalwide Approach

Integrating Risk Management and Quality Assurance
A hospital should have an effective malpractice prevention program which identifies potential liabilities, prevents patient injuries, and maximizes the hospital's defense in nonmeritorious malpractice litigation.

1.   The hospital should have adequate orientation, training, and inservice programs for all its professional employees and all other staff who have patient contact.

2.   The hospital should have a meaningful and effective quality assurance program which:

   a.   identifies patient care problems prospectively, concurrently, and retrospectively;

   b.   objectively assesses the patient care problems identified;

   c.   includes mechanisms to effectively resolve identified patient care problems;

   d.   includes mechanisms for ongoing monitoring of patient care activities;

   e.   includes documentation that substantiates the effectiveness of the quality assurance program.

3.   The hospital should ascertain that the medical staff has developed a consistent, appropriate informed consent policy which has been adopted and is used by the physicians on the medical staff.

4.   The hospital staff in cooperation with the medical staff should have a meaningful and effective patient education program.

5.   The hospital should ensure that ancillary departments operate appropriately and communicate with each other to avoid errors which could lead to patient injury.

6.   The hospital should ascertain that the medical staff has a meaningful and effective credentialing and re-credentialing policy.

7.   The nursing and medical staffs should have open, constructive, and purposeful communication to coordinate all levels of patient care.

8.   The hospital should have a sound policy for the maintenance and servicing of all biomedical equipment and ensure that all hospital personnel who use the equipment have been adequately trained and supervised to use it.

9.   The hospital should have sufficiently detailed plans to prevent patient and employee injuries which could result from fire, internal disaster, premise hazards, or safety deficiencies.

10.   The hospital and medical staff should receive current and detailed information about medical and legal issues which affect their practice. The information should include data about past claims experience against comparable hospitals and similar medical and nursing specialists.

11.   The quality of medical record documentation by physicians, nurses, and other health professionals should be reviewed frequently to ensure that patient care has been appropriately recorded. The quality of documentation must be reviewed to ensure that it will assist, rather than impair, the defense of the hospital and physicians in malpractice litigation.

12.   The hospital should have mechanisms for period review of policies and procedures to ensure their clarity and to determine that all personnel are familiar with the policy and with revisions.

13.   The hospital should have an efficient mechanism for responding to patient and family complaints and for addressing and resolving the problems which led to these complaints.

14. If medical residents are permitted to participate in patient care, the hospital should ensure that the medical staff has developed meaningful, defensible guidelines for supervision of the residents. A mechanism should be established and followed for orienting the residents to the facility, for evaluating residents' performance, for disclosure to patients of the residents' status and level of participation in patient care, and for assuring that residents comply with all hospital policies and medical staff bylaws.

15. In developing its marketing strategy, the hospital should look inward as well as outward. The marketing effort which includes improving the hospital's image and its resources in the public's eye should ensure that all staff understand and cooperate in the marketing effort.[2]

VERBAL ORDERS

Recently, verbal and telephone order policies have received much attention. Telephone orders differ from verbal orders and are discussed separately in this book. Verbal orders are those given by the physician to the nurse to record on the physician's behalf. The usual scenario involves the physician giving orders to the nurse as the physician leaves the nurse's station or walks down the hall.

Verbal orders often lead to questions of liability.[3] Nurses are especially alarmed over the problems inherent in receiving verbal orders, and the concern is well justified, because most of them have encountered a problem in this area at one time or another.

Verbal orders, often given for the convenience of the physician, are a risky business. Their use should be and has been forbidden by many hospitals and health care facilities, except in emergency situations. First of all, verbal orders are legal and binding. However, a problem arises if the nurse fails to hear an order correctly, since this increases the potential for patient injury. The inconvenience of having the physician write his/her own orders is insignificant when considering the risks to the patient and the legal hazards. Implementation by the hospital of a policy requiring written orders will assist in keeping all parties out of the courtroom.

It is extremely difficult to defend verbal orders in court. For one thing, a jury may find it hard to understand why the physician did not take the time to write the order. Also, in almost every case where the defendants have disagreed as to what the verbal order was, the plaintiff has won. It is a less-than-optimal situation in the courtroom when the defendants are pointing fingers at each other.

As previously mentioned, verbal orders are not illegal, but they greatly increase the probability of error. Nurses should make every effort to have physicians write their orders.

The JCAH *Accreditation Manual for Hospitals* states that when a verbal order is given, any authorized person may accept it and record it on the physician's order sheet.[4] Medical staff rules and regulations should set forth those personnel who are authorized to do this. Nurses have always been deemed to be the appropriate persons to accept and transcribe verbal orders.

The JCAH manual also states that "the medical staff defines any category of diagnostic and therapeutic verbal orders associated with any potential hazard to the patient."[5] Additionally, all verbal orders must be authenticiated or signed by the physician within twenty-four hours.

A local attorney recently tried to defend a physician in a case where a patient was severely injured as the result of a verbal order which was incorrectly written by the nurse. The physician was sued as well as the nurse and the hospital. The physician saw the patient and then gave the verbal order because "he was in a hurry." The court was unimpressed with this argument and felt that, had the physician written the order, the injury could have been prevented.

"No Code Blue" (NCB) or "Do Not Resuscitate" (DNR) orders should always be put in writing.[6] This policy should be written and contained in the health care facility's policy manual. The American Medical Association has been advocating to physicians since 1974 that all NCB orders be written in the patient's medical records, and the National Conference on Standards has been advocating since as early as 1973 that all NCB orders be written. (This is discussed in more detail in the section on NCB orders.)

TELEPHONE ORDERS

Telephone orders are to be differentiated from verbal orders. Telephone orders are often necessary for the patient's well-being. For example, a patient whose condition has become critical may be in severe need of receiving prompt treatment to survive. Telephone orders in a case like this are certainly warranted and are easily justified. However, misinterpretation of instructions given over the telephone is a common cause of errors. The potential for this can be decreased by the nurse repeating the instructions back to the physician.

It is always best that telephone orders be given directly from the physician to the nurse. Unfortunately, a number of hospitals still allow ward secretaries to take telephone orders, which must then be co-signed by the nurse. This puts the nurse and his/her employer in a difficult legal position because the nurse has no opportunity to verify the correctness of the telephone order.[7] It also increases the risk to the physician. The ward clerk is at risk of making an error in transcribing the orders. If such an error occurs, the physician as well as the hospital may be sued.

Many hospitals now have policies requiring that all telephone orders be taken by the nurse and monitored by another health care staff member. Both staff members should sign the order. The physician should then co-sign the telephone order as soon as possible. Most policies dictate that all telephone orders be signed within twenty-four hours, which is consistent with JCAH and A.H.A. policies. This procedure has significantly decreased the number of patient injuries, as well as the number of lawsuits against hospitals, nurses and physicians.

There are a number of cases that exemplify the hazards of both verbal and telephone orders. In the *Thomas* case, a patient was brought into the emergency room after being involved in an automobile accident.[8] The patient had a frontal scalp abrasion and was unable to move his right leg. The emergency room nurse called the physician on call and advised him of the patient's condition. The patient was admitted to the hospital which was filled with influenza patients, and given some pain medication. He was taken to the floor at 11:45 p.m. and placed in the hall outside the nurses' desk. At 12:05 a.m., the floor nurse took the patient's blood pressure and found it to be 70/50 with a pulse rate of 120 and respirations of 40. He was cool and perspiring. By 1:30 a.m., he was quieter. At 2:00

a.m., the nurse found him in Cheyne-Stokes respirations and with no pulse. Cardiopulmonary resuscitation was not successful.

A conflict arose between the physician and the emergency room nurse regarding telephone orders. The nurse denied telling the physician that he did not need to see the patient. The court found that if the floor nurse had notified the physician of the patient's vital signs at 12:05 a.m., the patient could have been saved.

The *Cortez* case also illustrates the legal risk of telephone orders.[9] Dr. Chi delivered a child on June 5, 1973. On June 18, the child was taken to Dr. Chi's office for a routine follow-up visit. Later the same day, the child was crying a lot, and the mother took him back to the doctor's office and received several prescriptions. The child continued to be ill and had a fever. Finally, after having two prior telephone conversations with Dr. Chi, the mother said she would take the child to the hospital.

The mother went to La Casita Hospital, where the child was born. They refused to admit him. She then took the child to the emergency room at Indio Community Hospital, arriving at about 7:20 a.m. on June 19. Nurse Sakemi recorded a rectal temperature of 104.8 degrees. The nurse called the doctor at 7:45 a.m. to let him know that the patient was in the emergency room and that his temperature was 104.8 degrees. The doctor prescribed some medications, including Dipuron. He said he couldn't come to the hospital because he was in the shower. He told the nurse to send the child to "my office at 9:00 a.m., whether the temperature is down or not."

At 8:30 a.m., the nurse rechecked the baby's temperature and it was 106.4 degrees. The nurse tried unsuccessfully to reach the doctor. The child died at 8:55 a.m.

The director of nursing called Dr. Chi shortly after the death and asked him to come to the hospital to talk to the parents, who were very upset. Though he lived two blocks from the hospital, he refused to come. A pathologist concluded that the child's death was caused by a febrile convulsion.

The trial court entered judgment against Dr. Chi for $150,000. The court said, "Assuming the doctor was irritated for the number, hour, and times of the telephone calls, and assuming he was irritated because Mrs. Cortez decided to take the child to the hospital rather than wait for his office to open at 9:00 a.m., and assuming these were the reasons he refused to come at 7:45 is enough to allow the jury to infer the doctor's conduct is outrageous."

This case, as Regan says, is a strong condemnation of "telephone medicine."[10] This is also the reason why most emergency rooms are now staffed with a physician on duty twenty-four hours a day.

Summary

The nurse should be aware of the legal risks of verbal and telephone orders, and should be familiar with his/her employer's policy in this area. Since it is in the best interest of the physician, the nurse and their employer, the nurse should encourage the physician to write all verbal orders. For example, the emergency room physician asks the nurse to administer lidocaine 50 mg. I.V. and morphine sulfate 2.0 mg. The nurse replies politely, "I'll go draw that up if you'll write the order for me." The physician obliges and now everyone has just decreased their liability exposure.

Telephone orders, when the physician is not present, are certainly more warranted than verbal orders. If time and circumstances allow, the nurse or a second nurse can read back the order. The nurse should always enter the physician's order as soon as possible on the physician's order sheet. He/she should note the date and time the order was received and sign his/her name as follows:

```
2/2/87   16:00   Lasix 40 mg. I.V. stat
                 ABG's stat
                 Portable chest x-ray
                 I.V. D₅W at a K.O. rate
                 Foley catheter to straight drain
                 T/O Dr. Mark Miller/S. Dill
                 Calloway, R.N.
```

Verbal orders are usually abbreviated "V.O." or "V/O," and telephone orders "T.O." or "T/O." The nurse should always document in the nursing notes which physician was notified, the time of notification and information relayed to the physician by the nurse. This will help prevent what happened to the nurse in the previously discussed *Thomas v. Corso* case. The nurse should also chart if orders were received and if they have been carried out. If the physician doesn't order anything, the nurse can chart, "Dr. Miller desires no further orders at this time. Instructed to continue to observe patient's condition." Some nurses also document in the nursing notes that the orders were read back and confirmed by the physician.

THE RIGHT TO REFUSE TREATMENT AND ADVISING PATIENTS WHO SIGN OUT AGAINST MEDICAL ADVICE (A.M.A.)

Patients who want to sign out against medical advice (a.m.a.) can present a dilemma for nurses, physicians and hospitals. Patients who are alert, oriented, competent and under no legal commitment have a right to refuse medical treatment. A competent adult's right to refuse medical treatment emanates from the individual's right to privacy and, in some cases, freedom of religion.[11] The Massachusetts Supreme Judicial Court summed up the patient's right to privacy as follows:

> The constitutional right of privacy, as we conceive it, is an expression of the sanctity of individual free choice and self-determination as fundamental constituents of life. The value of life as so perceived is lessened not by a decision to refuse treatment, but by the failure to allow a competent human being the right of choice.[12]

A growing number of courts have acknowledged the right of a competent adult to refuse treatment, even where the refusal is likely to result in the patient's death.[13] This is especially true when the patient is terminally ill. (A detailed discussion of these cases and the effect of living wills is contained in the book *Nursing Ethics and the Law*.)

111

The patient who wants to sign out against medical advice brings many considerations into play. The nurse is concerned that any attempt to detain a competent patient against his/her will could be considered false imprisonment or assault and battery, and could be actionable.[14] The patient's common-law right of autonomy is embodied in the legal doctrine of informed consent.

The JCAH *Accreditation Manual for Hospitals* reiterates, in the section on patient rights and responsibilities, that the patient may refuse treatment to the extent permitted by law. The Patient's Bill of Rights put out by the American Hospital Association states, "The patient has the right to refuse treatment to the extent permitted by law, *and to be informed of the medical consequences of his action.*" (Emphasis added.) The Pregnant Patient's Bill of Rights, promulgated by the International Childbirth Education Association, has a similar provision. Section 7 states the following:

> The Pregnant Patient has the right to determine for herself, without pressure, whether she will accept the risks inherent in the proposed therapy or refuse a drug or procedure.

In addition, many state legislatures have drafted patients' bills of rights which reiterate that a competent adult has a right to refuse treatment. California, Colorado, Illinois, Maryland, Massachusetts, Michigan, Minnesota, New York, Pennsylvania and Rhode Island are among some of the states that have already passed laws on patients' bills of rights.[15]

The Department of Health and Human Services has incorporated the bill of rights language into nursing home regulations, and the American Hospital Association has been encouraging many institutions to adopt bills of rights. In response to this, many hospitals have drafted their own bills of rights and have disseminated them to their patients and staff. Most of these bills reiterate the patient's right to refuse treatment as long as the patient is informed of the consequences of his/her actions.

So, now that it is established that the competent adult patient has a right to refuse treatment, what does the nurse do first? The nurse should communicate with the patient to determine why the patient wants to leave. Having a good interpersonal relationship with the patient is the best way to minimize a nurse's liability exposure. The nurse, as a patient advocate, should try to resolve the problem. The nurse may be able to address the patient's concerns and provide him with a new perspective on the situation. In one instance, I can recall a female patient who wanted to sign out against medical advice after reading the brochure describing visiting hours from 2 p.m. to 8 p.m. Her husband worked during these hours, and she could not imagine being in the hospital for one week without seeing her husband. The nurse intervened and arranged for special visiting hours for her husband. The patient was appreciative and no longer desired to sign out a.m.a.

Many medical insurance companies will not pay the hospital bill if a patient signs out a.m.a. While the nurse has no way of knowing for sure what each patient's policy of insurance will cover, he/she can mention that many insurers will not pay the hospital bill if the patient signs out a.m.a., and that this would mean that the patient may be personally responsible for the bill.

112

If the resolution of the problem is outside the nurse's scope of responsibility, the nurse should notify the patient's physician or the nursing supervisor. Many health care facilities have policies and position statements concerning patients who want to sign out a.m.a. The nurse should be familiar with his/her employer's policy, which is drafted to decrease the nurse's liability exposure.

In dealing with patients who want to sign out a.m.a., a nurse should use good common sense. Sometimes this means contacting the patient's spouse or family to apprise them of the situation. If the patient still insists on leaving, the nurse should explain his/her employer's early discharge procedure.

The patient should also be given an a.m.a. release form to sign. Most a.m.a. forms contain information which specifically sets out that the patient's leaving is against medical advice. They generally include a statement that the patient is relieving the physicians, nurses and hospital or other employer of all responsibility that may result from the early discharge.

It is important for the a.m.a. release form to state that the patient has been informed of the risks involved. As you will recall, the American Hospital Association Bill of Rights states that the patient has not only the right to refuse treatment, but also the right to be *informed of the medical consequences* of that action. This means that the patient must be informed of the implications and risks if he/she decides to leave. The alternatives available should also be discussed. This, of course, is easier said than done and sometimes presents a dilemma for the nurse.

Approximately three months ago, I was working in the emergency room when a 55-year-old man arrived. He complained of substernal chest pain radiating down his left arm, accompanied by nausea and diaphoresis. I immediately escorted him from the triage desk to a cart. I assisted him in removing his garments, and connected him to the monitor and checked his vital signs. Pursuant to our hospital policy, I ordered an EKG and promptly reported my nursing assessment to the physician. The physician was busy caring for a multiple-trauma victim and indicated that he would see the patient shortly.

I gathered the I.V. equipment in order to start a keep-open I.V. of D_5W. When I entered the patient's room, I saw that he had removed the monitor electrodes and was getting dressed. He indicated that he was leaving. I asked the patient a series of questions to ascertain why he was so insistent on leaving. He simply replied that he was feeling better and had not wanted to come to the hospital at all.

I went out to the waiting room and discussed the situation with his wife. The patient refused to talk to the physician since he was not going to stay. Finally, the patient was told that he had all the symptoms of a heart problem or heart attack and that additional tests would be necessary to confirm this diagnosis. He was informed of the possibility that a cardiac arrhythmia could result in death. The patient and his wife acknowledged these risks and both signed the a.m.a. release form. The doctor and I then signed as witnesses. We also documented this on the emergency room record. The patient was instructed to return to the hospital if he changed his mind.

I wondered that entire evening what might happen to the patient. One thing I felt comfortable with was that, had he died during the night, no liability would have resulted. The next day, the patient's pain became progressively increased, and he returned and was admitted with an acute anterior myocardial infarction.

If the patient refuses to sign the a.m.a. release form, the nurse should document this on the form and in the medical record. The nurse should not forget to document the fact that the medical risks were disclosed to the patient.

Most health care institutions will still provide the patient with written discharge instructions even if he/she signs out a.m.a. Several years ago, a patient came to the emergency room after sustaining a head injury which rendered him momentarily unconscious. The doctor wanted to admit the patient for observation, but the patient adamantly refused. The patient signed the a.m.a. form, which listed all of the risks. The patient was still given an instruction sheet dealing with care of a head injury and care of sutures, and he was still given a referral physician who would remove the sutures. The patient was also advised that he could return if he changed his mind.

If the patient wishing to refuse treatment is a minor, the nurse should immediately notify his/her supervisor, risk manager or the employer's attorney. If the minor's life would be in jeopardy without the treatment, the hospital or health care institution may request a court order.

In summary, the alert, competent adult patient has a right to refuse treatment, but this right is not absolute where the refusal of treatment is likely to result in the patient's death. Each hospital or other institution should have a written policy on a.m.a. releases and the nurse should be familiar with and follow his/her employer's policy. The nurse should attempt to resolve any problems within the scope of nursing practice. The physician should be notified if the resolution is outside of the nurse's scope of responsibility. Each hospital or health care facility should have a written a.m.a. release form. The risks and alternatives should be disclosed to the patient and this disclosure should be documented. Most institutions will provide discharge instructions to patients even if they sign out a.m.a., and invite patients to return if they change their minds.

CONFIDENTIALITY

The patient's right of privacy and confidentiality is protected by law. This right to privacy is reflected in many sources. There are, for example, a number of cases which support the patient's right to privacy. Some states have specific statutes which impose restrictions on the disclosure of information. Basic support for this proposition is even found in the Constitution of the United States.

The nurse, in her unique and critical role as a professional, is very much affected by the doctrine of confidentiality. This role is reinforced by the American Nurses' Association Code for Nurses. Number 2 of the A.N.A. Code states, "The nurse safeguards the client's right to privacy by judiciously protecting information of a confidential nature." (A copy of the Code for Nurses is included in the appendix.) The interpretive statements under this section state that the right to privacy is an inalienable human right.[16] The client trusts the nurse to hold all information in confidence — the client's welfare could be jeopardized and trust destroyed if the nurse nonjudiciously discloses such confidential information. However, the nurse's duty of confidentiality is not absolute if innocent parties could be harmed.

114

The interpretive statements stress that the nurse should consider the rights, well-being and safety of the client in making a judgment concerning the disposition of confidential information. Providing quality nursing care mandates that relevant and important information be shared with other practitioners. This is consistent with nursing standards and codes of responsibility. Information which is not pertinent to a client's treatment should not be disclosed, and disclosure of any information is made only to those directly involved in the patient's care or treatment.

Information for peer review, third-party payment or other quality assurance mechanisms must be disclosed only under defined policies, procedures or protocol. These guidelines should be written to assure that the patient's rights, safety and well-being are maintained and protected.

The third interpretive statement corresponding to Number 2 of the A.N.A. Code addresses the issue of access to records. In situations where the nurse needs access to the records of a person not under his/her care, the person should be notified first for permission to review the necessary records. As mentioned previously in the section discussing access to medical records, the health care facility owns and physically possesses the medical records. However, the patient maintains a right of control and has an interest in the information contained in those records.

If the patient's medical record is needed for research or nonclinical purposes for which anonymity cannot be guaranteed, consent must first be obtained. This is necessary to ensure the patient's right to privacy.

"A Patient's Bill of Rights" was approved in 1972 by the American Hospital Association, and has been adopted by many hospitals as official policy. (A copy is attached in the appendix.) Number 5 of the "Patient's Bill of Rights" states, "The patient has the right to every consideration of his privacy concerning his own medical care program. Case discussion, consultation, examination, and treatment are confidential and should be conducted discreetly. Those not directly involved in his case must have the permission of the patient to be present."

Number 6 states, "The patient has the right to expect that all communications and records pertaining to his care should be treated as confidential." This closely parallels the language contained in the A.N.A. Code for Nurses, Number 2, discussed above, and similar language is also found in the JCAH "Rights and Responsibilities of Patients," a copy of which is attached in the appendix.

Nurses and physicians are at risk for liability for the unauthorized disclosure of patient information under several different legal theories. These three theories have previously been discussed in detail in the intentional torts section.

First, practitioners can be liable under the tort of defamation, which is injury to a person's reputation through oral or written communication. It is possible that if a patient's medical records were published, his/her reputation in the community could be adversely affected. To prove defamation, the patient must demonstrate that the disclosure of information was unauthorized and untrue. For example, the mayor of Columbus was picked up several years ago for driving erratically. He was taken to the hospital, where his blood alcohol level was determined. Someone in the lab leaked to the press that the mayor's blood alcohol level was .30, a level which demonstrated legal intoxication. He was not able to sue for defamation when the results of his blood alcohol level were disclosed because the lab statistics were correct.

The second area under which practitioners can be sued is the invasion of the patient's right to privacy. An invasion of privacy is an unwarranted exploitation of one's personality or publication of one's private affairs. To be actionable, the invasion must be of a nature such that it causes outrage, mental suffering, shame or humiliation to a person of "ordinary sensibilities."

Generally, the release of information to a patient's family members, attorney or insurance company is not a violation of the right of privacy. Most lawsuits arise from the taking of photographs which are published without the patient's permission. Photographs are often important to record a patient's condition, and it is generally advisable to get the patient's written consent prior to taking such photographs.

In one case, a psychiatrist was sued after publishing a book which reported verbatim a patient's thoughts, feelings, emotions and fantasies.[17] The book was not published until eight years after treatment was terminated. The court found the plaintiff was damaged as a result of the publication and had not consented to the publication. The publication of the book violated the patient's right to privacy the court said.

The third area under which practitioners are at risk for liability is that of willful betrayal of professional secrets. Disclosure of a patient's secrets to the detriment of the patient may result in liability. There are very few cases in this area. One of the few involved a nurse who told a patient's landlord the patient had gonorrhea. The patient, who was consequently evicted, sued the nurse for liability.

Courts allow disclosure when the welfare of the patient or the public is at risk. For example, in all fifty states, confidential information obtained concerning a case of suspected child abuse must be reported. Each state also has a list of communicable diseases which must be reported. The federal government can collect medical information regarding employees under the Occupational Safety and Health Act (OSHA).[18] However, this information is limited to that which is relevant and necessary to accomplish a lawful purpose.[19]

In 1976, a court decided the controversial *Tarasoff* case.[20] The court held that a doctor has a legal duty to inform a third party about information learned from his patient if it would protect the third party from threatened harm. In the case at bar, a woman was murdered by a mentally ill patient who had told his psychotherapist that he intended to kill her. The victim's parents sued because the doctor had not warned their daughter. The court found the doctor liable for not disclosing this information.

Sometimes, the plaintiff in a medical malpractice case requests the records of other patients to be used as evidence. In the *Ziegler* case, the plaintiff made a claim against the hospital for the unnecessary implantation of a pacemaker.[21] Her claim against the hospital was for breach of its duty to supervise and control the administration of medical services within its facility. She claimed the hospital was aware or should have been aware that its doctors were committing acts of malpractice. The plaintiff wanted the charts of twenty-four other patients in order to show other cases where pacemakers were unnecessarily implanted.

The hospital and doctors were concerned about unwarranted disclosure. They felt the former patients were entitled to be left to their privacy, secure in the belief that their confidences, treatment and records were protected from disclosure.

The court noted that other courts have held that confidentiality can be protected by concealing the identity of the patients.[22] The court ordered the following in order to provide the necessary safeguards to balance the concerns of both parties:

1.   That all references on any chart to the name, address, marital status and occupation or employment of the patient which have not yet been removed shall be removed from the file. Any additional information that would tend to identify the patient shall be removed from the file except for age, sex and race (i.e., place of employment, spouse's name, number of children, ages of children, etc.).

2.   That upon review by plaintiff's counsel the records will be filed with the court and sealed by the court, not to be opened except upon order of the court.

3.   That no attempt will be made by any of the attorneys or parties to learn the identity of the patients, or to in any way attempt to contact these patients.

4.   That any information gained as a result of this review will not be communicated to any person not a party to this action, except as may occur during the trial of this case, or except in consultation with experts employed by the plaintiff to review and analyze the information.

There are several federal statutes that protect the confidentiality of patient records when treatment is received for drug and alcohol problems. For example, 42 C.F.R., Part 2, requires that a special medical records authorization form be signed. This special release form should contain the following information:

1)   patient's name, address, date of birth;
2)   the person or organization to whom disclosure is to be made;
3)   the purpose of the disclosure;
4)   the extent of information to be disclosed; and
5)   a statement that the consent is subject to revocation upon notice.

REFERENCES

1. Head, George and Horn, Stephen, 1 *Essentials of the Risk Management Process* 6 (Insurance Institute of America, 1985).
2. Vergamini, Stephen J., Materials prepared for lecture titled "Medical Malpractice Perspectives and Prevention, a Conference on Risk Management Issues," presented at Doctors Hospital, Columbus, Ohio, November 1, 1986.
3. *See also* Creighton, Helen, *Law Every Nurse Should Know*, 5th ed. (Philadelphia, W.B. Saunders Company, 1986).
4. Joint Commission on Accreditation of Hospitals, "Medical Record Services," *Accreditation Manual for Hospitals*, Section 9.2.2.6.2 (1986).
5. *Id.* at 9.2.2.6.3.
6. Hirsch, Harold, "Oral Orders," 11 *Legal Aspects of Medical Practice*, No. 6 (June 1983).
7. *See* Creighton, *supra* note 3.
8. *Thomas v. Corso*, 288 A.2d 399 (Md. 1972).
9. *Cortez v. Chi*, 167 Cal. Rptr. 905 (Cal. Ct. App. 1980). *See also Childs v. Greenville Hospital Authority*, 479 S.W.2d 399 (Tex. 1972).
10. Regan, Williams, "Telephone Orders: Legal Risks," 21 *Regan Report on Nursing Law*, No. 12, at 1 (Dec. 1980).
11. *See In re Osborne*, 294 A.2d 372 (D.C. 1972); *In re Estate of Brooks*, 32 Ill. 2d 361 (1965); *In re Melideo*, 88 Misc. 2d 974, 390 N.Y.S.2d 523 (1976).
12. *Superintendent of Belchertown State School v. Saikewicz*, 373 Mass. 728, 742 (1977). *See also* Swartz, Martha, "The Patient Who Refuses Medical Treatment," 11 *American Journal of Law and Medicine*, No. 2 (1985).
13. *Bartling v. Superior Court*, 163 Cal. App. 3d 186, 209 Cal. Rptr. 220 (1984).
14. *Rice v. Mercy Hospital Corp.*, 275 So. 2d 566 (Fla. Dist. Ct. App. 1973); *Long Island Home v. Rotondi*, 324 N.Y.S.2d 834 (N.Y. App. Div. 1971).
15. Cal. Admin. Code tit. 22, Section 70707 (1977); Colo. Rev. Stat. Section 25-1-121 (1976); Ill. Rev. Stat. ch. 111, Section 5401 *et seq.* (1979); Md. Ann. Code Section 565F (1978); Mass. Gen. Laws Ann. ch. 111, Section 70E (1979); Mich. Comp. Laws Ann. Section 333.20201 (1978); Minn. Stat. Ann. Section 144.651-652 (1973, am. 1976); N.Y. Comp. Codes R. & Regs. tit. 10, Section 405.25 (1977); 28 Pa. Admin. Code Section 102.21-24 (1978); R.I. Gen. Laws Section 23.16-19.1 (1978).
16. American Nurses' Association, *Code for Nurses with Interpretive Statements* 4, (1985).
17. *Doe v. Roe and Poe*, 400 N.Y.S.2d 668 (1978).
18. 29 U.S.C. Section 657 (1976).
19. 5 U.S.C. Section 552 d(e)(l) (1976). *Cf.* 5 U.S.C. Section 552 (j), (k).
20. *Tarasoff v. Regents of University of California*, 131 Cal. Rptr. 14; 551 P.2d 334 (1976).
21. *Ziegler v. Superior Court of the State of Arizona*, 134 Ariz. 390, 656 P.2d 1251 (1982).
22. *District Court in and for the County of Boulder*, 194 Colo. 98, 570 P.2d 243 (1977); *Rudnick v. Superior Court of Kern County*, 11 Cal. 3d 924, 114

Cal. Rptr. 603, 523 P.2d 643 (1974); *Hyman v. Jewish Chronic Disease Hospital*, 15 N.Y.2d 317, 258 N.Y.S.2d 397, 206 N.E.2d 338 (1965); *Osterman v. Ehrenworth*, 106 N.J. Super. 515, 256 A.2d 123 (1969); *Williams v. Buffalo General Hospital*, 28 A.D.2d 777, 280 N.Y.S.2d 699 (1967). *But see contra, Parkson v. Central Dupage Hospital*, 435 N.E.2d 140 (Ill. App. 1982) and *Lewin v. Jackson*, 108 Ariz. 21, 492 P.2d 406 (1972).

CHAPTER EIGHT

RECENT NURSING LIABILITY CONCERNS

Improper Orders — Duty to Defer
Restraints
Abandonment
"No Code Blue" Orders and Withholding Treatment
Consent

IMPROPER ORDERS — DUTY TO DEFER

Traditionally, the law has not held the nurse liable if the patient sustains injury as a result of an act by a nurse that was in conformance with a physician's order.[1] However, exceptions to this rule have recently been advocated. It is clear that the nurse has a duty to follow the physician's order,[2] and if he/she negligently fails to follow such appropriate order, liability can result.[3]

The nurse has a duty to follow the physician's orders unless the orders are so obviously improper that the ordinary prudent nurse would not obey them.[4] As previously discussed, a verbal order is a legal order and the nurse must follow it unless he/she is concerned that the order may be in error. Just following orders, whether oral or written, is *not enough* if the nurse knows or should have known the orders to be a mistake. If the nurse knows that the doctor's orders are clearly contradicted by normal practice, then ordinary prudence requires inquiry into their correction. The nurse and hospital will not be liable for negligence in following physicians' orders as long as the staff has no reason to suspect the orders are contrary to normal practice.[5]

There have recently been a number of cases that exemplify that the nurse has a legal duty to defer orders when he/she feels they are inappropriate. For example, in the *Czubinsky* case, a 28-year-old woman had been operated on for an ovarian cyst.[6] She was still in the operating room and just beginning to come out of her anesthetic. The surgeon had left the room to prepare for another case. He called for the circulating nurse to accompany him. The circulating nurse told him that she could not leave because she had not completed her postoperative monitoring of the patient.

The physician persisted and the circulating nurse left the room. While she was out of the room, the patient had a cardiac arrest. The anesthesiologist sent the operating room technician to obtain help. He immediately started CPR (cardiopulmonary resuscitation). The anesthesiologist could not optimally resuscitate the patient alone, and the patient was left completely paralyzed and semicomatose.

The hospital had a policy which required that the circulating nurse be on hand to assist the anesthesiologist during the entire postoperative procedure. The plaintiff argued that not only did the nurse abandon the patient, but she also violated hospital policy. It was no defense for the nurse that she was just "following orders." The jury awarded the plaintiff $982,000.

In another case, the court held that the nurse's following of orders was not enough, especially in light of an applicable hospital policy.[7] Mr. Utter was admitted through the emergency room after he suffered injuries from a fall. He had a comminuted fracture of the right wrist, a posterior dislocation of the right elbow, and a compression fracture of the second lumbar vertebra.

Mr. Utter's personal physician, Dr. Mills, applied a right long arm cast. On the third day, the arm became progressively edematous and discolored. A foul-smelling discharge was noted, and the patient was running a fever. The nurse realized that the patient was seriously ill and called Dr. Mills. Dr. Mills made no further orders.

The patient's condition worsened, and the next day he was evaluated by a physician who specialized in infectious disease. In order to save the patient's life, he was flown to another hospital where a hyperbaric oxygen tank was available. The patient survived but required an above-the-elbow amputation.

The hospital had the following policy:

> If a registered nurse has any reason to doubt or question the care provided to any patient or feels that appropriate consultation is needed and has not been obtained, she shall direct such question of doubt to the attending practitioner. If, after this, she still feels that the question has not been resolved, she shall call this to the attention of the Department Chairperson.

The court found the nurse liable to comply with the procedure contained in the nursing manual. A nurse is charged with the duty to observe the condition of his/her patient, and with the obligation to take some positive action when the patient shows signs of condition change.

This case is illustrative of several legal principles: Violation of an institution's policy can result in liability; following orders is no longer enough, especially when the situation involves life-threatening decisions; each nurse is accountable for his/her own actions; and each nurse must adhere to the standards of good nursing practice.

Suburban Hospital v. Hadary is another case illustrating that the nurse can be held liable for following orders which he/she knows or should have known were improper.[8] This case involved a patient who was admitted for a liver biopsy. The physician scheduled the patient for a biopsy which would require the insertion of a special needle into the liver.

The needles were kept in the cabinet of the minor surgery room. The two upper shelves were used for nonsterile needles and the bottom two for sterile needles. The shelves were not marked in any way. When the physician came down to do the liver biopsy, the nurse was busy in the next room assisting another physician. The physician asked for a needle. The nurse replied that she would get it for him in just a minute. The physician replied that he would get it himself. The nurse repeated that she would get the needle, but the doctor left the room.

He took one of the nonsterile needles off the shelf and performed the biopsy. This nonsterile needle had been used on a patient with liver disease. Because the patient who underwent the liver biopsy was exposed to infectious hepatitis, she had to undergo a number of globulin injections.

Both the physician and the nurse were held liable. The nurse admitted that it was standard practice for the nurse to obtain the needle for the physician.

There are numerous other cases that make it clear that the nurse has a legal duty to defer orders when it is reasonably certain that the orders will result in harm to the patient.[9] The more life-threatening the situation, the more concerned the nurse must be.

What should the nurse do when faced with an order that concerns him/her? First, the nurse should try to discuss it with the physician who has given the order. The nurse should explain specifically when he/she is concerned with the order and not just merely repeat the order. If the order violates a hospital policy or procedure, the physician must be informed. If the nurse is unable to receive an adequate explanation and attempts to change the physician's mind are unsuccessful, the nurse should call his/her supervisor. The nurse should also be aware of and follow the institution's policy for clarifying ambiguous or inappropriate orders, if one exists. The nurse should objectively document his/her actions.

RESTRAINTS

It has already been discussed that patient falls are a common cause of liability among nurses. The question of when to use restraints continues to challenge the nurse's best judgment. Decisions to restrain patients must be made on a case-by-case basis.

Sometimes it is necessary to restrain a patient's movement. This is legally justified when it is done to protect the safety of the patient, nurse, hospital, staff and other patients. Sometimes, when the need for restraints manifests itself, there is not time to contact the physician. Modern courts frequently recognize an independent duty on the nurse's part to evaluate the patient professionally. This encompasses a duty to properly assess the patient's condition and take appropriate precautions. If a patient's injury should have been foreseeable by the nurse, liability may result.

Lawful detention in order to protect the patient, staff or society has been found in cases involving psychiatric patients or prisoners. If a prisoner attempts to leave, the nurse should immediately notify the police or the custodial institution. They are responsible for sending personnel to guard the patient or otherwise make the necessary arrangements for that patient's continued care.

Lawful detention has also been found in cases involving patients with communicable diseases. The nurse should notify his/her supervisor immediately if he/she feels that such a patient might want to leave. The nursing supervisor or administrator can then decide if notification of the health department is in order. Some health care institutions elect to detain the patient until health department authorities arrive or a court order is obtained.

The decision regarding the necessity of restraints is not an easy one. Many states have made it easier by passing statutes which outline the appropriate situations for using restraints. Also, many state nursing associations have promulgated written policies and procedures outlining the use of restraints. The Ohio Nurses' Association has recently released such a policy. Additionally, many hospital and health care institutions have internal policies on the use of restraints. This type of policy is advised and should reflect each state's law and specifically answer such questions as the following:

1. When can and should a restraint be applied?
2. How long can the restraint be used?
3. How often should restraints be checked?
4. Is a physician's order always necessary, absent an emergency situation?
5. Who may apply the restraints?
6. Is there any difference in the law between using sheet restraints, soft hand restraints, Posey vests or leather restraints?

The nurse has a duty to follow the physician's order regarding the use of restraints. The nurse should be very careful about removing restraints that have

125

been ordered by the physician, unless they have been ordered p.r.n. Many states in the past five years have passed specific laws about the use of restraints in nursing homes. Some restrict the ordering of p.r.n. restraints in the nursing home facility. This is especially true for the disoriented, confused and mentally ill patient. In the *Cramer* case, the nurse removed the limb restraints and Posey vest after they had been ordered by the physician.[10] The nurse left the patient unattended in his room. The patient got up and fell, fracturing his hip. Patient falls are a recurrent cause of liability among nurses.

Many nurses think that after the application of restraints, they do not have to observe the patient as closely. However, many patients have strangled themselves in Posey vests. Patients with limb restraints should be checked to ensure that the restraints are not too tight and are not interfering with circulation. Almost every nurse has encountered at least one "Houdini patient." The Houdini patients somehow manage to free themselves of their Posey vests and limb restraints. This is more frequently seen by night nurses during a full moon.

Therefore, once restraints are applied, the patient should be closely monitored. Documentation on the flow sheet or nurses' notes should be done. This should include information regarding the type of restraints, where they are used and a description of the patient's behavior that warrants the use of restraints. Documenting the times the restraints are used is also advisable. Many authors advocate that leather restraints should at least be examined at fifteen- to thirty-minute intervals, and soft restraints at two-hour intervals.

The nurse should also be aware of his/her hospital's or health care institution's policy on the use of restraints. Violations of his/her own institution's policy are indicia of negligence. This is illustrated well by the *Washington Hospital Center* case.[11] In this case, a 93-year-old patient was recovering from a fractured right hip. Several days after surgery, she fell out of bed, fracturing her hip. The physician had prescribed restraints for the patient, but there was no evidence presented to show that the patient was in restraints. Also, the hospital had a policy dictating that patients should be checked every hour while in restraints, and there was evidence that the patient had been left unattended for a longer period of time. The jury found for the patient and the court of appeals affirmed the judgment.

In summary, the nurse should not hesitate to apply restraints temporarily in emergency situations. Generally, restraints that are used over an extended period of time are ordered by a physician. The nurse should not forget to closely observe the patient when restrained, and should be aware of his/her institution's policy, which should be drafted to reflect each state's law.

ABANDONMENT

Abandonment is the unilateral termination of a professional relationship without the patient's consent and without making arrangements for appropriate follow-up care. This means the nurse can be liable for an incident that takes place in his/her absence.

The nurse has a legal duty to continually monitor and care for his/her patients while on duty. The nurse transfers the care of the patients to the oncoming nurse at the end of the shift, and cannot abandon the patients if the replacement nurse is late or does not show up. The nurse must continue to provide care until coverage can be arranged. Most hospitals have written policies covering such situations. If the replacement nurse does not report for duty, most policies dictate that someone in nursing administration be notified.

The hospital is under a legal duty to provide adequate patient care coverage during shift changes, break time and code situations. For example, in the *Laidlaw* case, which has been discussed previously, the supervisor permitted one nurse to leave the recovery room for a coffee break just before three patients were admitted.[12] One of the patients suffered a respiratory obstruction that was not observed in a timely fashion. The patient was alleged to be abandoned by the nurse.

The plaintiff in the *Czubinsky* case also alleged abandonment by a nurse.[13] The patient was just coming out of anesthesia after having an ovarian cyst removed. The nurse was doing the postoperative monitoring when she was called away by the surgeon who was in the adjoining room. The patient, left in the presence of an anesthesiologist, had a cardiac arrest and suffered brain damage. The jury returned a verdict in favor of the plaintiff for $982,000. This case was discussed previously under the section on improper orders.

The claim of abandonment is most frequently raised in the following situations:

1. Failure to adequately supervise patients, especially the confused, disoriented, young or elderly patient.
2. Leaving patients unattended for an unreasonable amount of time. Leaving the hospital or health institution before the replacement shows up can also raise an allegation of abandonment.
3. Inadequate observation of the patient or inadequate follow-up care. The *Czubinsky* case is a typical scenario. Patients have also claimed abandonment after sustaining severe infiltrations of I.V. solutions.
4. Failure to provide adequate patient care coverage during change of shift, break time and code resuscitation efforts.
5. Failure to take adequate precautions when a unit is understaffed. The nurse should call this situation to the attention of the nursing supervisor.

"NO CODE BLUE" ORDERS AND WITHHOLDING TREATMENT

Recent medical and scientific technology has enabled the practitioner to extend a patient's life beyond the natural course of a terminal illness. Death can often be postponed by an I.V. insertion, hyperalimentation, gastrotomy tube insertion, a pacemaker, endotracheal tube insertion, or a respirator. Circulation can sometimes be maintained in a patient without a heartbeat by external cardiac massage. Many patients who go into ventricular fibrillation are successfully resuscitated after being defibrillated.

Cardiac arrest occurs at some point in the dying process of every person, whatever the underlying cause of death. Hence, the decision is whether or not to attempt resuscitation. The President's Commission reported that resuscitation grants only a small number of patients both survival and recovery.[14] One author collected all the cases in the literature and found 39 percent were *initially* successful but only 17 percent were able to be discharged home.[15] Two other authors found only a 3 percent success rate in a general hospital where virtually all deaths were attended by resuscitation efforts.[16]

One prospective study found a 4.9 percent long-term survival rate following resuscitative efforts after cardiac arrest.[17] Another study led to the discovery that one in every twenty patients who survived resuscitation had severe brain damage and one in four had some serious and permanent injury.[18] In 1983, Bedell published an article in the *New England Journal of Medicine* (309:501-8), which was entitled "Survival after Cardiopulmonary Resuscitation in the Hospital." Bedell found 44 percent survived the initial resuscitation efforts, 33 percent survived for twenty-four hours, 14 percent were discharged from the hospital, and 11 percent were alive six months later. Where cardiopulmonary resuscitation lasted more than fifteen minutes, only 5 percent survived.

Recently, there has been a concern that cardiopulmonary resuscitation is being used too frequently and that patients are harmed more than they are helped.[19-23] The President's Commission found that although resuscitation grants a small number of patients both survival and recovery, attempts at it usually fail; even when a heartbeat is re-established, such attempts can cause substantial morbidity.[24]

The Commission indicated that the prevalence of written "No Code" policies nationwide is not known. During hearings and in review of the letters received, the Commission's experience was that many hospitals are drafting "No Code" policies.

Policies on "No Code" orders started being published in 1976.[25-28] "The policies followed the recognition by professional organizations that non-resuscitation was appropriate when the patient's well-being would not be served by an attempt to reverse cardiac arrest."[29] An example is the 1974 version of the "Standards for Cardiopulmonary Resuscitation (CPR) and Emergency Cardiac Care (ECC)" of the American Heart Association and the National Academy of Science. These standards state, "Cardiopulmonary resuscitation is not indicated in certain situations, such as in cases of terminal irreversible illness, where death is not unexpected.[30]

In one recent article, Younger found a willingness among physicians in a large university hospital to write "No Code Blue" (NCB) orders for patients residing in the medical intensive care unit.[31] In fact, 14 percent of the patients had received NCB orders. It was reassured that the patients were given optimal care. In fact, the issues of overtreatment and appropriate allocation of limited medical resources were raised.

Robert Veatch wrote an accompanying editorial to Younger's article which raised ethical concerns on how the decision to write an NCB order was reached.[32] The author noted that although NCB orders are administratively encouraged, and even mandated by most hospitals, it was unclear whether competent patients were indeed given the opportunity to participate in the NCB decision. Bedell wrote an article which confirmed Veatch's concerns.[33] He found that only 10 percent of the physicians had discussed this issue with their patients. It was also interesting to note that one-third of the patients who were successfully resuscitated later stated they had not wanted resuscitation and would prefer not to be resuscitated in the future.

In a commentary which appeared in the January 10, 1986, issue of the *Journal of the American Medical Association*, the author advocated that all patients should have the opportunity to express their desire for resuscitation on routine admission to the hospital.[34] The living will could be used to support such a decision for terminal patients in the states that have implemented a living will statute. The President's Commission recommended that competent patients' wishes not to be resuscitated be honored.[35]

In the January 17, 1986, edition of the *Journal of the American Medical Association*, researchers studied 7,265 intensive care unit (ICU) admissions at thirteen hospitals.[36] All of the hospitals used NCB orders. This study found that 39 percent of all in-unit deaths were preceded by an NCB order. Most of the patients were elderly and had multiple organ failure. The researchers advocate that NCB orders are an *accepted practice* in ICUs and their use follows basic ethical and scientific guidelines.

Sample "No Code Blue" Policies

Several medical associations have drafted guidelines to help establish a standard of care for "No Code Blue" orders. The Interprofessional Committee of the Bar Association of San Francisco Medical Society drafted such a policy. The No Code Subcommittee first did a study and discovered that all of the hospitals in San Francisco County had a written "No Code Blue" policy with the exception of the Veterans Administration and the U.S. Army Hospital. The committee found considerable diversity in these policies.

The Medical Society of the State of New York approved its "No Code Blue" policy on September 20, 1982. All New York hospitals were encouraged to develop policies consistent with their respective bylaws and rules and regulations.

It is important to note that the physician has the responsibility for writing these orders. *All* "No Code Blue" orders should be written! All three of the "No Code" policies which were drafted by the above-mentioned medical associations concur in this opinion. The San Francisco Medical Society's statement contains the following commentary:

> All general acute care institutions in San Francisco now require the physician to enter the DNR Order in the record. This practice, formerly avoided on the basis of fear of liability, is now universally recommended. The order and its reasons, together with comments about discussion with patients, colleagues and family, is, in fact, the best defense against liability. In addition, the order allows all who are responsible for the care of the patient to act with unanimity in this situation and avoids confusion and uncertainty. It is reasonable also to require some regular review of the order, should conditions change unexpectedly. The extent of regular review should be determined by the institution in a prudent and reasonable way.

The New York State Medical Society requires that once the DNR decision has been made, the directive shall be written as a formal order by the attending physician. The policy further states, "A verbal or telephone order for DNR cannot be justified as a sound medical or legal practice."

The Minnesota Medical Association's policy also requires that the directive be written as a formal order once the DNR decision has been made. The attending physician is charged with the duty of writing the "No Code" order.

"No Code Blue" Orders

As early as 1973, physicians have been advised to write all "No Code" orders. In 1973, the National Conference on Standards for Cardiopulmonary Resuscitation suggested that all NCB orders be written. The Conference recognized the necessity of establishing a procedure by which physicians could indicate that additional medical treatment was not advantageous to the patient.

In 1974, the American Medical Association proposed that all NCB orders be written in the medical record by the physician. The fact that nurses continuously and currently question whether the NCB order should be written is an indication that the recommendation is not being followed. This problem has resulted from the fact that nurses have failed to assert their authority by accepting verbal NCB orders. Accepting verbal orders on anything other than an emergency basis is risky business for the nurse.

"No Code Blue" (NCB) or "Orders Not to Resuscitate" (ONTR) are legal and valid orders when written by the physician. This is true as long as the order is justified, medically indicated, and meets certain criteria. It is important for the nurse to be familiar with the institution's policy and make sure that policy is being followed. Any deviation from the policy should be reported to the nursing supervisor or administrator.

If no written order exists, and the nurse does not code the patient, he/she is, in effect, making a medical decision. This amounts to practicing medicine without a license.

For the protection of the physician, consultation regarding the writing of an NCB should be discussed with alert and oriented patients and their families. The courts have repeatedly reviewed this area and have sustained that mentally competent patients have a right to decide what is to be done with their own bodies. Generally, a patient has the right to refuse medical treatment even if it would result in death. The physician's decision to allow death to occur without consulting the patient or family poses a dilemma both legally and medically.[37-40]

Witholding Life Support and Treatment Cases

The writing of "No Code" policies has received little attention in court.[41] There are only a few cases in this area which provide direction for the nurse. The *Dinnerstein* case was the first to discuss the issuance of an NCB order.[42] Before explaining the *Dinnerstein* case, a discussion of several other cases is in order. The major cases of importance will be discussed. It is important for the nurse to pay attention to the cases in his/her state, if there are any. Many states have yet to decide any cases in this area. Many times, other states will just adopt the holding of one of the below cases.

New Jersey Approach

In 1976, the New Jersey court decided the *Quinlan* case.[43] Karen was the

130

21-year-old female who lapsed into a permanent coma after ingestion of an overdose of drugs and alcohol. Karen was placed on a respirator upon admission to the hospital. Her parents requested that the respirator be discontinued once it became apparent that she was in a "vegetative state" and would never return to a "cognizant and sapient state."

The physician refused to disconnect the respirator, so the parents went to court to have Karen declared incompetent. The father was then appointed guardian and permission was granted to authorize withdrawal of the respirator.

The court found that there is no requirement to prolong the life of an *irreversibly* ill person. The court recognized that Karen had a constitutional right to privacy. Her right to privacy could be exercised by her father on the theory of "substituted judgment." Under this theory, one can act on the same motives or considerations as would have moved the ill person. The court presumed Karen would have wanted the respirator disconnected.

Massachusetts Approach

In 1977, a year later, the Massachusetts court decided the *Saikewicz* case.[44] Joseph Saikewicz was a profoundly retarded 67-year-old patient who resided in a state mental health facility. He was suffering from acute myeloblastic monocytic leukemia.

At issue was whether to order chemotherapy, even though he would eventually die from the leukemia. The reason it was considered was because there was a 30 to 50 percent chance of a two- to thirteen-month remission with the chemotherapy. However, the chemotherapy was not without its side effects.

The Massachusetts Supreme Judicial Court held that the constitutional right to privacy would allow Saikewicz to refuse treatment if he desired. However, since he was incompetent, the court held that an incompetent patient's wishes could only be determined by the probate court. The court ruled that by using the subjective test, the patient would have chosen to forego chemotherapy.

Many saw the requirement of prior court approval as an unwarranted judicial intrusion. It is very costly and time-consuming to petition the court. If the person is incompetent, then he/she must wait for appointment of a guardian *ad litem*. The guardian is to present all reasonable arguments in favor of administering life-prolonging treatment. After this, the court could make its decision.

Within a year, the Massachusetts court was presented with the opportunity to answer the physicians' and nurses' complaints and concerns about the *Saikewicz* case. In 1978, the Massachusetts Appellate Court decided the *Dinnerstein* case.[45] The health care community hoped that this case would help to clarify and perhaps modify the *Saikewicz* decision.

Shirley Dinnerstein was a 67-year-old nursing home resident who was suffering from Alzheimer's disease. Alzheimer's is a type of senile dementia that results in the progressive destruction of brain tissue. There is no known cure. The disease leads to loss of all intellectual and motor functions and death is inevitable.

Her condition progressed to the point where she was immobile and speechless. She was catheterized and fed by a nasogastric tube. She was essentially in a vegetative state. The family, including her son who was a physician, wanted to make her a "No Code." However, in light of the *Saikewicz* case, all were unsure of the legal status of a "No Code" order. Both the physician and the family sought an action for declaratory relief.

The court held that an order not to resuscitate a "patient in an unremitting, incurable terminal illness" was appropriate and "peculiarly within the competence of the medical profession . . . in light of the patient's history, condition, and family wishes."

At first glance, the *Dinnerstein* case may appear at odds with *Saikewicz*. However, the two cases can be reconciled by looking at the factual differences. First of all, Shirley Dinnerstein was suffering from an incurable and terminal illness. Her care was only custodial and there was no chance of a remission as in *Saikewicz*. In the *Dinnerstein* case, there were close family members who concurred. In *Saikewicz*, there were no family members, he resided in a state facility, and finally, the proposed resuscitative efforts would have been painful and intrusive.

Saikewicz is interpreted as requiring judicial approval for withholding treatment from an incompetent individual when there is at least some reasonable expectation of effecting a permanent or temporary cure of relief from the illness or condition. If the person is suffering from an incurable or terminal illness, where death is imminent, then it is believed that prior court approval is not needed. *Dinnerstein* was not a "right to treatment" case because there was no treatment available. The Massachusetts court took the opportunity to emphasize the validity of this distinction when it decided the *In re Spring* case two years later.[46]

Earle Spring was senile, 77 years old, and suffering from end-stage kidney disease. The kidney disease was permanent and irreversible. Despite his resistance, he was receiving hemodialysis treatment to filter his blood to keep him alive. He would often kick the nurse and pull out his I.V.s. He resisted being transported to treatments.

His wife and son requested that treatment be stopped, but his physicians were opposed. The wife, son and physician sought a judgment decree regarding the termination of treatment.

The court felt that the first step was to decide whether there was a "right to treatment." Is the patient presently and irrevocably in the process of dying? If the patient is *not* presently dying, no matter how certain his death is, it is a "right-to-treatment" case. The courts, using substituted judgment, must decide what the patient's rights are whenever there is a right to treatment. Using the test of substitute judgment, the court concluded that Spring wanted his treatment discontinued.

The court went on to list criteria that the medical profession should consider when deciding if prior probate court approval must be obtained. The factors that the court considered to be important included the degree of impairment, the complexity and risk involved in the proposed medical treatment, the patient's level of understanding, how quickly the treatment decision must be made, the family's wishes, and whether the treatment or the withholding of treatment is good medical practice.[47]

The court stated that the medical profession's second-guessing as to whether the patient's condition was treatable or not would not be actionable unless it was "grievously unreasonable" or in bad faith.

132

The persuasiveness that the Massachusetts cases would have on other states was questioned. In 1981, New York vacated an appellate court decision that endorsed the Massachusetts decisions: *In re Storar* and its companion case, *In re Eichner*.[48]

In re Storar was the case involving the 52-year-old, profoundly retarded, institutionalized patient who was terminally ill with bladder cancer. The mother and legal guardian refused to consent to blood transfusions for the patient. The trial court ruled that New York would not recognize a family member's power to refuse treatment on a patient's behalf.

The Court of Appeals said it was unrealistic to attempt to determine whether the patient would want to continue treatment if he were competent. The New York court rejected the Massachusetts approach of "substitute judgment." Rather, the court held that because a parent could not deprive a child of lifesaving treatment, the blood transfusions had to be continued.

The court then took the opportunity to discuss the issue of when court approval should be obtained. The court stated,

> We emphasize, however, that any such procedure is optional. Neither the common law nor existing statutes require persons generally to seek prior court assessment of conduct which may subject them to civil and criminal liability. If it is desirable to enlarge the role of the courts in cases involving discontinuance of life sustaining treatment for incompetents by establishing . . . a mandatory procedure of successive approvals by physicians, hospital personnel, relatives and the courts, the change should come from the Legislature.[49]

The *Storar* court established a high standard when it required that there must be clear and convincing evidence to determine a patient's own wishes if treatment is to be terminated. To ensure that one's right to decline treatment is honored and to prevent problems, a living will can be completed in the states that have living will laws.

Other States

Florida

In states that have living wills or where the patient is still competent, the problems have been minimized. For example, the Florida Supreme Court recognized a competent patient's right to refuse treatment when suffering from a terminal condition.[50] The court authorized the removal of a respirator even if it resulted in death. The Georgia court discussed a similar case and came to the same holding.[51]

Connecticut

In Connecticut, in the *Foody* case, the court authorized removal of the respirator from a multiple sclerosis patient who had become comatose.[52] The court ruled that the parents could authorize the removal of the respirator even though the daughter had not previously discussed her wishes. The discontinuance of treatment was deemed appropriate when:

1. the incompetent person's condition is permanent and irreversible with no reasonable probability that the person will ever return to a cognitive state;

2. the patient's attending physician and at least two others unanimously agree on the patient's condition; and

3. there are concerned family members who, in good faith, wish to exercise through substitute decision making the patient's right to discontinue treatment.

Minnesota

In the *Hoyt* case, June Hoyt, a friend of 41-year-old Sharon Siebert, sought court review of Siebert's "No Code" order.[53] Siebert suffered brain damage and was unable to care for herself. In fact, she required total care, including a nasogastric tube. Her father consented to the "No Code" order but thought that it meant his daughter would not be put on a ventilator. He did not understand that she would not receive cardiopulmonary resuscitation. The court issued a restraining order to prevent the entering of a "No Code" order and appointed her friend as guardian. The court found there was insufficient evidence to determine what Siebert would have wanted.[54] (See also the Minnesota Supreme Court case of *In re Torres* which provides further direction on when court orders should be obtained.[55])

If there has been no advance deliberation regarding the code statute, the presumption in favor of resuscitation is justified. However, this presumption has been weakened. On June 13, 1982, the *Washington Post* printed an article titled "Doctor Sees Trend Not to Resuscitate." It is advisable to discuss the subject in advance to avoid using resuscitation in circumstances where it would be appropriate to omit it. This is especially important in light of a recent Ohio appeals court decision.

Ohio

In *Leach v. Akron General Medical Center*, the Probate Division of the Common Pleas Court approved the discontinuance of a life support system for a patient who was in a permanent vegetative state.[56]

Mrs. Leach entered the hospital on July 27, 1980. She was afflicted with amyotrophic lateral sclerosis and was suffering from respiratory distress. Later that day, she suffered a cardiopulmonary arrest. She was resuscitated but remained in a permanent vegetative state. On August 1, 1980, Mrs. Leach was placed on a ventilator. She was transferred from the intensive care unit to her room.

Prior to her admission, she had numerous conversations about life support systems. There was clear and convincing evidence that she did not want to be maintained on a respirator. The family asked the physician to remove her from the respirator but he refused. Mrs. Leach's husband, as her guardian, petitioned the Summit County Probate Court for an order to terminate the life support system. The court issued the order on December 18, 1980. On January 6, 1981, the respirator was disconnected and Mrs. Leach died. The court had stated, however, that before life support could be withdrawn, advance notice of a required medical examination and notice of the withdrawal of the respirator had to be given to the coroner's office and prosecutor's office, so that those offices could have witnesses present.

The family members were very angry because the physician did not abide by their request. Mrs. Leach's estate subsequently brought an action against the hospital and physician for damages for wrongfully placing and maintaining the patient on life-support systems.[57] The estate alleged that a battery had been committed because no consent was given to place Mrs. Leach on a respirator.

The hospital and physician moved for dismissal of the case or for summary judgment. The trial court agreed and dismissed the case for failure to state a claim upon which relief could be granted.

On appeal, the court said that treatment by a physician or hospital, in knowing contravention of that patient's wishes, would be an actionable battery for which liability in damages could result. While the patient's right to refuse treatment is qualified because it may be overridden by competing state interests, the patient's right to refuse treatment is absolute until the quality of the competing interests is weighed in a court proceeding. The physician owes his patient a fiduciary duty of good faith and fair dealing. These obligations require the patient's consent to medical treatment. If the patient is not competent to consent, an authorized person many consent on the patient's behalf.

The merits of the family's claim were dependent upon the facts that would be determined in the case. The existence and nature of consent or refusal of treatment were facts to be considered. The case was sent back to the trial court to determine these facts.

In September, 1984, the hospital settled out of the case. Two days later, the trial court judge directed a verdict in favor of the physician. Ohio is currently considering implementing a living will law. If it would have had a living will law at the time of the *Leach* case, chances are this situation would not have occurred. The physician would not have refused withdrawal of life-support systems because of the fear of being sued. A living will law would have provided the physicians and nurses with some clear directives to follow.

In the above case, the relatives sued for the expenses incurred in putting the patient on a life-support system. Such resuscitation commonly costs more than $1,000. The cost of caring for the surviving patients who suffer side effects is also high. Typically, hospitals have developed emergency mobilization procedures and specially trained teams of physicians and nurses to be able to immediately respond to calls for resuscitation. Typically, the call for assistance in a "Code Blue" is broadcast over the hospital's paging system so that the various members can converge upon the patient. This tends to be a very costly endeavor.

Delaware

In re Severns was decided in Delaware in 1980.[58] Mrs. Severns had sustained a broken neck and irreversible brain damage in an auto accident. Prior to the accident, she had executed a living will which stated she did not want to be kept alive as a vegetable. The husband applied to the court for an order to discontinue all treatment and that a "No Code" order be put on her chart. The trial court issued both orders and also ordered that those who honored them would be free of liability.

Washington

In 1983, the Washington Supreme Court approved removal of life support from a patient in a chronic vegetative state in *In re Colyer*.[59] The court appointed a guardian to assert the personal right of the incompetent patient. The "substitute judgment" standard was used in order to determine if life-sustaining treatment could be refused. The guardian was in the position of determining what the patient would choose if able to make the choice. The character and personality of the incompetent patient, prior statements and general attitutdes toward medical assistance are factors in the determination process.

The court also discussed the necessity of concurrence of the prognosis review board. If there is a disagreement among the board members as to whether there is reasonable probability that the patient will return to a sapient state, then court intervention may be required. This case supplemented the Washington Natural Death Act.

In 1984, the Washington Supreme Court in part clarified and in part overruled the above case when it decided *In re Guardianship of Joseph Hamlin*.[60] The court made it clear that life support could be withdrawn if there was an agreement between the family, physician and prognosis committee and the patient was in a persistent vegetative state with no reasonable hope of recovery. The decision-making process was not predicated upon the appointment of a guardian if the patient is incompetent. A guardian can be appointed if there are no family members. Judicial involvement is not required, even in the case of a severely retarded patient, unless there is a disagreement between the parties or the decision makers.

New York

In New York in 1984, a grand jury recommended state regulation of NCB procedures as a result of an egregious example of mishandling them in a hospital.[61] The case involved a failure to resuscitate a patient. It was discovered that the nurses would attach a purple dot to the cards of patients who were not to be coded. Doctors verbally communicated to the nurses which patients were "No Codes" so the purple dots could be placed on the cards. When the patients died, the cards were thrown out. One patient's card had two purple dots and it was not known if one had fallen on the card by accident. The policy concerned and astonished the grand jurors. After this, a special task force was appointed to study this problem and to make recommendations regarding NCB orders.

"Slow Code" Orders

Some nurses have been advised to accept "Slow Code" orders. No legal authority exists for the policy. Since the law does not recognize the concept, a "Slow

Code'' should never be ordered. The acceptable standards established by the National Conference on Cardiopulmonary Resuscitation does not include "Slow Codes."[62]

Summary

There are still many unanswered questions in the area of "No Code" orders, although the *Dinnerstein* case did much to clarify some of them. The most fundamental question yet to be answered is whether other states will agree that resuscitation may be withheld from a terminally ill and incurable patient without first obtaining court approval. In the thirty-six states that currently have living will laws, the answer becomes much clearer.

It also bears watching to see how many other states will hold that prior court approval is required before treatment can be withheld from an incompetent patient when such treatment can improve the prognosis.

It is worth noting that, to date, no physician has been found civilly or criminally liable for causing a patient's death by withholding treatment. One reason is that it is extremely difficult to prove that a terminally ill patient actually would have lived had resuscitative measures been attempted.[63, 64]

The nurse should remember that the duty and responsibility for ordering an NCB rests with the physician. However, if the institution has a "No Code" policy, the nurse should ensure that the policy is followed. All "No Code" orders should be written. The nurse should not accept a "Slow Code" order because the law does not recognize this concept. "No Code" policies are best drafted by a bioethics committee, and should be consistent with the nurse's state's laws. Typical "No Code" policies contain some of the following:

1. The patient should be resuscitated unless there is an order to the contrary.

2. Appropriate knowledge of the serious nature of the patient's medical condition is necessary.

3. The attending physician should determine the appropriateness of the NCB order.

4. All NCB orders should be given by the attending physician.

5. All NCB orders should be in writing.

6. NCB orders are compatible with maximal therapeutic care. This means the patient may receive vigorous support and yet an NCB order may be justified.

7. When the patient is capable of making his/her own judgments, the NCB decision should be reached in consensus by the patient and physician.

8. If the patient is not capable of making his/her own decision, then consultation between appropriate family members and the physician should be held before reaching a decision. An NCB order may be written if family members concur in the decision.

9. Many have the patient, if competent, or the family authorize in writing the NCB order.

137

10. The facts and considerations relevant to this decision are recorded by the attending physician in the progress notes.

11. The NCB order shall be subject to review at any time by all concerned parties on a regular basis and may be rescinded at any time.

12. Many add the disclaimer that the drafters of the Standards and Guidelines for Cardiopulmonary Resuscitation recommended:[65]

> The guidelines, procedures, or policies described here do not represent the only medically or legally acceptable approach but rather are presented with the recognition that acceptable approaches exist. Deviations under appropriate circumstances do not represent a breach of a medical standard of care. New knowledge, new techniques, clinical or research data, clinical experience, or clinical or bioethical circumstances may provide sound reasons for alternative approaches, even though they are not described in this document.

13. Some hospital policies require a second physician's opinion as to the irreversible nature of an incompetent patient before entering an "No Code" order.

14. States like Massachusetts usually have a section regarding when prior court approval is necessary. Because of the cases previously discussed, prior judicial approval should be sought if

a. an incompetent patient is not suffering from a terminal illness or death is not imminent; or

b. family members do not concur in the entry of an NCB order.

CONSENT

Informed consent is a concept that has given rise to much confusion on the part of doctors, patients, judges, and attorneys. Few subjects in today's world have generated so many articles, books, and lectures as the topic of informed consent. Originally, it was a judicially created doctrine. Now, many states have passed statutes or laws on informed consent. Some of the state laws are addressed to physicians, whereas others speak to a broader spectrum of health care providers. Most state statutes require that an informed consent be provided by the physician. Your states's status on informed consent is contained in the attached booklet.

There are two types of consent. The first type is general consent. General consent is needed to treat a patient on admission to the hospital. It prevents the hospital and staff from being sued for assault and battery. (Assault and battery have been discussed previously.) It advises the patient of procedures that will be performed. General consent allows the staff to perform examinations on the patient, which will allow a diagnosis to be made.

Nurses generally are able to give information only for general consent. Nurses do not give informed consent information due to the nature of the nurses' practice. For example, the nurse does not advise the patient undergoing a hysterectomy about the complications of hemorrhage, infection, ureter and bladder damage, fistual formation, anesthesia complications, paraplegia, and death. This is the responsibility of the physician.

Informed consent usually is obtained when invasive procedures are used for diagnostic or therapeutic purposes. As previously discussed, the physician generally has the responsibility for obtaining informed consent in most states.

There are several different types of consent: implied, expressed, and written. The patient implies consent by submitting to the procedure. Oral consent is when the patient verbally agrees to the procedure. Both of these forms are legally sufficient but create many evidentiary problems. It becomes difficult to prove in court, years after the fact. Therefore, written consent is far superior and should be obtained whenever possible. If it is an emergency or a life-threatening procedure or if the patient is comatose, it may be impossible to obtain a written consent. Consent usually is obtained from the spouse or next of kin as soon as feasible.

The patient should be given sufficient information so that a reasoned and intelligent decision can be made. Justice Cardozo wrote, "Every human being of adult years and sound mind has a right to determine what shall be done with his own body. A surgeon who performs an operation without the patient's consent commits an assault of which he is liable in damages."[66]

It is permissible for nurses to witness the patient's signature to the informed consent form. The nurse should actually see the patient sign his/her name to the form. It is the general consensus of experts that the nurse is merely witnessing the patient's signature. Witnessing the consent form does not mean that the nurse verifies that all risks have been explained and that the patient comprehends the physician's explanations.

A patient can revoke consent at any time. The patient may revoke the consent orally or in writing. This rule requires a sense of reasonableness. If the patient is halfway through the procedure, and if terminating the procedure would result in injury to the patient, then the procedure should be completed.

Minors cannot give consent, in most states, without a specific state statute. Absent an emergency situation, minors should not be treated until the parent or legal guardian gives consent. There are several exceptions to this general rule. Emancipated minors, in most states, are treated as adults and can provide consent. Many states allow minors to seek treatment for venereal disease, drug abuse, and alcohol abuse without parental consent. Each nurse should be familiar with his/her hospital's policy on consent and treatment of minors.

The emergency doctrine of consent has already been referred to several times. In an emergency situation, the law implies consent. What constitutes an emergency depends on the specific circumstances. If another physician or nurse in the same or similar circumstances would consider the situation to be an emergency, then the legal requirements are met.

When the parents of minor children are divorced, generally only the parent with legal custody can give consent for treatment. Generally, I have the noncustodial parent sign the consent form. I then attempt to reach the custodial parent by phone. In cases where the custodial parent is out of state, or out of the country, then verbal permission to treat is accepted. It's a good idea to have two witnesses anytime the taking of verbal consent is necessitated.

REFERENCES

1. *City of Somerset v. Hart*, 549 S.W.2d 814 (Ky. 1977); *Toth v. Community Hospital at Glen Cove*, 22 N.Y.2d 255, 292 N.Y.S.2d 440 (1968).
2. *Abile v. U.S.A.*, 482 F. Supp. 703 (1980); *Carlsen v. Janvurek*, S26 F.2d 202 (1975).
3. *Peeples v. Sargent*, 77 Wis. 2d 612, 253 N.W.2d 459 (1977); *Beardsley v. Wyoming County Community Hospital*, 79 A.D.2d 1110, 435 N.Y.S.2d 862 (1981).
4. *Czubinsky v. Doctors Hosptial*, 188 Cal. Rptr. 685, 139 Cal. App. 361 (1983).
5. *Toth v. Community Hospital at Glen Cove, supra* note 1.
6. *Czubinsky v. Doctors Hospital, supra* note 4.
7. *Utter v. United Hospital Center, Inc.*, 236 S.E.2d 213 (W. Va. 1977).
8. *Suburban Hospital v. Hadary*, 322 A.2d 258, 22 Md. App. 186 (1974).
9. Norman, "Nurses and Malpractice," 33 *Defense L.J.* No. 1, at 103 (1984); *Poor Sisters of St. Francis Seraph v. Cantron*, 435 N.E.2d 305 (Ind. App. 1982); *Killan v. Reinhardt*, 71 A.D.2d 851, 419 N.Y.S.2d 175 (1979).
10. *Cramer v. Theda Clark Memorial Hospital*, 45 Wis. 2d 147, 172 N.W.2d 427 (1969).
11. *Washington Hospital Center v. Martin*, 454 A.2d 306 (D.C. 1983).
12. *Laidlaw v. Lions Gate Hospital*, 8 D.L.R.3d 730 (B.C. Sup. Ct. 1969).
13. *Czubinsky v. Doctors Hospital, supra* note 4.
14. President's Commission for the Study of Ethical Problems in Medicine and Biomedical and Behavioral Research, *Deciding to Forego Life-Sustaining Treatment* 236 (March 1983).
15. DeBard, M., "Cardiopulmonary Resuscitation: Analysis of Six Years' Experience and Review of the Literature," 10 *Annals Emerg. Med.* 408 (1981).
16. Hershey, C. and Fisher, Linda, "Why Outcome of Cardiopulmonary Resuscitation in General Wards Is Poor," 1 *Lancet* 31 (1982).
17. Messert, Bernard and Quaglieri, C., "Cardiopulmonary Resuscitation Perspectives and Problems," 1 *Lancet* 410, 411 (1976).
18. Clark, C., *et al.*, "Criteria for Cessation of CPR in the Emergency Department," 10 *Annals Emerg. Med.* 11, 14 (1981).
19. Castagna, J., *et al.*, "Cardiac Arrest in the Critically Ill Patient," 2 *Heart and Lung* 847 (1973).
20. Fusgen, I., *et al.*, "How Much Sense Is There to Resuscitate an Aged Person?" 24 *Gerontology* 37 (1978).
21. Petty, T., "Mechanical Last 'Rights,'" 142 *Arch. Int. Med.* 1442 (1982).
22. Editorial, "Cardiac Resuscitation in Hospitals: More Restraint Needed?" 7 *Lancet* 27 (1982).
23. National Institute of Health Clinical Center, Policy and Communications Bull. No. 82-4 (July 12, 1982).
24. Nagel, E.L., "Complications of CPR," 9 *Crit. Care Med.* 424 (1981).
25. Mitchell, T., *et al.*, "Orders Not to Resuscitate," 295 *New Eng. J. Med.* 364 (1976).
26. "Optimum Care for the Hopelessly Ill Patients: A Report of the Critical

Care Committee of the Massachusetts General Hospital," 295 *New Eng. J. Med.* 362 (1976).

27. Kirchner, M., "How to Go on Prolonging Life: One Hospital's Systems," *Med. Econ.* (July 12, 1976).

28. Arena, F.P., *et al.*, "Initial Experience with a 'Code-No Code' Resuscitation System in Cancer Patients," 8 *Critical Care Medicine* 733 (Dec. 1980).

29. *Deciding to Forego Life-Sustaining Treatment, supra* note 14, at 236.

30. National Conference Steering Committee, "Standards for Cardiopulmonary Resuscitation (CPR) and Emergency Cardiac Care," 227 *J.A.M.A.* 837, 864 (1974).

31. Younger, S.J., Lewandowski, W., McClish, D.L., *et al.*, "Do Not Resuscitate Orders: Incidence and Implications in a Medical Intensive Care Unit," 253 *J.A.M.A.* 54 (1985).

32. Veatch, R.M., "Deciding Against Resuscitation: Encouraging Signs and Potential Dangers," 253 *J.A.M.A.* 78 (1985).

33. Bedell, S.E. and Delbanco, T.L., "Choices About Cardiopulmonary Resuscitation in the Hospital: When Do Physicians Talk with Patients," 310 *New Eng. J. Med.* 1089 (1984).

34. "Do Not Resuscitate Orders, A Commentary," 255 *J.A.M.A.* 240 (Jan. 10, 1986).

35. *Id.* at 244.

36. Zimmerman, J.E., *et al.*, "The Use and Implication of Do Not Resuscitate Orders in Intensive Care Units," 255 *J.A.M.A.* 351 (Jan. 17, 1986).

37. Collins, D., "Limits of Medical Responsibility in Prolonging Life," 206 *J.A.M.A.* 389 (1968).

38. Corbett, R., "Withholding Life-Prolonging Medical Treatment," 46 *New Eng. J. on Prison Law* 47 (1976).

39. Gillerman, *et al.*, "Orders Not to Resuscitate," 295 *New Eng. J. of Med.* 364 (1976).

40. "No Code Orders v. Resuscitation: The Decision to Withhold Life-Prolonging Treatment from the Terminally Ill," 26 *Wayne L. Rev.* 139 (1979).

41. *Deciding to Forego Life-Sustaining Treatment, supra* note 14, at 238.

42. *In re Dinnerstein*, 380 N.E.2d 134 (Mass. App. 1978).

43. *In re Quinlan*, 70 N.J. 10, 355 A.2d 647 (1976).

44. *Superintendent v. Saikewicz*, 373 Mass. 728, 370 N.E.2d 471 (1977).

45. *In re Dinnerstein, supra* note 42.

46. *In re Spring*, 8 Mass. App. 831, 399 N.E. 493 (1979), *superseded, In re Spring*, 380 Mass. 629, 405 N.E.2d 115 (1980).

47. *Id.* at 1216-17, 405 N.E.2d at 121.

48. *Eichner v. Dillon*, 73 A.D.2d 431, 426 N.Y.S.2d 517 (App. Div. 1980), *rev'd sub nom. In re Storar*, 52 N.Y.2d 363, 438 N.Y.S.2d 266 (1981).

49. *Id.* at 382-83, 438 N.Y.S.2d at 276.

50. *Satz v. Perlmutter*, 262 So. 2d 160 (Fla. Dist. Ct. App. 1978) *aff'd*, 379 So. 2d 359 (Fla. 1980).

51. *Young v. Emory University*, No. 83-6143-S (Ga. 1983).

52. *Foody v. Manchester Memorial Hospital*, 40 Conn. Supp. 127, 482 A.2d 713 (Conn. 1984).

53. *Hoyt v. St. Mary's Rehabilitation Center*, D.C. File No. 774555, Hennepin County Minnesota District Court (Feb. 13, 1981).

54. "June Hoyt: No Code Blue/Do Not Resuscitate," 3 *Bioethics Q.* 129 (Summer 1981).

55. *In re Torres*, 357 N.W.2d 332 (Minn. 1984).

56. *Leach v. Akron General Medical Center*, 68 Ohio Misc. 1, 22 Ohio Op. 3d 49, 426 N.E.2d 809 (Com. Pl. 1980).

57. *Leach v. Shapiro*, 13 Ohio App. 3d 393, 13 Ohio B. 477, 469 N.E.2d 1047 (1984).

58. *In re Severns*, 425 A.2d 156 (Del. Ch. 1980).

59. *In re Colyer*, 99 Wash. 2d 114, 660 P.2d 738 (1983), overruled in part, *In re Guardianship of Hamlin*, 102 Wash. 2d 810, 689 P.2d 1372 (1984).

60. Messert, *supra* note 17.

61. Society for the Right to Die, *The Physician and the Hopelessly Ill Patient, Legal, Medical and Ethical Guidelines* 31 (250 W. 57th Street, New York, N.Y. 1985).

62. National Conference on Cardiopulmonary Resuscitation, "Standards for Cardiopulmonary Resuscitation," 244 *J.A.M.A.* 453 (1980).

63. Teckleburg, Nancy, "Medico-Legal Implications of 'Orders Not to Resuscitate,'" 31 *Catholic University Law Review* 515 (1982).

64. Memel, L., *et al.*, "The Legal Status of 'No Code Orders,'" 7 *Hosp. Med. Staff* 2 (May 1978).

65. National Conference on Cardiopulmonary Resuscitation, *supra* note 62.

66. *Canterbury v. Spence*, 464 F.2d 772 (D.C. Cir.) *cert. den'd*, 409 U.S. 1064 (1972).

CHAPTER NINE

COMMON CAUSES OF NURSING NEGLIGENCE

Hospital and Nursing Home Cases
Operating Room Nurses
Orthopedic Nurses
Obstetrical Nurses
Anesthesia Errors by a CRNA
Occupational Health Nurses
School Nurses
Liability of the Hospice Nurse

INTRODUCTION

At least twenty-two recurring situations exist in which nurse liability is found. These situations occur in all fields of nursing. By being aware of such problem areas, hopefully the nurse can avoid liability. Not all of the recurring situations which cause nurse liability are discussed and defined in this chapter. Many of the situations have already been covered elsewhere in this book. Some of the more common cases against nurses involve the following:

1. Errors in the administration of treatments and medications (wrong medication, wrong dosage, wrong route, wrong technique, wrong patient or wrong time).

2. Failure to adequately supervise patients.

3. Failure to remove foreign objects from patients after surgery (errors in sponge, instrument and needle counts).

4. Burns to patients (hot water bottles, K-pads, scalding hot water, douches, sitz baths, etc.).

5. Failure to monitor, observe and report changes in a patient's condition.

6. Drug distribution as opposed to drug administration by nurses (in violation of the state's pharmacy act).

7. Mistaken identification of a patient.

8. Errors by a certified registered nurse anesthetist (CRNA).

9. Use of defective equipment.

10. Abandonment of a patient.

11. Loss or damage to a patient's property.

12. Failure to function within the scope of nursing education or a job description.

13. Failure to report known or suspected incompetent care and incompetence of a practitioner.

14. Failure to use aseptic techniques, resulting in patient infections.

15. Failure to monitor the use of restraints.

16. Failure to keep abreast of nursing knowledge.

17. Failure to defer execution of improper orders.

18. Failure to take an adequate patient history, including failure to note patient allergies.

19. Failure to follow established policies and procedures.

20. Failure to chart adequately and promptly; alteration of records.

21. Failure to resuscitate promptly and properly.

22. Failure to communicate concerns to physicians or to the nursing supervisor.

HOSPITAL AND NURSING HOME CASES

There are many common areas of recurring liability that involve hospital and nursing home nurses. It is interesting to note that it is not in the practice of sophisticated, technical procedures that nursing liability generally results. Rather, errors in the most basic nursing tasks most often result in nursing liability. Generally, errors in carrying out the procedures, care and treatment learned in nursing school get nurses into trouble. As soon as we get out of nursing school, we no longer check the patient's name band or double check to be sure that we have the right medication. Prevention of many nursing errors can be accomplished by "getting back to basics." The following illustrate well many of the errors that can result from the care and treatment rendered by the nurse on a frequent basis.

Errors in the Administration of Treatment and Medication

Drug errors are the most common allegations of negligence against nurses. Every nurse will recall learning the standard of care for administering medication and treatment to patients. This entails administering the following:

1. The *right* medication;
2. to the *right* patient;
3. at the *right* time;
4. in the *right* dosage;
5. by the *right* route; and
6. by the *right* technique.

Most medication errors could be avoided if the nurse followed the basic guidelines taught in nursing school. The nurse is expected to know a drug's safe dose, toxicity, indications and potential side effects.

There is a plethora of cases involving the administration of wrong medications. In one case, a judgment was affirmed against a nurse for injuries caused when hydrochloric acid was inserted in a patient's nose instead of nose drops.[1] In another case, a nurse erroneously administered a solution of 10 percent sodium hydroxide instead of saline during a gastric analysis.[2] The patient suffered some serious injuries and permanent disability.

There are a number of cases that result from the improper administration of I.M. or I.V. medications. In the *Guthrie Hospital* case, a patient was admitted for a hernia repair.[3] Postoperatively, the physician ordered penicillin and Chymar I.M. The patient was given both drugs I.V. instead of I.M., and suffered a grand mal seizure.

The court held the hospital liable for negligence. There was testimony that the introduction of the Chymar I.V. was the direct cause of the patient's injury. This case illustrates, first, that the nurse is under a legal duty to know how to administer specific drugs. Second, the nurse should always make sure that the medication is given by the right method.

In the *St. Francis Hospital* case, a physician wrote an order for "Dramamine 50 mg. hypodermically."[4] The nurse administered the Dramamine subcutaneously instead of intramuscularly. The patient developed a fat necrosis and sued the hospital, alleging negligence.

The court held for the plaintiff. Testimony demonstrated that the subcutaneous administration of Dramamine is not good nursing practice because Dramamine is irritating to the tissues. This case is another illustration of a nurse's responsibility to administer medications in the right route and by the right technique.

The nurse is also under a duty to administer patient medication accurately and on time. In the *St. James Hospital* case, the plaintiff's only claim against the nurse was her alleged delay in administering the medication prescribed to the plaintiff's 14-month-old daughter.[5]

The time at which the medication is administered is the time that should be charted. Every medication given should be charted. For example, Keflex 250 mg. P.O. is ordered at 9:00 a.m. If the nurse gives the medication at 9:10 a.m., it is better to chart the exact time. Charting either time would be within the acceptable standard of practice; however, the nurse's credibility may be enhanced by charting the exact time. For example, a jury may wonder how a nurse administered 140 medications at exactly 9:00 a.m.

A frequent source of liability is damage to the sciatic nerve during injections in the buttocks. For example, in the *Wilmington General Hospital* case, a nurse negligently administered an I.M. injection in the wrong quadrant of the patient's buttocks.[6] The patient developed a permanent footdrop and atrophy of the calf muscle as a result of the nurse's negligence.

In the *Bernardi* case, the nurse was found negligent for the improper administration of an I.M. injection to a 7-year-old child.[7] The nurse administered tetracycline into the right gluteal area, striking the sciatic nerve. The child developed a complete footdrop.

In the *Tucson General Hospital* case, the plaintiff claimed that the nurse was negligent in administering an I.M. injection of Vistaril, resulting in damage to his sciatic nerve.[8] The nurse had appropriately given Vistaril 50 mg. I.M. "Z-track" as ordered by the physician. The nurse had also appropriately charted that it was administered in the right gluteus. The hospital and nurse were granted summary judgment.

Sciatica can be from a number of different causes. The nurse and hospital are liable for a patient's sciatica only if it is demonstrated that the nurse deviated from the acceptable standard of care and that his/her negligence caused the sciatica. For example, in one case, the nurse administered an intramuscular injection of Demerol and Phenergan.[9] This was administered in the upper, outer quadrant of the left gluteus before the patient went for a colonoscopy. Immediately after the injection, the patient complained of burning and pain down his left leg. He subsequently developed a footdrop.

Testimony was presented that the needle used was not long enough to have pierced the sciatic nerve. In addition, it was possible that the patient had a slight anatomical abnormality in the location of his sciatic nerve. Evidence was also presented that the medication could have diffused through the sheath surrounding the sciatic nerve, with the results being the same as had the nerve been pierced.

The court found for the defendant in this case. As a practical point, many cases are won or lost because of the talent, experience or preparation of the attorneys representing the parties. It is up to the plaintiff's attorney to allege the

147

proper grounds for recovery. The presence and quality of expert witnesses are also factors in determining whether the suit will be won or lost.

There are numerous cases of alleged negligence resulting from patients who sustained sciatic nerve injury. This is one reason why it is imperative that the nurse document in the medical records where injections are given. Recently a case was successfully dismissed because of excellent documentation by the nurse. The patient was involved in an automobile accident and admitted overnight for observation. The chart indicated that the patient received a tetanus toxoid .5 cc. in the right deltoid and Demerol 50 mg. and Phenergan 25 mg. I.M. in the right gluteus. The patient developed a left sciatica. Since no injection was administered in the left gluteus, the case was dismissed. Had the nurse failed to document where the Demerol and Phenergan were administered, it would have become an issue of fact for the jury to decide.

Nurses should also be familiar with the *Physician's Desk Reference* (P.D.R.) or packet inserts regarding how fast an I.V. medication can be pushed. In the *Mohr* case, a nurse anesthetist was sued after administering Valium I.V.[10] The patient testified that the nurse administered the Valium I.V. push rapidly and in less than one minute. He alleged that the phlebitis and thrombosis that developed in his right arm were due to the nurse injecting the medication too rapidly.

The nurse testified that it was her practice to always administer Valium slowly and in accordance with the manufacturer's recommendation. The package insert stated that the drug should be administered slowly, at least one minute for each five milligrams given. The nurse testified that she gave it slowly in order to judge its effect.

The court ruled in favor of the nurse, considering the amnesic qualities of Valium. The court found the nurse's estimate of time to be more likely than the plaintiff's estimate.

This case illustrates that the nurses is responsible for administering patient medications appropriately, which includes administering the drug over the correct period of time pursuant to good clinical nursing practice. Package inserts and the P.D.R. are only two sources for the nurse to use in determining what establishes good nursing practice. Charting the time period over which the drug was administered may have prevented the *Mohr* suit from being filed against the nurse. For example, instead of charting, "Valium 10 mg. I.V. at 10:00," write, "Valium 10 mg. I.V. push start, 10:00-10:02 in #18 angio in Rt. antecubital fossa."

The correct I.V. solution should be infused and at the right rate. It is so easy, especially when the nurse is busy, to forget to monitor the patient's I.V. This is especially important with infants and the elderly.

In *Wyoming County Community Hospital*, a 6-year-old boy was admitted for a splenectomy following a sledding accident.[11] The nurse postoperatively infused the wrong I.V. solution and in the wrong amount. The infusion of an excessive amount of salt-free fluid resulted in the dilution of body salts. This caused severe cerebral edema, which resulted in two grand mal seizures and brain damage.

The court awarded the plaintiff $340,000. Part of the judgment, $100,000, was awarded for pain and suffering. The New York Supreme Court stated that the $100,000 award for pain and suffering was not excessive, because this amount did not deviate from what would be considered to be fair compensation so as to shock the conscience of the court.

In the *Doctors Hospital* case, the court gave the jury the following charges:

> If you are reasonably satisfied from the evidence in this case that a nurse employed by Doctors Hospital of Mobile, Inc., made a medication error in administering a drug or other medicine to Mrs. Kirksey's right thigh, then the hospital would be liable for injuries and damages proximately resulting from such error, as nurses are bound to know the fatal dosage of all drugs and the danger of an overdose of any type of drug and the proper way to administer any drug, and nurses must be familiar with the usually acceptable routes of drug administration.[12]

In this case, the hospital appealed because of the court's failure to define what constituted reasonable and ordinary care. The Supreme Court of Alabama reversed and remanded the case (sent it back to be tried again). This is only one of the many cases which illustrate the nurse's expanded role in the administration of drugs.

Failure to Adequately Supervise Patients and Patient Falls

An increasing number of cases have been filed against nurses for injuries to patients caused by leaving them unattended.[13-29] In fact, no other type of injury gives rise to as many malpractice suits against nurses, hospitals or nursing homes as patient falls. The May 1986 edition of *Medical Liability Advisory Service* stated, "As many lawsuits against hospitals involve falls by patients as any other category of lawsuit."[30] The August 1986 edition of *Law, Medicine and Health Care* stated that the problem of patient falls has reached a proportion such that it clearly deserves careful and in-depth industry study.[31] The question of when to provide side rails and restraints continues to perplex the best minds in hospital management and to challenge the best judgment of nurses.

Nurses, hospitals and other health institutions are not liable for all patient falls. The standard of care for nursing generally requires the use of side rails for most elderly patients. Sedated, mentally impaired, young or confused patients require an even higher degree of care. The nursing standard of care generally requires that safeguards such as side rails be utilized for these classes of patients as well.

The nurse is under a duty to follow the physician's order regarding the use of side rails and restraints. Additionally, courts have frequently recognized an independent duty on the part of the nurse to evaluate the patient's needs. The nurse has a duty to properly assess a patient's condition and take appropriate precautions. If the patient's injury was foreseeable and steps were not taken to protect the patient, liability may result. The emphasis on preventive medicine and risk management has resulted in the compilation of hospital rules and standards whereby the use of bed rails has passed beyond the mere following of physicians' orders.[32] Jane Greenlaw, a nurse attorney, summarized this well when she wrote the following:

> Today, it is generally accepted that when a nurse reaches a "nursing diagnosis" and feels that due to a patient's age, medication, post-surgical weakness or disorientation, a bedrail should be in the up position, it is the nurse's responsibility to see that the rail is raised.[33]

149

This is illustrated well by the *Bleiler* case, which was decided by a New York Court of Appeals on May 2, 1985.[34] The court held as follows:

> The role of the registered nurse has changed in past few decades, from that of a passive, servile employee to that of an assertive, decisive health care provider. Today, the professional nurse monitors complex physiological data, operates sophisticated lifesaving equipment and coordinates the delivery of a myriad of patient services. As a result, the reasonable and prudent nurse no longer waits for and blindly follows the physician's orders.

In the *Cavenaugh* case, the patient had an EKG done and was placed in the treatment room some distance from the nursing station.[35] The patient was left on a hospital stretcher for more than an hour, sitting up and with no side rails. She had to urinate and attempted to get assistance from one of the staff. Finally, while trying to reach the bathroom on her own, she fell and fractured her hip.

In *Favalora*, the patient sued the hospital and the radiologist for injuries sustained as a result of a fall during an x-ray examination.[36] Mrs. Favalora had been admitted for a checkup and a G.I. series. She complained of weakness, fatigue and stomach pains and had a syncopal (fainting) episode.

The patient was standing at the base of the x-ray table getting ready to drink the second glass of barium. The x-ray technician was standing at the opposite side of the room depositing the exposed x-ray film into the pass-box. The patient fainted and fell.

Mrs. Favalora suffered a cervical and femur fracture. She underwent an open reduction and internal fixation of the femoral fracture. She developed a pulmonary embolism and required a ligation of the inferior vena cava.

The court found both the hospital and radiologist negligent. The nurses had a duty to obtain a history from the newly admitted patient and should have communicated to the radiology department the fact that the patient had previously fainted, the court said. The radiologist was negligent because he was under a duty to obtain a history from the patient, which he failed to do.

Every hospital or institution must exercise the degree of care and skill that the patient's condition requires. Patients who are handicapped, disoriented, mentally ill or very young require special attention.

A 70-year-old patient was sent to the radiology department for an abdominal film.[37] The patient was overweight and had bilateral above-the-knee amputations. Because of her condition, a decision was made to obtain the x-ray with the patient lying on her side.

The patient was placed on her side on the stretcher with her abdomen resting against the x-ray table. The wheels of the cart were reportedly in a locked position. While the x-ray technician was taking the film, the patient fell off the cart. She fractured both her pelvis and femur in the fall.

The court of appeals applied the doctrine of *res ipsa loquitur* (this doctrine has been explained earlier), and found that the hospital's negligence was the most likely cause of the accident.

In *Polonsky*,[38] an 81-year-old female was transferred from the C.C.U. unit to the medical floor. That night the nurse gave her Dalmane, a sleeping pill. During the night she awoke to go to the bathroom. She was confused and thought she was at home. The side rails on her bed were down, and she fell and fractured her right hip.

The hospital had a policy requiring that the side rails be up on the beds of all confused or disoriented patients. The nurse acted unreasonably by failing to put up the side rail, the court said. She was also found liable for violating her hospital's own internal policy.

In the *Smith* case,[39] the patient was under the influence of a sedative. The side rails were down, and the patient got out of bed and fell. The hospital had a policy requiring that the side rails be up. The court held the nursing staff liable, and said the nurses should have foreseen that a heavily sedated patient might fall from the bed if the side rails were down.

In *Parkview Estate Nursing Home*, a senile, elderly patient fell after her side rails had been left down.[40] On one prior occasion, the patient had fallen after her side rails were left down. The nurses testified that she needed her side rails up to prevent her from falling. The court found the nurses liable for the damages attributable to the injuries from her fall.

In *Jenkins*, a fully alert patient was instructed repeatedly not to get out of bed without assistance.[41] The patient disregarded the nurses' warnings. The court denied the patient recovery, stating that he caused his own injuries. The court concluded that a hospital is not an insurer of a patient's safety.

Other courts have found that the nurse and the hospital were not liable for patient falls.[42-43] A patient who was alert and oriented was medicated for sleep. He got up in the night to go to the bathroom and fell. Another patient got up during the night to go to the bathroom and also fell. The court said that the hospital was not under a duty to remain a constant guard over sleeping patients.

In *Albany Medical Center Hospital*, a patient was recovering from surgery on his leg.[44] It was the ninth postoperative day when he fell out of the hospital bed and sustained serious injury. The patient was alert and oriented. The nurses testified that they had no reason to suspect or foresee his fall. The physician testified that the patient's condition did not warrant the use of side rails. The court denied recovery to the patient.

In *Shannon*, a mental patient fell out of bed and fractured his leg.[45] He had been in the hospital for eight months prior to his fall and never had side rails on his bed. The court denied recovery. The court found that the patient had never fallen before and that the nurses had no reason to suspect that he might fall.

In *Butler*, a woman was admitted to the hospital for a fractured hip.[46] She was given crutches to use with only a few words of instruction. The patient fell the first day she used the crutches.

The court permitted recovery in this case because the nurses failed to supervise the patient or provide crutch instructions. Testimony was presented that the standard of care is to provide crutch instructions and supervise patients when crutches are given. This is one of many cases which illustrate that the nurse's failure to provide adequate instruction may result in nursing liability.

One author studied the activity of alert patients at the time of their falls.[47] These were recorded as follows:

1. 49 percent fell from bed;

2. 8 percent fell from a chair;

3. 18 percent fell while ambulating; and

4. 25 percent were bathroom related.

Nineteen percent of the patients were acting against doctor's orders. Because of the comparative negligence principle, nurses should always document the patient's failure to follow the physician's order.

The problem of patient falls is compounded by the patient's need to feel in control. Patients who feel that they have lost all control over their lives exhibit a sense of helplessness. This can adversely affect their lack of functioning. They are told when and what they will eat, what they can wear, when they are to arise and when they can have visitors. As the nurse pulls up the side rails, the patient feels a lack of control. Having to wait for the nursing staff's availability for assistance can present a physiological problem. A speedy response to a patient's call can assist in resolving this problem and can decrease the incidence of patient falls.

In summary, the nurse's duty to protect the patient is largely determined by the patient's condition and ability to safeguard himself/herself. The fact that patients fall from their beds and sustain injury is not, without more evidence, determinative of nursing negligence.

In finding negligence, the court will consider the facts of each case. The type and dosage of medication administered is only one factor that will be considered by the court. The patient's age, mental status and diagnosis are additional factors. Physician orders and hospital policies are also considered. The breach of a hospital policy or procedure is not conclusive evidence of negligence. If an alert and oriented patient falls from a bed, wheelchair or cart, there is generally no liability on the part of the nurse, hospital or institution. The patient's own carelessness is a factor in this determination. If the patient is confused, disoriented, debilitated, heavily sedated or is a child or elderly person, the nurse must take adequate safeguards or face liability. The nurse must conform to the applicable standard of care or face the risk of liability.

Burns to Patients

Burns may be caused by multiple sources, including heating pads, vaporizers, hot water bottles, hot enemas, douches, showers and sitz baths.

In *McEachern*, the nurse was held liable for placing a vaporizer too close to a baby.[48] The child had third-degree burns to her body. In *Capasso*, liability also resulted from burns caused by a vaporizer.[49] In *Starnes*, the anesthetist was liable for a burn to an infant undergoing surgery.[50] In that case, the plaintiff alleged negligence in the use of a hot water bottle instead of a thermal blanket to heat the infant patient during surgery.

In *Milner*, the patient was burned by a heating pad which someone had turned up too high.[51] The facts of the *Foster* case are similar,[52] where the patient was also burned by a heating pad. Burns to patients have been reduced by using heating pads with temperature-locking devices.

A surgeon in another case was sued when an electric cautery machine burned a patient during a hemorrhoidectomy.[53] The surgeon had used the machine four times that day. The first two times, the machine did not deliver sufficient heat to cauterize the vessels. The surgeon requested the operating room nurse to check it. After the nurse checked it, the machine worked satisfactorily. The court held that the surgeon was not liable. The court found that it was the hospital's responsibility to check the machine to make sure it was in proper working order.

In the *Bing* case, the operating room nurses were aware that an alcoholic antiseptic that was painted on the patient, tincture of Zephiran, was potentially dangerous.[54] The nurses had received instructions to be careful that none of the liquid got on the linen. If this occurred, they were to replace the sheets with dry linens. The nurses failed to do this. As a result, the patient was seriously burned when the sheets were set on fire by an electric cautery machine.

In the *Monk* case, the patient was admitted to Doctors Hospital for abdominal surgery.[55] Before the surgery, the patient also asked the doctor to remove three moles from her right arm and one from her right leg.

The operating room nurse prepared the Bovie machine. She placed the contact plate of the Bovie machine under the patient's right calf. The patient claimed burns resulted from contact with the Bovie plate. There was evidence that the nurse was aware that other patients at the same hospital who had moles removed had been burned by the same type of electrosurgical machine when there was insufficient contact between the patient's body and the contact plate of the machine.

The judge did not let the jury decide if the nurse was negligent. The trial court directed a verdict for the hospital. The plaintiff appealed.

The U.S. Court of Appeals, District of Columbia, sent the case back to the trial court. The appeals court said that the jury should decide if there was any negligence.

In the *Tucson Medical Center* case, the parents of a 4-year-old boy filed suit after the child sustained a burn on his leg after heart surgery.[56] The court held that the doctrine of *res ipsa loquitur* should apply since a lay person could conclude as a matter of common knowledge that burns do not result if due care has been exercised. Because of the frequency of burns during the operative period, the surgery nurse should take all necessary precautions. Proper grounding, the removal of wet linens from the operating room table and the immediate removal of defective equipment are some of the steps the operating room nurse can utilize.

Many patients are burned by cigarettes or pipes. In the *Bowers* case, a paraplegic patient was given his pipe.[57] He was unable to remove the pipe from his mouth safely. The nurse left the room for a few minutes. While she was gone, the pipe fell from his mouth, setting the bed on fire. The court held that nurses have a duty to ensure the safety of their patients, especially from a known hazard.

In *Kent*,[58] the patient's family advised the nurses that he often burned himself while smoking. The patient was suffering from chronic brain syndrome. The nurses had him restrained in a chair and left him alone while he was smoking. The patient was severely burned and died after his gown and cover blanket caught fire. The hospital was held liable for his death.

Liability has also resulted from burns received by patients from scalding bathtub water. In *Kopa*, an 83-year-old patient was burned by hot water while in the bathtub. There was evidence that he was partially blind, feeble and senile.[59] He was being removed from the bathtub when he started kicking. The patient accidentally turned the hot water on and, before he could be retrieved from the tub, he had suffered first-, second-, and third-degree burns on his buttocks, legs and feet.

The court found the hospital liable. The injuries had been caused by the hospital permitting scalding water to stand in the pipes, the court said.

In another case, the court reversed a lower court decision and held the doctrine of *res ipsa loquitur* was applicable against a nursing home. In that case, a patient suffered burns while taking a bath.[60]

Burns caused by hot enemas and hot water bottles have also resulted in hospital and nursing liability.[61] Liability has also resulted from burns sustained during surgery.[62]

The above cases are illustrative of the number of nursing malpractice cases that are filed as a result of patient burns. Special care should be taken to prevent burns in the cases of young, elderly, confused, sedated or mentally ill patients. Liability is frequently imposed on nurses for burns to these individuals because of their inability to protect themselves.

Nurses should have cautery equipment checked at the earliest sign of any problem. Equipment with obvious defects should never be used on patients. Nurses should also evaluate patients who smoke. Disoriented and confused patients should never be left unattended while smoking — not even for a second.

Failure to Observe and Report Changes in a Patient's Condition

The Ohio case of *Richardson v. Doe* illustrates what can happen when the nurse fails to observe and report changes in a patient's condition.[63] The patient entered Good Samaritan Hospital in active labor. The physician delivered the baby without any complications. After a recovery period, the patient was sent to her room. The postpartum nurse permitted the mother to hemorrhage for eight hours after discovery without notifying her physician.

As a result of her blood loss, the patient required two units of blood. From the transfusion, the patient developed hepatitis. The nurse was held liable for her failure to timely report a change in the patient's condition, which resulted in the need to administer two units of blood, which then caused the patient's hepatitis.

The *Goff* case was very similar to the *Richardson* case.[64] The patient developed postpartal vaginal bleeding after delivery because the physician had failed to suture her properly. The physician specifically instructed the nurses to call him if there was any change in the patient's condition. The patient died. The nurses testified that they were aware of the patient's dangerous condition. Both nurses knew that the patient would die if nothing was done. They were liable for failure to notify the physician of a change in the patient's condition.

A nurse has the responsibility to do an adequate initial patient evaluation. The nurse also has a responsibility to continually monitor the patient's condition, and should report changes in the patient's condition as the situation warrants. If the patient reaches a condition that could have been prevented, the question becomes whether the nurse should have detected it earlier. The law implies the use of a sense of reasonableness. It is impossible to continuously monitor most patients. The frequency of the nurse's observations is determined by the patient's needs, the type of institution, customary practice, the physician's orders and the hospital's or institution's policy. The nurse must assess each patient and formulate a nursing diagnosis to meet the patient's needs.

In the *Yorita* case, an 8-year-old boy had a tonsillectomy and adenoidectomy.[65] The surgery was uneventful, and he was sent to the recovery room, where he suffered a cardiac and respiratory arrest. The child was left with brain damage due to the nurse's failure to detect the arrest situation earlier. Failure to monitor and report changes in the patient's condition is the most common cause of liability against recovery room nurses.

In the *Mundt* case, the nurse's early evaluation and care was excellent.[66] However, the nurses breached their duty to continuously monitor the patient's condition and to report condition changes.

Mildred Mundt was admitted for a chronic circulatory disorder. A "cutdown" was performed on Mrs. Mundt's right lower leg to infuse the I.V. containing ACTH.

The nurse observed the cutdown site initially for signs of redness and infiltration, and informed the physician on April 5 that the I.V. was not infusing properly and that some slight tissue edema was developing. The physician evaluated the patient's leg but ordered to continue the infusion.

The next day, the nurse noted that the entire right leg was noticeably larger. The physician was not called this time. Due to compartment syndrome, tissues in the leg became necrotic. The nurse was found negligent for failure to notify the physician of a new or progressive change.

Unattended infants and postoperative patients are two classes which require more frequent observations by the nurse. In the *Crowe* case, the nurse was held liable for leaving a 22-month-old child unattended for a prolonged period of time.[67] The infant vomited and aspirated.

In the *Thomas* case, the patient had been struck by a speeding car.[68] A friend witnessed the accident and stated that Thomas was initially unconscious. The patient, with complaints of right hip pain, was transported to the emergency room by the rescue squad.

The patient's blood pressure was 80/60 upon admittance into the E.R. at 11:10 p.m. At 11:25 p.m., the nurse rechecked the vital signs and charted that his blood pressure was 90/60. At this time, she contacted the physician who was on call, and reported the patient's condition and vital signs. The on-call physician ordered the patient's admission to the hospital. Pursuant to instructions, the emergency room nurse transferred the patient to the floor.

There were no beds available, and the patient was placed in the hall by the nurses' station at 11:45 p.m. The nurses continued to monitor the patient's vital signs, which started to fall. They did not notify the doctor of the changes. The patient coded and died.

The patient was in hypovolemic shock, as evidenced by his dangerously low blood pressure. The nurse was held liable for her failure to notify the physician of the patient's changing condition. Had the nurse given prompt notice, the physician may have been able to save the patient's life.

The emergency room nurse is under a duty to obtain all pertinent information from the medics who have transported the patient to the hospital. For example, in the *New Biloxi Hospital* case, the emergency room nurse observed that the medics brought in a patient who was bleeding profusely.[69] She did not check the patient's vital signs. She made no effort to examine the extent of the bleeding, and no attempts were made to control the bleeding. The nurse transferred the patient to a veteran's hospital, where he died secondary to hypovolemic shock.

In *Vasey*, a patient came into the emergency room with complaints of abdominal pain and vomiting.[70] The nurse took the patient's history and vital signs, and called the emergency room physician on the phone. The physician prescribed medication and discharged the patient. The next day the patient's appendix ruptured. He subsequently developed peritonitis.

The patient sued the hospital and the nurses, claiming that the nurses should have made a medical diagnosis of appendicitis. The court denied recovery because making a medical diagnosis is outside of the scope of nursing practice.

In summary, a nurse has a duty to observe and report changes in a patient's condition. A nurse should notify her supervisor, the house physician or the attending physician pursuant to hospital policy and promptly report any change in a patient's condition. This communication "up the chain of command" is very important. Failure to do so which results in a patient injury can lead to a finding of negligence.[71]

Drug Distribution and Drug Administration

There is a difference between drug distribution and drug administration. Nurses on evening and night shifts, especially nursing supervisors, often find themselves in the dilemma of practicing pharmacy without a license.

Each state has its own pharmacy act. The pharmacy act basically states that the pharmacist's function is to identify, compound, package, label and preserve medication. No one but a licensed pharmacist can fulfill the pharmacist's tasks.

Dispensing refers to taking a drug from the pharmacy supply and giving it or selling it to another person. Drug distribution or dispensation is the filling of the nurses' station container. It can only be performed by a pharmacist and is outside of the nurse's role.

This contrasts with drug administration. Nurses are licensed to administer medication and not to dispense medication. Drug administration is defined as actually giving the medication to the patient pursuant to the physician's order. It is therefore permissible for the nurse to go to the pharmacy and take one dose of a drug for a specific patient since this is drug administration. This is within the nurse's role. A state's nurse practice act is the authority that allows nurses to administer medication.

In rare instances, adequate patient care may require the nurse to give a certain drug that is not available on the floor or in the patient's medicine cart. It may have been accidentally omitted or it may have been a new order. The patient also may have been a recent admission. Often the nursing supervisor will have to go to the pharmacy if a pharmacist is not on duty.

Many hospitals and nursing homes have a written policy and procedure that permits the nurse to do this under special circumstances. However, even though the institution has a policy, a nurse who dispenses drugs does so unlawfully unless the state pharmacy practice act specifically authorizes this practice. If the nurse makes a mistake in dispensing the drug, the fact that she was practicing pharmacy without a license may be admissible in court.

This practice is risky business. Many hospitals and nursing homes, as a result, have rearranged the staffing in their pharmacies. They have readjusted the scheduling to provide pharmacy staffing on a twenty-four-hour basis.

Of course, in extraordinary circumstances and the more life threatening the situation, the nurse will have to weigh concern for the patient's health against concern for loss of licensure.

Mistaken Identity of Patient

One of the first lessons that every student nurse is indoctrinated in is that of checking the identity of the patient before any medicine is given or any procedure is performed. Generally, most hospitals place arm bands on all of their patients so that they can be readily identified. Many hospitals also use name plates either on or above the patient's bed. As previously mentioned, it is often the failure to remember the "basics" which lands the nurse in court.

For example, in the *Southeastern Kentucky Baptist Hospital* case, the surgical technician arrived on the floor to transport the patient to the operating room.[72] Mrs. Bruce was scheduled for a conization of the cervix at the same time another patient was scheduled for a thyroidectomy. They had already made the incision on Mrs. Bruce's neck before anyone realized the error.

None of the surgical staff had bothered to check Mrs. Bruce's name band. They had erroneously relied on the patient, who had answered to the wrong name. The plaintiff was allowed to recover damages due to the staff's failure to ascertain her correct identity.

On the renal floor at Genesee Hospital, a postnephrectomy patient was recovering well.[73] In fact, she was anticipating discharge in a few days. The nurse and intern informed Ms. Necolayeff that she would be receiving a unit of blood soon. They stated that the blood had been donated by her daughter. Ms. Necolayeff insisted she did not have a daughter. During the infusion of the blood she suffered an incompatibility reaction. The blood was stopped after she experienced severe chills and an elevated temperature.

The patient subsequently became ill and required admittance to a psychiatric hospital. The court found both the nurse and the intern negligent for the error. The blood transfusion was supposed to be for another patient in the same unit.

In the *Ebaugh* case, the surgical technician accidentially mixed up the patient's charts on the way to the operating room.[74] The patient with an abnormal gallbladder had a breast biopsy instead of a cholecystectomy. The patient scheduled for the breast biopsy had her normal, functioning gallbladder removed. Both patients sued and were awarded damages.

Failure to identify a patient before taking a blood sample has resulted in a plethora of cases. This is illustrated by the *Walker* case.[75] After aorta-femoral bypass surgery, the doctor decided that the patient needed a blood transfusion. The phlebotomist went into the patient's room. She did not ask which patient was Mr. Walker. She withdrew blood, which was typed and cross-matched as being Mr. Walker's.

Based on the blood sample, Mr. Walker was transfused with a unit of packed cells; within minutes, he started jerking violently. The nurse discontinued the blood. It was discovered that his reaction was due to getting the wrong blood type.

These cases illustrate the importance of patient identification bracelets and checking them before any procedure. The nurse should not rely on the fact that the patient answers to a name.

Use of Defective Equipment

The hospital or nursing home is under a legal duty to maintain proper medical equipment. Most hospitals and institutions have a policy that provides for routine examination of equipment to insure patient safety. Some equipment checks are done by the maintenance department, while others are delegated to nursing staff. Intubation equipment, monitor and defibrillator checks are usually done by nursing staff.

In one case the hospital had a policy requiring that monitors and defibrillators be checked every shift. Pursuant to this policy, the day shift nurse started to check the defibrillator. She charged up the paddles and observed that there was an inadequate discharge. She was going to have the other nurse check the monitor when she became busy and forgot about it.

Approximately two hours later, the emergency squad brought in a patient having an acute inferior myocardial infarction. The patient was transferred onto the E.R. cart, and the monitor was attached. Shortly after this, the patient went into ventricular fibrillation. The nurse charged up the paddles only to discover that nothing happened.

The E.R. only had one defibrillator. By the time the nurse secured the defibrillator from the C.C.U., the patient had expired.

Nurses should be aware of any hospital policy that requires them to do equipment checks. Any defective equipment should be fixed as soon as possible. Broken equipment should never be left for the unsuspecting staff member to discover.

In another case, the operating room nurse discovered in her morning check that the cautery unit may not have been working properly. Later that morning, an unsuspecting physician used the unit during a B.P.S. surgery to cauterize a woman's fallopian tube.

Postoperatively, the patient was discovered to have bowel burns, which are a known complication of the surgery and can occur even in the best of hands. A defensible case became indefensible because of the nurse's failure to have the unit removed or checked by the hospital's maintenance department.

A hospital is generally not liable for defective equipment if adequate checks are made and there is no reason to suspect that the equipment is defective. Hospital liability for defective equipment is generally predicated on negligence, since the hospital is not a guarantor of the safety of its equipment.[76]

In the *Emory University* case, an infant's foot was severely burned by an unshielded light bulb in an incubator.[77] The court in *Emory University* said, "A hospital owes to its patients only the duty of exercising ordinary care to furnish equipment and facilities reasonably suited to the uses intended. The hospital is not required to furnish the latest or best appliances, or to incorporate in existing equipment the latest inventions or improvements even though such devices may make the equipment safer to use."

In the *Bellaire General Hospital* case, a hospital was held liable for the death of a patient when the wall oxygen connection failed to work.[78] The nurses moved the patient to a private room and did not discover the defective outlet until after the transfer.

In the *Lauro* case, the plaintiff claimed the hospital was negligent in not using modern equipment in the pathology department.[79] The plaintiff had a breast lump, and a biopsy was performed. The pathologist erroneously diagnosed the biopsy specimen as cancerous.

Subsequently, the breast was removed. The plaintiff alleged the hospital was negligent in having a freezing microtome system instead of a cryostat. The court disagreed, since there was no testimony that the freezing microtome was an unsafe factory device.

The hospital or other health care facility has a legal duty to maintain properly working medical equipment. The nurse should insure the patient's safety by removing any defective equipment. If a patient is injured and the nurse suspects it is due to defective equipment, the nurse should notify her supervisor or the risk manager, if the institution has one. Many times the sales representative will offer to take the equipment back and replace it. However, it may be very important to preserve the defective equipment in the event of a lawsuit against the nurse or the health care institution.

Lack of Adherence to Aseptic Techniques, Resulting in Patient Infection

Nurses can be a causal factor in infection or cross-infection when they fail to use sterile or aseptic techniques. Nurses are legally bound to follow the established standard of care in regard to infection control. Hand washing between patient visits, sterile technique during Foley catheter insertion and sterile dressing changes are among the procedures taught in nursing training and education. If a nurse deviates from acceptable practice, causing a patient infection, the nurse is liable. There has been an increasing number of cases filed against nurses for injuries caused by failure to use aseptic technique.[80]

In the *De Falco* case, the nurse retrieved an eye patch from the floor. The patient was recovering from cataract surgery. The plaintiff alleged that the nurse applied it directly to the eye, and the patient subsequently developed a serious eye infection. The jury found for the plaintiff. However, the judge overruled the jury because the plaintiff did not establish that each and every one of the four elements of negligence was present.

The plaintiff failed to show proximate cause, and he produced no expert, the judge said. The court felt it was beyond the ordinary understanding of a jury to know that "Enterobacter and staph germs are frequently found on hospital floors and these virulent microbes enter the body and can cause an infection."[81]

The professional nurse is responsible for supervising the safety and security of the patient. This means that the nurse must be concerned with the hospital environment.[82] In one case, matters such as the cleanliness of the floor (cleaned by sweeping with a broom, causing dust), improper sterilization of equipment and improper dressing changes were all admissible into a court of law.[83]

In another case, a mother was erroneously given another infant by the nurse.[84] The infant was suffering from impetigo, and her own baby subsequently became infected with impetigo and died. The nurse was held liable for cross-contamination which resulted from her negligence.

In yet another case, a patient underwent hip surgery after being involved in an automobile accident.[85] His roommate had a boil which was discharging pus. There was evidence that the nursing staff administered care to both patients without observing aseptic technique as prescribed by hospital infection control policies.

Eventually, a culture of the boil was performed, which showed Staphylococcus aureus in the boil. He was then moved into isolation. However, by this time, the patient who had undergone hip surgery had an infection which had penetrated into the joint. This infection was caused by Staphylococcus aureus. The patient required a second surgery for the osteomyelitis, in which his hip had to be fused in a nearly immobile position. This was enough to establish the plaintiff's case.

In *Kalmus*, the nurse came in, inserted a needle into the patient's buttocks, removed the needle, and reinserted it.[86] The patient subsequently developed a staph infection. Testimony established that standard practice required that a sterile needle be used and that the skin should be scrubbed with an alcohol sponge. The court found against the nurse.

In *Cohran*, the patient was given an I.M. injection and subsequently developed a staph infection.[87] In this case, however, the nurse had used a prepackaged needle and syringe. She testified that she cleansed the area of the injection before inserting the needle, and that the needle was used once and promptly discarded. There was evidence presented at trial that the nurse's hands never touched the needle.

The court found for the nurse. There was no evidence that the nurse deviated from the acceptable standard of care, the court said. If the needle had been contaminated, the nurse would have had no way of knowing this, since it was a prepackaged kit.

In the past, the nurse has frequently been held liable for failure to adequately sterilize needles and other equipment.[88] Now that most hospitals and institutions are using prepackaged equipment, this has reduced liability in this area. If a patient is injured by a contaminated needle or syringe, it is now the manufacturer who is at risk for liability (unless, of course, the nurse contaminated the needle or knew or had reason to know that it was contaminated).

The JCAH has recognized the problem of nosocomial infections and has set forth guidelines to encourage infection control. Chapter 7 of the 1986 edition of the JCAH *Accreditation Manual for Hospitals* is entitled "Infection Control." The JCAH standards dictate that there be an active, effective, hospitalwide infection control program. The basic elements of the infection control program include the following:

1. definition of nosocomial infection to provide uniform identification and reporting of infections;

2. a system for reporting, evaluating and maintaining records of infection among patients;

3. an ongoing review of all aseptic, isolation and sanitation techniques employed in the hospital;

4. written policies defining the specific indications for isolation; and

5. preventive, surveillance and control procedures that relate to the inanimate hospital environment, including sterilization and disinfection practices and central services.

Documentation of all in-services relative to infection prevention and control should be made. All new employees should be oriented to the importance of infection control and personal hygiene.

The mere fact that a patient has contracted an infection while in the hospital does not establish negligence. The patient has to come forth with expert testimony to demonstrate that the infection was negligently caused or improperly treated.[89]

Generally, because of the nature of the injury, it has become very difficult, if not impossible, for the plaintiff to prove liability for nosocomial or hospital-acquired infections. There are certain bacterial infections that are impossible to prevent.[90] Staph infections, for instance, can occur in postoperative patients because bacteria is found within the sweat glands, in hair follicles and on the skin. This is true even if the skin is cleansed with antiseptics prior to surgery.[91]

Failure to Take an Adequate Patient History, Including Failure to Note Patient Allergies

A nurse is responsible for knowing what is important in eliciting a patient history. The nurse is under a duty to exercise due care and make the appropriate inquiries.[92] Information regarding the patient's current medication and any known allergies should be obtained.

A mother brought her two boys to the emergency room.[93] Each had a chest and head rash accompanied by a high fever. The mother told the nurse that she had removed two ticks from the head and one from the stomach of one of her two sons. The nurse did not chart this, nor did she relay this history to the emergency room physician. The physician evaluated the boys and made a diagnosis of measles. Aspirin was prescribed and they were discharged.

One of the boys was found dead two days later. An autopsy report showed the cause of death to be Rocky Mountain spotted fever. The second son was treated for the same and survived.

Evidence supported that the failure of the nurse to notify the physician of the patient history regarding the removal of the ticks violated her duties as a nurse.

In the *Kenyon* case, Mrs. Kenyon had a routine blood test done in 1971 during her first pregnancy. Dr. Hammer ordered a blood test, which revealed that she had Rh-negative blood.[94] Dr. Hammer's office nurse erroneously marked Mrs. Kenyon's chart to indicate that she had Rh-positive blood.

On July 10, 1972, Mrs. Kenyon delivered a normal, healthy baby with Rh-positive blood. If Dr. Hammer would have known Mrs. Kenyon's Rh factor was negative, he would have administered RhoGAM. RhoGAM is administered to prevent immune reactions in subsequent pregnancies due to the mixing of a child's Rh-positive blood cells in the mother.

Mrs. Kenyon became pregnant with her second child in 1978. The baby was stillborn as a result of the destruction of its blood cells by the mother's Rh antibodies. To prevent future tragedies, Mrs. Kenyon underwent a tubal ligation.

Mr. and Mrs. Kenyon filed suit against Dr. Hammer, alleging vicarious liability for the acts of the nurse in incorrectly recording Mrs. Kenyon's Rh factor. The doctor was granted summary judgment by the trial court on the grounds that the action was barred by the statute of limitation. However, the case was reversed and remanded on a separate issue by the Arizona Supreme Court.

In obtaining a patient history, the nurse should also ask the patient about over-the-counter drugs. Benadryl, Actifed, Sudafed, Nuprin and Advil can now be purchased without a prescription, and patients often don't think of such over-the-counter drugs as medication. This is illustrated well by the following.

One day the emergency room was very quiet, and I volunteered to go the the medical floor to start an I.V. The nurses on the floor had been unsuccessful after several attempts and wanted to be sure to maintain the patient's blood level since she was on heparin.

After starting the I.V., I noticed three round white pills on the bedside table. I then asked the patient what the white pills were, and she replied they were aspirin. She had been taking twelve aspirin per day for her arthritis. Since she purchased the aspirin at the grocery store without a prescription, she did not regard it as medicine. She did not realize that the aspirin were contraindicated because she was on I.V. heparin.

OPERATING ROOM NURSES

One of the most common allegations against the operating room nurse revolves around the retention of foreign objects in patients after surgery. Liability usually results when needles, instruments, sponges or other foreign objects are left in a patient after surgery.[95] The Association of Operating Room Nurses, Inc., has promulgated standards and recommended practices with which operating room nurses should be familiar.[96]

The recommended practices outline procedures to be used in accounting for sponges, needles and instruments during surgery. Safe practice ensuring high-quality care for the patient undergoing surgery should include procedures for counting these items. The standards further require that each hospital have specific written policies and procedures which define the material to be counted, the times when counts must be made and the documentation required.

Many courts apply the doctrine of *res ipsa loquitur* to retained foreign bodies cases. This doctrine has been discussed previously in Chapter 2. Basically, *res ipsa loquitur* is used to shift the burden of proof to the nurse. Normally it is the *plaintiff* who must prove all of the elements of negligence. In *res ipsa loquitur* cases, the *nurse* must prove that she is *not* negligent.

Some states hold that the nurse is solely responsible for retained sponges and instruments. However, there are some states that hold the physician jointly or solely liable. For example, in the *Hestbeck* case, where a sponge was left in the patient during a cholecystectomy, the court awarded the plaintiff $12,500 in damages.[97] Sixty-five percent was applied against the surgeon and 35 percent against the nurse.

A California court held that a hospital could be liable for a clamp left in the patient even though it was not local practice at that time to do instrument counts.[98] The standard of practice can usually be evidenced by showing custom. However, custom is not an absolute defense. In this case, the court found that the custom was inadequate and that hospitals should require counts by their nurses.

In the 1985 case of *Rubeck v. Wright*, liability resulted after the nurse failed to inform the surgeon of an unaccounted sponge.[99] The radiologist was also held liable for failing to detect the sponge in postsurgical x-rays. The patient was a 74-year-old male who underwent surgery for a hernia repair. A lap mat measuring 30 × 30 centimeters was left inside.

Postoperatively, the patient developed anorexia, weight loss and fluid build-up in his legs. By the time the retained sponge was detected by another hospital, the patient was too weak for immediate surgery. Before the sponge could be removed, he died.

Two other 1985 cases held that the doctrine of *res ipsa loquitur* is applicable to medical malpractice involving leaving surgical instruments or supplies inside the body. Both cases involved leaving a sponge inside the patient following a cesarean section.[100]

As previously stated, leaving foreign objects in the patient undergoing surgery is a common cause of liability among operating room nurses. Either the nurse fails to count the sponges or does so incorrectly. Another example is the *Truhitte* case, where the nurse reported that the sponge count was correct.[101] The patient who had surgery for a vaginal hysterectomy, subsequently experienced abdominal pain, and it was discovered that a long narrow sponge known as a "GYN tape" had been left in the patient's abdomen. The patient suffered a total bowel perforation as a complication of the retained sponge.

The jury found that the nurse was 55 percent liable and the physician 45 percent liable, and specifically found that the nurse was under the control of the hospital and was not an agent for the physician.

The hospital's position was that the physician should be totally liable under the "captain-of-the-ship doctrine." The trial judge agreed and reapportioned the negligence, making the physician 100 percent negligent. The physician had participated in the sponge count.

The captain-of-the-ship doctrine has been previously discussed in Chapter 3. It is a doctrine in which the physician, as captain, is held liable for the actions of all members of the health team. It is an expansion of the borrowed-servant doctrine. The captain-of-the-ship doctrine has, for the most part, been discarded or severely eroded by most of the states.

Under this doctrine, the surgeon was responsible for all the negligent acts of the nurses. It was felt that the surgeon should be responsible since he or she is viewed as the person "in charge." Also, surgery is a special situation because the unconscious patients cannot assist themselves and are totally dependent on another for their safety.

The reason that the captain-of-the-ship doctrine has eroded is historical in nature.[102] This doctrine arose at a time when most hospitals enjoyed charitable immunity, and the courts wanted to give the patient some avenue for recovery. Since charitable immunity is no longer present, the need for the captain-of-the-ship doctrine is no longer present.

Another area of alleged negligence against operating room nurses concerns burns during surgery. These have been discussed in detail in the earlier section on burns to patients.

ORTHOPEDIC NURSES

One of the most common areas where there are findings of liability against orthopedic nurses involves the failure to monitor and report changes in the patient's circulation. The *Darling* case, which has been discussed previously, is illustrative of this point.[103] In *Darling*, the patient had a cast on his leg. The nurse failed to perform circulation checks. The patient's cast occluded his blood flow, which resulted in below-the-knee amputation.

In the *Kolakowski* case,[104] the patient had undergone a diskectomy. Several hours after the operation, he complained to the nurse that he could not bend his left leg and that his right side was weak and numb. The nurse charted his complaints four times over the next four hours. Once the nurse attempted to call the neurosurgeon but was unable to locate him.

The neurosurgeon saw the patient the next day and attributed his symptoms to spinal cord edema. He was taken to surgery two days later, when extruded bits of the disk were removed. The patient was left a quadriplegic as a result.

The court held that the nurses were under a duty to report the unusual signs and symptoms to the physician. The nurses breached their duty to the patient by their failure to timely notify the physician of the change in condition, the court said.

OBSTETRICAL NURSES

There are a number of cases against obstetrical nurses for failure to adequately observe and monitor patients on Pitocin. For example, in *Long*, a patient in active labor was admitted to the hospital. The nurse started an I.V. drip of Pitocin about an hour later.[105] The mother testified that no one monitored her contractions for the next two hours. The nurse's notes did not reflect any monitoring during this period. The patient experienced severe abdominal cramping. The child was born with cerebral palsy.

Testimony was presented that the infant's oxygen supply was diminished by the severe uterine contractions caused by the Pitocin, and the infant's cerebral

164

palsy was the result of the anoxic episode. The jury found for the plaintiff and awarded $350,000.

In *Mertsaris*, the plaintiff was awarded $7.5 million due to the defendant's failure to monitor the patient while the Pitocin drip was infusing.[106]

In the *Stack* case, the physicians and the hospital were found liable for failure to monitor the administration of Pitocin.[107] The Pitocin I.V. drip was started, and the records reflect that for the next three hours the patient was not checked. Following delivery, the patient began to bleed heavily, necessitating a hysterectomy. The patient required a blood transfusion. She contracted hepatitis from the blood and suffered a partial hearing loss in both ears.

The American College of Obstetricians and Gynecologists (ACOG) has promulgated standards for obstetric-gynecologic services. The 1982 standards indicate the following:

> [I]nduction or augmentation of labor with oxytocin should be inititated only after the attending physician has determined that it is required for the benefit of the mother or fetus. When labor is augmented, the obstetrician should review the course of labor, examine the patient and establish the indication and plan of action. The patient must be examined prior to starting the infusion. Examination of the patient may be delegated to another physician or a qualified nurse if the obstetrician has examined the patient within the last four hours.[108]

The 1982 standards further dictate that only qualified personnel familiar with effects of oxytocin agents and able to identify both maternal and fetal complications should be in attendance while oxytocin agents are being administered. Once oxytocin has been started, a responsible physician should be present in the labor area during the first twenty minutes to manage any unexpected effects. Thereafter, the obstetrician should be readily accessible for the management of any complications that may arise.

Oxytocin should be administered by the I.V. route only, the ACOG standards state. An I.V.A.C. or I.V. infusion control device should be used to ensure the correct rate. An electronic fetal monitor should also be used when oxytocin is adminstered. If this equipment is not available, the fetal heart tone, frequency and character of contractions, rate of oxytocin flow and maternal pulse should be recorded at regular intervals — preferably no less than every fifteen minutes. Maternal blood pressure should be recorded every half-hour and more frequently if indicated.

It is important to note that the ACOG revised these standards in 1985. For births occuring after 1985, these revised standards should be followed:

> Induction or augmentation of labor with oxytocin may be initiated only after a responsible physician has evaluated the patient, determined that induction or augmentation is beneficial to the mother or fetus, recorded the indication, and established a prospective plan of management. Only a physician who has privileges to perform cesarean deliveries should initiate these procedures. A physician or qualfied nurse should examine the patient vaginally immediately prior to the oxytocin infusion.

> A written protocol for the preparation and administration of the oxytocin solution should be established by the obstetric department in each institution. Oxytocin should be administered only intravenously, with a device that permits precise control of the flow rate. While oxytocin is being administered, an electronic fetal monitor should be used for continuous recording of fetal heart rate and uterine contractions.[109]

There are a number of recurring causes of obstetrical malpractice against physicians and nurses. Although this book is about *nursing* law, the obstetrical area is a prime example of a situation where *everyone* who has cared for the plaintiff is included in the lawsuit. It has almost gotten to the point that whenever there is a brain-damaged baby, there is concern that a lawsuit may be filed. It is for this reason that both nurses and physicians should be jointly aware of the recurring areas of obstetrical liability. The following are some examples:

1. **Ante partum care**
   a. Teratogenesis
   b. Toxemia of pregnancy
   c. Amniocentesis
   d. Ectopic pregnancy
   e. Fetal maturity
   f. Chorioamnionitis

2. **Labor**
   a. Oxytocin drugs, induction of labor
   b. Cephalopelvic disproportion
   c. Fetal distress
   d. Fetal monitoring
   e. Placental hemorrhage
   f. Prolonged (post maturity) pregnancy
   g. Breech presentation
   h. Labor difficulties and dystocia
      — uterine dysfunction
      — uteroplacental dysfunction
      — forceps operation
      — prolapse of the umbilical cord
      — abruptio placentae and placenta previa
   i. Obstetrical anesthesia
   j. Cesarean section

3. **Newborn and postpartum care**
   a. Resuscitation and immediate care of newborn
   b. Hemolytic disease of the newborn
   c. Postpartum hemorrhage

Recurring Obstetrical Malpractice

This discussion of obstetrical nursing has been broken down into three phases: ante partum care, labor, and newborn and postpartum care. There are a number of areas of care that are the source of recurrent obstetrical malpractice. Hopefully, by making the practitioner aware of these volatile areas, malpractice incidents can be reduced.

Ante partum Care

The ante partum or prenatal care phase is considered to be from the time the pregnancy is confirmed until the onset of labor. There are six significant areas of recurring malpractice associated with the prenatal period.

Teratogenesis is a term that denotes the physical defects that occur in the fetus *in utero*. Generally, the cause of the majority of congenital malformations appears to be dual in nature. Both environmental and genetic factors are known to exist.

The embryo's susceptibility to a known teratogen also depends on the developmental age of the fetus.[110] To cause a congenital malformation, the teratogen must be in a specific amount and administered during the period when the embryo is at a susceptable stage of development.[111] Drugs administered in the first trimester and during organogenesis are considered to have the greatest teratogenetic effect. (Organogenesis is the development or growth of body organs which occurs during the thirteenth to fifty-sixth day after fertilization. The embryo is sensitive to teratogens during this time.)[112] Therefore, it is considered to be a deviation from the standard of care to administer any drugs to a pregnant woman in early pregnancy unless "urgently indicated."[113]

Drugs that are administered later on can also affect fetal functioning. Many will recall the thalidomide babies. Alcohol, folic acid, aminopterin, methotrexate, androgens, progestogens, anti-thyroid drugs, iodides, barbiturates and smoking are known to produce fetal malformation.[114] Bendectin has been implicated as a teratogen by some researchers. However, other studies suggest that Bendectin does not significantly affect the fetus.[115]

Toxemia of pregnancy is the second area of recurring malpractice associated with the prenatal period. This, of course, is a complication of pregnancy that occurs during the third trimester. It is a hypertensive disorder which in the past claimed a number of maternal lives. Today, many experts are advocating that this disorder is "largely preventable."[116]

Pre-eclampsia is a toxemia of pregnancy diagnosed on the basis of hypertension, proteinuria and/or edema that occurs after the twentieth week of pregnancy. Untreated, it can lead to eclampsia with its seizure disorder. Therefore, the main objective of the treatment of pre-eclampsia is the prevention of eclampsia, and as one leading author wrote, "The obstetrical failure to prevent eclampsia represents a grievous failure of antepartum care."[117]

Incidentally, maternal deaths are categorized by maternal mortality committees as to whether they are preventable or not preventable. Minnesota and Ohio have led the United States in specifying problems that pertain to maternal deaths.[118] In the past thirty-five years, hemorrhage, infection, toxemia and anesthesia have been the four leading causes of maternal deaths.[119] A survey of maternal mortality in major hospitals reflects a significant decline in maternal deaths from infection, hemorrhage and toxemia. However, it is noted that continued vigilance is necessary since 58 percent of direct obstetric deaths were considered to be preventable.[120]

Amniocentesis involves the removal of amniotic fluid from the intrauterine cavity. Amniocentesis is one of the advances that has altered the practice of medical genetics, and, like both ultrasound and fetoscopy, has increased the investigation and early detection of congenital anomalies.

A recent study of 3,000 amniocentesis procedures concluded that "prenatal diagnosis is safe, highly reliable, and extremely accurate."[121] In 1978, the National Institute of Health noted and supported two studies that showed that midtrimester amniocentesis does not increase neonatal or maternal morbidity or mortality. The institute also discounted a British study that showed significant increases in fetal deaths and obstetrical complications. Therefore, amniocentesis is "an acceptable part of clinical practice for the specific assessment of certain at-risk fetal conditions in specified pregnancies."[122] The American College of Obstetricians and Gynecologists concur in the view that amniocentesis is part of the acceptable medical standards. It also adds that the patient has a right to make decisions about the use of these techniques.[123]

An *ectopic pregnancy* refers to implantation of the zygote outside of the uterus or in an abnormal location within the uterus. The incidence of ectopic pregnancy has almost doubled in the past ten years and accounts for 10 percent of all maternal deaths. Early diagnosis and aggressive surgical management have been estimated to save as many as 75 percent of all patients. Irregular bleeding and pain are two symptoms which warrant an evaluation for ectopic pregnancy. Leukocytosis, shock, decreased hemoglobin and hematocrit, and decreased blood pressure may also be present. Only approximately 75 percent of all the patients have the classic triad of pain, bleeding and an adnexal mass. The risk of recurrent ectopic pregnancy is increased after any tubal surgery,[124] which may account for the increased incidence of this problem. The primary treatment for ectopic pregnancies remains surgical.[125]

When confronted with the proper symptoms, the obstetrician may engage in a process of differential diagnosis to rule out P.I.D., threatened or incomplete abortion, ovarian cyst or acute appendicitis. If the practitioner is faced with a situation where the patient dies during the differential evaluation, no matter what the problem is, he/she should point this out.

Fetal maturity evaluation is another area where there has been recurring obstetrical malpractice. Obviously, the goal is to deliver the fetus at term. A term infant is one born after thirty-seven weeks through forty-one weeks of gestation. A preterm or premature infant is one born after nineteen but before thirty-seven completed weeks of gestation, with weight of less than 5½ pounds (2,500 grams) at birth. An infant is post-term if born after the beginning of the forty-second week of gestation.[126]

Liability in this area can result from inadequate objective history taking and serial clinical examinations. Normally these tests start in early pregnancy and, with appropriately timed follow-up exams, will yield an accurate assessment of gestational age. Clinical evaluation of menstrual history and uterine size, sonography and amniocentesis aid in an accurate prediction of maturity of pulmonary function. The measurement of the fetal biparietal diameter before the third trimester and, of course, the use of multiple tests give more reliable results than any single test.[127]

An important cause of perinatal morbidity and mortality is the premature rupture of membranes. There is currently much debate on the proper treatment of this occurrence. Some sources advocate that if labor does not begin within twelve hours after the premature rupture, labor should be induced. In any event, there are a large number of cases that evolve from the treatment of the premature rupture of membranes.

One authority advocates that in repeat elective cesarean sections, an amniocentesis should be performed to preclude inadvertent early delivery of the fetus.[128] The goal is to make sure that in this situation the obstetrician is not iatrogenically delivering a premature infant.

Legal problems can also result from the post-term baby. The post-term baby is often in the high-weight category, which can cause dystocia and birth injury. These pregnancies are often monitored with repeated estriol measurements and an oxytocin challenge test, which helps to determine whether the fetus can withstand the stress of labor. It is standard to admit the patient to the hospital for delivery once forty-two weeks of gestation have been completed.

The specific infections of the membranes, amniotic fluid and fetus are included in the general term of *chorioamnionitis*. Infection is most commonly seen following rupture of the membranes. The longer the time period after the rupture, the more likely that chorioamnionitis will occur.

Signs may include an increased pulse, fever, cloudy or purulent amniotic fluid, and uterine irritability. Patients with amnionitis can go on to develop septic shock without adequate treatment.

Chorioamnionitis can be minimized by observing strict indications for the vaginal procedure and using aseptic technique.[129] Vaginal exams should only be performed when absolutely necessary.

Guidelines for Perinatal Care

The *Guidelines for Perinatal Care* are put out by the American Academy of Pediatrics and the American College of Obstetricians and Gynecologists. Adherence to these standards helps the practitioner to support the view that the standard of care has been met. If the practitioner is involved in a malpractice action, it is important to point out these standards to the attorney representing him/her in order to indicate the practitioner's compliance. Also, any medical articles that explain the issue and that would help to support the care rendered should be provided to the attorney.

Often, the practitioner who is faced with a legal malpractice action tends to withdraw or ignore the problem. It is not comforting for anyone to be sued. Unfortunately, many nonmeritorious cases are settled because the practitioner does not take an active interest in the matter or withdraws. If faced with a frivolous claim, the practitioner should review and summarize the records, point out the strengths of the case to his/her attorney, and provide the medical literature to support his/her view.

Below are a few examples of some of the useful information that is contained in the *Guidelines for Perinatal Care*:

1. Organization of perinatal health care
2. Physical facilities for perinatal care

3. Personnel for perinatal service
   a. Nursing and medical staff for the different level hospitals
   b. In-service and continuing education (states that there should be at least one joint teaching session each month concerning maternal and neonatal health)
4. Perinatal care services
   a. Ante partum care (history, establishing the EDC, physical exam, lab tests, etc.)
   b. Intrapartum care (admission procedure, medical records, patient consent forms, managing labor and delivery, assessing fetal maturity before a c-section, vaginal delivery after a cesarean childbirth, Apgar scores)
   c. Normal postpartum and newborn care
5. Maternal and neonatal follow-up care
   a. Maternal follow-up care
   b. Normal neonatal follow-up care
   c. High-risk neonatal follow-up care
   d. Child abuse
6. Control of infections in obstetric and nursing areas
   a. Colonization of newborn infants
   b. Surveillance for nosocomial infection
   c. Measures for prevention and control of infection
      — hand washing
      — dress codes
      — preventive measures of an O.B. service (vaginal exams, fetal monitoring, intrauterine pressure and prophylactic antibiotics for O.B. patients)
      — neonates (invasive procedures on neonates, intravascular flush solution, antibiotics for neonates)
   d. Specific infections during pregnancy
      — gonorrhea
      — herpes simplex
      — rubella
      — hepatitis
      — group B streptococcus
      — cytomegaly, toxoplasmosis
      — TB, varicella-zoster
      — chorioamnionitis
7. Maternal and newborn nutrition
   a. Nutrition history
   b. Weight gain
   c. Specific nutritional needs (iron, folic acid, etc.)
   d. Lactation and the nursing mother
8. Interhospital care of the perinatal patient
   a. Indications for tranfer
   b. The organized approach to transport
   c. Patient care in transit

9. Evaluation of perinatal care
   a. Definitions
   b. Statistical evaluation
10. Special considerations
   a. Antenatal detection of genetic disorders
      — amniocentesis
      — fetoscopy
      — laboratory studies
   b. Clinical considerations in the use of oxygen
   c. Hyperbilirubinemia
   d. Thermal regulation
      — hyperthermia
      — hypothermia
   e. Stillbirth, neonatal deaths and congenital abnormalities
   f. Adoption
11. Appendix
   a. Categories of perinatal services
   b. Equipment and supplies for resuscitation
   c. Preconceptional care
   d. Perinatal conditions that increase perinatal morbidity
   e. Prevention of opthalmia neonatorum
   f. Maternal consultation/transfer record

Pregnant Patient Bill of Rights

The International Childbirth Education Association has promulgated the following bill of rights for the pregnant patient:

(1) The Pregnant Patient has the right, prior to the administration of any drug or procedure, to be informed by the health professional caring for her of any potential direct or indirect effects, risks, or hazards to herself or her unborn or newborn infant, which may result from the use of a drug or procedure prescribed for, or administered to her during pregnancy, labor, birth or lactation.

(2) The Pregnant Patient has the right, prior to any proposed therapy, to be informed, not only of the benefits, risks and hazards of the proposed therapy but also of known alternative therapy, such as available childbirth education classes which could help to prepare the Pregnant Patient physically and mentally to cope with the discomfort or stress of pregnancy and the experience of childbirth, thereby reducing or eliminating her need for drugs and obstetric intervention. She could be offered such information early in her pregnancy in order that she may make a reasoned decision.

(3) The Pregnant Patient has the right, prior to the adminstration of any drug, to be informed by the health professional, who is prescribing or administering the drug to her, that any drug which she receives during pregnancy, labor and birth, no matter how or when the drug is taken or administered, may adversely affect her unborn baby, directly or indirectly, and that there is no drug or chemical which has been proven safe for the unborn child.

(4) The Pregnant Patient has the right if cesarean birth is anticipated, to be informed prior to the administration of any drug, and preferably prior to her hospitalization, that minimizing her, and in turn her baby's intake of nonessential pre-operative medicine will benefit her baby.

(5) The Pregnant Patient has the right, prior to the administration of a drug or procedure, to be informed of the areas of uncertainty if there is no properly controlled follow-up research which has established the safety of the drug or procedure with regard to

its direct and/or indirect effects on the physiological, mental and neurological development of the child exposed, via the mother, to the drug or procedure during pregnancy, labor, birth or lactation (this would apply to virtually all drugs and the vast majority of obstetric procedures).

(6) The Pregnant Patient has the right prior to the administration of any drug, to be informed of the brand name and generic name of the drug in order that she may advise the health professional of any past adverse reaction to the drug.

(7) The Pregnant Patient has the right to determine for herself, without pressure, whether she will accept the risks inherent in the proposed therapy or refuse a drug or procedure.

(8) The Pregnant Patient has the right to know the name and qualification of the individual administering a medication or procedure to her during labor or birth.

(9) The Pregnant Patient has the right to be informed, prior to the administration of any procedure, whether that procedure is being administered to her for her or her baby's benefit (medically indicated) or as an elective procedure (for convenience, teaching purposes, or research).

(10) The Pregnant Patient has the right to be accompanied during the stress of labor and birth by someone she cares for, and to whom she looks for emotional comfort and encouragement.

(11) The Pregnant Patient has the right, after appropriate medical consultation, to choose a position for labor and for birth which is least stressful to her baby and to herself.

(12) The Obstetric Patient has the right to have her baby cared for at her bedside if her baby is normal, and to feed her baby according to her baby's needs rather than according to the hospital regimen.

(13) The Obstetric Patient has the right to be informed, in writing, of the name of the person who actually delivered her baby and the professional qualifications of that person. This information should also be on the birth certificate.

(14) The Obstetric Patient has the right to be informed if there is any known or indicated aspect of her baby's care which may cause her or her baby later difficulty or problems.

(15) The Obstetric Patient has the right to have her and her baby's hospital medical records complete, accurate and legible, and to have their record, including Nurses' Notes, retained by the hospital until the child reaches at least the age of majority, or alternatively to have the records offered to her before they are destroyed.

(16) The Obstetric Patient, both during and after her hospital stay, has the right to have access to her complete hospital medical records, including Nurses' Notes, and to receive a copy upon payment of a reasonable fee and without incurring the expense of retaining an attorney.[130]

The International Association of Insurance Counsel recently published an interim report of a committee of the National Association of Insurance Commissioners which studied 295 claims involving babies with neurological deficiencies.[131] The committee that issued the report was composed of physicians, attorneys and claims experts. The report was made with the encouragement and support of the American College of Obstetricians and Gynecologists.

The report found the obstetrical area to be one in which practitioners are highly vulnerable to liability. This is partially based on the fact that many states have longer statutes of limitations for minors. Also, many plaintiffs' lawyers may accept a case involving a brain-damaged baby regardless of liability because of the potential for sympathy and large damage awards. There have been many educational programs and books that teach lawyers about the management of pregnancy, labor and delivery. In fact, the July 1986 edition of *Medical Liability Advisory Service* reports that the Practicing Law Institute now offers a 5½-hour video cassette titled *Brain-Damaged Infants: Case Evaluation and Management.*[132]

Obstetrics is in a constant state of change, with abandonment or modification of previously accepted procedures such as electric induction and mid-forceps delivery, the increased incidence of cesarean sections, the decreased use of analgesia and anesthesia, and the newer modalities such as ultrasound and fetal monitoring. Add to these the enhanced patient expectations, the right of the patient to be informed, media education, childbirth preparation classes like Lamaze and fathers in the delivery room. This results in greater liability exposure in the obstetrical arena.

In its report, the NAIC committee made nine observations and suggestions. These were primarily directed to physicians but have a direct impact on nursing.

The *first* observation was that the documentation appearing in patient medical records was inadequate. There was insufficient documentation on the ante partum record regarding the patient's history. The committee found that in 56 percent of the cases, the mother was not even asked about smoking habits. In 65 percent of the cases, there was no documentation about alcohol consumption. Obstetrical office nurses could remedy this situation by drafting standard sheets that list all vital information, and thus prevent important omissions.

The committee also found that the description and timing of significant events before and during labor were incomplete. Infant records were sketchy and of little assistance in establishing the infant's condition postpartum. This type of situation makes it very difficult to defend a claim, for example, that neurological problems were due to birth trauma.

The committee recommended that all physicians and nurses must improve their record keeping in these vital areas. This is not only in the interest of good patient care, but it also helps to put them in a more defensible medical-legal position, the committee said.

The *second* observation focused on the timely identification and management of high-risk patients. The primary problems were said to be the identification of risk factors, underemployment of antenatal screening and inadequate consultation.

The NAIC committee reiterated the importance of identifying, documenting and monitoring the high-risk patient throughout pregnancy. This encompasses necessary consultation and referral to tertiary centers where appropriate.

The *third* observation concerned dysmaturity, which was noted to be a significant problem. The committee urged the use of all available modalities to confirm the presence of prematurity and postmaturity.

Ultrasonography was used in 32 percent of all cases studied. It was used in 23 percent of the cases to determine fetal age. However, in several of the cases it was not done early enough (before the thirtieth week of gestation) to be of value. In other cases, there was no follow-up sonography when a need for it was indicated.

The committee emphasized the use of ultrasound as one important method to be employed in cases where there is doubt about gestational age. However, clinical evaluation is always essential.

The *fourth* area concerned the problems of communication among partners in group practice. This also included problems in communication with consultants and covering physicians. The NAIC committee urged doctors to carefully coordinate patient care with partners, consultants and covering physicians. The office nurse can be of assistance in this matter by being observant and bringing any questions regarding the patient's care to her physician employer.

The *fifth* area discussed was liability exposure resulting from serious communication problems between obstetricians and pediatricians. This resulted in the absence of the pediatrician in the delivery room during complicated cases.

The committee recommended notifying pediatricians early and securing their continued involvement. Timely follow-up reports from pediatricians to obstetricians were noted to be most important.

Sixth, the committee observed that the belated arrival of the physician during the labor process increased liability exposure. This was true whether or not the reasons for the delay were valid. Accordingly, the committee urged physicians to be responsive to a nurse's report about the patient's condition and to be prepared to be in attendance or provide for immediate coverage.

Seventh, the committee found the use of fetal monitoring and the interpretation of tapes as key factors in cases involving fetal distress. The data showed inadequate use of internal fetal monitors. Of the 295 cases studied, external monitoring was done in 50.8 percent of the cases. Internal monitoring was only done in 22.7 percent of the cases.

The committee felt that electronic fetal monitoring is of great value during labor. It particularly urged the use of internal monitoring when the need is indicated. Personnel competent to read the fetal monitor strips should be available at all times, the committee said.

The nurse, physician and hospital should also be alerted to the need to save the fetal monitor strips. Some cases have been harmed because the monitor tapes had been discarded.

Eighth, the committee noted the claims it studied were replete with allegations of delay. These included delay in appreciating and responding to evidence of fetal stress. There were also delays in arriving at a decision to do a c-section and in performing the c-section once the decision was made.

Last, but not least, the committee observed with dismay that in many cases, subsequent treating pediatricians have attributed infants' neurological problems to "hypoxia during the birth process" or "birth trauma." This is charted by some pediatricians without even thinking about it and without "having conducted any investigation." Therefore, these diagnoses are made without any medical justification. Careless statements such as these make the defense of a case very difficult.

The committee was not suggesting that a diagnosis, scientifically determined, should be withheld. Rather, it was suggesting that pediatricians should be judicious in this regard and refrain from making loose statements without foundation.

Any attorney who has defended many brain-damaged baby cases can appreciate the wisdom of the advice given by the NAIC committee. Physicians and nurses can significantly decrease their liability exposure by following this advice.

Also, it is important to consult an excellent book, *Perinatal and Prenatal Factors Associated with Brain Disorders* by Robin Freeman. It has been extremely helpful in defending brain-damaged baby cases. It points out recent research which has demonstrated that often the brain damage occurs in the first trimester and is unrelated to the delivery process. This book, released in April 1986, is an excellent resource and is available for a fee from the National Institute of Health in Bethesda, Maryland.

There is also an article which may be of particular interest, entitled "The Lawyer's Perspective on the Use of Ultrasound in Obstetrics and Gynecology."

It appeared in the October 1985 edition of *Law, Medicine, and Health Care*. Another excellent book available is titled *Obstetrics, Gynecology, and the Law* by Feinberg. (See also the book *Handling Birth Trauma Cases* by Stanley Schwartz. It was published by John Wilery & Sons Inc. in 1985.) Last is an article entitled "Electronic Fetal Monitoring and Obstetrical Injury," which appeared in the June 1985 edition of *Law, Medicine, and Health Care*. This would be important to read in light of the many recent cases filed in this area.

ANESTHESIA ERRORS BY A CRNA

The letters *CRNA* stand for a "certified registered nurse anesthetist." A nurse anesthetist is a registered nurse who has completed a program of clinical training in anesthesia. Most states have a statute concerning the nurse anesthetist's practice.

Nurse anesthetists function in a high-risk class. In fact, there are more cases involving nurse anesthetists than any other nursing subspecialty. A common cause of liability among nurse anesthetists and anesthesiologists is the misplaced endotracheal tube. The presence of the endotracheal tube in the esophagus instead of in the trachea prevents oxygenation of vital tissues. If left undetected, the patient can die. Death in this situation is frequently due to anoxic encephalopathy, or brain death.

Cases of liability resulting from such errors have large damages attributable to them. For example, permanent brain damage was sustained by a 48-year-old patient after he was given an overdose of narcotics by the nurse anesthetist during surgery.[133] At the completion of surgery, an inadequate amount of reversal drugs was given. He suffered a respiratory depression that lasted four or five hours. He was awarded $750,000.

In another case, the plaintiff was awarded $500,000 due to the negligence of the nurse anesthetist, who was having difficulty ventilating the patient, and failed to call the anesthesiologist for assistance.[134] The patient died shortly thereafter. In *Hughes*, an attempted nasal intubation failed.[135] This resulted in the patient's death. An out-of-court settlement was reached for $264,728.

In *Parks v. Perry*, Mrs. Parks went to surgery for a hysterectomy by Dr. Perry.[136] The nurse anesthetist administered a general anesthetic and placed the patient in the lithotomy position. The next day the patient experienced numbness and weakness of the right fourth and fifth fingers. She was diagnosed as having ulnar nerve damage in her right arm.

Mrs. Parks sued the surgeons, the nurse anesthetist and the hospital. The defendants filed a motion for a summary judgment, which was granted by the trial court. The court of appeals affirmed the granting of summary judgment in favor of Dr. Perry. However, the supreme court stated that the *res ipsa loquitur* doctrine applied. (This doctrine was previously discussed in Chapter 2.) Therefore, there remained a genuine issue of fact for the jury with respect to the care rendered by the nurse anesthetist.

In *St. Clair Medical Center*, the patient was admitted for an arthroscopy.[137]

The nurse anesthetists were not employed by the hospital but by a professional service corporation named Cave Run Clinic.

Generally, patients undergoing an arthroscopy would have a spinal anesthetic. However, Ed Johnson, the nurse anesthetist, decided that since Mr. Williams had previously had a myelogram, he would administer a general anesthetic.

Johnson had just graduated from nurse anesthetist school and was uncertified. He was given temporary privileges which were limited to those instances where he was under the direct supervision of Jerri Reis, a CRNA.

Johnson induced anesthesia in the absence of the CRNA and the surgeon. Shortly after the anesthetic was started, the nurse anesthetist noted that the patient was cyanotic from the head up. He asked the surgeon to step into the room. The patient went into a coma for ten days and then died.

Not all cases involving CRNAs result in liability. In *Airco*, a patient was given preoperative medication.[138] This depressed the patient's respirations. The CRNA placed the patient on a respirator. During the surgery, the respirator malfunctioned for several minutes. This resulted in serious lung injury and irreversible brain damage to the patient.

A hose had been attached to the right-hand part of the selector valve. The other end of the hose was open so that it could later be connected to the absorber. The other hose had erroneously been connected to the middle part.

The trial court found the respirator manufacturer liable, and said the device was inherently dangerous. The manufacturer appealed, alleging the damage resulted from the negligence of the nurse anesthetist. The Supreme Court affirmed the judgment of the trial court.

In *Barth*, a 5-year-old went in for an open reduction of her arm, which was injured when she fell off her bicycle.[139] Mr. Rock, a nurse anesthetist, administered a general anesthetic with sodium pentothal, succinylcholine chloride drip and nitrous oxide. The child began to move during the surgery and additional Pentothal was given. Immediately after, her blood pressure and pulse dropped. Atropine was immediately administered without response. Epinephrine was administered with an immediate response.

The case was tried before a jury for three weeks. The jury returned a verdict for the surgeon, hospital and nurse anesthetist. The plaintiff moved for a new trial, which was granted. The defendants appealed, but the Court of Appeals affirmed the trial court's order for a new trial. An expert had reported during the trial that there are fifty-five documented cases of sodium pentothal reactions. However, it was later determined there were fifty-five reported allergic reactions to barbiturates in general. Since this information was not heard by a jury, ordering a new trial was proper.

In *Forray*, a nurse anesthetist was sued after the posterior aspect of the patient's trachea was perforated during a tracheotomy.[140] The surgeon indicated he thought the tear occurred when the tracheotomy tube was inserted.

The medical malpractice panel found no negligence on the part of the CRNA. Her motion for summary judgment was granted by the trial court and affirmed by the supreme court.

The standard of care for nurse anesthetists was described in a 1980 Michigan case.[141] Nurse anesthetists are professionals who have expertise which is similar to the practice of medicine. Their responsibilities are greater than that of floor nurses. Since their responsibilities lie in the area of "medical" expertise, the standard of care is based on the skill and care normally expected of those with the same education and training.

In *Otts v. Bryant*, the patient was scheduled for orthopedic surgery.[142] During the patient's surgery, the CRNA had difficulty ventilating the patient through the endotracheal tube. Dr. Lane, an anesthesiologist, was in the next room administering anesthesia. He was not called by the CRNA until Otts suffered a cardiac arrest. After surgery, he suffered severe brain damage and was in a coma until he died six weeks later.

The plaintiff alleged that Otts' death resulted from an uncorrected airway obstruction. The plaintiff's expert alleged that the failure of the CRNA to call for help at the moment she had difficulty ventilating Otts was a departure from acceptable medical standards. The defendant alleged that Otts' death was caused by an air embolus.

The case went to trial but the jury was unable to reach a verdict. During the second trial, the jury returned a verdict in favor of the plaintiff in the amount of $500,000.

In *Brown v. Allen Sanitarium, Inc.*, the plaintiff died of a cardiac arrest after receiving a general anesthetic.[143] The diagnosis was an adverse Anectine reaction. The plaintiff alleged negligence on the part of Dr. Chillow, who did the preoperative visit, for failing to perceive from the decedent's medical history that a problem could occur if an Anectine reaction was experienced because of a known prior reaction to sulfa drugs.

An autopsy was performed which showed the decedent had a cardiac condition known as myocarditis. The pathologist concluded in his report that the patient would have survived had it not been for the inflammation of the heart muscle.

At trial, the court entered judgment for the hospital, physician and CRNA. The decedent's family appealed.

There are numerous cases against nurse anesthetists regarding failure to intubate the patient while administering a general anesthetic, which results in aspiration pneumonitis. The 1986 case of *Keys v. Mercy Hospital of New Orleans* is an example.[144] The court awarded the decedent's family $350,000, and noted that pregnant patients, like the one in this case, pose a high risk of regurgitation during surgery.

In summary, a nurse anesthetist is a recognized specialist, who has a duty to carefully monitor the patient undergoing anesthesia. Communication should be made with the surgeon about the anesthetic agent being used. This should be done at the earliest feasible time should a complication arise. Reasonable care must be taken in the administration and selection of the statutes affecting nurse anesthetists' practice.

OCCUPATIONAL HEALTH NURSES

Today, occupational health nurses may be employed not only in the industrial work place, but also in a variety of other settings, such as employee health services for hospitals, colleges and health care centers. Some have positions with enormous responsibility.

The Occupational Safety and Health Act (OSHA) of 1970 has resulted in an increase in the number of occupational health nurses.[145] Under OSHA, industry is required to provide a safe and healthful environment, and the occupational health nurse is instrumental in maintaining professional services— from caring for injured workers to counseling and health education. Many occupational health nurses are also responsible for performing pre-employment physicals and periodic health assessments.[146]

It is important for the occupational health nurse to have written policies and procedures upon which to rely. These should be medically approved by the company's physician. All standing orders should also be written, signed and dated. All policies and orders must be within the scope of the state's nurse practice act. Without such protocol, a nurse risks being found guilty of practicing medicine without a license.[147] These policies and standards should be consistent with industry standards and what is advocated in nursing textbooks.[148] They should also be consistent with the OSHA standards.

Negligence actions are the most common allegations against occupational health nurses. Such actions often arise because it can be difficult for the nurse to ascertain when the patient should be referred for further care. The *Cooper v. National Motor Bearing Co., Inc.* case is illustrative of this point.[149]

In this case, the nurse, acting under standing order, treated the patient's puncture wound. The worker had sustained the wound to his head after a piece of metal had been dropped by another worker. The nurse cleansed the area with an antiseptic and applied a bandage. The wound was not explored for a possible foreign body. It appeared to be closed and healing but a small red area remained. It began to spread and became puffy. After ten months, the worker asked the nurse to send him to a physician because the wound was not healing properly. The physician performed a biopsy of the area, which revealed a basal cell carcinoma. After the growth was surgically removed, the patient sued the nurse and her employer.

The nurse had failed to recognize one of the seven classic danger signals of cancer: a sore that does not heal. She also had failed to refer the patient for follow-up treatment when his condition was not improving. The court said:

> A nurse in order to administer first aid properly and effectively must make a sufficient diagnosis to enable her to apply the appropriate remedy. Usually she receives some history from the patient, inspects a wound, and bases her choice of treatment on the deductions thus made. She has been trained but to a lesser degree than a physician, in the recognition of symptoms of disease and injuries. She should be able to diagnose . . . sufficiently to know whether it is a condition within her authority to treat as a first aid case or whether it bears danger signs that should warn her to sent the patient to a physician.[150]

The nurse failed to formulate a diagnosis and violated the acceptable standard of care. Based on this deviation, the court awarded the plaintiff $15,000. This case illustrates well the principle that the occupational health nurse should refer any patient who is not responding to nursing treatment or whose diagnosis is uncertain.

The occupational health nurse should also be familiar with the workers' compensation laws in his/her state.[151] Generally, workers' compensation laws provide for a fixed schedule of benefits to the employee or the employee's dependents in case of industrial accidents or disease.[152] These laws are meant to compensate the employee for work-related injury or illness without regard to the negligence of either the employer or employee. This compensation is meant to be the sole remedy, and the employee then waives the right to sue his or her employer. In exchange, the employer cannot allege contributory or comparative negligence on the part of the employee. However, a few states still allow the worker to collect workers' compensation benefits and then later sue if the injury was intentionally caused.[153]

Most states grant immunity to the employer and co-workers of the injured worker when the injured worker receives workers' compensation benefits. Thus, if the nurse is a co-worker of the injured worker, she is generally immune.[154] This is why there are few cases of liability against occupational health nurses.

However, liability can attach against the occupational health nurse if she is not a co-worker or if she is an independent contractor. The nurse also does not have protection if excluded by the state's workers' compensation law. For example, in states such as Alabama, Arizona, Minnesota, Wisconsin, Nebraska, Rhode Island, South Dakota and Vermont, and under the Federal Employees' Compensation Act, only the employer has immunity.[155]

Another area of liability involving the occupational health nurse is the breach of the duty of confidentiality. Many occupational health nurses are involved in employee drug and alcohol testing or AIDS testing, which present confidentiality considerations. The information contained in the medical records is confidential, and many advocate that this information should not even be disclosed to the employer.[156] Physicians have been held liable for unwarranted disclosure, a risk which also could affect nurses.

The *Horne v. Patton* case illustrates well the physician's duty of confidentiality.[157] The Alabama Supreme Court held there was a confidential relationship between the doctor and the patient, even in the occupational setting. This imposed a duty on the physician not to disclose any information to the employer which was obtained in the course of treatment.

The physician had wrongfully disclosed to the employer that the employee suffered from a long-standing nervous condition which caused the employee to have feelings of anxiety and insecurity. Because of the disclosure of this information, the employee was dismissed. The court said that a physician who enters into a patient-physician relationship implicitly contracts to keep confidential all disclosed information.

The other area of liability exposure has to do with the occupational health nurse's responsibility to advise the physician of all abnormal findings. This duty to inform is present even if the finding regards an applicant who does not get the job or regards an employee who is seen for an independent problem. This has become a source of liability exposure in light of the fact that more nurses are conducting pre-employment or periodical physical exams.

This is illustrated well by the case of *Betesh v. United States*,[158] in which a widow brought a medical malpractice action against the United States. Her husband had had a chest x-ray done as part of a preinduction physical. Government doctors found an abnormality in the chest x-ray but failed to notify him. Her husband assumed that he was rejected because of a knee injury. Actually, he had Hodgkin's disease which was in an early, curable state when the chest x-ray was taken. However, when the doctors first notified him six months later, it had progressed to an incurable and terminal state.

The district court held the United States liable for the decendent's death. It found the doctors had violated the government regulation requiring physicians to notify rejected candidates who need immediate medical attention. The widow was awarded $100,000.

In *Coffee v. McDonnell-Douglas Corporation*,[159] a pilot sued, alleging that he should have been notified of an elevated sedimentation rate. Later, he was found to have multiple myeloma. The pilot was awarded damages resulting from the failure of physicians to discover the disease during his pre-employment physical. This physical was done to certify that he was physically fit to serve as a pilot. The lab result was never seen by the defendant corporation's medical personnel because its procedure allowed the report to be filed without evaluation.

SCHOOL NURSES

The decision of whether school nurses should administer medication to schoolchildren and other school personnel has always been a sensitive subject. Recently there have been new federal and state statutes requiring the mainstreaming of many physically handicapped children.[160] This has made the administration of medication and issue of even greater concern for the school nurse and school administrators.

One recent article reported that approximately one-half of all trainable mentally retarded students were receiving medication.[161] Many nurses express concern in administering medication for controversial disorders such as hyperactivity.

One author conducted a survey of all fifty states regarding the existence of medication-related procedures.[162] At least sixteen states have passed laws which set out guidelines for the administration of medication in the schools.[163] It is advisable for every school district to have a written policy on the administration of medication in the school. The policy should be consistent with any applicable state-required guidelines. Many policies include some of the following:

1. The school nurse or nurse's designee will assist in dispensing medication.
2. All medication, even over-the-counter medication, must be prescribed by a physician.
3. Assistance in dispensing medication must also be requested by the parent in writing.
4. The parent request should be written on a form which is approved by the board of education.
5. The parent's written request should include the following:
   (a) the signature of the parent;
   (b) the child's name;
   (c) name of medication;
   (d) parent's phone numbers, if any, and address;
   (e) dosage of medication;
   (f) route;

(g) date signed; and

(h) exculpatory clause regarding liability.

6. The physician's written form should include the following:

(a) name of child and address;

(b) name of drug;

(c) dosage;

(d) route;

(e) times of administration;

(f) any specific instructions for storage;

(g) possible side effects;

(h) parent's address and phone number, if any;

(i) action to be taken if side effects observed;

(j) date signed;

(k) physician's signature; and

(l) physician's phone number.

7. The nurse or his/her designee should be responsible for supervising the storage of the medication.

8. Medication must be in original containers (childproof) and have affixed labels including the student's name, name of medication, dosage, route and time of administration.

9. New request forms should be submitted each school year and as necessary for changes in medication order.

10. Accurate records must be kept in the student's file. This includes the name of the student, medication given, date and time.

11. In the case of an extreme allergic reaction, the nurse or nurse's designee shall immediately call the emergency squad.

12. If, in the judgment of the nurse, an injection of Adrenalin must be administered prior to the arrival of the squad, it should be given. (This should be established by a written standing order. Some prefer to use Ana-Kit or Epi-Pen.)

13. Medication should be stored in a secure location.

14. Provisions for the disposal of unused medication should be made.

Many states have passed laws requiring that school districts develop specific policies regarding the administration of medication. Additionally, the Joint Committee on Health Problems in Education of the National Education Society, the American Academy of Pediatrics and the American Medical Association have urged the adoption of such policies.[164]

In addition, the school nurse may be involved in performing clean intermittent catheterization for physically handicapped children. School nurses also provide nursing care for sick or injured students, help the physican with routine exams, give annual screening tests (such as vision, audiometry and scoliosis), enforce state immunization policies, counsel parents and students, and meet with staff about health problems and health education.

LIABILITY OF THE HOSPICE NURSE

Hospice Standards

It is a basic fact of life that even with the quality of modern medicine, a cure is not always possible. The hospice concept has provided a holistic approach to patient care by encompassing the medical, nursing, psychosocial and spiritual needs of terminally ill patients and their families. The hospice concept was developed to meet the specific needs of terminal cancer patients and patients with chronic diseases such as chronic obstructive pulmonary disease, cardiac disease and musculoskeletal disease. Recently, these patients and their families have embraced the hospice philosophy of palliation and comfort. It has helped to re-establish some dignity and autonomy in their lives.

Hospice care is a relatively new field. It has only been available in the United States since 1974,[165] when it was introduced because of public dissatisfaction with the care rendered to terminally ill patients in the hospital setting. The first hospice program was established at Connecticut Hospice of New Haven in conjunction with a study project at Yale University.[166] The 1974 National Health Planning and Resources Development Act mandated that health planning agencies encourage the development of less costly and more appropriate plans of care for the terminally ill. This was effective, and the number of hospice programs rose from one program in 1974 to more than 1,600 programs in 1985.[167] Before this time, little was known about hospice as a health care entity.

The National Hospice Organization (NHO) was formed in 1978. Its primary purpose was education and support. However, since that time the program has expanded to set standards for the development of hospice programs. Even though the NHO does not have any legal authority, it continues to oversee the development of hospice care and to suggest standards.

In June 1980, the General Accounting Office did a survey on existing U.S. hospices.[168] Seven of the programs surveyed required a certificate of need from their respective states.[169] The Health Resources Administration and the Department of Health and Human Services advised state certificate-of-need agencies to treat hospice programs as developmental rather than service efforts.

In the April 1986, edition of *Nursing Management*, author Marilyn Halthons wrote that hospice care was rendered to provide support to the patient and family during the dying process and to maintain the integrity of the dying person. Some commonly reported goals of the hospice include the following:

1. To help the patient and the family cope with the approach of death.

2. To help the patient live as fully as possible within that individual's physical and emotional limitations.

3. To emphasize the management of pain and other symptoms.

4. To support the desires of terminally ill cancer patients to remain at home, if this is their choice.

5. To familiarize other disciplines with the hospice philosophy so that they will be able to use these concepts in the care of the terminally ill.[170]

The Hospice Project was funded from March 1981 to December 1983 by a grant from the W.K. Kellogg Foundation of Battle Creek, Mich. This 2½-year study was conducted by the Joint Commission on Accrediation of Hospitals (JCAH). The purpose of the project was to study the need for and the delivery of hospice care in the United States. The project was also aimed at the identification of common principles, services and standards. This was the first large-scale study of the characteristics of hospices in the United States.

It was discovered that, in early 1981, there were more than 800 hospice programs operating at some capacity in the United States. Fifty-one percent of these hospice programs had become operational after January 1980. The majority of the hospice programs were noted as being small — the average monthly census was 17. Sixty percent of the programs reported yearly budgets of less than $75,000.

The JCAH survey showed that the hospice programs throughout the United States were operated out of a variety of organizational settings. Hospital-based operations comprised 46 percent of all hospice programs. Hospice patients were cared for 26 percent of the time by visiting nurses' associations, skilled nursing facilities or community-based home care organizations. Home health agencies provided 23 percent and volunteer community-based programs comprised the remaining 4 percent of the hospice care rendered.

The survey showed the licensure of hospice programs in 1981 varied. Home health agencies licensed 160 of the hospice programs. There were 147 hospice programs which were licensed as acute care hospitals. Other health care services accounted for the licensure of 80. There were 146 programs which were not licensed by any type of health care provider.

The hospice programs were staffed by interdisciplinary teams composed of physicians, registered nurses, social workers, clergy and volunteers. Most of the programs had medical direction. Most offered skilled nursing, social work, spiritual counseling and bereavement services. The hospice care rendered emphasized the management of the patients' pain and symptoms. The hospices also provided psychosocial counseling to not only patients, but also their families.

All the hospice programs treated the patient and family as a unit of care. Most required that one primary care person — usually a family member — be available to the patient. All the programs required the approval of the patient's physician before acceptance into the program.

Interviews conducted as part of the JCAH study uncovered that each hospice had or was developing written policies and procedures. Each hospice also had or was in the process of developing written job descriptions for the hospice team members.

One of the objectives of the Hospice Project was to gather information so that hospice standards could be developed. Committees were formed, surveys were mailed and reviewed, regional conferences were held, and pilot surveys were conducted in order to accomplish this objective. Standards were drafted and evaluated in five different areas: patient/family as a unit of care, interdisciplinary team services, continuity of care, symptom management, and home care and inpatient services. The fourth draft of the hospice standards became the standards that are

183

now included in the JCAH *Hospice Standards Manual* and the *Hospice Self-Assessment and Survey Guide.*

In June 1982, a survey was done to evaluate compliance with the established JCAH standards. Those who responded reported problems with compliance in these standard areas: continuity of care and utilization review and quality assurance. Thirty-eight percent of the hospice programs that responded to the survey said they were unable to comply with the continuity of care standard. Thirty-nine percent of the independently owned programs, 21 percent of hospital-owned programs, and 31 percent of community home health agency programs said they could not comply with the utilization review requirements.

In summary, approval of hospice standards led to JCAH's accreditation program for hospice care. This was the first accreditation program for hospices in the United States. The new accreditation program began conducting surveys in February 1984.

Increased Hospice Participation

Nurses will most likely see an increase in the number of patients who participate in hospice programs. One reason is that Medicare patients are affected by the current diagnosis-related group (DRG) cost-containment program, which is aimed at putting pressure on hospitals to expedite patient discharges. This program will increase the need for hospice home care.[171]

The recent Hospice Medicare Reimbursement Act is a landmark in social welfare legislation.[172] This act will also increase the number of patients who will be participating in hospice programs. However, to date, only a small number of the patients eligible for this benefit have actually received it.[173] This is due, in part, to the many restrictions in the regulation and reimbursement levels of the bill.

The third reason for the expected increase in the number of patients participating in hospice programs is that many health insurance companies have added this coverage to their policies. Insurance companies have supported hospice programs because they have been shown to be cost-effective.[174] A 1983 study found that only a small percentage of eligible patients made use of their hospice coverage.[175] However, this was largely attributable to the fact that neither the patient nor the physician knew of the coverage and the availability of hospice programs. With the increased popularity of hospice programs, this is likely to change.

Legal Issues and Nursing Issues in Hospice Care

Increased numbers of hospice patients represent increased liability exposure. Today, many hospice team members are performing a wider variety of highly skilled and specialized services and thus are being exposed to greater liability risks. With more responsibility comes more accountability. A review of related literature failed to turn up any recorded cases of liability against a hospice team member or institution. Part of this is due to the fact that hospice care is a relatively new field and has only been available in the United States since 1974. The potential for liability exists, especially in view of the litigious nature of our society. The complicated nature of the law surrounding the critically ill patient is also a factor which establishes the potential for liability exposure.

The humanitarian purpose underlying the hospice program will not prevent the institution or team worker from being legally liable if the plaintiff can prove each of the four elements of negligence. For example, say a hospice nurse accidentally administers the wrong dose of Roxanol. Roxanol is a morphine sulfate intensified oral solution used for pain control which contains 20 mg. per ml. The physician wrote an order for 20 mg. and the nurse accidentally and erroneously administers 20 ml., which is equivalent to 400 mg. The patient suffers a respiratory arrest as a result of the nurse's error and dies.

The patient's family files suit against the nurse for the wrongful death of the decedent. The plaintiff must prove each of the four elements in order to prove legal liability. In evaluation of these elements, it can be said that the hospice nurse had a *legal duty* to the decedent since he was participating in the hospice program. The nurse *breached her legal duty* to the patient by administering an incorrect dose of medication. Nurses are always under a legal duty to administer to their patients the right medication, in the right dose, in the right route, and at the right time. The nurse's failure to administer the right dose of medication proximately caused the decedent to suffer a respiratory arrest which *proximately* and directly caused his death. The only remaining issue is the *damages*. Critically ill patients are bound to have less damages since they have a markedly decreased life expectancy. If the plaintiff can show that the decedent's life expectancy would have been a year, then damages may be recoverable for this time period. The four elements of negligence are discussed in more detail in Chapter 2.

In a JCAH *Quality Review Bulletin* article entitled "Hospice: A New Arena for Legal Liability," the author cited four specific liability problems that could arise for a hospice.[176] The first problem includes nontreatment policies regarding terminally ill patients. Hospices, like any other health institution, should draft a policy and procedure manual. This should include clear policies of nontreatment. This policy should be written, medically sound, and consistent with the standard of practice. The policy should be well researched and reflective of applicable state law. Failure to have such policies could result in legal liability in the event a patient could have been saved by routine curative therapy, such a surgery, chemotherapy or radiation therapy.[177]

Natural death statutes that allow for living wills and the durable power of attorney will help to provide clear directions in the drafting of nontreatment policies. A hospice that follows its state's statutory requirements in this regard will receive immunity and protection from legal liability.

The hospice team should also be familiar with the hospice standards which have been developed by the JCAH. Recently, there has been a body of law developed regarding failure to comply with the applicable standards. In the *Darling* case, the court allowed the JCAH standards and hospital bylaws to be admitted into evidence to show custom.[178] These standards were admitted in order to aid the jury in determining if that institution had met the required standard of care.

The hospice team should also be familiar with its employer's policies. If the employer has a policy, the hospice team member must make sure the policy is enforced. If the policy or procedure is not representative of good practice or is not being followed, it should be eliminated and replaced with one reflecting current practice. Many recent cases have shown that violation of an employer's policy may result in a negligence action being filed against the employer hospice institution or hospice team member.[179] Written policies of the institution are admissible into evidence in a court of law.[180]

State licensure laws and regulations should be incorporated into the employer's policies and procedures. If a hospice is a Medicare-certified program, the conditions of participation should be reflected in the policies and procedures. A violation of either may be admissible in a court of law to show negligence.

The second specific liability problem identified in the article mentioned above regards application of the informed consent doctrine. The patient's selection of hospice care should be made only after all the applicable information has been provided, so that a reasoned and intelligent decision can be made. Justice Cardozo once wrote, "Every human being of adult years and sound mind has a right to determine what shall be done with his own body."[181] Generally, the patient should be given information about the hospice program, the services provided, the participation of the various team members, the frequency and times of services and their costs.

A written plan of care evidencing the above-mentioned items will assist in decreasing the hospice's liability exposure. This will help to establish the adequate disclosure which is not only necessary under each state's consent law and case law but also under Medicare certification requirements.[182]

Medicare requires the beneficiary-patient to sign a formal "election statement" that includes, among other things, an acknowledgement that the patient is waiving other Medicare benefits by selecting hospice care.[183] It is advisable to specifically identify, in writing, those Medicare benefits which are waived. The patient may also want to include in the election statement the fact that the election may be revoked. This will entitle the patient to then receive Medicare coverage for other health services.[184]

The third specific liability problem identified in the *Quality Review Bulletin* article concerns purchasing an individual liability policy. It will suffice to say that every professional associated with the hospice program should have a professional liability policy. This topic is discussed at length in Chapter 5.

The fourth specific liability problem identified involves corporate malpractice liability. This is liability that is imposed on the incorporated hospice program because, as a corporation, it has failed to meet some duty which is recognized by law. The hospice program, as a corporate entity, could be held liable for negligent conduct.

The principles of corporate liability began to develop in the early 1960s, and the theory is still considered to be in its early stages. The landmark case that recognized corporate liability was the *Darling* case.[185]

The law recognizes the hospice corporation as a "person." As such, the hospice institution has to meet its legal duty. There are five basic obligations which have commonly been relied upon to support a claim founded on corporate liability. First, the institution is under a legal duty to maintain proper medical equipment, supplies and medications.[186] Second, there is a duty to exercise reasonable care to provide safe physical premises for the patients. This means the hospice institution's buildings and grounds should be adequately maintained.[187] This also means that the hospice has a duty to make sure the patients are safely treated in their homes. Third, internal policies and procedures should be adopted which are reasonably calculated to protect the safety and interests of patients.[188] Fourth, there is a duty to exercise reasonable care in the selection and retention of employees and in granting staff privileges.[189] Fifth, there is a duty to take reasonable steps in ensuring that adequate patient care is being given.[190]

Under the doctrine of *respondeat superior*, the employer is responsible for the negligent acts of an employee.[191] This means that the hospice is liable for the negligent acts of its employed nurses who are acting within the scope of their responsibility. Of course, the individual team worker or nurse is also personally liable for his/her independent act of negligence.

The independent contractor is an exception to this rule. The employer is not responsible for the self-employed person. The independent contractor is legally defined as a person who contracts with another to do something. If the hospice physician or other staff member is an independent contractor, then there is generally no liability on the part of the hospice institution for his/her negligent acts.

Many hospice programs rely heavily on volunteers. The Medicare regulations for certified programs specify that volunteers are to be classified as employees.[192] This raises an interesting question as to whether the negligent acts of volunteers subject the hospice institution to liability. There is now strong legal precedent that the institution is liable for the negligent acts of its volunteers.[193]

In summary, it is important to note that there has not yet been any litigation in this area. This is attributable to the fact that the hospice is a new concept. However, our modern society is litigious and it is only a matter of time until a suit will be filed against a hospice institution or team member. The complexities and nature of hospice treatment make it susceptible to liability exposure. Hopefully, the liability exposure can be minimized by the following:

1. Each hospice institution should be familiar with the JCAH Accreditation Standards for Hospice Care Programs. Each should be aware that violations of the standards may be admitted into evidence in a court of law.

2. Each institution should adopt internal policies and procedures.

3. Each institution should be familiar with its state's statutes. For example, a policy of nontreatment should be consistent with the natural death statute, living will law, or durable power of attorney, if the state has one. The policy should also be consistent with the case law in that state in addition to the applicable federal laws such as Medicare provisions.

4. A written consent form is advisable. In drafting the consent form, the nurse should keep in mind the points mentioned in the above discussion.

5. Each hospice institution should evaluate its insurance needs. Individual team members may also want to consider purchasing insurance policies.

6. Each hospice institution should be aware of the emerging theory of corporate liability. Each institution should take the necessary precautions in the employment and retention of its employees. References should be verified after a written consent form is received to allow this verification.

7. Each hospice institution should check to make sure its employees are duly licensed when licensure is required.

8. Each hospice institution should make sure its medical equipment is properly maintained. Employees should remove all equipment that is malfunctional. This will prevent patient injury.

9. Each hospice institution should exercise reasonable care to provide safe physicial premises for its patients.

10. Each hospice institution should take reasonable steps in ensuring that adequate patient care is being given. An effective quality assurance system is of paramount importance in attaining this result.[194]

REFERENCES

1. *Penaloza v. Baptist Memorial Hospital*, 304 S.W.2d 203 (Tex. 1957).
2. *Gault v. Poor Sisters and St. Joseph Hospital*, 1967 C.C.H. Neg. Cases 1223.
3. *Moore v. Guthrie Hospital*, 403 F.2d 366 (1968).
4. *Barnes v. St. Francis Hospital and School of Nursing*, 507 P.2d 288 (Kan. 1973).
5. *Sheils Gasbarra v. St. James Hospital*, 406 N.E.2d 544 (1980).
6. *Wilmington General Hospital v. Nichols*, 210 A.2d 861 (Del. 1965).
7. *Bernardi v. Community Hospital Association*, 433 P.2d 708 (Colo. 1968).
8. *McWarn v. Tucson General Hospital*, 137 Ariz. 356, 670 P.2d 1180 (1983).
9. *Kord v. Baystate Medical Center*, 429 N.E.2d 1045 (1985).
10. *Mohr v. Jenkins*, 393 So. 2d 245 (1982).
11. *Beardsley v. Wyoming County Community Hospital*, 425 N.Y.S.2d 862.
12. *Doctors Hospital of Mobile, Inc. v. Kirksey*, 275 So. 2d 651 (1973).
13. *Jenkins v. Bogalusa Community Medical Center*, 340 So. 2d 1065 (La. Ct. App. 1976).
14. *Ephraim McDowell Community Hospital Inc. v. Minks*, 529 S.W.2d 360 (Ky. 1975).
15. *Collins v. Westlake Community Hospital*, 312 N.E.2d 614 (Ill. 1974).
16. *Fernandez v. State of New York*, 45 A.D.2d 125, 356 N.Y.S.2d 708 (N.Y. App. Div. 1974).
17. *Fatuck v. Hillside Hospital*, 45 A.D.2d 708, 356 N.Y.S.2d 105 (N.Y. App. Div. 1974).
18. *Myers v. Hospital Association of City of Schenectady*, 45 A.D.2d 780, 356 N.Y.S.2d 720 (N.Y. App. Div. 1974).
19. *Fleming v. Baylor University Medical Center*, 554 S.W.2d 263 (Tex. Civ. App. 1977).
20. *Favalora v. Aetna Casualty and Surety Co.*, 144 So. 2d 544 (1962).
21. *Sabella v. Baton Rouge General Hospital*, 408 So. 2d 382 (1982).
22. *D'Antoni v. Sara Mayo Hospital*, 144 So. 2d 643 (1962).
23. *Polonsky v. Union Hospital*, 418 N.E.2d 620 (Mass. App. Ct. 1981).
24. *Smith v. West Calcasieu-Cameron Hospital*, 251 So. 2d 810 (La. Ct. App. 1968).
25. *De Blanc v. Southern Baptist Hospital*, 207 So. 2d 838 (La. Ct. App. 1968).
26. *Weipert v. General Rose Memorial Hospital Association*, 487 P.2d 615 (Colo. Ct. App. 1971).
27. *Powell v. Parkview Estate Nursing Home*, 240 So. 2d 53 (La. Ct. App. 1970).
28. *Burks v. Christ Hospital*, 249 N.E.2d 829 (Ohio 1969).
29. *Hilzendager v. Methodist Hospital*, 596 S.W.2d 284 (Tex. Civ. App. 1980).
30. 11 *Medical Liability Advisory Service* 1 (May 1986).
31. "Prevention of Patient Falls Through Perceived Control and Other Techniques," 14 *Law, Medicine, and Health Care* 21 (Aug. 1986).
32. *Haber v. Cross County Hospital*, 378 N.Y.S.2d 369 (1975).
33. Greenlaw, J., "Failure to Use Siderails: When Is It Negligence?" 10 *Law, Medicine, and Health Care* 125 (June 1982).
34. *Bleiler v. Bodnar*, 65 N.Y.2d 65, 489 N.Y.S.2d 885 (1985).

35. *Cavenaugh v. S. Broward Hospital Dist.*, 247 So. 2d 769 (Fla. Dist. Ct. App. 1971).

36. *Favalora, supra* note 20.

37. *D'Antoni, supra* note 22.

38. *Polonsky, supra* note 23.

39. *Smith, supra* note 24.

40. *Powell, supra* note 27.

41. *Jenkins, supra* note 13.

42. *Ephraim, supra* note 14.

43. *Collins, supra* note 15.

44. *Mossman v. Albany Medical Center Hospital*, 311 N.Y.S.2d 131 (N.Y. 1970).

45. *Shannon v. State of New York*, 289 N.Y.S.2d 462 (1968).

46. *Butler v. Lutheran Medical Center*, 36 A.D.2d 640, 319 N.Y.S. 291 (2d Dept. 1971).

47. "Prevention of Patient Falls Through Perceived Control and Other Techniques," *supra* note 31.

48. *McEachern v. Glenview Hospital, Inc.*, 505 S.W.2d 386 (Tex. Civ. App. 1974).

49. *Capasso v. Square Sanitarium*, 3 Misc. 2d 273, 155 N.Y.S.2d 313 (N.Y. 1956).

50. *Starnes v. Charlotte-Mecklenburg Hospital Authority*, 221 S.E.2d 733 (N.C. 1976).

51. *Milner v. Huntsville Memorial Hospital*, 398 S.W.2d 647 (Tex. 1966).

52. *Foster v. Delgrave*, 129 Cal. App. 2d 525, 277 P.2d 408 (1954).

53. *May v. Brown*, 492 P.2d 776 (Or. 1972).

54. *Bing v. Thunig*, 2 N.Y.2d 656, 143 N.E.2d 3, 163 N.Y.S.2d 3 (1957).

55. *Monk v. Doctors Hospital*, 403 F.2d 580 (1968).

56. *Carranza v. Tucson Medical Center*, 135 Ariz. 490, 662 P.2d 455 (1983).

57. *Bowers v. Olch*, 260 P.2d 997 (Cal. 1953).

58. *Kent v. County of Hudson*, 245 A.2d 747 (N.J. 1968).

59. *Kopa v. United States* , 236 F. Supp. 189 (Haw. Ct. App. 1964).

60. *Franklin v. Collins Chapel Correctional Hospital*, 696 S.W.2d 16 (1985).

61. *City of Shawnee v. Roush*, 101 Okla. 60, 223 P. 354 (1924); *Norwood Hospital v. Brown*, 219 Ala. 445, 112 So. 411 (1929).

62. *Bing v. Thunig, supra* note 54; *Oldis v. La Societe Francaise de Bienfaisance Mutuelle*, 130 Cal. App. 2d 461, 279 P.2d 184 (1955).

63. *Richardson v. Doe*, 176 Ohio St. 371 (1964).

64. *Goff v. Doctor's Hospital*, 166 Cal. App. 314, 333 P.2d 29 (1958).

65. *Yorita v. Okumoto*, 643 P.2d 820 (Haw. Ct. App. 1982).

66. *Mundt v. Alta Bates Hospital*, 35 Cal. Rptr. 848 (Cal. Ct. App. 1963).

67. *Crowe v. Provost*, 52 Tenn. App. 397, 374 S.W.2d 645 (1963).

68. *Thomas v. Corso*, 265 Md. 84, 288 A.2d 379 (1972).

69. *New Biloxi Hospital v. Frazier*, 245 Miss. 185, 145 So. 2d 882 (1962).

70. *Vasey v. Burch*, 262 S.E.2d 865 (N.C. 1980).

71. *Hiatt v. Groce*, 215 Kan. 14, 523 P.2d 320 (1974); *Franz v. San Luis Medical Clinic*, 81 Cal. App. 3d 34, 146 Cal. Rptr. 146 (1978).

72. *Southeastern Ky. Baptist Hospital, Inc. v. Bruce*, 539 S.W.2d 286 (Ky. 1976).

73. Bergen, Richard, "Mistaken Identity," 221 *J.A.M.A.* 74 (Aug. 14, 1972).

74. *Ebaugh v. Rabken*, 99 Cal. Rptr. 706 (1972).

75. *Walker v. Humana Medical Corp.*, 415 So. 2d 1107 (Ala. App. 1982).

76. *Bellaire General Hospital, Inc. v. Campbell*, 510 S.W.2d 94 (Tex. 1974); *Jones v. City of New York*, 57 A.D.2d 429, 395 N.Y.S.2d 10 (N.Y. App. Div. 1977); *Tucson General Hospital v. Russell*, 7 Ariz. App. 193, 437 P.2d 677 (1968); *Davison v. Bernard McFadden Foundation*, 4 A.D.2d 978, 167 N.Y.S.2d 784 (N.Y. App. Div. 1957); *Mt. Sinai Hospital of Greater Miami, Inc. v. Wolfson*, 327 So. 2d 883 (Fla. Dist. Ct. App. 1976); *Mattair v. St. Joseph's Hospital, Inc.*, 234 S.E.2d 537 (Ga. Ct. App. 1977); *Arterkurn v. St. Joseph's Hospital and Rehabilitation Center*, 551 P.2d 886 (Kan. 1976).

77. *Emory University v. Porter*, 103 Ga. App. 752, 755, 120 S.E.2d 668 (1961).

78. *Bellaire General Hospital, supra* note 76.

79. *Lauro v. Travelers Insurance Co.*, 261 So. 2d 261 (La. 1972).

80. *City and County of Denver v. Madison*, 351 P.2d 826 (1960); *Cohran v. Harper*, 115 Ga. App. 277, 154 S.E.2d 461 (1967); *Casey v. Penn*, 362 N.E.2d 1373 (Ill. App. Ct. 1977); *Garrison v. Hotel Diew*, 319 So. 2d 557 (La. Ct. App. 1975); *Taaje v. St. Olaf's Hospital*, 271 N.W. 109 (Minn. 1937); *Thompson v. Methodist Hospital*, 211 Tenn. 650, 367 S.W.2d 134 (1963); *Valentine v. Kaiser Foundation Hospital*, 15 Cal. Rptr. 26 (1961); *Kapuschinsky v. United States*, 248 F. Supp. 732 (D.S.C. 1966); *Lane, v. Otis*, 412 So. 2d 254 (Ala. 1982); *Kenyon v. Hammer*, 688 P.2d 96, (Ariz. 1984).

81. *DeFalco v. Long Island College Hospital*, 90 Misc. 2d 164, 393 N.Y.S.2d 859 (N.Y. App. Div. 1977).

82. Lesnik, Milton and Anderson, Bernice, *Nursing Practice and the Law* 261 (2nd ed., J.B. Lippincott Co., Philadelphia, 1962).

83. *Woodlawn Infirmary v. Byers*, 216 Ala. 210, 112 So. 831 (1927).

84. *Criss v. Angelus Hospital Association*, 12 Cal. App. 2d 412, 56 P.2d 1274 (1936).

85. *Helman v. Sacred Heart Hospital*, 62 Wash. 2d 69, 381 P.2d 605 (1963).

86. *Kalmus v. Cedars of Lebanon Hospital*, 132 Cal. 2d 243, 281 P.2d 875 (1955).

87. *Cohran v. Harper, supra* note 80.

88. *Kalmus, supra* note 86.

89. *Kieswetter v. Center Pavillion Hospital*, 662 S.W.2d 24 (Tex. Civ. App. 1983); *St. Paul Fire and Marine Insurance Co. v. Prothro*, 266 Ark. 1020, 590 S.W.2d 35 (1979); *Wilson v. Stilwil*, 411 Mich. 587, 309 N.W.2d 898 (1981); *Adams v. Eye, Ear, Nose, and Throat Hospital*, 346 So. 2d 327 (La. Ct. App. 1977); *Morse v. Moretti*, 403 F.2d 564 (D.C. Cir. 1968); *Lefort v. Mass. Bonding and Ins. Co.*, 358 F.2d 341 (5th Cir. 1966).

90. *Sommers v. Sisters of Charity of Providence in Oregon*, 277 Or. 549, 561 P.2d 603 (1977); *Roark v. St. Paul Fire and Marine Insurance Co.*, 415 So. 2d 295 (La. Ct. App. 1982).

91. *See* Cruse, "A Five-Year Perspective Study of 23, 649 Surgical Wounds," 107 *Archives of Surgery* 206 (1973).

92. *Lhotka v. Larson*, 307 Minn. 121, 238 N.W.2d 870 (1976).

93. *Ramsey et al. v. Physicians Memorial Hospital, Inc., et al.*, 373 A.2d 76

(Md. 1977); *Toth v. Community Hospital at Glen Cove,* 22 N.Y.2d 255, 239 N.E.2d 368, 292 N.Y.S.2d 440 (1968).

94. *Kenyon v. Hammer, supra* note 80.

95. *Dinsmore, Richard, "OR Nurse's Liability in Needle Count," 20 AORN Journal* 1002 (Dec. 1974).

96. Standard 111:12-1, Association of Operating Room Nurses, Inc., Denver, Colo.

97. *Hestbeck v. Hennepin County,* 212 N.W.2d 361 (Minn. 1973).

98. *Leonard v. Watsonville Community Hospital,* 47 Cal. 2d 509, 305 P.2d 36 (1956).

99. *Rubeck v. Wright,* 709 P.2d 621 (1985).

100. *Sullivan v. Methodist Hospital of Dallas,* 699 S.W.2d 265 (Tex. 1985) and *Powell v. Mullins,* 479 So. 2d 1119 (Ala. 1985).

101. Truhitte v. French Hospital, 180 Cal. Rptr. 152 (Cal. Ct. App. 1982).

102. Payne, William H. and Mayes, K., "Vicarious Liability and the Operating Room Surgeon," 17 *S. Tex. L.J.* 367 (1976); Hendrickson, Calvin W. and Laughlin, Nancy, "The Sponge Count, the Surgeon's Vicarious Liability and Other Fictions," 25 *Federation Ins. Coun. Q.* 34 (1974).

103. *Darling v. Charleston Memorial Hospital,* 33 Ill. 2d 326, 211 N.E.2d 253 (1965).

104. *Kolakowski v. Voris,* 395 N.E.2d 6 (Ill. App. Ct. 1979).

105. *Long v. Johnson,* 381 N.E.2d 93 (Ind. 1978).

106. *Hippocrates Mertsaris v. 73rd Corp.,* 482 N.Y.S.2d 792 (N.Y. 1984).

107. *Stack v. Wapner,* 368 A.2d 292 (Pa. Super. Ct. 1976).

108. American College of Obstetricians and Gynecologists, *Standards for Obstetric-Gynecologic Services* 29 (5th ed. 1982).

109. American College of Obstetricians and Gynecologists, *Standards for Obstetric-Gynecologic Services* 35 (6th ed. 1985).

110. Warkany, Joseph, *Congenital Malformation* 101 (Year Book Medical Publisher 1971).

111. Catz, C., *et al.,* "Drugs and Pregnancy," *Drug Therapy* (April 1984).

112. *Id.*

113. Pritchard and MacDonald, *Williams Obstetrics* 829 (15th ed. 1976).

114. Pegales, Steven and Wachsman, H.F., "Obstetrics and Obstetrical Malpractice," *American Law of Medical Malpractice* 97 (Supp. 1983); Forfar, J., "Epidemiology of Drug-Induced Malformations," 2 *Biochemical Society Transactions,* No. 4 (1974); American Medical Association Department of Drugs, *AMA Drug Evaluation* 17 (3rd ed. 1977); Schenkel, L., "Nonprescription Drugs During Pregnancy, Potential Teratogenic and Toxic Effects upon Embryo and Fetus," 12 *Journal of Reproductive Medicine* (Jan. 1974); Nora, J., *et al.,* "Exogenous Progestrogen and Estrogen Implicated in Birth Defects," 240 *J.A.M.A.* 843 (1978).

115. Bleakley and Peters, "Bendectin," 16 *Trial Magazine* (May 1980); Moslock, M., *et al.,* "Bendectin and Fetal Development," 142 *Journal of Obstetrics and Gynecology* 209 (1982); Mitchell, A., *et al.,* "Birth Defects Related to Bendectin Use in Pregnancy," 245 *J.A.M.A.* 2311 (1981).

116. Hellman and Pritchard, *Williams Obstetrics* 685 (14th ed. 1971).

117. *Id.* at 686, 687, 696.

118. Quilligan, Edward and Zuspan, Fred, *Practical Manual of Obstetrical Care* 122 (C.V. Mosby Co. 1982).

119. *Id.*; American College of Obstetricians and Gynecologists, *An Update in Obstetrics and Gynecology* 29 (1981).

120. Varner, "Maternal Mortality in a Major Referral Hospital," 143 *American Journal of Obstetrics and Gynecology* 325 (June 1, 1982).

121. Globus, M., *et al.*, "Prenatal Diagnosis in 3,000 Amniocenteses," 300 *New Eng. Journal of Medicine* 157 (1979).

122. *Id.*

123. "Antenatal Diagnosis: What Is Standard?" 241 *J.A.M.A.* 1665 (April 20, 1979).

124. Queenan, John T., *Managing OB-Gyn. Emergencies* 63 (C.V. Mosby Co. 1982).

125. McElin, Thomas, "Ectopic Pregnancy," *Obstetrics and Gynecology* 336 (3rd ed., Harper and Row).

126. *Supra* note 113, at 2.

127. Pitkin, R., "Estimation of Fetal Maturity," *Perinatal Medicine: Disease of the Fetus and Infant* 14 (2nd ed. 1977).

128. Taylor, Stewart, *Beck's Obstetrical Practice in Fetal Medicine* 552 (10th ed. 1976).

129. *Protocols for High-Risk Pregnancy* 213 (J. Queenan and J. Hobbins ed. 1982).

130. International Childbirth Education Association, Inc., ICEA Publication/Distribution Center, P.O. Box 9316, Midtown Plaza, Rochester, N.Y. 14601.

131. National Association of Insurance Commissioners, 2 *NAIC Malpractice Claims* 3 (1978).

132. *Brain-Damaged Infants: Case Evaluation and Management* (Available from Practicing Law Institute, Dept. AG, 810 Seventh Ave., New York, N.Y. 10019.)

133. *Wagner v. Kaiser Foundation Hospitals*, 589 P.2d 1106 (1979).

134. *Lane v. Otis*, 412 So. 2d 254 (Ala., 1982).

135. *Hughes v. St. Paul Fire and Marine Ins. Co.*, 401 So. 2d 448 (La. Ct. App. 1981).

136. *Parks v. Perry*, 314 S.E.2d 287 (N.C. 1984).

137. *Williams v. St. Claire Medical Center*, 657 S.W.2d 590 (Ky. Ct. App. 1983).

138. *Airco v. Simmons*, 638 So. 2d 660 (Ark. 1982).

139. *Barth v. Rock*, 674 P.2d 1265 (Wa. Ct. App. 1984).

140. *Forray v. New York Hospital*, 475 N.Y.S.2d 57 (N.Y. 1984).

141. *Whitney v. Day*, 100 Mich. App. 707, 300 N.W.2d 380 (1980).

142. *Otts v. Bryant*, 412 So. 2d 254 (Ala. 1982).

143. *Brown v. Allen Sanitarium*, 364 So. 2d 661 (La. Ct. App. 1978).

144. *Keys v. Mercy Hospital of New Orleans*, 485 So. 2d 514 (La. Ct. App. 1986).

145. Occupational Safety and Health Act of 1970, 29 U.S.C. Sections 651-677 (1976 and Supp. 1981).

146. Brown, M.L., *Occupational Health Nursing: Principles and Practices* (Springer Publishing Co., New York, 1981).

147. Bruce, J. and Snyder, Elizabeth, "The Right and Responsibility to Diagnosis," 82 *American Journal of Nursing* 645 (April 1982).

148. Fiesta, Janine, *The Law and Liability: A Guide for Nurses* 28 (John Wiley and Sons, New York, 1983).

149. *Cooper v. National Motor Bearing Co., Inc.*, 288 P.2d 581 (Cal. 1955).

150. *Id.*

151. Manicini, M., "The Law and the Occupational Health Nurse," 79 *American Journal of Nursing* 1628 (Sept. 1979).

152. Larson, A., *Workmen's Compensation for Occupational Injuries and Death*, Sections 72 and 100 (Matthew Bender & Co., New York, 1983).

153. Cushing, M., "The Occupational Nurse's Liability," 81 *American Journal of Nursing* 2207 (Dec. 1981).

154. Bowyer, Elizabeth, "The Liability of the Occupational Health Nurse," *Law, Medicine, and Health Care* 224 (Oct. 1983).

155. Creighton, Helen, "Occupational Health Nurse's Liability," *Nursing Management* 49 (Feb. 1985).

156. Brown, *supra* note 146; Bowyer *supra* note 154.

157. *Horne v. Patton*, 287 So. 2d 824 (Ala. 1973).

158. *Betesh v. United States*, 400 F. Supp. 238 (D.C. 1974). *See also Union Carbide and Carbon Corp. v. Stapleton*, 237 F.2d 229 (6th Cir. 1956).

159. *Coffee v. McDonnell-Douglas Corp.*, 105 Cal. Rptr. 358, 503 P.2d 1366 (Cal. 1972).

160. Caulfield, James, "Administering Emergency Treatment and Medication," *Ohio Elementary Principal* 16 (June 1980).

161. Gadow, J., *et al.*, "Administration of Medication by School Personnel," *Journal of School Health* 178 (March 1983).

162. Appleman, M.A., "The Legal Issues Involved in the Use of Stimulants on Hyperactive Children," 35 *Dissertation Abstracts International* 5161A (1975).

163. Courtnage, L., "Managing Medication in the School: A Survey of State Policies," 49 *Exceptional Child* 75 (1982); *see also* Kinnison, J., "An Analysis of Policies Regarding Medication in the Schools," 49 *Journal of School Health* 280 (1979).

164. Baum, Pat, "The Administration of Medication in Schools," 10 *Administrator* No. 2, at 11 (1981).

165. McCann, B.A., *The Hospice Project Report* (Joint Commission on the Accreditation of Hospitals, Chicago, 1985).

166. Wald, Florence, *et al.*, "The Hospice Movement as a Health Care Reform," *Nursing Outlook* 175 (March 1980).

167. McCann, B.A. and Hill, K.L., "The Hospice Project," in "Quality of Care for the Terminally Ill: An Examination of the Issues," *Quality Review Bulletin* 9 (Joint Commission on the Accreditation of Hospitals, 1985).

168. Brooks, T.A., "Legal and Regulatory Issues in Hospice Care," *The Hospital Medical Staff* 15 (June 1980).

169. *Id.*

170. McNerney, W., *et al.*, "A Comprehensive Comparative Study of Hospice Service in the United States," 72 *AJPH* 455 (May 1982).

171. Levy, Michael, "Pain Control: Bridging the Gap Between Medical Science and Patient Comfort," in "Quality of Care for the Terminally Ill: An Examination of the Issues," *Quality Review Bulletin* 19 (Joint Commission on the Accreditation of Hospitals, 1985).

172. *Id.*

173. Amenta, M.O., "Hospice U.S.A. 1984 — Steady and Holding," 11 *Oncol. Nurs.* 68 (Sept.-Oct. 1984).

174. Hospice Council for Northern Ohio, "Hospice Care Cost Savings to Third-Party Insurers" (Cleveland, 1984).

175. Hawthorne, "1983 Hospice Reimbursement Survey" (Frank B. Hall Consulting, New York, 1984).

176. Blum, John, "Hospice: A New Arena for Legal Liability," in "Quality of Care for the Terminally Ill: An Examination of the Issues," *Quality Review Bulletin* 154 (Joint Commission on the Accreditation of Hospitals, 1985).

177. *Burks v. Christ Hospital, supra* note 28.

178. *Darling, supra* note 103.

179. *Williams, supra* note 137; *Kohoutek v. Hafner*, 366 N.W.2d 633 (Minn. Ct. App. 1985); *Foley v. Bishop Clarkson Memorial Hospital*, 185 Neb. 89, 173 N.W.2d 881 (1970); *Haber, supra* note 32; *Hunt v. King County*, 481 P.2d 593 (Wash. 1971).

180. *Smith, supra* note 24; *Gourdene v. Phelps Memorial Hospital*, 366 N.Y.S.2d 316 (N.Y. 1972).

181. *Canterbury v. Spence*, 464 F.2d 772 (D.C. Cir. 1972).

182. 48 Fed. Reg. 56,027 (1983).

183. 42 C.F.R. Section 418.26 (1982); *see also* O'Neil, E.A., "Risk Management and Hospice Care," in "Quality of Care for the Terminally Ill: An Examination of the Issues," *Quality Review Bulletin* 160 (Joint Commission on the Accreditation of Hospitals, 1985).

184. 42 C.F.R. Section 418.26 (1982).

185. *Darling, supra* note 103.

186. *See* 54 A.L.R.3d 358 (1973); *see also Silverhart v. Mt. Zion Hospital*, 20 Cal. App. 2d 1022, 98 Cal. Rptr. 187 (1971); *Shivers v. Good Shepherd Hospital, Inc.*, 427 S.E.2d 104 (Tex. Civ. App. 1968); *Mauran v. Mary Fletcher Hospital*, 318 F. Supp. 297 (Vt. 1970); *Starnes, supra* note 50.

187. *Smith v. Travelers Insurance Co.*, 287 So. 2d 576 (La. 1973); *Carrasco v. Bankoff*, 33 Cal. Rptr. 673 (Cal. 1963).

188. *Bornman v. Great S.W. General Hospital, Inc.*, 453 F.2d 616 (5th Cir. 1971); *Johnson v. Grant Hospital*, 32 Ohio St. 2d 169, 291 N.E. 440 (1972); *see also* 60 A.L.R.3d 380 (1974).

189. *Hipp v. Hospital Authority of Marietta, Georgia*, 121 S.E.2d 273 (Ga. 1961); *Corletto v. Shore Memorial Hospital*, 138 N.J. Super. 302, 350 A.2d 534 (1975); *Purcell v. Zimbelman*, 18 Ariz. App. 75, 500 P.2d 335 (1972).

190. *Darling, supra* note 103; *Lundahl v. Rockford Memorial Hospital Association*, 93 Ill. App. 2d 461, 235 N.E.2d 671 (1968); *Gridley v. Johnson*, 476 S.W.2d 475 (Mo. 1972); *Tuscon Medical Center, Inc. v. Misevch*, 113 Ariz. 34, 545 P.2d 958 (1976).

191.   Southwick, A.S., *The Laws of Hospital and Health Care Administration* (Health Administration Press, Ann Arbor, Mich., 1978); Blum, *supra* note 176, at 154-159.
192.   48 Fed. Reg. 56,027 (1983).
193.   Blum, *supra* note 176.
194.   Kranz, D. and Lamb, C.M., "A Quality Assurance System for Hospice Programs," in "Quality of Care for the Terminally Ill: An Examination of the Issues," *Quality Review Bulletin* 108 (Joint Commission on the Accreditation of Hospitals, 1985).

CHAPTER TEN

LAW FOR NURSE MANAGERS

Staffing
Floating
Reporting Incompetence
The Impaired Professional
Drafting Policies and Procedures
Standing Orders
Liability of Nurse Supervisors
Liability of Student Nurses

STAFFING LEVELS

The 1986 edition of the JCAH *Accreditation Manual for Hospitals* sets forth the following statements regarding staffing:

1. It is a required characteristic that the hospital have a *sufficient number* of qualified registered nurses on duty at all times . . . .

2. There should be *sufficient nursing staffing* to assure prompt recognition of any untoward change in a patient's condition and to facilitate appropriate intervention by the nursing, medical, or hospital staff.[1]

Unfortunately, the JCAH does not state any nurse/patient ratios or other guidelines regarding what constitutes a "sufficient number"; nor have the courts been able to come up with a reliable standard to use when inadequate staffing is alleged.

Inadequate staffing is often an area of concern for the nurse. In fact, inadequate staffing is probably the most difficult management problem within the health care system. In the 1970s and early 1980s, much of the inadequate staffing problem was due to vacant nursing positions. However, the nursing shortage has, for the most part, resolved itself nationwide. Today, inadequate staffing is mostly due to faulty scheduling practices, which are the result of either an inadequate number of positions or the wrong mix of hospital positions. The problem has been compounded by issues such as specialization, special certification, unionization, DRGs, collaborative practice acts and accreditation requirements.

The constant race for nurses to stay on top of things when faced with inadequate staffing situations has resulted in fatigue and growing morale problems. The problem has become so frequent that it has been called "the burnout syndrome."

Recently, there have been many articles in nursing literature about this burnout syndrome. A recent study of fifteen hospitals in six cities was conducted by the University of Maryland.[2] During this study, the nurses said they felt that patient care was not affected by working with less than adequate staff. However, while the nurses were overworking themselves to prevent the patients from suffering, psychosocial aspects of care were being overlooked. The study found that there was a decrease in the careful monitoring of patients' conditions as well as an increase in medication errors. The study also showed that when nurses worked under these circumstances, they tended not to develop care plans and they did not know their patients as well. It also showed that the sicker patients were attended to, but the ambulatory patients were neglected.

The hospital, as a corporation, has a legal duty to make sure that its institution is adequately staffed. Administration usually delegates this chore to nursing services. Ordinarily, inadequate staffing levels are an internal problem. The issue is rarely raised as a source of liability against the hospital by the plaintiff's attorney. Alleging that the patient did not receive enough care is not raised unless the patient can show that he or she was directly damaged in some way.

The hospital's duty to provide adequate staff is illustrated well in the *Darling* case. In that case, a patient with a broken leg was treated in the emergency room by the physician on call.[3] A cast was applied. The patient was then admitted to the orthopedic floor. Obvious danger signals and progressive worsening of the patient's circulation occurred over the next two weeks. The nurses checked the leg only a few times per day. On at least one occasion, one of the nurses contacted the physician about the patient's circulation checks. However, she was not persistent and did not bring the problem to the attention of her nursing supervisor.

The leg became gangrenous, and the young athlete's lower leg was amputated. The Illinois Supreme Court held that the hospital was negligent for failing to provide a *sufficient number of trained nurses*. Also, the hospital staff failed to review the treatment rendered by the attending physician, and failed to require the appropriate consultation on examination by hospital staff physicians.

The *Sanchez* case is another one that illustrates what happens when the hospital fails to have an adequate number of trained nurses.[4] The patient had surgery for a laminectomy. During surgery, a catheter was placed in the right atrium of the heart, to minimize the chances of an air embolism forming in the heart.

She was observed in the recovery room from about 12:35 p.m. to 3:15 p.m., and then was transferred to her room. At 3:30 p.m., her vital signs were checked and showed a substantial decrease in blood pressure (96/60). No comparison was made with her prior vital signs record. Her chart was not examined. No neurological exams were made, and no examination of the pupils or check of medications were made.

Requests by friends for assistance and medication were ignored. The nurse was informed that the patient was vomiting but never left the nursing station to verify the patient's condition.

The patient continued vomiting and later jerked violently, her pupils dilated, and went into cardiac arrest. The nurse panicked, did nothing to open the patient's airway, and did not initiate CPR. The emergency room physician arrived minutes later. The nurses had thought that the atrial catheter was a peripheral I.V. and that all medications were administered through that line. The patient was pronounced brain dead at 5:00 a.m.

The court found against the nurses in the amount of $400,000. The nurses failed to check the patient's chart and her neurological status. They failed to recognize her deteriorating vital signs and to timely notify the physicians.

This scenario can occur when staffing is short and nurses do not have enough time to adequately check their patients. Many institutions have discovered that their attempts to save money by short staffing have backfired. Their short staffing has resulted in liability claims which have dramatically increased their cost of liability insurance. Courts hold hospitals primarily liable in suits where nursing understaffing is the key issue.

Hospitals have asserted several defenses for their understaffing. None have been accepted by the courts. Some hospitals have argued the unavailability of staff. Others claim insufficient funds to adequately staff. These have been repeatedly rejected by the courts.

There is one defense asserted by hospitals that has sometimes been successful. This is the sudden emergency exception. This defense might be used, for example, if the night nurse is in an accident on the way to work or calls in ill, and this causes a shortage for that particular day. Courts that have accepted this defense have done so only if there has not been a problem of chronic understaffing.

Nurses who are aware of a staffing problem which could compromise patient care should place their supervisors on notice. They should request additional assistance. If the assistance is not available, they should try other alternatives in order to solve the problem. Perhaps a nurse who is off that day could come in and work. Trading shifts is another alternative. For example, if the supervisor notes that there is an extra nurse scheduled the next day, that nurse might be able to work on the understaffed day and take the next day off. This system works better in situations where overtime restrictions apply.

The *Horton* case is illustrative of what can happen when the nurse who is aware of a staffing problem does not place his/her supervisor on notice.[5] The importance of communication cannot be overemphasized. Any time a nurse has a serious concern about the patients or their care, no matter what the problem, his/her supervisor should be notified.

In the *Horton* case, a charge nurse, an L.P.N. and one aide were responsible for nineteen patients. It was a very busy evening. One of the patients became disoriented and attempted to climb down the balcony of his room. The attending physician was notified and instructed the nurse to have someone sit with the patient.

The nurse called the patient's wife. She arranged to have the patient's mother sit with him, but it would be a little while before she could get there. During this period, the nurse provided no supervision of the patient. The charge nurse did not even notify her supervisor of the problem to see if any staff member or volunteer would be available to sit with the patient. Before the patient's mother arrived, the unsupervised patient jumped off the balcony and injured himself. The court had no difficulty finding the charge nurse liable, because she was aware of the temporary staffing problem and failed to put her supervisor on notice.

Every nurse at some time will be faced with a sudden overload. This may result because of frequent admissions or the fact that the patients are much sicker and require more intensive care. A nurse faced with this situation should, as previously mentioned, first notify his/her supervisor of the situation. If help is not available, the nurse can refuse to work and risk suspension or being fired. This also places the nurse at risk for adandonment. The other option is to stay on the job and do the best he/she can. Some prefer, in such a situation, to write a memo outlining the situation, what was done, what was said and a summary of the facts. This can be filed with the director of nursing.

This report may not protect the nurse from being legally responsible if an injury should occur. However, most courts would not allow the hospital to seek indemnification since the situation was caused by understaffing.

In summary, the doctrine of *respondeat superior* makes the hospital liable for the negligence of the nurses. In view of this doctrine, a nursing shortage can be risky for the hospital. Adequate staffing is one protection the hospital has against errors which can result in malpractice suits.

FLOATING

Floating is the process by which a nurse is pulled from one area of duty to another. Today, the practice of "pulling" a nurse is common practice. However, pulling a nurse from an area which is familiar, where he or she is competent, to an area which is foreign is a real concern for that nurse.

Nursing specialization has compounded the problem of floating. If a nurse is pulled to a medical floor, for example, where the patients' care does not require more specialized knowledge or skill, the potential for that nurse to get into legal problems is minimal. Consider, however, the effect of pulling a nurse who has no prior critical care experience from a medical floor into an area such as the I.C.U., C.C.U. or E.R. Consider also the effect of pulling the nurse who has worked with alcohol and drug abuse patients on the psychiatric floor for the past five years to cover the recovery room or I.C.U. In these instances, the chance for error, as well as the nurse's anxiety level, increases.

As previously discussed, the hospital has a legal duty to ensure that all areas of the hospital are adequately staffed. This often places the hospital in a position where floating staff members is the only way to balance the needs of the hospital's units and its responsibility to ensure patient safety. However, nurses should never be floated to areas or given assignments that they have never been taught to handle. This is exemplified by the JCAH standards.

The JCAH *Accreditation Manual for Hospitals* sets out criteria upon which staffing and assignments are to based. These are necessary in order to assure quality nursing care and a safe environment. One of these criteria states, "The patient care assignment is commensurate with the *qualifications of each nursing staff member*, the identified nursing needs of the patient, and the prescribed medical regimen."[6]

This standard is violated when a nurse is floated to an area with which he/she is completely unfamiliar. Another of the JCAH criteria calls for units such as surgery, obstetrics, emergency and ambulatory care to be staffed with nursing personnel who have the appropriate "staff expertise" to meet the patient care requirements.[7]

Nurses always ask if they can refuse to float. The answer depends on several factors. A nurse who accepts a position at the hospital with the understanding that he/she will not be floated can refuse to float. The hospital is bound by its prior contract, whether it is implied or express. In recent years, collective bargaining agreements have included a clause which states that no nurse will be floated to an area in which he/she is not professionally competent. However, unless there is a written hospital policy to the contrary, a nurse has no legal grounds to refuse to float. Legally, the nurse can't refuse to float simply because he/she feels that his/her skills needed for the assignment have diminished. If the nurse refuses to float, he/she may face the possibility of discharge on grounds of insubordination. The nurse should fully understand his/her professional limitations and be prepared to act in the best interest of the patient. The patient should never be left, as the nurse could be accused of abandonment.

A nurse who feels uncomfortable with floating should advise his/her supervisor, and should voice his/her limitations and concerns. The nurse should clarify what his/her duties and responsibilities will be in the area to which he/she is pulled. Unfamiliar procedures should never be performed. If the supervisor insists, after being informed, that the nurse perform a task that the nurse doesn't know how to do, the nurse, of course, must refuse. If the nurse is reprimanded or fired, she may be able to appeal the action in court.

Helen Creighton, in her book titled *Law Every Nurse Should Know*, cites a recent example.[8] A critical care nurse was asked to go to the emergency room. She agreed to float as long as she was given an orientation. The hospital failed to give her an orientation, and she refused to go. She resigned because she was going to be fired. She sued and won. The court felt that a nurse who is floated to another unit is entitled to an orientation.

Management and the professional nurse may be able to resolve these types of problems through a number of options. Through the problem-solving approach, the nurse may be able to remedy the situation. For example, suppose Nurse Jones is asked to float to I.C.U., where she has never worked. She knows that one of the I.C.U. nurses is off duty and available to work overtime. Perhaps, by suggesting this, her problem could be solved. Another possible solution might be to let Nurse Jones go to the surgical floor, with which she is more familiar, so that a surgical nurse with prior critical care experience could go to the I.C.U.

Another solution, especially for smaller hospitals that tend to float staff more frequently, is to provide continuing education programs. These will assist nurses in learning and maintaining clinical skills. Some hospitals rotate their nurses through the various units.

As previously mentioned, the doctrine of *respondeat superior* makes the hospital liable for the negligence of its nurses. Floating of staff members to unfamiliar areas can be risky for the hospital. The *Dessauer* case is a good example of this.[9] An obstetrical nurse was pulled to the emergency room, and a patient came in complaining of substernal chest pain and diaphoresis. The emergency room physician made a diagnosis of acute myocardial infarction and ordered 50 mg. of lidocaine. The nurse looked around and found a vial of lidocaine, which read, "Lidocaine for dilution only. Not for direct injection." The nurse administered the entire vial of lidocaine I.V. (The vial contained a total of 800 mg. of lidocaine.) The patient went into cardiac arrest as soon as this drug was given. The patient suffered brain damage and eventually died.

The *Norton* case is also a good example of a situation that occurred when a nurse was floated to an area with which she was unfamiliar.[10] A nursing supervisor went to the pediatric unit to assist the nurse because she was unusually busy. The nursing supervisor was transcribing some of the physicians' orders. One chart read, "Lanoxin 3.0 cc.'s now." The nursing supervisor, unfamiliar with pediatric dosages, administered 3.0 cc.'s of injectable Lanoxin. (She was unaware that there was an oral elixir.) The child went into cardiac arrest and died.

The two examples above illustrate the hazards that arise when a nurse floats to an unfamiliar unit. Mistakes are more likely to occur, and the practice can result in increased liability for the nurse and the hospital.

REPORTING INCOMPETENCE

Is the nurse under any ethical, moral or legal duty to report another whom she knows to be incompetent? The American Nurses' Association Code for Nurses states, "The nurse acts to safeguard the client and the public when health care and safety are affected by the incompetent, unethical, or illegal practice of any person." Therefore, it is clear that the nurse has at least a moral and ethical obligation to report another that he/she knows to be incompetent. The nurse should carefully document the incidents of the practitioner's incompetence, and these should be communicated to his/her nursing supervisor.

Many cases of nursing incompetence center around the alcoholic nurse. A recent article reported that there are about 40,000 alcoholic nurses in the United States.[11] Recently there also have been an increasing number of nurses who have become addicted to narcotics. One author stated that health care professionals are four times more likely to be narcotic dependent than any other professional.[12]

Many state nursing societies have started programs for their alcoholic or narcotic-dependent nurses. Many state licensure boards are requiring the reporting of nurses who are addicted to alcohol or narcotics. They also are suspending or terminating these nurses' licenses. Many hospitals and health institutions are also starting programs to help the impaired nurse.

It already has been discussed that the nurse is under an *ethical* and *moral* duty to report another he/she knows to be incompetent.[13] The next question becomes whether the nurse is under any *legal* duty to report the incompetence of another. The law regarding the incompetence of a hospital employee may be described as unsettled. There generally are many questions surrounding the nurse's consideration to report the incompetence of another. What should you do if you suspect that the nurse you are working with is impaired? When and to whom should you report your observations? What happens if you did not report the nurse you knew was incompetent and a patient died or was injured as a result?

The likelihood of a successful suit against the reporting nurse is very minimal, especially if the report is carefully and accurately made. Failure to report an impaired nurse increases danger to patients, places the hospital at risk, and allows the impairment to grow worse.[14]

Many hospitals have a written policy dictating what the nurse should do if he/she has a reasonable suspicion that his/her co-worker is impaired. Generally, a report is given to the nursing supervisor. The report should be objectively written, stating all known facts. After a report is made it should not be discussed with other staff members.

In the *Judge* case, already discussed,[15] the court held that the nursing director had a duty to make statements concerning the loss of narcotics while Nurse Judge was working. The statements were communicated in a proper way and the applicable facts recorded. The court found that a qualified privilege attached.

THE IMPAIRED PROFESSIONAL

In recent years, there has been a rapid escalation in attempts to deal with the impaired professional.[16] The impaired nurse has been discussed in the previous section. The impaired professional recently has been an increased concern of hospitals, especially those professionals who are radiologists, anesthesiologists, pathologists and emergency room physicians. This is due to recent changes in the law.

The hospital is no longer held accountable only for the acts of its employees. The corporate liability theory that emerged from the *Darling* case has expanded the potential for hospital liability. One author wrote, "[This] means the nurses must overview the physician's activities, and actively and affirmatively intervene if they believe it to be below the accepted standard, but not, however, when they merely disagree with the approach."[17]

Even before the *Darling* case, courts agreed that there is no automatic right to staff privileges at a hospital. In the *Dayan* case, the court upheld the right of a hospital to deny staff privileges for physical infirmities, advancing years or personal habits.[18] The court indicated that liability might fall on the hospital if its personnel were subject to control of one lacking in some of the necessary professional skills.

The hospital is not liable for the acts of physicians who are not its employees, as long as there is no reason to know that the physician is incompetent.[19]

In the *Corleto* case, the plaintiff sued the physician for his alleged negligence in the performance of abdominal surgery.[20] He also sued the 141 physicians on staff. He alleged the staff knew or should have known the defendant physician was incompetent. The New Jersey Court agreed. Liability attaches, the court said, because the physicians allowed the wrongful act to occur by leaving an incompetent in a position to do harm.

Any physician on the medical staff should make sure that the medical staff has adequate mechanisms for reviewing the performance of its members, or he/she faces the potential for liability. Generally, this process is performed by peer review committees.

DRAFTING POLICIES AND PROCEDURES:
CONFLICTS WITH EMPLOYER POLICY

As I take pen to paper, I can't help but reminisce about days gone past. I remember wondering why my nursing supervisor insisted that each of the staff nurses write a policy for the procedure book. I was there to practice nursing, and this seemed like a waste of time. Why was she so concerned with revising our policies? They looked fine to me. Each of us had to sign statements that we had reviewed new and changed policies. Why the hassle?

It was not until I was out of law school and worked on my first case that I could appreciate and understand the importance of having written nursing policies and procedures. Then I could understand why employer policies need to be periodically reviewed. Most nurses believe that the only reason for writing and reviewing employer policies is to satisfy the JCAH inspectors. However, there is an even more important reason. Establishing and periodically reviewing policies to ensure that one's nursing practice conforms to the policies may very well help to keep the nurse out of the courtroom! Lawsuits are a fact of life, and nurses need all the assistance they can get in this litigious society.

The May 30, 1986, edition of *Hospital Week* featured an article in which the American Hospital Association advised hospitals to draft explicit policies on I.C.U.

admissions and discharges. Such policies should be developed and followed to optimize I.C.U. treatment outcomes, prevent staff burnout, reduce liability claims and cut costs.

If an employer has a policy, it must make sure that the policy is enforced. Violation of an employer's policy may result in a negligence action being filed against the employer or the nurse. Many hospital policies are mandated by specific laws in each state. Violations of these policies are known as "negligence per se."

Plaintiffs' attorneys are becoming more experienced. They frequently will subpoena copies of the employer's policies and procedures. Any discrepancies between the written policy and actual practice are indicia of negligence. Note that such discrepancies only suggest negligence and are not determinative. For example, suppose that an employer has a policy stating that only plain tetanus toxoid 0.5 cc. I.M. is to be administered. The policy is five years old and has never been revised. Suppose that the standard of practice changes and the treatment of choice becomes diphtheria toxoid 0.5 cc. I.M. A nurse administers this to a patient who has an anaphylactic reaction to the diphtheria toxoid and dies. The plaintiff subpoenas the employer's policies and discovers the policy stating that only plain tetanus is to be given. The plaintiff has now determined that there has been a breach of the employer's own policy.

As previously mentioned, a violation of the employer's own policy only suggests negligence. In this case, the plaintiff would probably not win, assuming the patient was asked and did not indicate that he was allergic to diphtheria toxoid. This problem could have been alleviated simply by ensuring that the policy was consistent with nursing practice.

The *Williams* case is an example of a case where the court imposed liability for failure to follow hospital policy.[21] The patient was having problems with his left knee and was admitted on October 29, 1980, for an arthroscopy.

The hospital had a number of written policies concerning anesthesia. First, CRNAs were under the direct supervison of the chairman of anesthesia service. Second, when giving anesthesia, the CRNA was to be in direct communication with the anesthesiologist or surgeon. Third, anesthesia was to be administered only by a CRNA or qualified physician.

St. Claire Hospital did not have an anesthesiologist on staff. Dr. Fossett, one of the surgeons, was chairman of the department of anesthesiology. The CRNAs were not employees of the hospital but were independent contractors. They were employed by Cave Run Clinic, a corporation owned by doctors.

Ed Johnson had just graduated from nurse anesthetist school and was uncertified. He was given temporary privileges, which were limited to those instances when he was under the direct supervision of Jeri Reis, a CRNA. The night before surgery, Johnson made a preoperative visit to the patient. Spinal anesthetics were usually administered for an arthroscopy, but Johnson planned a general anesthetic because the patient had previously had a myelogram. Johnson did not discuss this decision with anyone.

The next day, the patient went to the operating room, where Johnson administered a general anesthetic. After twenty minutes, the patient became cyanotic and coded. He remained in a coma for ten days and died.

The deceased patient's family sued Johnson, Dr. Fossett and the hospital.

The hosital was granted summary judgment because Johnson was an independent contractor and not an employee. The plaintiff appealed. The court then inquired whether the hospital owed a duty to its patients to ensure that its rules and regulations were met. Neither Dr. Fossett nor Johnson were aware of the hospital's policy restricting Johnson's practice. The hospital strenuously argued it had no liability because Johnson was an independent contractor. The court did not accept this argument and said that the *hospital had a legal duty to enforce its policies*. This case illustrates a situation in which the violation of standards ended in disaster.

In the *Foley* case, the hospital had a policy that a written history and physical be done within twenty-four hours on all patients admitted.[22] Another policy stated, "All necessary admission information is collected with particular attention to the possibility of infection. Suspicion of infection is to be reported to the physician immediately." Another rule provided that the intern should immediately evaluate any patient whose condition changes and that the attending physician should be notified of all significant changes.

Mrs. Foley entered the hospital in active labor at 5:20 a.m. She had been treated by her physician during the last 1½ months for a sore throat. Nine hours after admission, she delivered. Five hours after delivery she developed a temperature of 102.2 degrees. The intern evaluated the patient but did not notify the attending physician.

The attending physician had ordered that a blood count be taken within twenty-four hours of admission. This was not taken until thirty-two hours after admission and after the patient's condition had become critical. The patient died at 9:15 p.m. on the day following admission.

The court said that a jury might reasonably infer that if the patient's infection had been treated earlier she might have survived. Had a history been taken, as required by the rules, the hospital staff would have discovered her cold and sore throat condition. The court further stated that standards and regulations fixed by the State Department of Health and by such organizations as the American Hospital Association, as well as the employer's own rules, standards and regulations, may be used to develop the standard of care.

In the *Utter* case, which has been discussed previously, the nurses failed to abide by the hospital's policy.[23] The court found the nursing staff negligent for its failure to comply with the policy and procedure contained in the nursing manual. The nursing manual said that a nurse should notify a physician of any adverse condition. If the physician did not do anything about the adverse condition, the nurse was to call the department chairman. The nurses failed to follow this policy, and liability resulted.

The results in the *Union Hospital* case were identical.[24] The hospital had a policy requiring that side rails be used for all confused patients. The nurse failed to meet the hospital's own standard and was liable for the patient's injuries.

In the *Hicks* case, the hospital had an internal policy that appropriate progress notes and a diagnostic medical conference be performed on all committed psychiatric patients.[25] Mr. Morgan was admitted to the hospital for a condition which would send him into a violent rage. Progress notes were not kept, and a diagnostic medical conference was never scheduled. Subsequently, the court determined that Mr. Morgan was competent since there was no evidence to the contrary. When Mr. Morgan was released, he went home and killed his wife.

The court held that Mr. Morgan would not have been considered competent and released had the hospital followed its own internal standards. Therefore, the negligent failure to follow these standards was the proximate cause of Mrs. Morgan's death.

In the *Haber* case, the hospital had a policy requiring that side rails be up at night for all patients over fifty years of age.[26] When the patient fell out of bed and injured himself, the hospital was liable for failure to follow its own internal policy.

In the *Hunt* case, a 20-year-old patient was brought to the psychiatric ward after he had demolished part of his family's house with a hatchet.[27] The patient was brought to the hospital in restraints, accompanied by the police. The father told the staff that the patient would try to escape any way possible. The hospital had a written policy requiring the nursing staff to keep the utility room door locked at all times. The windows in the utility room were not covered by metal safety screens, as were the patients' rooms. The patient found the utility room unlocked one day and climbed out the window, falling five floors to the ground and injuring himself. The court held that the hospital was liable for the failure to follow its own rule. Had the utility room door been locked, the patient would not have fallen.

If a hospital policy should ever conflict with a state's nurse practice act, the nurse should defer in following the hospital policy. She should immediately notify her nursing supervisor. This is necessary to prevent the nurse's loss of licensure.

An employer cannot avoid liability for failure to follow rules merely by not having any. If there is no internal policy, the court will decide if a policy should have been in effect for the patient's safety or treatment.

The Ohio Supreme Court decided the *Burks* case along those lines.[28] An obese lady was medicated and placed in a bed that didn't have any side rails. She rolled over and fell out of bed. The hospital did not have a written policy and procedure manual for the nurses at that time. However, the school of nursing affiliated with the hospital had a nursing procedure manual. This manual had a procedure which required that side rails be used for any patient who was obese, restless or sedated. The jury was instructed, in determining negligence, to consider the absence of any procedural rule governing the use of side rails. The court adopted the school of nursing policy as applicable to the hospital.

The written rules of a hospital are admissible into evidence in a court of law.[29] In the *Smith* case, the hospital had a written policy requiring that side rails be used for all patients under sedation. When the patient fell out of bed, the nurse was sued.[30] The court was unimpressed with the argument that the use of side rails requires a specific order from a physician. The hospital had an internal policy which was violated, the court said.

Failure to Follow State, Federal or JCAH Standards

Employer policies should not be so specific and burdened with so much detail

208

as to pose legal dangers. Excessive detail is often needless, serves no useful purpose and is only a detriment to the employer.

If there is a state licensing agency rule requiring that a minimum number of nurses be on duty for each specified number of patients and an employer fails to comply, it may be liable if a patient is injured.

Courts since the *Darling* case are giving great weight to the JCAH standards and hospital bylaws in defining the standard of care. This was reaffirmed in the recent case of *Pedroza v. Bryant.*[31] Therefore, hospital policies should be consistent with JCAH requirements if the hospital is a JCAH-accredited facility. (The American Osteopathic Association has very similar guidelines for its accredited facilities.)

In the *Kakligian* case, the state licensing agency required that there be a written hospital policy stating when a consultation should be obtained.[32] All consultations were then to be recorded. The hospital in this case had no consultation policy. The court held, "Ample evidence was before the jury to show that there was no hospital policy denoting when consultations should be held. The plaintiff's case against Ford Hospital is largely based on an alleged defect in hospital procedure, *independent of the accuracy of treatment."* (Emphasis provided.)

JCAH policy states that all policies and procedures that reflect optimal nursing care should be written. The JCAH requires that the policies and procedures be
1. reviewed at least annually;
2. revised as necessary;
3. dated to indicate the time of last review;
4. signed by the responsible reviewing authority; and
5. implemented.[33]

The JCAH also requires, as a minimum, policies and procedures that relate to the following:
1. assignment of nursing care that is consistent with patients' needs;
2. acknowledgment and implementation of the diagnostic and therapeutic orders of medical staff members;
3. medical administration;
4. confidentiality of information;
5. the role of the nursing staff in patient and family education;
6. the maintenance of required records, reports and statistical information;
7. cardiopulmonary resuscitation;
8. patient, employee and visitor safety; and
9. the scope of activity of volunteers or public attendants.[34]

In summary, the following points should be remembered:
1. Every employer should have a written policy and procedure manual.
2. This manual should not be unnecessarily detailed.
3. Policies are generally more applicable and functional if staff members to whom the rules apply have input into policy drafting.
4. All written policies and procedures should be medically sound. They should be consistent with the standard of practice. Policies should be well researched. They should never be "thrown together" in response to a JCAH mandate that something be in writing for accreditation.

5. All policies and procedures should be realistic and within the capabilities of the staff to perform.
6. All policies and procedures which are not being followed should be eliminated and replaced with ones reflecting current standards.
7. JCAH-accredited facilities are required to date each policy and procedure to indicate the time of last review.
8. Each policy and procedure should be signed by the responsible reviewing authority (also a JCAH requirement).
9. If there is some reason why the employer policy or procedure must deviate from a responsibility mandated by an outside agency, the reason should be stated. This should be so integrated that one cannot be read without the other.
10. Before any policy or procedure is adopted, it should be processed through the appropriate hospital approval system.
11. In-services should be conducted on all new policies and procedures. Many employers post new policies and procedures and require each staff member's signature to verify that a review has been made. Employees are obligated to know the policies and procedures and to follow them.
12. The employer should appoint persons whose responsibility it is to periodically review the standards to make sure that the institution is current.
13. Newly employed nurses should have an orientation to existing policies and procedures. Written documentation should be made that all of the policies and procedures were reviewed.
14. Copies of the policies and procedures that affect the nursing staff's provision of care should be available in each patient care unit.

STANDING ORDERS

Recently, many questions have been asked by nurses concerning preprinted and standing orders. The law surrounding preprinted orders is more defined than that of standing orders. Preprinted orders are a set of standard medical directives written for a specific patient. They are implemented after contact and review by a physician, and are frequently used in intensive and coronary care units.

Preprinted orders are signed by the physician. The nurse has the same responsibility for implementing, documenting and clarifying preprinted orders as for any other medical orders. Each health care institution should have a written policy on the use of preprinted orders. The value and use of preprinted orders have been recognized by the medical and nursing community as long as they are consistent with the applicable standard of care. Preprinted orders should be reviewed and updated on a yearly basis.

Standing orders can present some unique legal questions. Standing orders are defined as medical directives to be implemented in situations requiring nursing judgment. Nursing judgment is premised on an understanding, recognition and interpretation of the patient's condition.

Standing orders are often utilized in life-threatening or serious conditions when physician intervention is not available. Many health care practitioners are certified in advanced cardiac life support and have standing orders regarding cardiac or respiratory emergencies. Standing orders may also be appropriate in non-life-threatening situations and when they are pursuant to approved protocol.

The standing order, to be valid, must involve an appropriate nursing function. For example, it would be inappropriate for a physician to leave a standing order with the office nurse to administer antibiotics to anyone with strep throat. This would require the nurse to perform acts of medical diagnosis. However, if based on a nursing diagnosis, the nurse decides the patient should have an air mattress, most institutions would hold this to be appropriate. Health care institutions should have written policies covering standing orders which should be updated and reviewed on a yearly basis.

Some physicians fill out cards listing standing orders that can be ordered for their patients. These generally involve nonprescription items such as aspirin, tucks and laxatives. These cards should be signed by the physician. The JCAH requires that standing orders be written in the medical record. This is generally written by using the abbreviation for standing orders, "S.O." The medical staff should authenticate and sign the order within twenty-four hours.

LIABILITY OF NURSE SUPERVISORS

Nurse supervisors are liable for their own independent acts of negligence. The hospital or employer will be liable for the supervisor's negligent acts which are created within the scope of his/her employment under the doctrine of *respondeat superior*. For example, in the *Norton* case, the nursing supervisor administered Lanoxin 3.0 cc.'s I.M. instead of the elixir form.[35] This proximately resulted in the patient's death. Liability resulted in this case because of the supervisor's own acts of negligence.

The *Valentin* case is another example where liability resulted directly from the nursing supervisor's own acts of negligence.[36] The nursing supervisor was liable for her three-day delay in notifying a physician of complications that a postoperative patient was having. For three days, the patient had demonstrated signs of tetanus following surgery for a hernia repair. The nursing supervisor had been duly informed of these complications by the floor nurse. A nursing supervisor also was liable for her acts of negligence when she administered an injection incorrectly to a patient while covering in the emergency room.[37]

It is a general proposition of law that no one is responsible for another's negligence unless one contributed to or participated in the negligence. The law allows that liability for the acts of one person can be transferred to another only under certain legal conditions. There is no liability on the part of the nursing supervisor under the doctrine of *respondeat superior* because the nursing supervisor is not the employer. Liability results either from the supervisor's own acts of negligence or from negligent acts of supervision.

The *Bowers* case exemplifies this situation.[38] After a patient's surgery, it was discovered that a needle had not been removed from the patient's abdomen during surgery. The patient filed suit against the hospital, the surgeons, the operating room nurses and the nursing supervisor of the operating room. The nursing supervisor was not present during the surgery and did not participate in the patient's care. Evidence was presented that she had no reason to suspect that the two nurses assigned to the case were anything other than competent.

The court dismissed the nursing supervisor, finding that she was not liable by reason of the assignment. The court ruled that the doctrine of *respondeat superior* is not applicable to the relationship between a supervisor and subordinate employees. The supervisor did not participate in the patient's care and had assigned competent nurses.

Nurse supervisors have a legal duty to ensure that the staff members under them are performing in a manner consistent with the standard of practice. Nurse supervisors are therefore liable if they are negligent in carrying out their supervisory duties. If a nurse supervisor makes an assignment to one he/she knows is not competent to perform that assignment, he/she will be liable if the patient is injured. The employer will also face liability through the doctrine of *respondeat superior*. Therefore, the supervisor should assign duties that are within the competence level of the staff member.

For example, a graduate nurse has just been employed. It is a busy day and the supervisor instructs the graduate nurse to start an I.V. on a patient. The graduate nurse remarks that she has never inserted an I.V. before. The nursing supervisor briefly explains the procedure stating, "there's nothing to it." The graduate goes to the patient's room, and in the process of inserting an I.V., punctures an artery. This results in amputation of the patient's arm. The nursing supervisor is at risk since she knew the graduate nurse was not competent to perform the procedure. The nursing supervisor should not request the nurse to do any procedure in which the nurse is untrained or unqualified. The supervisor should also provide the nurse with the degree of supervision he/she knows or should know is needed.

Lack of adequate supervision is frequently cited by the courts as contributing to a patient's injury. However, there is no clear-cut list which sets forth the legal requirements for adequate nursing supervision. Nursing supervisors should use common sense in their delegation of duties. For example, in the Canadian case of *Lions Gate Hospital*, a nursing supervisor was held liable for the patient's injuries which resulted from inadequate monitoring in the recovery room.[39] There were two recovery room nurses on duty, which the court accepted as adequate staffing. The nursing supervisor permitted one of the nurses to leave for a coffee break just before three patients were admitted. The nursing supervisor was liable for not attending to the staffing needs of the area she supervised.

Nurse supervisors should ensure that their staff members are competent and qualified to practice. One method is to make sure that their nursing licenses are current. A photocopy of the current license may be made, and the copy placed on file to evidence that this was done.

Nurse supervisors should closely monitor employer policies and procedures. They should see that the staff complies with these internal policies. For example, if an employer requires that all staff members attend a CPR refresher course and be certified yearly, the supervisor should check to see that each of his/her staff members have complied with this policy. In one case, the family of a patient who had coded and died sued a hospital and the nurses, saying that the staff was inadequately trained in CPR. The nursing supervisor had yearly copies of her staff's recertification, and the jury found for the nurses as a result of this documentation.

Nurse supervisors should maintain lists of all continuing education courses taken by the staff. In a recent case, we were able to get the nurse's continuing education card introduced into court to show that she had indeed had training on the care of a patient with a P.A.P./M.A.P. line.

Nursing supervisors should make sure that their nursing staff members stay within the parameters of nursing as set forth in their state's nurse practice act. The nurse practice act is the authority by which the nurse can practice nursing, and sets out the duties and functions which can be performed by registered or practical nurses.

STUDENT NURSES: SUPERVISION AND LIABILITY

Student nurses can be sued along with their nursing instructors. For this reason, most nursing schools require their nursing students to maintain a professional liability policy. Many insurance companies give students discounted rates.

Student nurses, as part of their educational preparation, are entrusted with the responsibility of providing different levels of patient care. While the student nurse is rendering nursing care, he/she is considered an employee of the hospital. This is true whether he/she is a student of a hospital school of nursing or of a university affiliated with the hospital. A student nurse who commits malpractice is personally responsible for his/her own acts of negligence. The hospital is also responsible through the doctrine of *respondeat superior*. For this reason, most hospitals mandate that the student nurse carry professional liability insurance.

Student nurses are held to the same standard of care as registered professional nurses. For this reason, student nurses should make sure they are adequately prepared to care for assigned patients. Student nurses should not perform any act or procedure in which they are untrained or inadequately prepared.

In one case, a nursing student was held liable for improperly administering a medication.[40] The label indicated that the medication was for I.V. use only. The student nurse injected the infant intramuscularly with the medication, causing the patient injury.

The same principles discussed under the above section, "Liability of Nurse Supervisors," apply to the nursing instructor who supervises the student nurse. A nursing instructor should check off the students as they demonstrate each nursing procedure. The instructor should make sure that each student is capable of performing in a manner consistent with the standard of care.

Instructors are under a legal duty to make sure they have provided adequate instruction to their students. The test for determining whether a clinical instructor has deviated from the acceptable standard of care is to compare his/her actions with what another prudent instructor would have done in the same or similar circumstances. For example, suppose that a nursing student is about to insert

213

a Foley catheter and that she advises her clinical instructor that she has never catheterized a patient. If the instructor replies that it is a simple procedure and advises the student to proceed unsupervised, and the patient develops an infection or complication from the procedure, the instructor is at legal risk. The instructor has a duty to make sure that the students are competent to perform any procedure or treatment rendered.

Instructors who have given adequate training to their nursing students are not liable if a student commits negligence.[41] This is true as long as the instructor has not contributed to the injury and has no reason to believe that the student is incompetent.

REFERENCES

1. Joint Commission on Accreditation of Hospitals, *Accreditation Manual for Hospitals* 133 (1986).
2. *Inadequate Staffing Seen as New Type of Nurse Shortage in Hospitals* 52-55 (January 1, 1985).
3. *Darling v. Charleston Community Memorial Hospital*, 33 Ill. 2d 326, 211 N.E.2d 253 (1965).
4. *Sanchez v. Bay General Hospital*, 172 Cal. Rptr. 342 (Cal. Ct. App. 1981).
5. *Horton v. Niagara Falls Memorial Medical Center*, 380 N.Y.S.2d 116 (N.Y. App. Div. 1976).
6. Joint Commission on Accreditation of Hospitals, *supra* note 1, at Section 12.4.3.4.
7. *Id.* at Section 12.4.4.1.
8. Creighton, Helen, *Law Every Nurse Should Know* 69 (5th ed., W.B. Saunders, Philadelphia, 1986).
9. *Dessauer v. Memorial General Hospital*, 628 P.2d 337 (N.M. Ct. App. 1981).
10. *Norton v. Argonaut Insurance Co.*, 144 So.2d 249 (La. 1962).
11. *American Journal of Nursing* 212 (April 1982).
12. Bissell, Leclair, *Alcoholism and the Professional*, Oxford University Press.
13. Stroedel, Robert, "Thy Brother's Keeper, Responsibility for the 'Impaired Physician,'" 10 *Legal Aspects of Medical Practice* (December 1982).
14. Horty, John, *Patient Care Law* 1 (Pittsburg, Pa., August/September 1983).
15. *Judge v. Rockford Memorial Hospital*, 150 N.E.2d 202 (Ill. App. Ct. 1958).
16. Norman, Jane, "So-Called Physician 'Whistle-Blowers' Protected," 11 *Legal Aspects of Medical Practice* (February 1983).
17. Stroedel, *supra* note 13.
18. *Dayan v. Wood River Township Hospital*, 152 N.E.2d 205 (Ill. 1958).
19. *Tuscon Medical Center, Inc. v. Misevch*, 545 P.2d 958 (Ariz. 1976).
20. *Corleto v. Shore Memorial Hospital*, 350 A.2d 534 (N.J. Super. Ct. 1975).
21. *Williams v. St. Claire Medical Center*, 657 S.W.2d 590 (Ky. Ct. App. 1983).
22. *Foley v. Bishop Clarkson Memorial Hospital*, 185 Neb. 89, 173 N.W.2d 881 (1970).
23. *Utter v. United Hospital Center, Inc.*, 236 S.E.2d 213 (W. Va. 1977).
24. *Polonsky v. Union Hospital*, 418 N.E.2d 620 (Mass. App. Ct. 1981).
25. *Hicks v. United States*, 357 F. Supp. 434 (D.D.C. 1973).
26. *Haber v. Cross County Hospital*, 378 N.Y.S.2d 369 (N.Y. 1975).
27. *Hunt v. King County*, 481 P.2d 593 (Wash. 1971).
28. *Burks v. Christ Hospital*, 249 N.E.2d 829 (Ohio 1969).
29. *Smith v. West Calcasieu-Cameron Hospital*, 251 So. 2d 810 (La. 1971); *Gourdine v. Phelps Memorial Hospital*, 366 N.Y.S.2d 316 (N.Y. 1972).
30. *Smith, id.*
31. *Pedroza v. Bryant*, 677 P.2d 166 (Wash. 1984).
32. *Kakligian v. Henry Ford Hospital*, 210 N.W.2d 463 (Mich. 1973). *See* Mich. Admin. Code Section 7.12, rule 325.1027.
33. Joint Commission on Accreditation of Hospitals, *supra* note 1, at 136.
34. *Id.* at 137.

35. *Norton, supra* note 10.
36. *Valentin v. La Societe Francaise de Bienfaisance Mutuelle de Los Angeles,* 76 Cal. App. 2d 1, 172 P.2d 359 (1946).
37. *Lewis v. Davis,* 410 N.E.2d 1363 (Ind. Ct. App. 1980).
38. *Bowers v. Olch,* 120 Cal. App. 2d 108, 260 P.2d 997 (1953).
39. *Laidlaw v. Lions Gate Hospital,* 8 D.L.R.3d 730 (B.C. Sup. Ct. 1969).
40. *O'Neil v. Glens Falls Indemnity Co.,* 310 F.2d 165 (8th Cir. 1962).
41. *Aubert v. Charity Hospital of Louisiana,* 363 So. 2d 1223 (La. 1978).

CHAPTER ELEVEN

THE NURSE IN A LAWSUIT

The Complaint
The Answer
Pretrial Discovery and Motions for Summary Judgment
Arbitration
Trial
Appeals
Settlement

THE COMPLAINT

Lawsuits must be brought within a certain time or they are barred. The time period during which a suit must be filed is called a statute of limitation. The specific statute of limitation for actions against nurses differs from state to state and will be discussed later.

A plaintiff initiates a lawsuit by filing a complaint and a summons. The receipt of the complaint is the way in which the nurse discovers that she has been sued. The complaint contains the allegations upon which the plaintiff bases his or her claim to damages.

The complaint may state only that the nurse was negligent and that her conduct fell below the acceptable standard of care. Many times the nurse is unable to recall the patient and wonders what the plaintiff's specific allegations are against her. Discovery would then be initiated by her attorney to find out specifically what the plaintiff's allegations are. Other complaints are more specific and may give an outline of the facts supporting the plaintiff's allegations.

The plaintiff's allegations may draw upon more than one legal theory. For example, in medical and nursing malpractice actions, common allegations include negligence, breach of contract, loss of consortium, lack of informed consent and unnecessary treatment. The plaintiff must prove each of the elements of each theory in order to recover.

The summons notifies the defendant that a lawsuit has been started against him/her and explains that the defendant must respond within a certain period of time. Failure to respond can result in a default judgment against the defendant. The time period for answering varies from state to state. Most states provide either a twenty- or twenty-eight-day period in which to answer.

The complaint is sent by the manner described in the state's court rules. The summons and complaint are usually sent by registered mail or are personally delivered by a legal messenger to the defendant's home or place of employment. Because the period of time for a response is short, it is important for the nurse who is served with a summons and complaint to *immediately* notify her employer, insurance carrier or personal attorney.

The employer, through its own insurance policy, will hire an attorney to defend and represent the defendant's interests. Generally, the employer's policy will provide the nurse with a defense if the act of alleged negligence was within the scope of his/her responsibility. If the nurse has his/her own professional liability insurance policy, that company will hire an attorney to defend and represent his/her interests at no expense.

An attorney may object to the complaint. For example, the defendant may allege that the summons was incorrectly served or that suit was brought in the wrong state. These are called pre-answer motions. If no pre-answer motions are filed, the nurse's attorney must then file the answer within the designated time period to avoid a default judgment.

Many nurses have never seen a complaint. In the appendix of this book is a sample complaint which was filed against a nurse. The plaintiff alleged that the nurse failed to use aseptic technique in administering an I.M. injection.

THE ANSWER

The answer is the nurse's response to the plaintiff's complaint. The answer is drafted by the attorney representing the nurse. It is a document in which the nurse admits or denies each of the allegations made by the plaintiff. Some allegations may be denied because the nurse does not have enough knowledge to form a belief as to whether the allegation is true or false. Any allegation that is admitted as true by the defendant does not have to be proven by the plaintiff at trial. Thus, it is highly unusual to admit to the plaintiff's allegation of a violation of the standard of care, proximate cause and damages.

In addition to admitting or denying the allegations made by the plaintiff, the nurse may assert certain defenses. For example, the nurse may allege that the action is barred by the statute of limitation or that injury, if any, was caused or contributed to by the plaintiff or by another person.

In addition to asserting defenses, the nurse may file counterclaims or cross-claims. For example, a private duty nurse is employed by Mrs. Jones to provide home care. One night, Mrs. Jones falls out of bed and fractures her hip. Mrs. Jones sues the nurse for negligence. The nurse answers, stating she is not negligent, and files a counterclaim for $400, which is owed to her for her professional nursing services.

A cross-claim is filed by one of the defendants against another defendant. For example, an emergency room physician is sued for failing to diagnose a plaintiff's fracture. The hospital is also sued based on the apparent authority doctrine previously discussed in Chapter 3. The bottom line is that the wrongdoer is ultimately responsible for his or her own acts of negligence. The hospital files a cross-claim indicating that if it has to pay part of the judgment, it is seeking indemnification from the physician.

The pleading may raise factual questions along with questions on the law. In a jury trial, the judge will settle questions of law, and the jury will decide questions of fact. An example of a factual question would be whether a patient's dressing was changed and how often. The jury will listen to the evidence, evaluating those who testify, and decide what occurred. A sample answer has been attached in the appendix. Thus, the nurse can be familiar with not only what a summons and complaint look like, but also the answer that is filed on his/her behalf in the event he/she is ever named a defendant.

PRETRIAL DISCOVERY AND
MOTIONS FOR SUMMARY JUDGMENT

Pretrial discovery is used to investigate the claim and to discover information related to the adversary's case. Pretrial discovery is used by the plaintiff to fully develop the allegations listed in the complaint, and by the defendant to develop information to support denials and affirmative defenses as listed in the answer. The parties must conduct pretrial discovery pursuant to the rules of the court. Pretrial discovery puts to use devices such as interrogatories, depositions, requests for admissions and requests for production of documents.

A number of procedural remedies are also available during this time. Either party may ask the court for a judgment on the pleadings. When this motion is made, the court will examine the case and decide if a judgment can be made based upon the complaint and the answer. The nurse's attorney will sometimes ask for a motion to dismiss the action. Motions for a more definite statement may also be made.

The nurse's attorney may also file a motion for summary judgment. A summary judgment is generally granted by the judge when a party is entitled to judgment according to law and when there are no material facts in dispute. For example, a nurse stopped on her way home at an accident and rendered emergency care. Under the Good Samaritan law in her state, she has civil immunity even if she was negligent. The facts are not in dispute. The plaintiff's only allegation is that she was negligent in performing CPR. The nurse's attorney files a summary judgment motion saying that even if everything the plaintiff alleges is true, the nurse is still entitled to judgment in her favor. The judge agrees and the case is over.

Interrogatories

Interrogatories are written questions submitted to one party by the other party. The party to whom the interrogatories are directed must answer the written questions within the period set by the court rules, usually twenty to twenty-eight days. Frequently, the defendant nurse will ask the plaintiff to identify the specific allegations of negligence against him/her. The nurse may ask for the name of the plaintiff's expert witness and what that expert witness's testimony is expected to be, the names and addresses of persons having relevant knowledge of the facts or allegations, or an explanation of the alleged damages.

The plaintiff also may send interrogatories to the defendant nurse. The interrogatories may ask the defendant to describe the care and treatment given or to give information about the defendant's training and experience. A sample set of interrogatories is contained in the appendix.

Depositions

A deposition is a face-to-face questioning session, in which the person answering the questions is called the deponent. Depositions can be taken of witnesses or parties to an action. A party requesting a deposition is usually represented by an attorney, who asks the questions. There is a court reporter present to transcibe the proceeding. Attorneys for the named parties are present and may ask questions. Questions regarding any information which could lead to discoverable evidence may be asked.

The plaintiff usually starts out the nurse's deposition by asking his/her name, address, marital status and educational background. The plaintiff generally asks if he/she has any children and for information concerning his/her past employment. Many nurses are surprised that they are asked these types of questions. These are generally asked just to provide background information.

Usually, the plaintiff's attorney will not only depose all the named defendants, but also any other important witnesses. For example, if the hosital is sued for the negligence of a nurse, but the nurse is not personally named in the lawsuit, the nurse will probably be deposed.

The defendant nurse's deposition is the most important part of discovery. The deposition will be used to "lock in" the nurse's testimony. The deposition can be transcribed and used by the plaintiff at trial and read to the jury to point out inconsistent statements. This is why the nurse should always review a copy of the deposition testimony prior to trial.

It is important for the defendant nurse to be adequately prepared for the deposition. The nurse has a right to review the notations made in the plaintiff's medical record. The nurse's attorney should meet with him/her prior to the deposition to explain the procedure, to discuss anticipated questions and to make sure the nurse is prepared to testify. The attorney for the defendant nurse should object to any improper questions at the deposition. The constant objections made by the attorneys often confuse the nurse. These objections are made based on the rules of evidence and are to be decided by the judge. The nurse need not be concerned with these objections. Rather, he/she should concentrate on the questions. After the objections are made, he/she should then answer each question. This is true unless the nurses's attorney specifically advises him/her not to answer. If the nurse forgets the question, he/she can ask the court reporter to repeat it.

The plaintiff's attorney often tries to intimidate and put words in the nurse's mouth. The nurse should pause and take a deep breath if he/she becomes nervous and should listen closely to the recharacterization of his/her prior testimony. If he/she has been incorrectly quoted, he/she should merely state what it was that was said.

If the nurse does not understand a question he/she can simply state that he/she does not understand and ask the plaintiff's attorney to rephase the question. The nurse should take as much time as necessary to answer. If he/she does not know the answer, he/she should simply say so.

The nurse's attorney usually deposes the plaintiff as well as any other witnesses having knowledge about the claimed injury. The defense attorney may also depose any subsequent treating physicians.

Later in the discovery period, when each side has retained expert witnesses, each attorney may depose the opposing side's expert witnesses to determine their opinions and the assumptions upon which they base their opinions.

The nurse should dress appropriately for the deposition. Patched jeans and old T-shirts are not advised. This is probably the first time the nurse will have a chance to meet opposing counsel, who will be evaluating him/her and sizing up what type of witness he/she will make before the jury.

Nurses should avoid shaking their heads and nodding during the deposition. The court reporter will be transcribing everything said, and a nod of the head may not be recorded and may give the appearance that the nurse has failed to answer the question. Also avoid such responses as "uh-uh" and "uh-huh," since they do not paint a good image of the nurse on paper.

The nurse should always be courteous. This does not mean that the nurse should be overly friendly or "chummy" with opposing counsel. Many plaintiff's attorneys attempt to lure the nurse into this trap by giving this appearance. The nurse should remember the relative positions of the parties — the individual across the way just sued him/her for professional negligence.

Nurses are generally so used to being part of a helping profession that they want to "tell it all." However, the nurse should not volunteer any information. He/she should listen to each question and answer that question only. The nurse should always tell the truth; however, the truth should and can be stated in a light which is most favorable to the nurse. This does not mean that the nurse should exaggerate. If the jury believes the nurse is exaggerating many points, it could damage his/her credibility.

Requests for Production of Documents

A request for production of documents is used to obtain tax returns, medical records, reports or other relevant documents. The requesting party makes a list of the items desired. If the requested material is outside the scope of discovery, the other party merely objects. Objections to the requests are ruled on by the judge. Some attorneys also prefer to request what is known as a "protective order."

The plaintiff may request production of relevant hospital policies and procedures and even hospital bylaws. Thus it is imperative for each nurse to be aware of his/her institution's policies and procedures. This is discussed in more detail in the section on policies and procedures in Chapter 10. There is also an example of a request for production of documents in the appendices.

Other Discovery Devices

Independent Medical Examinations and Subpoenas
If the plaintiff claims physical or psychological injury, the defense attorney is entitled to have the plaintiff examined by a physician or psychologist. The independent medical examination is performed to rebut the plaintiff's testimony about the cause or extent of the plaintiff's injury.

There are two types of subpoenas. A subpoena *ad testificandum* is a written order commanding a person to appear and give testimony at trial. The more common type is a subpoena *duces tecum*. A subpoena *duces tecum* is a written order commanding a person to appear, give testimony and bring all the documents, papers, books or records described in the subpoena. A subpoena *duces tecum* may be used by either party to obtain medical records or other relevant records kept in the course of business. A copy of a sample subpoena is attached in the appendices.

A valid subpoena usually includes the following:
1. names of the plaintiff and defendant;
2. case number;
3. name of the court;
4. name and address of the person commanded to attend;
5. date, time and place of the requested appearance;
6. name and telephone number of the attorney who had the subpoena issued; and
7. a list of the items that the recipient is ordered to bring (if it is a subpoena *duces tecum*).

The attorneys for each party are allowed to interview and talk with witnesses. However, it is improper for the plaintiff's attorney to discuss the case with the named defendants without first obtaining permission from defense counsel. Nurses are cautioned that if they are approached by a plaintiff's attorney, they should contact their risk manager or hospital attorney before discussing a patient's care and treatment. This is especially important in cases where the nurse's employer has already been sued.

ARBITRATION

In an attempt to minimize the volume of litigation for nursing and medical malpractice claims, many states have legislation that requires review by a screening or arbitration panel. There are two types of arbitration panels: mandatory and voluntary. The purpose of the arbitration or screening panel is to reduce litigation and settle claims expeditiously. The statutes vary dramatically from state to state.

In theory, screening panels are somewhat different from arbitration panels, though in many states this distinction is blurred. Screening panels do not make final and binding determination of claims. The purpose of the screening panel is to make findings of fact and assist in determining the merits of cases.

Arbitration is defined as the reference of a dispute to an impartial third person chosen by the parties to the dispute.[1] The parties agree in advance to abide by the arbitrator's award. By definition, arbitration is binding; however, many states provide for nonbinding arbitration.

Each state has a statute defining a panel's composition. In Alabama,[2] Georgia,[3] Illinois,[4] Louisiana[5] and Maine,[6] the defendant and the plaintiff each choose an arbitrator. Those two arbitrators then select a neutral third arbitrator agreeable to each side.

Some states have a specific law setting out the composition of the panel. This is true in Puerto Rico,[7] Virginia,[8] Vermont[9] and South Dakota.[10] Puerto Rico has an interesting procedure. Panels are composed of a physician, an attorney and a lay person. All three panel members are selected by the Secretary of Health. Panels in Virginia consist of three attorneys, three physicians and one circuit court judge.

Binding arbitration of malpractice disputes is provided by twelve states and Puerto Rico.[11] Some states provide for voluntary binding arbitration. Many of the state statutes providing for mandatory binding arbitration, as opposed to voluntary binding arbitration, have been ruled unconstitutional since they interfere with the individual's right to a trial.

As previously mentioned, there is a great deal of variance in the different arbitration statutes. Arizona's arbitration statute is entitled "Medical Liability Review Panels."[12] In that state, in the case of a claim involving nursing negligence, the panel would be made up of a nurse, a lawyer and a judge. These three hear the evidence much the same as during a trial.[13] This is nonbinding arbitration, because if the nurse is found not negligent, the plaintiff can go on to trial. As in most other states, the panel's finding is disclosed to the jurors during trial.

Hawaii's arbitration panel is entitled the "Medical Claim Conciliation Panel."[14] Each Medical Claim Conciliation Panel includes a chairperson who is selected from among persons who are familiar with and experienced in personal injury claims. The second member is an attorney who is experienced in trial practice, and the third person is a physician or surgeon. The Medical Claim Conciliation Panel reviews and renders findings and advisory opinions on the issue of liability and damages in medical tort claims against health care providers.

Michigan's arbitration statute was enacted in 1975.[15] Both hospitals and physicians can take advantage of the arbitration statute. Under Michigan law, the patient can sign forms to have the case arbitrated.[16] However, this means the right to trial has been given up. The arbitration panel is composed of three arbitrators. The panel consists of an attorney, a member of the public and either a physician or a hospital employee, depending upon who is being sued.

TRIAL

Jury Selection

Most medical malpractice trials are jury trials. The number of jurors may differ from state to state. Most states have between six and twelve jurors. Frequently, jurors' names are selected from the voter registration list. Usually the attorneys are permitted to ask the potential jurors questions to assist each side in selecting appropriate jurors. The questions are designed to determine whether the juror will be able to hear and understand the evidence, weigh the evidence objectively and follow the judge's instructions. The questioning of jurors is called *voir dire*.

Jurors can be removed "for cause." Usually an attorney will request a removal for cause if he/she feels the juror will not be objective. For example, if the potential juror is a relative of one of the parties, he/she is likely to be biased and would be removed for cause. Perhaps the juror has been treated by the defendant nurse or doctor in the past. That juror might be considered automatically biased and would be dismissed. There is usually no limit to the number of potential jurors who can be dismissed "for cause."

In addition, each side is allowed a certain number of "peremptory challenges." Most statutes allow two or three peremptory challenges to each party. The peremptory challenges allow the attorneys to remove prospective jurors without stating any reason. Usually the attorneys will pre-empt jurors who they believe will be more sympathetic to the other side's case.

Opening Statement

After selection of the jury, each side gives an opening statement. The plaintiff's attorney goes first unless he/she waives opening statement.

The opening statement provides each attorney with an opportunity to explain to the jury the evidence that he/she expects to present and gives the jury an overview of what the evidence will be, which is important because witnesses do not always testify in order. Opening statements are not evidence, but merely the attorney's statement of what he/she expects the evidence to show.

Presentation of Evidence

After the opening statement, the plaintiff presents his/her evidence. The defendant follows. Witnesses are called by each side and are first examined by the attorney calling them to testify. The attorney asks the witness a series of questions; this is known as a "direct examination." When the direct examination is completed, opposing counsel cross-examines the witness in an effort to challenge the testimony or present additional facts to the jury. The plaintiff may then ask additional questions, "redirect," and the defendant may "recross."

After the plaintiff's case is presented, the defendant may move for a directed verdict when the plaintiff has failed to prove the necessary elements of the case. If the judge grants the motion, the trial is over and the defendant wins. If the motion is overruled, the defendant presents his/her case.

The defense attorney will call the defendant to testify along with any defense expert witnesses, and the plaintiff's attorney will be given the opportunity to cross-examine each witness.

Closing Argument

After all of the evidence is presented, each attorney will summarize the case by making a closing argument. This is the final chance for each side to persuade the jury to resolve the case in its favor. The lawyers may make conclusions or draw inferences from the material presented. Facts which have not been introduced into evidence cannot be argued.

Jury Instructions

If the case is being tried by a jury, the judge instructs the jury on the law. The judge reads written instructions to the jurors, and the jurors will be permitted to take the instructions into the jury room to aid in their deliberation. The jury is to find the facts from the evidence presented. The judge instructs the jurors to apply these facts to the law as it was explained to them.

In a negligence action against a nurse, the instructions define each of the four elements that must be present to prove liability. An instruction will be given that the plaintiff has the burden of proof, which means that if the jury does not find the plaintiff's version more probable than not, a decision must be rendered for the defendant.

Jury Deliberations

The judge's instructions require the jurors to first elect a foreperson. In a malpractice case, the jurors must then vote on the presence of each of the four elements of negligence. After the jury reaches a verdict, it returns to the courtroom, and the foreperson announces the verdict.

APPEALS

Sometimes the side that loses at trial may request a new trial. If that motion for a new trial is denied, the party may appeal the decision to a higher court. The appellate court reviews a case by looking at written briefs of both counsel, which outline their positions. The appellate court also reviews the trial transcript.

The appellate court listens to oral arguments made by each side. Frequently the basis for appeal is that the trial court judge made a mistake in admitting or excluding evidence, in instructing the jury or in otherwise conducting the trial. The appellate court enters a written opinion which either affirms or reverses the trial court's decision.

The party losing the appeal may appeal to the state supreme court. If the case is accepted by the supreme court, the appellate procedure is followed again. The supreme court justices then write an opinion. Supreme court opinions are very important sources of case law.

SETTLEMENT

The case may be settled at any time. A settlement means the plaintiff agrees to dismiss the claim against the named defendant and releases him/her from future liability, usually in exchange for money.

As a matter of simple economics, it is good to settle deserving cases early. The plaintiff's attorney has invested time in preparing the case and will expect more money when more work has been expended. Out-of-pocket expenses have been incurred in soliciting expert testimony. The nurse's attorney should make an investigation early in the case to attempt to evaluate liability. Defense counsel will also save time and money by early settlement of cases in which liability is likely.

In addition to economic loss and inconvenience to the defendant nurse, the lawsuit can cause anxiety. The anxiety level is higher when the nurse knows that he/she may be liable or may have problems proving that he/she was not negligent.

For these reasons, the nurse must relate both the favorable and unfavorable facts of the case to his/her attorney. In a meritorious case, the plaintiff will have to be compensated, whether it is today or tomorrow.

REFERENCES

1. *Black's Law Dictionary*, 96 (5th ed. 1979).
2. Ala. Code Section 6-5-485(b) (1977).
3. Ga. Code Ann. Section 7-408(a) (Supp. 1982).
4. Ill. Ann. Stat. ch. 10, para. 213(a) (Smith-Hurd Supp. 1983-1984).
5. La. Rev. Stat. Ann. Section 9:4231 (West 1983).
6. Me. Rev. Stat. Ann. tit. 24, Section 2705(1) (Supp. 1982-1983).
7. P.R. Laws Ann. tit. 26, Section 4111 (Supp. 1982).
8. Va. Code Ann. Section 8.01-581.3 (1983).
9. Vt. Stat. Ann. tit. 12, Section 7002(a) (Supp. 1983).
10. S.D. Codified Laws Ann. Section 21-25B-4 (1979).
11. Ala. Code Section 6-5-485 (1977); Alaska Stat. Section 09.55.535 (Supp. 1982); Cal. Civ. Proc. Code Section 1295 (Deering 1982); Ga. Code Ann. Section 7-402, -403 (Supp. 1982); Ill. Ann. Stat. ch. 10, Section 201 (Smith-Hurd Supp. 1983-1984); La. Rev. Stat. Ann. Section 9:4230-4236 (West 1983); Me. Rev. Stat. Ann. tit. 24, Section 2701, 2702 (Supp. 1982-1983); Mich. Comp. Laws Ann. Section 600.5040, 5041 (Supp. 1983-1984); Ohio Rev. Code Ann. Section 2711.21 (1981); S.D. Codified Laws Ann. Section 21-25B-1 (1979); Vt. Stat. Ann. tit. 12, Section 7002 (Supp. 1983); Va. Code Ann. Section 8.01-581.1 (Supp. 1983).
12. Ariz. Rev. Stat. Ann. Section 12-567 (am. 1982).
13. Perin, Robin, *Arizona Statutes Affecting Nursing Practice* 2 (Professional Education Systems, Inc., 1986.)
14. Hawaii Rev. Stat. Section 671(1)-(17) (am. 1983).
15. Lutz, Sharon, *Michigan Statutes Affecting Nursing Practice* 20, (Professional Education Systems, Inc., 1986).
16. Mich. Comp. Laws Ann. Section 600.5041.

CHAPTER TWELVE

APPENDICES

A.N.A. Code for Nurses
A.M.A. Principles of Medical Ethics
A.H.A. Patient's Bill of Rights
JCAH Patient's Bill of Rights
Standards for Nursing
Primary Nursing
Sample Professional Liability Policy
Common Areas of Liability for Physicians
Complaint
Answer
Sample Interrogatories
Demand for Production of Documents and Things for Inspection
Case Example of Common Charting Errors
Case Study: Advising Patients Who Want to Sign Out A.M.A.
Glossary of Legal Terms

APPENDIX A

The A.N.A. Code for Nurses

Preamble

The Code for Nurses is based on belief about the nature of individuals, nursing, health, and society. Recipients and providers of nursing services are viewed as individuals and groups who possess basic rights and responsibilities, and whose values and circumstances command respect at all times. Nursing encompasses the promotion and restoration of health, the prevention of illness, and the alleviation of suffering. The statements of the Code and their interpretation provide guidance for conduct and relationships in carrying out nursing responsibilities consistent with the ethical obligations of the profession and quality in nursing care.

Code for Nurses

1. The nurse provides services with respect for human dignity and the uniqueness of the client unrestricted by considerations of social and economic status, personal attributes, or the nature of the health problem.
2. The nurse safeguards the client's right to privacy by judiciously protecting information of a confidential nature.
3. The nurse acts to safeguard the client and the public when health care and safety are affected by the incompentent, unethical, or illegal practice of any person.
4. The nurse assumes responsibility and accountability for individual nursing judgments and actions.
5. The nurse maintains competence in nursing.
6. The nurse exercises informed judgment and uses individual competence and qualification as criteria in seeking consultation, accepting responsibilities, and delegating nursing activities to others.
7. The nurse participates in activities that contribute to the ongoing development of the profession's body of knowledge.
8. The nurse participates in the profession's efforts to implement and improve standards of nursing.
9. The nurse participates in the profession's efforts to establish and maintain conditions of employment conducive to high-quality nursing care.
10. The nurse participates in the profession's efforts to protect the public from misinformation and misrepresentation and to maintain the integrity of nursing.
11. The nurse collaborates with members of the health professions and other citizens in promoting community and national efforts to meet the health needs of the public.

APPENDIX B

American Medical Association Principles of Medical Ethics

Preamble

These principles are intended to aid physicians individually and collectively in maintaining a high level of ethical conduct. They are not laws but standards by which a physician may determine the propriety of his conduct in his relationship with patients, with colleagues, with members of allied professions, and with the public.

Section 1

The principal objective of the medical profession is to render service to humanity with full respect for the dignity of man. Physicians should merit the confidence of patients entrusted to their care, rendering to each a full measure of service and devotion.

Section 2

Physicians should strive continually to improve medical knowledge and skill, and should make available to their patients and colleagues the benefits of their professional attainments.

Section 3

A physician should practice a method of healing founded on a scientific basis; and he should not voluntarily associate professionally with anyone who violates this principle.

Section 4

The medical profession should safeguard the public and itself against physicians deficient in moral character or professional competence. Physicians should observe all laws, uphold the dignity and honor of the profession, and accept its self-imposed disciplines. They should expose, without hesitation, illegal or unethical conduct of fellow members of the profession.

Section 5

A physician may choose whom he will serve. In an emergency, however, he should render service to the best of his ability. Having undertaken the care of a patient, he may not neglect him; and unless he has been discharged, he may discontinue his services only after giving adequate notice. He should not solicit patients.

Section 6

A physician should not dispose of his services under terms or conditions which tend to interfere with or impair the free and complete exercise of his medical judgment and skill or tend to cause a deterioration of the quality of medical care.

Section 7

In the practice of medicine a physician should limit the source of his professional income to medical services actually rendered by him, or under his supervision, to his patients. His fee should be commensurate with the services rendered and the client's ability to pay. He should neither pay nor receive a commission for referral of patients. Drugs, remedies, or appliances may be dispensed or supplied by the physician provided it is in the best interest of the patient.

Section 8

A physician should seek consultation upon request; in doubtful or difficult cases; or whether it appears that the quality of medical service may be enhanced thereby.

Section 9

A physician may not reveal the confidences entrusted to him in the course of medical attendance, or the deficiencies he may observe in the character of patients, unless he is required to do so by law or unless it becomes necessary in order to protect the welfare of the individual or of the community.

Section 10

The honored ideals of the medical profession imply that the responsibilities of the physician extend not only to the individual, but also to society where these responsibilities deserve his treatment and participation in activities which have the purpose of improving both the health and the well-being of the individual and the community.

Principles of Medical Ethics of the AMA, adopted, AMA House of Delegates, June 1980. Reprinted with permission of the American Medical Association.

APPENDIX C

A Patient's Bill of Rights
(Reprinted with permission of the American Hospital Association, copyright 1972.)

The American Hospital Association presents a Patient's Bill of Rights with the expectation that observance of these rights will contribute to more effective patient care and greater satisfaction for the patient, his physician, and the hospital organization. Further, the Association presents these rights in the expectation that they will be supported by the hospital on behalf of its patients as an integral part of the healing process. It is recognized that a personal relationship between the physician and the patient is essential for the provision of proper medical care. The traditional physician-patient relationship takes on a new dimension when care is rendered within an organizational structure. Legal precedent has established that the institution itself also has a responsibility to the patient. It is in recognition of these factors that these rights are affirmed.

1. The patient has the right to considerate and respectful care.

2. The patient has the right to obtain, from his physician, complete current information concerning his diagnosis, treatment, and prognosis in terms the patient can be reasonably expected to understand. When it is not medically advisable to give such information to the patient, the information should be made available to an appropriate person in his behalf. He has the right to know by name, the physician responsible for coordinating his care.

3. The patient has the right to receive, from his physician, information necessary to give informed consent prior to the start of any procedure and/or treatment. Except in emergencies, such information for informed consent should include, but not necessarily be limited to, the specific procedure and/or treatment, the medically significant risks involved, and the probable duration of incapacitation. Where medically significant alternatives for care or treatment exist, or when the patient requests information concerning medical alternatives, the patient also has the right to know the name of the person responsible for the procedures and/or treatment.

4. The patient has the right to refuse treatment to the extent permitted by law, and to be informed of the medical consequences of his action.

5. The patient has the right to every consideration of his privacy concerning his own medical care program. Case discussion, consultation, examination, and treatment are confidential and should be conducted discreetly. Those not directly involved in his care must have the permission of the patient to be present.

6. The patient has the right to expect that all communications and records pertaining to his care should be treated as confidential.

7. The patient has the right to expect that within its capacity a hospital must make reasonable response to the request of a patient for services. The hospital must provide evaluation, service, and/or referral as indicated by the urgency of the case. When medically permissible a patient may be transferred to another facility only after he has received complete information and explanation concerning the needs for and alternatives to such

a transfer. The institution to which the patient is to be transferred must first have accepted the patient for transfer.

8. The patient has the right to obtain information as to the existence of any professional relationships among individuals, by name, who are treating him.

9. The patient has the right to be advised if the hospital proposes to engage in or perform human experimentation affecting his care or treatment. The patient has the right to refuse to participate in such research projects.

10. The patient has the right to expect reasonable continuity of care. He has the right to know in advance what appointment times the physicians are available and where. The patient has the right to expect that the hospital will provide a mechanism whereby he is informed by his physician or a delegate of the physician of the patient's continuing health care requirements following discharge.

11. The patient has the right to examine and receive an explanation of his bill regardless of source of payment.

12. The patient has the right to know what hospital rules and regulations apply to his conduct as a patient.

No catalogue of rights can guarantee for the patient the kind of treatment he has a right to expect. A hospital has many functions to perform, including the prevention and treatment of disease, the education of both health professionals and patients, and the conduct of clinical research. All these activities must be conducted with an overriding concern for the patient and, above all, the recognition of his dignity as a human being. Success in achieving this recognition assures success in the defense of the rights of the patient.

Approved by the House of Delegates of the American Hospital Association, February 6, 1972.

APPENDIX D

A Patient's Bill of Rights—JCAH

Reprinted with permission of the Joint Commission on Accreditation of Hospitals

Rights and Responsibilities Of Patients

The basic rights of human beings for independence of expression, decision, and action, and concern for personal dignity and human relationships are always of great importance. During sickness, however, their presence or absence becomes a vital, deciding factor in survival and recovery. Thus it becomes a prime responsibility for hospitals to endeavor to assure that these rights are preserved for their patients.

In providing care, hospitals have the right to expect behavior on the part of patients and their relatives and friends, which, considering the nature of their illness, is reasonable and responsible.

This statement does not presume to be all-inclusive. It is intended to convey JCAH's concern about the relationship between hospitals and patients and to emphasize the need for the observance of the rights and responsibilities of patients.

The following basic rights and responsibilities of patients are considered reasonably applicable to all hospitals.

Patient Rights

Access to Care

Individuals shall be accorded impartial access to treatment or accommodations that are available or medically indicated, regardless of race, creed, sex, national origin, or sources of payment for care.

Respect and Dignity

The patient has the right to considerate, respectful care at all times and under all circumstances, with recognition of his personal dignity.

Privacy and Confidentiality

The patient has the right, within the law, to personal and informational privacy, as manifested by the following rights:

- To refuse to talk with or see anyone not officially connected with the hospital, including visitors, or persons officially connected with the hospital but not directly involved in his care.

- To wear appropriate personal clothing and religious or other symbolic items, as long as they do not interfere with diagnostic procedures or treatment.

- To be interviewed and examined in surroundings designed to assure reasonable visual and auditory privacy. This includes the right to have a person of one's own sex present during certain parts of a physical examination, treatment, or procedure performed by a health professional of the opposite sex and the right not to remain disrobed any longer than is required for accomplishing the medical purpose for which the patient was asked to disrobe.

- To expect that any discussion or consultation involving his case will be conducted discreetly and that individuals not directly involved in his care will not be present without his permission.

- To have his medical record read only by individuals directly involved in his treatment or in the monitoring of its quality and by other individuals only on his written authorization or that of his legally authorized representative.

- To expect all communications and other records pertaining to his care, including the source of payment for treatment, to be treated as confidential.

- To request a transfer to another room if another patient or a visitor in the room is unreasonably disturbing him by smoking or by other actions.

- To be placed in protective privacy when considered necessary for personal safety.

Personal Safety

The patient has the right to expect reasonable safety insofar as the hospital practices and environment are concerned.

Identity

The patient has the right to know the identity and professional status of individuals providing service to him and to know which physician or other practitioner is primarily responsible for his care. This includes the patient's right to know of the existence of any professional relationship among individuals who are treating him, as well as the relationship to any other health care or educational institutions involved in his care. Participation by patients in clinical training programs or in the gathering of data for research purposes should be voluntary.

Information

The patient has the right to obtain, from the practitioner responsible for coordinating his care, complete and current information concerning his diagnosis (to the degree known), treatment, and any known prognosis. This information should be communicated in terms the patient can reasonably be expected to understand. When it is not medically advisable to give such information to the patient, the information should be made available to a legally authorized individual.

Communication

The patient has the right of access to people outside the hospital by means of visitors, and by verbal and written communication.

When the patient does not speak or understand the predominant language of the community, he should have access to an interpreter. This is particularly true where language barriers are a continuing problem.

Consent

The patient has the right to reasonable informed participation in decisions involving his health care. To the degree possible, this should be based on a clear, concise explanation of his condition and of all proposed technical procedures, including the possibilities of any risk of mortality or serious side effects, problems related to recuperation, and probability of success. The patient should not be subjected to any procedure without his voluntary, competent, and understanding consent or that of his legally authorized representative. Where medically significant alternatives for care or treatment exist, the patient shall be so informed.

The patient has the right to know who is responsible for authorizing and performing the procedures or treatment.

The patient shall be informed if the hospital proposes to engage in or perform human experimentation or other research/educational projects affecting his care or treatment, and the patient has the right to refuse to participate in any such activity.

Consultation

The patient, at his own request and expense, has the right to consult with a specialist.

Refusal of Treatment

The patient may refuse treatment to the extent permitted by law. When refusal of treatment by the patient or his legally authorized representative prevents the provision of appropriate care in accordance with professional standards, the relationship with the patient may be terminated upon reasonable notice.

Transfer and Continuity of Care

A patient may not be transferred to another facility unless he has received a complete explanation of the need for the transfer and of the alternatives to such a transfer and unless the transfer is acceptable to the other facility. The patient has the right to be informed by the practitioner responsible for his care, or his delegate, of any continuing health care requirements following discharge from the hospital.

Hospital Charges

Regardless of the source of payment for his care, the patient has the right to request and receive an itemized and detailed explanation of his total bill for services rendered in the hospital. The patient has the right to timely notice prior to termination of his eligibility for reimbursement by any third-party payer for the cost of his care.

Hospital Rules and Regulations

The patient should be informed of the hospital rules and regulations applicable to his conduct as a patient. Patients are entitled to information about the hospital's mechanism for the initiation, review, and resolution of patient complaints.

Patient Responsibilities

Provision of Information

A patient has the responsibility to provide, to the best of his knowledge, accurate and complete information about present complaints, past illnesses, hospitalizations, medications, and other matters relating to his health. He has the responsibility to report unexpected changes in his condition to the responsible practitioner. A patient is responsible for making it known whether he clearly comprehends a contemplated course of action and what is expected of him.

Compliance with Instructions

A patient is responsible for following the treatment plan recommended by the practitioner primarily responsible for his care. This may include following the instructions of nurses and allied health personnel as they carry out the coordinated plan of care and implement the responsible practitioner's orders, and as they enforce the applicable hospital rules and regulations. The patient is responsible for keeping appointments and, when he is unable to do so for any reason, for notifying the responsible practitioner or the hospital.

Refusal of Treatment

The patient is responsible for his actions if he refuses treatment or does not follow the practitioner's instructions.

Hospital Charges

The patient is responsible for assuring that the financial obligations of his health care are fulfilled as promptly as possible.

Hospital Rules and Regulations

The patient is responsible for following hospital rules and regulations affecting patient care and conduct.

Respect and Consideration

The patient is responsible for being considerate of the rights of other patients and hospital personnel and for assisting in the control of noise, smoking, and the number of visitors. The patient is responsible for being respectful of the property of other persons and of the hospital.

APPENDIX E

Standards for Nursing

1. Standards for Medical-Surgical Nursing Practice
    American Nurses' Association
    2420 Pershing Road
    Kansas City, Missouri 64108

2. Standards for Nursing Practice
    American Nurses' Association
    2420 Pershing Road
    Kansas City, Missouri 64108

3. Standards of Emergency Nursing Practice
    American Nurses' Association
    2420 Pershing Road
    Kansas City, Missouri 64108

4. Standards of Emergency Room Practice
    Emergency Nurses' Association
    C.V. Mosby Company
    11830 Westline Industrial Drive
    St. Louis, Missouri 63146   (1983)

5. Standards for Critical Care Nurses
    Second Edition
    C.V. Mosby Company
    11830 Westline Industrial Drive
    St. Louis, Missouri 63146   (1985)

6. Association of Operating Room Nurses, Inc.
    Recommended Practices for Perioperative Nursing
    10170 East Mississippi Avenue
    Denver, Colorado 80231

7. Joint Commission on Accreditation of Hospitals
    875 North Michigan Avenue
    Chicago, Illinois 60611

8. Guidelines for Perinatal Care
    American Academy of Pediatrics and
    American College of Obstetricians and Gynecologists
    600 Maryland Ave., S.W.
    Washington, D.C. 20024

9. Standards for Obstetric-Gynecologic Services
   American College of Obstetricians and Gynecologists
   600 Maryland Ave., S.W.
   Washington, D.C. 20024

10. Standards for Obstetrical Nursing
    American Nurses' Association
    2420 Pershing Road
    Kansas City, Missouri 64108

11. Accreditation Manual, 11th Edition
    American Osteopathic Association
    212 East Ohio Street
    Chicago, Illinois 60611   (1985)

12. Standards for Professional Nursing Education
    (Pub. No. NE-12)
    American Nurses' Association
    2420 Pershing Road
    Kansas City, Missouri 64108

13. Standards for Continuing Education in Nursing
    (Pub. No. COE-8)
    American Nurses' Association
    2420 Pershing Road
    Kansas City, Missouri 64108

14. Standards of Nursing Practice in Correctional Facilities
    (Pub. No. CH-11)
    American Nurses' Association
    2420 Pershing Road
    Kansas City, Missouri 64108

15. Standards of Practice for the Perinatal Nurse Specialist
    (Pub. No. MCH-15)
    American Nurses' Association
    2420 Pershing Road
    Kansas City, Missouri 64108

16. A Guide to JCAH Nursing Services Standards
    JCAH
    875 N. Michigan Avenue
    Chicago, Illinois 60611

17. Principles for Accreditation of Community
    Mental Health Services Programs
    JCAH
    875 N. Michigan Avenue
    Chicago, Illinois 60611

18. Long Term Care Standards Manual
    JCAH
    875 N. Michigan Avenue
    Chicago, Illinois 60611

19. JCAH Guide to Life Safety
    JCAH
    875 N. Michigan Avenue
    Chicago, Illinois 60611

20. Consolidated Standards Manual for Child, Adolescent,
    and Adult Psychiatric, Alcoholism, and Drug
    Abuse Facilities, *et al.*
    JCAH
    875 N. Michigan Avenue
    Chicago, Illinois 60611

21. Hospice Standards Manual
    JCAH
    875 N. Michigan Avenue
    Chicago, Illinois 60611

22. Ambulatory Health Care Standards Manual
    JCAH
    875 N. Michigan Avenue
    Chicago, Illinois 60611

Other ways to demonstrate the nurse has satisfied the standard of care:

Your state nursing association's standards and position statements

Expert Testimony

Nursing Practice Act

Nursing textbooks and literature

Hospital policies and procedures

Standards promulgated by the American Hospital Association

APPENDIX F

The History of Primary Nursing

Primary nursing is a professional commitment by the nurse to provide direct and comprehensive nursing care to specifically assigned patients and their families. For primary nursing to reach the position it has today in nursing literature and practice, it took years of building, changing, resisting, and redefining within the profession. It is an integration of attitude, knowledge, and skills.

Before World War I, most patients received nursing care in their home. The family nurse's duties included household chores in addition to rendering nursing care. Nurses at this time in history did not require a license to practice and were very unskilled and often uneducated.

Between 1873 and 1900, nurses started to increase their competence and their technical nursing skills. Hospitals came to prosper between 1900 and 1910. Physicians needed to staff these institutions. Nurses became the logical choice.

Hospitals began to provide a formal education for their nurses. However, the training received was very "task" oriented. This education lacked concepts such as the nursing process. There were no considerations to the patient's psychological well-being. Hospitals were not conducive to safe and therapeutic nursing care.

After World War II, functional nursing came into existence. During this war, there were large numbers of unskilled hospital workers who came into the hospital arena. Nurse's aides, orderlies, and practical nurses became the main source of inexpensive hospital labor.

Patient care was divided functionally. The task requiring the least skill was done by the least skilled worker. Tasks were assigned by the head nurse as opposed to particular patient assignments. Nurses were handmaidens of the physicians. Their only function was to "follow orders."

Eventually, the problems of functional nurses were felt. There were not enough nurses to adequately supervise the poorly trained personnel.

The concept of team nursing then came into existence. The nursing staff was divided into teams that provided care for a limited number of patients. Each team member had a team leader to coordinate work assignments. The patients had fewer staff members to get to know. Patient conferences provided continuing education for the staff members. The written nursing care plan provided more continuity of care.

In the 1960's, nursing education evolved and a number of changes were noted. Colleges of nursing were starting to develop. The nursing curriculum was geared toward incorporating theory and skills together to assist in meeting the patient's comprehensive needs.

The "nursing process" developed as a way of assessing, planning, intervening, and evaluating the patient and family needs and their responses to nursing care. This would assist in identifying and providing structure to nursing practice. Care plans were tools to assist the nurse to shift emphasis from performing routine chores to a goal-oriented focus to meet individual patient needs.

In the 1960's, the importance of the patient's family was advocated. This contributed to the development of primary nursing.

The model for primary nursing was established at the Loeb Center for Nursing and Rehabilitation at Montefiore Hospital in the Bronx in New York in the early 1960's. The model was based on the ideas of Lydia Hall. She believed nurses should have a greater role in nurturing and healing.

The Loeb model was implemented in 1963. This model concretely acknowledged the importance of registered nurses. Each nurse had eight patients. He/she directed all the care and gave a great deal of it personally.

In 1969, the term *primary nursing* was given a new pattern of nursing care at the University of Minnesota Hospital. Under the system, each R.N. and L.P.N. had primary responsibility for all nursing care rendered. They were assigned a group of from three to six patients. They performed all the daily care tasks for their patients.

Primary Nursing and Its Effect on Liability

Primary nursing offers a way to provide quality care that includes continuity and comprehensiveness for the patient, autonomy, authority, and accountability for the nurse.[1] Primary nursing provides an efficient, cost-effective system for the health agency and for society.[2] Primary nursing is important for another reason. Primary nursing tends to reduce the number of lawsuits filed because it decreases the amount of errors, and, if an error is made, the patient is less likely to sue.

The goal of any primary nursing unit is to provide optimum care and services to patients and their families by focusing nursing care on the individual patient's needs. When the individual patient's needs are met, the patient is more satisfied. A satisfied patient is less likely to sue even when an error is committed. (See the enclosed chart showing significant increased patient satisfaction from primary nursing.)

Primary nursing, as the main mode of distributing patient care responsibilities, transcends to a greater degree the various levels of intervention, which are treatment, restoration, and prevention. Prevention practices decrease the number of suits. The patient receives more of his/her care from fewer practitioners with primary care nursing than in functional nursing. For example, under a functional nursing approach, Mr. Jones will obtain his morning care from the nurse aide. The L.P.N. does the treatments and the pharmacy technician administers the medication. The staff nurse charts the patient and the head nurse makes rounds with the physicians and takes off the orders. The catheter care is done by a male orderly. Anytime you decrease the number of staff persons responsible for the patient's care, you decrease the potential for error. Primary care nursing offers a better coordination of patient care.

Authority, accountability, and autonomy in patient care foster professional identification and responsibility for patient care for the nurse. Primary nursing can assist in the organization of care delivery to reinforce growth and knowledge among staff members. This results in primary nurses being happier and more content with their occupations. Studies show that the level of satisfaction for nurses increased significantly after the implementation of primary nursing. (See Table 1.) Studies also show that satisfied nurses are less likely to make errors in patient care and treatment.[3] No other mode of organizing nursing care promises as much nurse accountability as primary nursing.

REFERENCES

1. Marram, Gwen; Barrett, Margaret; and Benis, E., *Primary Nursing—A Model for Individualized Care*, Second Edition, The C.V. Mosby Company, St. Louis 1979, p. 181; Corpus, T., "Primary Nursing Meets Needs, Expectations of Patients, Staff and Hospitals," *J. Am. Hosp., Assoc.*, 51: 95-100, 1977.
2. Marram, G., Flynn, K., *et al.*, "Cost-effectiveness of Primary Team Nursing," Wakefield, Mass., 1976, Contemporary Publishing, Inc.; Benton, D., and White, H., "Satisfaction of Job Factors for Registered Nurses," *Journal of Nursing Administration*, 2: 55-63, 1972.
3. "Inadequate Staffing Seen as New Type of Nurse Shortage," *Hospitals*, Jan. 1, 1985, p. 53.

BIBLIOGRAPHY LIST

1. Bailes, Jo., *et al.* "The Role of the Head Nurse in Primary Nursing," *Canadian Nurse*, March 1977, 73(3), pp. 26-30.
2. Bolder, J., "Primary Nursing: Why Not?" *Nursing Administration Quarterly*, Winter 1977, I(2), pp. 79-87.
3. Bower-Ferres, S., "Loeb Center and Its Philosophy of Nursing," *American Journal of Nursing*, June 1977, 74(6), pp. 1053-1056.
4. Elpern, E.H., "Structural and Organizational Supports for Primary Nursing," *Nursing Clinics of North America*, December 1969, 4, pp. 721-729.
5. Hegyvary, S.T., "Foundations of Primary Nursing," *Nursing Clinics of North America*, June 1977, 12(2), pp. 187-196.
6. Manthey, M., *et al.*, "Primary Nursing - A Return to the Concept of 'My Nurse' and 'My Patient,' " *Nursing Forum*, 1979, 9(1), pp. 65-83.
7. Marram, G., *et al*, *Primary Nursing, A Model for Individualized Care*, St. Louis, C.V. Mosby, 1974.
8. Mundinger, M., "Primary Nursing," *Nursing Administration Quarterly*, Winter 1977, I(2), pp. 69-77.
9. Pryma, R., "Primary Nursing: A Work Philosophy - An Organizational Style," *Magazine of Rush - Presbyterian - St. Lukes Medical Center*, Spring, 1978, (2), pp. 3-17.

NURSE SATISFACTION WITH PRIMARY NURSING

Nurses' satisfaction with the way their work is
organized on primary nursing and other nursing units

Level of satisfaction	Primary nursing units (N = 45)	Case method units (N = 25)	Team nursing units (N = 24)	Functional nursing units (N = 16)
Extremely satisfied	30%	10%	12%	10%
Very satisfied	60%	60%	40%	33%
Moderately satisfied	10%	30%	48%	50%
Slightly satisfied	0	0	0	7%
Not at all satisfied	0	0	0	0

Nurses' satisfaction with the way their work is
organized before and after the implementation of primary nursing

Level of satisfaction	Before primary nursing (N = 45)	After primary nursing (N = 45)
Extremely satisfied	0	10%
Very satisfied	25%	54%
Moderately satisfied	50%	36%
Slightly satisfied	15%	0
Not at all satisfied	10%	0

250

Professional orientation of nurses before
and after implementation of primary nursing

| | Frequency nurses agreed (percent) | |
Nurses' attitudes	Before primary nursing (N = 45)	After primary nursing (N = 45)
1. Ideals rather than rules and procedures should be followed	20%	50%
2. Emotional side of patient care should be more important than knowing technical skills	15%	50%
3. Being at work on time rather than quality care should influence promotion	50%	15%

From *Primary Nursing* by Gwen Marram, Margaret Barrett, and Em. Bevis

PATIENT SATISFACTION WITH PRIMARY NURSING

Patients' satisfaction with their nursing care

Level of satisfaction	Primary nursing units (N = 60)	Case method units (N = 30)	Team nursing units (N = 60)	Functional nursing units (N = 30)
Extremely satisfied	65%	40%	37%	48%
Very satisfied	32%	40%	41%	21%
Moderately satisfied	3%	15%	10%	12%
Slightly satisfied	0	5%	11%	9%
Not at all satisfied	0	0	1%	10%

Patients' perceptions of their nurses and nursing
care before and after primary nursing implementation

Patient's view of Nurses' attitudes	Percentage of patients agreeing or strongly agreeing	
	Before (N = 60)	After (N = 60)
1. Nurse gives emotional support frequently	35%	75%
2. Nurse treats patients like special human beings	30%	95%
3. Finishing on time is more important to nurse than giving good care	15%	0
4. Nurse spends more time with patient than with other tasks	5%	15%
5. Nurse is too concerned with others' perceptions and not with what patients think they need	15%	0

Patients' satisfaction before and after implementation of primary nursing

Level of satisfaction	Before (N = 60)	After (N = 60)
Extremely satisfied	29%	64%
Very satisfied	58%	24%
Moderately satisfied	0	12%
Slightly satisfied	0	0
Not at all satisfied	13%	0

What patients liked best
before and after primary nursing

| | Frequency nurses agreed (percent/rank) | |
Category of response	Before (N = 60)	After (N = 60)
1. Pleasantness of nurse	42.9%/1	20%/2
2. Promptness of nurse	28.6%/2	16%/3
3. Nurse's ability	4.2%/3	0%/5
4. Nurse's consideration of patient individuality	28.6%/2	44%/1
5. Physical care considerations (e.g. back rubs)	0%/4	4%/4

From *Primary Nursing* by Gwen Marram, Margaret Barrett, and Em. Bevis.

254

CHICAGO INSURANCE COMPANY
CHICAGO, ILLINOIS

PROFESSIONAL LIABILITY DECLARATIONS

INSURED
NAME
AND
ADDRESS

SPECIMEN

Policy No.

AFFILIATION:

PROFESSIONAL OCCUPATION	POLICY TERM	FROM	TO	BOTH DAYS AT 12:01 A.M. STANDARD TIME

The limit of the Insurers' Liability under each coverage, subject to all the terms of this insurance having reference thereto, shall be as stated here:

COVERAGE BY PROFESSION	LIMITS		PREMIUM
Coverage A – MALPRACTICE LIABILITY		Any One Claim	
		Any One Annual Period of Insurance	
Coverage B – PERSONAL LIABILITY		Any One Occurrence	
Coverage C – MEDICAL PAYMENTS	$250	Any One Person	
DATE LICENSED RESIDENT AGENT			

PROFESSIONAL COMPREHENSIVE LIABILITY
THE INSURERS

Hereby agree with the Insured, named in the Declarations made a part hereof, in consideration of the payment of the premium and of the statements contained in the Declarations and subject to the limits of liability, exclusions, conditions and other terms of this insurance:

INSURING AGREEMENTS

I. COVERAGE A—MALPRACTICE. To pay on behalf of the Insured all sums which the Insured shall become legally obligated to pay as damages because of injury arising out of

(a) malpractice, error or mistake in rendering or failing to render professional services, or

(b) acts or omissions of the Insured as a member of a formal accreditation or similar professional board or committee of a hospital or professional society in the practice of the Insured's professional occupation as stated in the Declarations, committed by the Insured during the policy period.

COVERAGE B—PERSONAL LIABILITY. To pay on behalf of the Insured, all sums which the Insured shall become obligated to pay by reason of the liability imposed upon him by law, for damages, including damages for care and loss of services, because of bodily injury, sickness or disease, including death at any time resulting therefrom, sustained by any person or persons, and for damages because of injury to or destruction of property, including the loss of use thereof.

COVERAGE C—MEDICAL PAYMENTS. To pay to or for each person who sustains bodily injury, sickness or disease, caused by accident,

(1) while on the premises with the permission of the Insured, or

(2) while elsewhere if such injury, sickness or disease

(a) arise out of the premises or a condition in the ways immediately adjoining.

(b) is caused by the activities of the Insured, or

(c) is caused by the activities of or is sustained by a residence employee while engaged in the employment of the Insured.

The reasonable expense of necessary medical, surgical, ambulance, hospital, professional nursing and funeral services, all incurred within one year from the date of accident.

II. DEFENSE, SETTLEMENT, SUPPLEMENTARY PAYMENTS. It is further agreed that as respects insurance afforded by this policy the Insurers shall, in addition to the applicable limit of liability of this policy:

(a) defend in his name and behalf any suit against the Insured alleging such injury, sickness, disease or destruction and seeking damages on account thereof, even if such suit is groundless, false or fraudulent; but the Insurers shall have the right to make such investigation, negotiation and settlement of any claim or suit as may be deemed expedient by the Insurers.

(b) pay all premiums on bonds to release attachments for an amount not in excess of the applicable limit of liability of this policy, all premiums on appeal bonds required in any such defended suit, but without any obligation to apply for or furnish such bonds, all costs taxed against the Insured in any such suit, all expenses incurred by the Insurers, all interest accruing after entry of judgment until the Insurers have paid, tendered, or deposited in court such part of such judgment as does not exceed the limit of the Insurer's liability thereon, and expenses incurred by the Insured, in the event of bodily injury, sickness or disease, for such immediate medical and surgical relief to others as shall be imperative at the time of accident.

CIC-44-36 (REVISED 10/83) ED. 6/85

EXCLUSIONS

This insurance does not apply:

(a) under Coverage A to liability of the insured as a nurse anesthetist or as a nurse midwife.

(b) under Coverage A in respect to any loss based on criminal acts or on services rendered while under the influence of intoxicants or drugs.

(c) under Coverage A (as respects Psychologists only) to claims resulting in Bodily Injury, including death to any person, arising out of direct or indirect physical contact when such physical contact results in injury or death from the Insured's profession as a Psychologist.

(d) under Coverages A, B and C to liability of the Insured, as a proprietor or executive officer of any hospital, sanitarium, nursing home, clinic or laboratory, in which the Insured has a pecuniary interest as owner, partner or stockholder, or to any business undertaking other than the Insured's professional occupation designated in the Declarations.

(e) under Coverages B and C except with respect to liability assumed under contract covered by this policy, to bodily injury to or sickness, disease or death of any employee of the Insured while engaged in the business, other than domestic employment, of the Insured, or to any obligation for which the Insured may be held liable under any workmen's compensation law or in respect to any loss caused by any automobile, recreational motor vehicle, tractor or trailer owned or operated by or on behalf of the Insured, or any aircraft or watercraft of any nature, or caused by any person employed by the Insured while engaged in the maintenance or use of such automobile, tractor, trailer, aircraft or watercraft. A recreational motor vehicle means a golf cart or snowmobile or any other land motor vehicle designed for recreational use off public roads, whether or not subject to motor vehicle registration; but this exclusion does not apply to golf carts while used for golfing purposes.

(f) under Coverages B and C:

1. to Bodily Injury or Property Damage which is either expected or intended from the standpoint of the Insured;

2. to liability assumed by the Insured under any contract or agreement;

3. to Property Damage to property occupied or used by the Insured or rented to or in the care, custody or control of the Insured or as to which the Insured is for any purpose exercising physical control;

4. to sickness, disease or death resulting therefrom of any residence employee unless written claim is made or suit is brought against the Insured within 36 months after the end of the policy term.

(g) 1. under any Liability Coverage, to injury, sickness, disease, death or destruction

(a) with respect to which an Insured under the policy is also an Insured under a nuclear energy liability policy issued by Nuclear Energy Liability Insurance Association, Mutual Atomic Energy Liability Underwriters or Nuclear Insurance Association of Canada, or would be an Insured under any such policy but for its termination upon exhaustion of its limit of liability; or

(b) resulting from the hazardous properties of nuclear material and with respect to which (1) any person or organization is required to maintain financial protection pursuant to the Atomic Energy Act of 1954, or any law amendatory thereof, or (2) the Insured is, or had this policy not been issued would be, entitled to indemnity from the United States of America, or any agency thereof, under any agreement entered into by the United States of America, or any agency thereof, with any person or organization.

2. under any Medical Payments Coverage, or under any Supplementary Payments provision relating to immediate medical or surgical relief, to expenses incurred with respect to bodily injury, sickness, disease or death resulting from the hazardous properties of nuclear material and arising out of the operation of a nuclear facility by any person or organization.

3. under any Liability Coverage, to injury, sickness, disease, death or destruction resulting from the hazardous properties of nuclear material, if

(a) the nuclear material (1) is at any nuclear facility owned by or operated by or on behalf of, an Insured or (2) has been discharged or dispersed therefrom;

(b) the nuclear material is contained in spent fuel or waste at any time possessed, handled, used, processed, stored, transported or disposed of by or on behalf of an Insured;

(c) the injury, sickness, disease, death or destruction arises out of the furnishing by an Insured of services, materials, parts or equipment in connection with the planning, construction, maintenance, operation or use of any nuclear facility, but if such facility is located within the United States of America, its territories or possessions or Canada, this exclusion (c) applies only to injury to or destruction of property at such nuclear facility; or

(d) as used in this exclusion:

"hazardous properties" include radioactive, toxic or explosive properties; "nuclear material" means source material, special nuclear material or byproduct material; "source material", "special nuclear material", and "byproduct material" having the meanings given them in the Atomic Energy Act of 1954 or in any law amendatory thereof; "spent fuel" means any fuel element or fuel component, solid or liquid, which has been used or exposed to radiation in a nuclear reactor; "waste" means any waste material (1) containing byproduct material and (2) resulting from the operation by any person or organization of any nuclear facility included within the definition of nuclear facility under paragraph (a) or (b) thereof; "nuclear facility" means (a) any nuclear reactor, (b) any equipment or device designed or used for (1) separating the isotopes of uranium or plutonium, (2) processing or utilizing spent fuel, or (3) handling, processing or packaging waste, (c) any equipment or device used for the processing, fabricating or alloying of special nuclear material if at any time the total amount of such material in the custody of the Insured at the premises, where such equipment or device is located consists of or contains more than 25 grams of plutonium or uranium 233 or any combination thereof, or more than 250 grams of uranium 235, (d) any structure, basin, excavation, premises or place prepared or used for the storage or disposal of waste, and includes the site on which any of the foregoing is located, all operations conducted on such site and all premises used for such operations; "nuclear reactor" means any apparatus designed or used to sustain nuclear fission in a self-supporting chain reaction or to contain a critical mass of fissionable material; With respect to injury to or destruction of property the word "injury" or "destruction" includes all forms of radioactive contamination of property.

CONDITIONS

1. **LIMITS OF LIABILITY.** The limits of liability stated in the Declarations for Coverage A on account of "Malpractice" arising in respect of any one person shall be limited to the amount stated applicable to any one person in respect of any one or more of the Insureds specified in this insurance. All claims arising from the same malpractice, error or mistake in rendering or failure to render professional services shall be considered a single claim for the purposes of this insurance. Further, it is specifically understood and agreed that subject to the foregoing limit in respect of any one person, the total liability of the Insurers for any and all claims howsoever arising under this insurance shall not exceed the amount stated in the Declarations in "any one annual period of insurance" in respect of all the Insureds specified in this insurance and on any endorsement attached thereto. The term "any one annual period of insurance" as used herein shall mean each complete consecutive period of twelve months commencing from the inception date of this insurance.

The limit of liability stated in the Declarations for Coverage B is the limit of the Insurers' liability for all damages, including damages for care and loss of services, arising out of one occurrence.

The limit of liability stated in the Declarations for Coverage C is the limit of the Insurers' liability for all expenses incurred by or on behalf of each person who sustains bodily injury, sickness or disease, including death resulting therefrom, in any one accident.

The inclusion herein of more than one Insured shall not operate to increase the limits of Insurers' liability.

2. **NOTICE OF ACCIDENT.** Upon the occurrence of an accident written notice shall be given by or on behalf of the Insured to the Insurers or their authorized representative as soon as practicable. Such notice shall contain particulars sufficient to identify the Insured and also reasonably obtainable information respecting the time, place and circumstances of the accident, the names and addresses of the injured and of available witnesses.

3. **NOTICE OF CLAIM OR SUIT.** If claim is made or suit is brought against the Insured, the Insured shall immediately forward to the Insurers every demand, notice, summons or other process received by him or his representative.

4. **ASSISTANCE AND COOPERATION OF THE INSURED.** The Insured shall cooperate with the Insurers and, upon the Insurers' request, shall attend hearings and trials and shall assist in effecting settlements, securing and giving evidence, obtaining the attendance of witnesses and in the conduct of suits; and the Insurers shall reimburse the Insured for expenses, other than loss of earnings, incurred at the Insurers' request. The Insured shall not, except at his own cost, voluntarily make any payment, assume any obligation or incur any expense other than for such immediate medical and surgical relief to others as shall be imperative at the time of accident.

5. **ACTION AGAINST THE INSURERS.** No action shall lie against the Insurers unless, as a condition precedent thereto, the Insured shall have fully complied with all of the terms of this policy, nor until the amount of the Insured's obligation to pay shall have been finally determined either by judgment against the Insured after actual trial or by written agreement of the Insured, the claimant, and the Insurers.

Any person or his legal representative who has secured such judgment or written agreement shall thereafter be entitled to recover under the terms of this policy in the same manner and to the same extent as the Insured. Nothing contained in this policy shall give any person or organization any right to join the Insurers as a co-defendant in any action against the Insured to determine the Insured's liability.

Bankruptcy or insolvency of the Insured or of the Insured's estate shall not relieve the Insurers of any of their obligations hereunder.

6. OTHER INSURANCE. If there is other valid and collectible insurance against a loss covered by this policy, the insurance provided hereunder shall be deemed excess insurance over and above the applicable limit of all such other insurance.

7. SUBROGATION. In the event of any payment under this policy the Insurers shall be subrogated to all the Insured's right of recovery therefor and the Insured shall execute all papers required and shall do everything that may be necessary to secure such rights.

8. CHANGES. No notice to any agent, or knowledge possessed by any agent or by any other person shall be held to effect a waiver or change in any part of this policy nor estop the Insurers from asserting any right under the terms of this policy; nor shall the terms of this policy be waived or changed, except by endorsement issued to form a part hereof, signed by an executive officer of the Insurers or their authorized representative.

9. ASSIGNMENT. No assignment of interest under this policy shall bind the Insurers until their consent is endorsed hereon; if, however, the named Insured shall die or be adjudged bankrupt or insolvent within the policy period, this policy, unless cancelled, shall, if written notice be given to the Insurers within sixty days after the date of such death or adjudication, cover the named Insured's legal representative as the named Insured.

10. In any case wherein the Insured has been in attendance or consultation, he will endeavor to notify the Insurers, or their authorized representative, before testifying at an inquest or public hearing.

11. This insurance may be cancelled on the customary short rate basis by the Insured at any time by written notice or by surrender of this insurance to the Insurers or their authorized representative. This insurance may also be cancelled, with or without the return or tender of the unearned premium, by the Insurers, or by their authorized representative on their behalf, by delivering to the Insured or by sending to the Insured by mail, registered or unregistered, at his address last known to the Company or its authorized agent, not less than thirty days' written notice stating when the cancellation shall be effective, and in such case the Insurers shall refund the paid premium less the earned portion thereof on demand, subject always to the retention by the Insurers of any minimum premium stipulated herein (or proportion thereof previously agreed upon) in the event of cancellation either by the Insurers or the Insured.

12. POLICY TERRITORY. This insurance applies only to occurrences happening within the United States of America, its territories or possessions or Canada.

In Witness Whereof, the Company has caused this policy to be executed and attested, but this policy shall not be valid unless countersigned by a duly authorized representative of the Company.

Secretary.

President.

APPENDIX H

Common Areas of Liability for Physicians

1. Failure to obtain the patient's informed consent.
2. Failure to recognize a perforation of the esophagus after a gastroscopy and after tracheal intubation.
3. Failure to diagnose appendicitis.
4. Inadequately performed tubal.
5. Failure to diagnose an ectopic pregnancy.
6. Failure to perform a C-section, resulting in a brain-damaged baby.
7. Failure to diagnose and inadequate treatment of fractures (especially a navicular fracture, imperfect or delayed union and complications such as Volkman's contractures).
8. Failure to diagnose cancer.
9. Negligence in prescribing a medicine to which the patient is susceptible or allergic.
10. Failure to diagnose meningitis.
11. Misplaced endotracheal tubes (endotracheal tubes in the esophagus).
12. Foreign objects left in wounds (especially glass, sponges, needles and instruments).
13. Failure to remove foreign objects from the eye.
14. Failure to perform an adequate history and physical, which results in an incorrect diagnosis being made and deprives the patient of the chance of proper treatment.
15. Alteration of medical records.
16. Failure to make referrals to a specialist.
17. Abandoning a patient.
18. Failure to keep abreast of current medical knowledge.
19. Failure to properly use laboratory, radiologic, and ancillary procedures.
20. Negligently performed abortions and inadequate follow-up.
21. Poor record keeping.
22. Failure to adequately monitor the patient during anesthesia.
23. Wrongful or excessive prescription of drugs.

APPENDIX I

Complaint

In the Court of Common Pleas,
Franklin County, Ohio

Ima Patient
100 Suethem Lane
Big Bucks, Ohio 43215   :   Case No. 85-001

     Plaintiff   :   Judge Ralph

   vs.

Jane Doe R.N.
100 Worried Ct.
Liability City, Ohio 43215   :

     and   :   **Complaint**

River Hospital
1 Hospital Lane
Hobbs, Ohio 43213   :

     Defendants

First Claim

1. Now comes Ima Patient and states that she was a patient at River Hospital on March 1, 1983 through July 1, 1983.
2. At all times alleged, the defendant River Hospital was an Ohio Corporation doing business in Franklin County and as such invited the public to come to its hospital for the purpose of obtaining medical and surgical care for a fee.
3. At all times, Jane Doe was a registered nurse licensed to practice in the state of Ohio.
4. At all times, Jane Doe was acting within the scope of her employment at River Hospital.
5. On or about March 1, 1983, the plaintiff was admitted to River Hospital. She was an in-house patient until July 1, 1983.
6. During this admission, Nurse Doe gave the patient an injection into the right buttocks. Nurse Doe failed to cleanse the skin. Nurse Doe also contaminated the needle. This proximately resulted in the patient contracting a staphlococcus infection in the right buttock.
7. While the plaintiff was a patient of these defendants, while in the scope of employment and agency, each defendant was negligent because his/her

care was below the customary and acceptable level as practiced in 1983.

8. As a direct and proximate result of the negligence of the defendants, Ima Patient was required to undergo extensive medical procedures and treatment. This caused great mental and physical pain.

9. By reason of all of the above, the plaintiff brings this action for extensive damages suffered by the plaintiff.

Second Claim — LACK OF INFORMED CONSENT

10. For purposes of the Second Claim, the plaintiff realleges all allegations previously stated in paragraphs 1-9 as if fully stated and set forth here.

11. Plaintiff was not informed of the inherent risks in obtaining an I.M. injection.

Wherefore, the plaintiff demands judgment against the defendants in the First Claim for an amount to be determined by the trier of facts, for the Second Claim for the sum of two hundred thousand dollars ($200,000), and for all interest and cost of this action.

Jury Trial

A trial by jury is hereby demanded.

_____
Plaintiff Attorney

APPENDIX J

Answer

In the Court of Common Pleas, Franklin County, Ohio

Linda A. Cord, *et al.*   :

     Plaintiffs   :   Case No. 84CV-09-5

   vs.   :   Judge Flowers

River Methodist Hospital,   :
   et al.,

     Defendants   :

Answer of Defendant, River Methodist Hospital

Now comes defendant, River Methodist Hospital (hereinafter referred to as "River"), and for its answer to plaintiff's complaint, avers, admits and denies as follows:

Answer to First Claim

1. River avers that it is without knowledge or information sufficient to form a belief as to the truth of the allegations contained in paragraph 1 and, therefore, denies same.
2. River admits that it is a corporation existing under the laws of, and licensed to do business in, the state of Ohio.
3. River avers that it is without knowledge or information sufficient to form a belief as to the truth of the allegations contained in paragraphs 3 and 4 and, therefore, denies same.
4. River admits that on or about August 31, 1982, Gordon Cord was admitted to River and further answering denies the remaining allegations contained in paragraph 5.
5. River avers that it is without knowledge or information sufficient to form a belief as to the truth of the allegations contained in paragraph 6 and, therefore, denies same.
6. Denying River's negligence, River denies the other allegations in paragraph 7.
7. River avers that it is without knowledge or information sufficient to form a belief as to the truth of the allegations contained in paragraphs 8, 9, 10, 11, and 12 and, therefore, denies same.

Answer to Second Claim

8. River hereby incorporates its answer to plaintiff's first claim, the same as if fully set forth herein.

263

9. River denies the allegations contained in paragraph 14.

10. River denies any and all allegations not heretofore specifically denied.

Second Defense

11. The injuries and damages, if any, of which plaintiff complains were proximately caused in whole or in part by the negligence of Gordon Cord.

Third Defense

12. Gordon Cord knowingly or intentionally assumed the risk of the injuries and damages, if any, of which plaintiff complains.

Fourth Defense

13. Plaintiff's Complaint fails to state a claim upon which relief can be granted as against defendant River.

Fifth Defense

14. River states that all or part of this claim is barred by the applicable status of limitations.

Sixth Defense

15. This defendant reserves the right to offer proof in support of the defenses provided by the law of comparative negligence.

Seventh Defense

16. The complaint fails to conform to the mandatory pleading requirements of the laws of Ohio governing medical claims.

WHEREFORE, having fully answered plaintiff's Complaint, defendant, River Methodist Hospital, prays that the Complaint in its entirety be dismissed and that they be permitted to go hence with costs to the plaintiffs.

LANE, ALTON & HORST
155 East Broad Street
Columbus, Ohio 43215
(614) 228-6885

_____

Sue Dill Calloway

APPENDIX K

Sample Interrogatories

In the Court of Common Pleas, Franklin County, Ohio

Ima Patient Admr.,	:	
	:	
	:	
Plaintiff,	:	Case No. 84CV-04-2282
vs. :		
	:	Judge LaWilliams
Chris B. Physician, M.D.,	:	
et al., :		
	:	
Defendants	:	

Pursuant to Rule 33 of the Ohio Rules of Civil Procedure, Defendant Mer Cey Hospital Association, hereby submits the following written Interrogatories to Plaintiff, Ima Patient, Administrator of the Estate of Gailen P. Patient, Deceased, to be answered in writing, under oath, within 28 days of service hereof.

1. Please state your name, date of birth, residential address, business address, social security number and relationship to decedent.

   ANSWER:

2. Please state the full name of decedent, decendent's date and place of birth and decedent's social security number.

   ANSWER:

3. Please state the address of each place at which decedent resided in the past ten years, and the inclusive dates of residence at each.

   ANSWER:

4. Was decedent ever married? If so, state as to each marriage:

   (a) the name and present address of each such spouse;
   ANSWER:

   (b) the date and place of marriage;
   ANSWER:

   (c) the date and place of termination of marriage, if terminated;
   ANSWER:

   (d) the name, address and date of birth of each child of issue of each such marriage.
   ANSWER:

5. Please state each and every fact upon which you base your claim in Paragraph Eleven of the Complaint that this Defendant's "agents and employees negligently failed in the performance and interpretation of certain diagnostic tests by negligently failing to identify the exact location of the tumor and/or failing to obtain thorough clinical information to make such diagnosis, negligently failing to provide proper and adequate treatment in a manner consistent with the standard of care and skill in its and similar communities."
   ANSWER:

6. With respect to your answer to the preceding Interrogatory, please state:

   (a) a description of the alleged negligent and unskillful conduct of the Defendant;
   ANSWER:

(b) a description of this Defendant's conduct as you claim it should have been so as not to have caused decedent's death;

ANSWER:

(c) the basis of your answer to (b) above.

ANSWER:

7. Please state each and every fact upon which you base your claim in Paragraph Ten of the Complaint that "Defendant Mer Cey Hospital Association was directly negligent and was negligent in permitting Defendant, Chris B. Physician, M.D. and/or Defendant Nurse Bean to remain on the staff of Mer Cey Hospital Association."

ANSWER:

8. Please state each and every fact upon which you base your claim that the conduct of this Defendant was a direct and proximate cause of any and all damages, as alleged in the Complaint, arising from medical care and treatment rendered to the decedent.

ANSWER:

9. Have you ever received information that this Defendant was negligent in the care and treatment of decedent or failed to exercise a degree of care and requisite skill ordinarily employed by members of the medical profession in attending and treating decedent? If so, for each such person who so informed you, please state:

(a) his/her name, address, occupation and qualification;

ANSWER:

(b) a summary of the information he/she gave you;

ANSWER:

(c) a summary of the information upon which the person based his/her information;

ANSWER:

(d) whether a record was ever made of the information and, if so, the name and address of the person presently having control or control of said record.

ANSWER:

10. Please produce with your answers to these Interrogatories a copy of each and every report and/or record which contains any criticism of the care and treatment rendered to decedent by this Defendant.

ANSWER:

11. Please itemize all medical expenses incurred by decedent's estate for all medical services rendered to decedent after he first presented himself to this Defendant, and by whom said amounts were paid.

ANSWERS:

12. Please indicate the total amount of expenses incurred for decedent's funeral.

ANSWER:

13. Prior to decedent's admission to Mer Cey Hospital on April 12, 1984, had decedent ever consulted any medical practitioner with regard to any medical problems? If so, as to each practitioner consulted, please state:

(a) his/her name, address and medical specialty;

ANSWER:

(b) each date on which decedent consulted him/her;

ANSWER:

(c) for each date listed in response to (b) above, the reason decedent consulted him/her;

ANSWER:

(d) the nature of the treatment given on each such date in response to (b) above.

ANSWER:

14. Prior to decedent's appearance at Mer Cey Hospital on April 12, 1984, had decedent ever been an inpatient and/or outpatient at any hospital, clinic or other medical facility? If so, please state as to each hospital, clinic or other medical facility:

(a) name and address of each;

ANSWER:

(b) inclusive dates of treatment, indicating inpatient or outpatient status;

ANSWER:

(c) reason(s) decedent was treated on each date listed in response to (b) above;

ANSWER:

15. Subsequent to decedent's death on May 20, 1985, have you or anyone else on decedent's behalf consulted any medical practitioners with regard to the specific cause of decedent's death? If so, for each practitioner consulted, please state:

(a) his/her name, address and specialty;

ANSWER:

269

(b) each date on which he/she was consulted;

ANSWER:

(c) a summary of the explanation and/or opinion given by each medical practitioner as to decedent's cause of death;

ANSWER:

(d) whether the opinion or explanation by each medical practitioner was written and, if so, who presently has custody or control of the written explanation or opinion.

ANSWER:

16. Please list each and every disease and/or illness which decedent suffered during his lifetime, including but not limited to cardiovascular disease, neurologic disorders and cephalic disorders.

ANSWER:

17. For each disease or illness listed in your response to the preceding Interrogatory, please state:

(a) its identity;

ANSWER:

(b) the approximate date it manifested itself;

ANSWER:

(c) the name, address and medical specialty of each and every physician or other medical person whom decedent consulted for such disease or illness;

ANSWER:

(d) describe any medication or treatment received by decedent for each disease or illness, indicating by whom it was prescribed and the inclusive dates between which decedent received it.

ANSWER:

18. Please list each and every occasion on which decedent suffered any trauma or blow to the head and, for each such instance, please state:

(a) the date and location where each such incident occurred;

ANSWER:

(b) the names and addresses of all witnesses to each such incident;

ANSWER:

(c) the name, address and medical specialty of each and every physician with whom decedent consulted following each such instance:

ANSWER:

(d) the nature of injury, disability, complaint or other reaction by decedent to each such incident;

ANSWER:

(e) a description of all medication and treatment received by decedent in response to each such incident, indicating by whom each was prescribed and the inclusive dates between which decedent received it;

ANSWER:

(f) a brief description of the incident in which decedent suffered head trauma or a blow to the head, including but not limited to a description of all instrumentalities involved therein.

ANSWER:

19. Regarding each employer from whom decendent worked during the ten years prior to his death, please state:

(a) the name and address of each employer;
ANSWER:

(b) the type of business in which each employer listed in answer to (a) above was engaged;
ANSWER:

(c) the inclusive dates of decedent's employment;
ANSWER:

(d) decedent's job title and description, indicating dates of promotion and new titles;
ANSWER:

(e) rate of renumeration at the time decedent left the employment of each.
ANSWER:

20. Please produce with the answer to these Interrogatories copies of federal and state income tax returns filed by decedent or on behalf of decedent for the years 1979 through 1985.
ANSWER:

21. In reference to the estate of the decedent, please state:

(a) the case number and county in which it was filed;
ANSWER:

(b) the date the administrator was appointed.

ANSWER:

22. Please identify by name, address, date of birth and relationship to decedent each individual who has a survivorship interest in the Estate of Gailen P. Patient.

ANSWER:

23. As to each individual listed in response to the above Interrogatory, please:

(a) define the manner in which decedent's death resulted in a "loss of society" to this individual, and state the dollar amount of that loss on a yearly basis;

ANSWER:

(b) define the manner in which decedent's death resulted in a "loss of services" to this individual, and state the dollar amount of that loss on a yearly basis;

ANSWER:

(c) define the manner in which the decedent's death resulted in a "loss of consortium" to this individual, and state the dollar amount of that loss on a yearly basis;

ANSWER:

(d) define the manner in which the decedent's death resulted in a "loss of companionship" to this individual, and state the dollar amount of this loss on a yearly basis.

ANSWER:

24. Had decedent or anyone on behalf of decedent ever made a claim against any other medical practitioner or hospital? If so, for each such claim, please state:

(a) the date and place it was made;

ANSWER:

(b) the name and address of each person or hospital against whom said claim was made;

ANSWER:

(c) the basis for each such claim;

ANSWER:

(d) the outcome of each such claim.

ANSWER:

25. State the name, present address and occupation of each person whom you will or may call as a lay witness at the trial or arbitration of this matter.

ANSWER:

26. With respect to all witnesses whom you will or may call as experts to give opinion testimony in the trial/arbitration of this matter, please state the following:

(a) name and address of said expert;

ANSWER:

(b) name and address of said expert's employer or the organization with which said expert is associated in any professional capacity;

ANSWER:

(c) the field in which said expert is to be offered as an expert;

ANSWER:

(d) a summary of said expert's qualifications within the field in which said expert is expected to testify.

ANSWER:

27. With respect to each such expert listed in your answer to the preceding Interrogatory, please state:

(a) the subject matter on which said expert is expected to testify;

ANSWER:

(b) the substance of the facts and opinions to which said expert is expected to testify:

ANSWER:

(c) a summary of the grounds upon which said expert bases such opinion;

ANSWER:

(d) whether said expert has submitted a written report concerning facts known or opinions held relative to this action;

ANSWER:

28. Please state the name and address of every person known to have witnessed the alleged incident at Mer Cey Hospital on or about April 23, 1984.

ANSWER:

29. Please state the name, address and occupation of each person known to you to have knowledge of any fact or record of any fact relating to this action.

ANSWER:

30. Please produce copies of any and all medical records, hospital records, medical reports and bills in the custody or control of you or your attorney for all treatment rendered to and hospitalization of decedent; or, in the alternative, please execute the attached authorization form so that this Defendant may obtain said records and reports.

ANSWER:

31. Pursuant to Rule 26(E) of the Ohio Rules of Civil Procedure, these Interrogatories shall be deemed continuing in character so as to require seasonable supplementation between the time Plaintiff's answers are served and the date of the commencement of the trial/arbitration of this action. Please state whether you agree to supplement said answers accordingly.

ANSWER:

By_____   LANE, ALTON & HORST
  Sue Dill Calloway   155 East Broad Street
  Attorney for Defendant,   Columbus, Ohio 43215
  Mer Cey Hospital Association Phone: (614) 228-6885

Certificate of Service

The undersigned hereby certifies that the original foregoing Interrogatories are being served upon Eugene L. Mad, Attorney for Plaintiff, 13 South Front Street, Columbus, Ohio, 43213; with a copy being served upon James S. Elephant, Attorney for Defendent Dr. Physician and Nurse Bean, 137 Broad Street, Columbus, Ohio, 43215, by ordinary United States mail, postage prepaid, on this 2nd day of July, 1985.

_____
Sue Dill Calloway

APPENDIX L

Demand for Production of Documents and Things for Inspection

In the Court of Common Pleas of Franklin County, Ohio

Alexis W. Lime, *et al.*, :

    Plaintiffs, :

vs. :   Case No 84CV-04-2184

River Methodist Hospital, :
  et al., :   Judge Britt

    Defendants :

Demand for Production of Documents and Things for Inspection

Pursuant to Rule 34 of the Ohio Rules of Civil Procedure, Defendant, River Methodist Hospital, demands that Plaintiff, Alexis W. Lime or his attorney produce for inspection by counsel for said Defendants not later than noon on February 14, 1985, at the offices of LANE, ALTON, & HORST, 155 East Broad Street, Columbus, Ohio 43215, or at such earlier date, time and place as may hereafter be agreed to between counsel for the parties, the following things:

1. Copies of any and all invoices or bills for medical examinations or treatment, prescriptions, or related expenses, comprising items of special damage which Plaintiff claims to have resulted from the incident described in his Complaint, which will be offered into evidence or for which special damages recovery will be sought at trial.

2. Copies of Plaintiff's federal, state or city income tax returns for 1979, 1980, 1981, 1982, 1983, 1984, and 1985.

3. Copies of any photographs showing or purporting to show any physical damage, injury or disability or the results thereof, claimed to have resulted to Plaintiff from the incident described in the Complaint, which Plaintiff intends to offer in evidence at the trial of this case.

4. Copies of all written reports from treating or examining physicians of Plaintiff for any injury or condition claimed to have resulted from the incident described in his Complaint, for which Plaintiff seeks recovery of damages from the Defendants.

5. Complete copies of all hospital records relating to examination or treatment of Plaintiff for any injury claimed received by him as a result of the incident described in his Complaint except the inpatient River Hospital records from November 12, 1984 and February 18, 1985.

6. Copies of any handwritten statements or transcripts of recorded statements of any agent, representative or employee of Defendant, River Methodist Hospital, (other than depositions) previously given to or in the possession of Plaintiff or his attorney or other representative (pursuant to Rule 26(b)(3), and particularly the sentence "a statement concerning the action or its subject matter previously given by the party seeking the statement...").

7. Copies of any and all paperwork submitted to the Ohio Bureau of Worker's Compensation by, or on behalf of, Plaintiff during the years 1979, 1980, 1981, 1982, 1983, 1984, and 1985.

The foregoing Demand for Production of the items specified is made separately as to each and every individual item and thing demanded to be produced.

LANE, ALTON & HORST
155 East Broad Street
Columbus, Ohio 43215

_____

John Alton

_____

Sue Dill Calloway
Attorney for Defendants,
River Methodist Hospital

Certificate of Service

I hereby certify that a copy of the foregoing was sent by regular U.S. Mail, postage prepaid to: Thomas L. High, Esq., Attorney for Plaintiffs, Two Riverside Plaza, 10th Floor, Columbus, Ohio 43215; Bradley LaHummel, Esq., Attorney for Defendant Nurse Jones, 311 East Broad Street, Columbus, Ohio 43215 and to Daniel J. Black, Esq., Attorney for Defendant Martin Kneeman, M.D., Suite 340, One Capitol South, 175 South Third Street, Columbus, Ohio 43215, this 4th day of December, 1984.

_____

Sue Dill Calloway

APPENDIX M

Case Example of Common Charting Errors

The purpose of this case example is to provide an illustration of common charting errors.

The medical record indicates that Ima Patient came to the emergency room at 1400 hours (2:00 p.m.) on September 6, 1984. She is a 20-year-old female who cut her right hand and arm severely at work today. She complains of pain of same. The notes also noted that the patient had a large amount of bleeding on her towel. Patient states she was unable to stop the bleeding initially. It says, "Patient appears pale and slightly diaphoretic," there is a slash in the notes, and then the emergency room nurse's initials followed by an entry that states "cut on" and there is a word which has been scratched out and is completely illegible.

Vital signs were taken at 2:10 p.m. and the blood pressure was recorded as 160/96 temperature 98.6 and respirations 18. The current medication was listed as coumadin and the patient was known to have no allergies. The last tetanus shot was given in 1974.

The physician then wrote that the patient had a laceration as above. She then charted that the wound was examined and sutured with 5-0 chromic (24 stitches) and 5-0 nylon (52 stitches). The patient had lacerated the arm while working on a meat slicer. The physician's diagnosis was "laceration." Orders and treatments included T.T. (tetanus toxoid) .5 cc I.M. and the application of a small sterile dressing.

The plaintiff is alleging that she developed an infection from inappropriate care in the emergency room. The emergency room nurse is being criticized, along with the emergency room physician, for inadequate charting. The nurse is unable to recall exactly where the laceration was or how long it was. The nurse also is unable to explain at what part of the hand or arm the patient was complaining of pain. The entry regarding the large amount of bleeding on the towel is not very descriptive. The entry regarding the inability to stop bleeding initially does not tell how long there was bleeding or what the estimated blood loss was.

The plaintiff also is alleging that she was treated inappropriately because she had a significant amount of blood loss, which was not picked up by the emergency room nurse or the physician. The patient testified as to the large amount of blood that she had lost, which may be due to the coumadin she was given. The patient was dismissed from the emergency room and was driven to her home approximately one mile away. As she was walking to the house, she became very nauseated and dizzy and passed out. The emergency squad came and took her to another hospital where she was admitted for forty-eight hours and given several units of blood.

The nurse also is criticized for failure to take a complete set of vitals pursuant to hospital policy. Nurse Nesman repeated the blood pressure because the first reading was high. She is unable to remember why she put a question mark beside the blood pressure reading of 160/96. The blood pressure subsequently was checked at some point in time and was found to be 90/60. Nurse Nesman cannot recall at what time this blood pressure was taken.

The plaintiff is alleging that she was too unstable too be dismissed. She also is saying that the nurse's failure to take vital signs pursuant to the hospital's policy resulted in her being dismissed in an unstable condition. She is alleging that, if the nurse had taken the pulse pursuant to hospital policy, she would have realized that it was a very rapid pulse rate. The rapid pulse rate, in addition to the blood pressure of 90/60, should have alerted the nurse that the patient was hypovolemic as a result of excessive blood loss due to the laceration.

The nurse testified that she soaked the arm for twenty minutes in a betadine solution. However, she failed to chart that this was done. She is attempting to testify that it is something that is commonly performed and that it does not need documentation. This does not go over well with the opposing counsel.

The nurse also has failed to document where the tetanus toxoid was given. She insists that it was given, although she failed to document this in the medical record.

The nurse is alleging that the patient developed an infection because she failed to follow her discharge instructions. The nurse indicates that, although it is not documented on the emergency room report, the patient was given discharge instructions. She specifically instructed the patient to look for any signs of redness, warmth, or purulent drainage. She instructed the patient to see the referral physician immediately if any of these signs occurred. The patient was given the name of a referral physician and told to have the stitches removed in seven days. The nurse did not write the referral physician's name on the chart and is unable to remember which physician she referred to.

The nurse also is criticized for making an obliteration in her triage notes.

TIME ENTERED	DATE	PATIENT'S NAME					PHONE NO.	ROOM NO.
1400	6/6/84	Ima Patient					222-8888	200

PATIENT'S ADDRESS	STREET	CITY	STATE	ZIP	STATUS	BIRTHDATE	AGE	INSURED SOCIAL SECURITY
12 Shot Street		Columbus,	OH	43222	(M) W S D	10/1/64	20	232-23-2323

EMPLOYER'S NAME	EMPLOYER'S ADDRESS	STREET	CITY	STATE	ZIP	PATIENT'S OCCUPATION
Rax Roast Meal	333 Chester Street		Columbus, OH	43000		Assistant Manager

EMPLOYER'S PHONE NO.	NEAREST RELATIVE (NOT SPOUSE) RELATIVE'S ADDRESS	RELATIVE'S PHONE NO.
888-8000	Jane Doe 20 Needle Dr. Columbus, OH 43111	898-9999

NAME OF INSURED	RELATIONSHIP TO PATIENT	PRIMARY INSURANCE	POLICY NO.	SECONDARY INSURANCE	POLICY NO.
Ima Patient	self	Blue Cross	232-23-2323	none	

MEDICARE NO.	INDUSTRIAL CLAIM NO.	PRIVATE PAY	DATE OF INJURY	INJURED AT WORK	BROUGHT BY	POLICE ATTENDED
none	none			✓	friend/ Shirley Ashton	

EMERGENCY	NON-EMERGENCY	NEW-INDUST. ACCIDENT	OLD-INDUST. ACCIDENT	HOME	AUTO	MISC.	EXPIRED IN ER	D.O.A.	NOTIFIED TIME	RELATIVE	POLICE	CORONER
X		X										

VALUABLES WITH PATIENT ☐ VALUABLES GIVEN TO FAMILY ☐ VALUABLES ENVELOPE #

FAMILY PHYSICIAN	REFERRAL PHYSICIAN
none	

TRIAGE: DESCRIPTION OF INJURY OR ILLNESS HISTORY

Cut Rt hand/arm severly @ work today. C/o's pain of same. Lg amt bleeding on towel. States unable to stop bleeding initially. Pt appears pale & slightly diaphoretic/ ERN Cut on ~~#~~

TIME	INITIALS	B/P	TEMP.	PULSE	RESP.	CURRENT MEDICATIONS
1410	SOC	160/96 90/60	98⁶		18	Coumadin

ALLERGIES	LAST TETANUS INJECTION	TRIAGE E.M.T. / RN SIGNATURE
NKDA's	1974	E. R. Nesman

PHYSICAL FINDINGS

Lac as above

Wound examined. Sutured c̄ 5-0 chromic x 24 and 5-0 Nylon x 52. Lacerated while working in meat slicer Neuro-status OK & good pulses.

DIAGNOSIS

Laceration

ORDERS AND TREATMENT

T.T. .5 cc Im

DSD

	X-RAY ORDERS			LAB ORDERS					
		INT	TIME		INT	TIME		INT	TIME
☐ CHEST PA & LAT.				☐ ELECTRO LYTES			☐ URINALYSIS		
☐ ABD. SERIES				☐ SMA-6			☐ EKG		
☐				☐ CCU			☐ ABG		
☐				☐ CBC			☐		
☐				☐			☐		
☐				☐			☐		

NO. OF SUTURES ▶		LACERATION LENGTH ▶	
IMPRINT IN THIS ▼ AREA ▼		No. 275879-5	

☐ DR. _____ HAS BEEN NOTIFIED @ _____ TIME   ☐ P.M. ☐ A.M.

CONDITION ON DISCHARGE (CIRCLE ONE)
FAIR   (STABLE)   IMPROVED   GUARDED   EXPIRED

DISPOSITION
ADMIT
(HOME)   MISC.

EMERGENCY PHYSICIANS SIGNATURE/PRIVATE PHYSICIANS SIGNATURE

Dr. Jane Fonda

NURSES SIGNATURE

E R Nesman

TIME DISCHARGE 20⁰⁰

EMERGENCY REPORT   HOSPITAL COLUMBUS, OHIO 43207

APPENDIX N

Case Study: Advising Patients Who Want to Sign Out
Against Medical Advice (A.M.A.)

A 54-year-old male came to the emergency room with complaints of severe sternal pressure and stabbing pain which started four hours prior to admission. The pain radiated down the right arm. The patient denied any shortness of breath but was slightly diaphoretic. The chest was clear bilaterally on auscultation. The pain was not affected by food. The patient complained of nausea but denied any vomiting or diarrhea.

The nurse placed the patient on a monitor which showed he had a normal sinus rhythm. Oxygen was applied at two liters per nasal cannula. The nurse related the history to the emergency room physician, who was with a critically ill patient and unable to leave. Lab tests, A.B.G.s, an E.K.G., and a keep-open I.V. of D_5W were ordered. The nurse went in to start the I.V. and found the patient had gotten off the cart and dressed. The patient stated that he was going to go home.

1. You are the emergency room nurse on duty. How should you respond?

2. What do you do if, after discussion with the patient, he maintains he feels better and wants to go home?

3. What do you do if the physician is unavailable?

4. Is there anything you can or should do that could help minimize potential liability exposure?

5. What should you discuss with the patient regarding insurance coverage?

6. What should you chart on the patient's medical record?

7. Should you and/or the physician talk to the patient's wife?

8. If the patient signs out A.M.A., should written discharge instructions be given?

9. Should an incident report ever be filled out for a patient who signs out A.M.A.?

An incident is any happening which is not consistent with the routine operation of the hospital or routine care of a particular patient. For each category mark as many items as are appropriate to adequately and completely describe the incident.

Hospital Attorney's Confidential Report of Incident (NOT PART OF MEDICAL RECORD)

100-64

James Patient Ama
146 John Doe Lane
Columbus, Ohio 43215

FLOOR	UNIT	INCIDENT DATE	REPORT DATE	INCIDENT TIME	SHIFT
ER		10-1-87	10-1-87	939 A.M. ___ P.M.	X 1st ___ 2nd ___ 3rd

PERSON INVOLVED	SEX	AGE	DIAGNOSIS
X 1 - Patient ☐ 2 - Visitor ☐ 3 - Employee ☐ 4 - Volunteer	☐ 1 - F X 2 - M	54	Chest pain-etiology UNKNOWN

No. 669909

For Patient Incidents: List Patient's Full Name or Use Addressograph Plate
For Employee and Visitor Incidents: List Full Name and Address

BRIEF DESCRIPTION OF INCIDENT; LIST WITNESSES: (Name, address, telephone - continue on reverse if necessary)

Pt. came in with complaints of chest pain which radiated down his right arm. Upon arrival the patient was immed. placed on a cart, his vitals (blood pressure et. al.) taken, and he was placed on a monitor. A brief history was obtained & into transmitted to the ER physician who was tied up with a critical pt. An EKG, lab & x-rays were ordered. As the R/V stepped into the room to start the IV the pt. had gotten dressed and stated he was feeling better. Pt. was advised that unless tests were done could not make a diagnosis. Both pt & wife advised of possibility without treatment. Pt signed out AMA

PRINT NAME AND PROFESSIONAL DESIGNATION OF PERSON COMPLETING REPORT
Pt also advised insur. may not cover bill if signed out AMA.
Nancy Headnurse RN

SUPERVISOR:

INCIDENT LOCATION

☐ 03 - CCU	☐ 21 - Laboratory	☐ 37 - Nursing-post partum	☐ 53 - Physical therapy	☐ 69 - Surgery
☐ 09 - Corridors	☐ 23 - Labor room (OB)	☐ 39 - Nursing-surgical	☐ 55 - Psychiatric unit	☐ 71 - Stairs
☐ 11 - Delivery room (OB)	☐ 24 - Laundry	☐ 41 - Occupational therapy	☐ 57 - Radiology	☐ 73 - Visitor's lounge
☐ 12 - Dietary	☐ 27 - Nuclear medicine	☐ 43 - Outpatient/clinics	☐ 59 - Recovery (Post-Anesthesia)	☐ 75 - Other ___
☐ 15 - Elevators	☐ 29 - Nursery	☐ 45 - Parking lots and sidewalks	☐ 61 - Respiratory therapy	
X 17 - Emergency room	☐ 31 - Nursing-medical	☐ 47 - Patient's bathroom	☐ 63 - Shower room/bathroom	
☐ 18 - ICU	☐ 33 - Nursing-orthopedic	☐ 49 - Patient's room	☐ 65 - Sitz bath	
☐ 19 - Extended care/geriatrics	☐ 35 - Nursing-pediatrics	☐ 51 - Pharmacy	☐ 67 - Special care unit	

PERSON MOST CLOSELY INVOLVED / SITE OF INJURY / CONDITION PRIOR TO INCIDENT

PERSON MOST CLOSELY INVOLVED			SITE OF INJURY		CONDITION PRIOR TO INCIDENT
☐ 04 - Aide/Orderly	☐ 20 - Pharmacist	☐ 32 - Resident	☐ 11 - Abdomen / ☐ 06 - Hand		X 00 - Alert
☐ 08 - Graduate Nurse	☐ 22 - Pharmacy Technician	☐ 34 - Respiratory Therapist	☐ 13 - Arm(s) / ☐ 01 - Head		☐ 01 - Agitated
☐ 10 - Intern	☐ 23 - Physical Therapy	☐ 36 - Student Nurse	☐ 07 - Back / ☐ 15 - Leg(s)		☐ 06 - Disoriented/confused
☐ 12 - I.V. Nurse	☐ 24 - Physician	☐ 38 - Technician/Technologist	☐ 14 - Buttocks / ☐ 05 - Neck		☐ 13 - Paralysis
☐ 14 - Licensed Practical Nurse	☐ 26 - Psychiatric Technician	☐ 39 - Volunteer	☐ 09 - Chest / ☐ 17 - None or NA		☐ 22 - Sedated
☐ 16 - Nurse Anesthetist (CRNA)	☐ 28 - Psychiatric Therapist	☐ 40 - Other - ___	☐ 03 - Face / ☐ 10 - Toe(s)		☐ 26 - Uncooperative
☐ 18 - Nurse and Pharmacist	X 30 - Registered Nurse		☐ 12 - Finger(s) / X 18 - Other -		☐ 29 - Weak/Faint/Dizzy
			☐ 08 - Foot / N/A		☐ 31 - Other -

INCIDENT TYPE - MEDICATION / INCIDENT TYPE - FALLS

INCIDENT TYPE - MEDICATION			INCIDENT TYPE - FALLS	
☐ 18 - Administered without order	☐ 30 - Medication theft/missing	☐ 44 - Wrong rate	☐ 01 - Ambulating/with permission	☐ 13 - Incontinent
☐ 20 - Adverse medication reaction	☐ 32 - Omission	☐ 46 - Wrong route	☐ 02 - Ambulating/without permission	☐ 17 - Lost Balance/Dizzy
☐ 22 - After discontinued	☐ 38 - Transfusion error	☐ 47 - Wrong site	☐ 03 - Bed-rails up/restrained	☐ 18 - Lowered side rail(s)
☐ 24 - Duplication	☐ 40 - Wrong dose	☐ 48 - Wrong time	☐ 04 - Bed-rails up/no restraints	☐ 19 - Refused restraints
☐ 26 - I.V. Infiltration	☐ 42 - Wrong medication	☐ 50 - Other - N/A	☐ 06 - Bed-rails down/restrained	☐ 21 - Refused side rails
☐ 28 - Medication on hold			☐ 08 - Bed-rails down/no restraints	☐ 23 - Removed restraint(s)
			☐ 05 - Call light not used	☐ 29 - Unable to follow instructions
☐ 02 - Analgesic	☐ 14 - Antihistamine	☐ 26 - Steroid	☐ 10 - Chair or equipment/restrained	☐ 33 - Violated activity order
☐ 04 - Antiarrhythmic	☐ 18 - Diuretic	☐ 28 - Unmedicated I.V. Solution	☐ 12 - Chair or equipment/no restraints	☐ 71 - Visitor assisted Pt. in ambulating
☐ 06 - Antibiotic	☐ 20 - Insulin	☐ 30 - Vasodilator	☐ 11 - Fainted	without staff assistance
☐ 08 - Anticoagulant	☐ 21 - Laxative	☐ 32 - Vasopressor	☐ 35 - Found on floor	☐ 81 - Other - ___
☐ 10 - Anticonvulsant	☐ 22 - Narcotic	☐ 34 - Other - ___	☐ 07 - Improper footwear	
☐ 12 - Antidepressant	☐ 24 - Sedative/Tranquilizer			

INCIDENT TYPE - OTHER

☐ 02 - Container contents not checked	☐ 44 - Patient not observed until medication (oral) was taken	☐ 52 - Assaults	☐ 86 - Patient escape
☐ 04 - Container improperly labeled	☐ 48 - Patient's allergies not checked	☐ 56 - Broken/malfunctioning equipment	☐ 87 - Smoking
☐ 06 - Container label not checked	☐ 50 - Patient's I.D. band not checked	☐ 58 - Caught In/On/Between	☐ 88 - Struck against
☐ 10 - Direct copy of physician's order not checked	☐ 58 - Route of administration not checked	☐ 60 - Contact with heat	☐ 90 - Struck by
☐ 14 - Blood crossmatching/typing	☐ 60 - Time lapse since last dosage not verified	☐ 62 - Diagnostic test at wrong time/sequence	☐ 92 - Surgery check list not completed
☐ 22 - Incorrect calculation of dosage	☐ 62 - Transcription error	☐ 64 - Needle stick	☐ 94 - Wrong diet
☐ 26 - IV not monitored	☐ 64 - Unclear order not reviewed with physician	☐ 66 - Fire	☐ 95 - Wrong treatment/diagnostic test
☐ 28 - Med. card not compared with unit med. profile/Kardex	☐ 66 - Unit med. profile/Kardex not checked frequently as reminder	☐ 71 - Consent	☐ 96 - Other - ___
☐ 30 - Med. cup not compared with med. card	☐ 68 - Unit med. profile/Kardex not compared with direct copy of physician's order	☐ 72 - Lost/damaged Pt./Visitor property	
☐ 34 - Med./IV placed in wrong location (shelf, unit dose tray, etc.)	☐ 72 - Wrong dosage or strength from pharmacy	☐ 74 - Lost specimens	**WAS PHYSICIAN NOTIFIED?**
☐ 40 - Patient drug profile not kept up-to-date and accurate on unit	☐ 74 - Wrong IV equipment used	☐ 76 - Missing instrument(s)	X YES ☐ NO
	☐ 76 - Wrong med. from pharmacy	☐ 78 - Missing needle(s)	**TIME NOTIFIED** ___ A.M.
	☐ 78 - Other - ___	☐ 80 - Missing sponge(s)	___ P.M.
		☐ 82 - Omitted diagnostic test	
		☐ 84 - Omitted treatment	

NATURE OF INJURY

☐ 01 - Abrasion	☐ 11 - Back	☐ 23 - Deceased	☐ 45 - Puncture	☐ 41 - No Apparent Injury
☐ 03 - Aggravation of pre-existing condition	☐ 15 - Broken tooth/teeth	☐ 25 - Fracture - Dislocation	☐ 47 - Sprain/strain	X 51 - Not Applicable
☐ 05 - Allergic Reaction	☐ 17 - Burns	☐ 27 - Head Injury	☐ 50 - X-Ray ordered	☐ 49 - Other - ___
	☐ 21 - Contusion	☐ 37 - Laceration		

PHYSICIAN'S STATEMENT
As above
Dr. Very Best

PRINT PHYSICIAN'S NAME
Dr. Very Best

HOSPITAL COPY - USE REVERSE SIDE IF NECESSARY

OHIC 10/80

285

☒ EMERGENCY ☐ NON-EMERGENCY	INDUSTRIAL ACCIDENT ☐ NEW ☐ OLD	ACCIDENT DATE	☐ HOME ☐ AUTO ☒ MISC.	☐ DOA ☐ EXPIRED IN E.R.	VALUABLES ENV. NO.	☐ WITH PATIENT ☐ GIVEN TO FAMILY	ALLERGIES: NKDA's	

| BROUGHT BY wife / Squad 14 | POLICE ATTENDED | NOTIFIED TIME ☐ RELATIVE ☐ POLICE ☐ CORONER | CURRENT MEDICATIONS ASA. gr X PO bid | | | | LAST TETANUS INJECTION N/A |

TRIAGE: DESCRIPTION OF INJURY OR ILLNESS

54 yo white ♂ amb. to ER c̄ c.c. of severe sternal pressure & stabbing pain which started 4 hrs PTA. Pain radiates down Rt arm. Denies SOB. Skin slightly diaphoretic. Pink fac. color. Bil radial & brachial pulses present. Chest clear on auscultation. Pain not effected by food. C/o's nausea. No vomiting or diarrhea. Placed on monitor = NSR. O₂ on @ 2 liters N/C 935 EKG notified. R.N. went in to start IV

TRIAGE E.M.T./R.N. SIGNATURE — Sue Will Calloway

PHYSICAL FINDINGS

and found pt. fully dressed - had removed hosp. gown stating he was feeling better & was leaving. ER dr. notified. Pt. informed of signs of ht. prob & informed a dx. could not be made unless tests performed. Informed if he signed out AMA he could die. Disc with wife who could not persuade pt. to stay. Signed out AMA being fully advised of signs & complications of signing out AMA.

ORDERS AND TREATMENT

931 Monitor = show NSR /SDC
931 O₂ 2 liters NIC /SDC
I.V. 500 cc's DₛW K.O. rate - pt. refused
Refused lab & ABG's & EKG /SDC

Signed out AMA

	TIME	INITIALS	B/P	TEMP.	PULSE	RESP.
	930	SDC	140/90	98⁶⁰	88	18

X-RAY ORDERS

	INT	TIME
☒ CHEST PA & LAT.		932 SDC
☐ ABD SERIES		

LAB ORDERS

	INT	TIME		INT	TIME
☐ ELECTROLYTES			☐ URINALYSIS		
☒ SMA-6	SDC		☒ EKG		932 SD
☒ CCU	930		☒ ABG		
☒ CBC			☐		

NO. OF SUTURES ▶ _____   LACERATION LENGTH ▶ _____

DIAGNOSIS Chest Pain, etiology unknown

☐ ADMIT _____   ☒ HOME AMA   ☐ MISC

EMERGENCY PHYSICIAN'S SIGNATURE	NURSE'S SIGNATURE Sue Will Calloway RN, CEN.	CONDITION ON DISCHARGE

☐ DR. _____ HAS BEEN NOTIFIED @ _____ TIME ☐ A.M. ☐ P.M.

CONDITION ON DISCHARGE: ☐ FAIR   ☐ STABLE   ☐ IMPROVED   ☒ GUARDED

PATIENT (LAST/FIRST/INT./MAIDEN) James Potient Ama	SPOUSE Sue	ADMISSION DATE 10-1-87	HOUR 930	ROOM NO. 1	HOSPITAL NO. 100-64

ADDRESS (STREET OR ROUTE) 146 John Doe Lane	PATIENT PHONE 459-1240	DISCHARGE DATE 10-1-87	HOUR 939	PATIENT'S SOC. SEC. NO. 297-54-2115

CITY Columbus, Ohio	STATE	ZIP 43215	SEX M	BIRTH DATE 1-27-33	AGE 54	MARITAL STATUS M	RELIGION 1	OCCUPATION Locksmith

PATIENT'S EMPLOYER Zero Locks	ADDRESS 146 Mercy Drive Col, Oh 43215	ZIP	PHONE 459-2010

FAMILY DOCTOR None	REFERRAL DOCTOR	E.R. DOCTOR Dr. Best

NEAREST RELATIVE (NOT SPOUSE) Brother, Left Ama 14 Anywhere St. Col. Ohio 43215	PHONE 459-2010	REG. TAKEN BY RCX

INSURANCE	F.C.	NAME OF INSURANCE CO. Blue Crosspers Insur.	POLICY/CLAIM NO. 146-54-2115
	F.C.	NAME OF INSURANCE CO.	POLICY/CLAIM NO.
	F.C.	NAME OF INSURANCE CO.	POLICY/CLAIM NO.

REV. 5-86   CHART COPY

1. *You are the emergency room nurse on duty. How should you respond?*

First, ask the patient why he wants to leave. This may help to establish a good interpersonal relationship between the patient and practitioner. In this case, the patient has no complaints about the care rendered so far. He indicates he feels much better and would like to go home.

2. *What do you do if, after discussion with the patient, he maintains he feels better and wants to go home?*

You ask the patient to wait a minute while you leave the room to discuss the situation with the physician. The physician is tending to another critically ill patient and is unable to leave. He advises you to do whatever you feel is appropriate.

3. *What do you do if the physician is unavailable?*

You return to the room, keeping in mind that an alert and oriented patient has the right to refuse treatment. However, you recall the emerging theory that the decision to refuse treatment must be an educated decision based on all the applicable and pertinent information. Since the physician is not available to disclose the risks of nontreatment, you, as an employee and representative of the hospital, are concerned about the potential for liability.

4. *Is there anything you can or should do that could help minimize potential liability exposure?*

Since the physician is not available and has not seen the patient, you could explain that without further examination and testing, a diagnosis cannot be made. You explain to the patient that he has symptoms which could be caused from a multitude of different conditions including, but not limited to, heart attack or heart disease. Without treatment there is always a possibility of death or damage to one of the body's organs. The patient indicates he is willing to accept those risks.

5. *What should you discuss with the patient regarding insurance coverage?*

As a general proposition, many insurance companies will not pay the hospital bill if the patient has signed out A.M.A. You have no way of knowing if the patient's insurance company will pay, and should inform the patient that he may be personally responsible for the bill if he signs out A.M.A. This has deterred many patients from leaving.

6. *What should you chart on the patient's medical record?*

It is important to note that a patient may refuse *part* of a recommended regimen of treatment. For example, a patient with chest pain agrees to having lab tests, a chest x-ray, E.K.G. and I.V. insertion but refuses to allow A.B.G.s to be drawn. After you explain the importance of blood gas analysis, the patient's refusal of the test should be noted in the medical record, along with the risks of nontreatment which were explained to the patient. Some physicians prefer that the patient sign the entry.

7. *Should you and/or the physician talk to the patient's wife?*

In this case, the nurse requested that the emergency room physician talk to the patient. However, the physician was attending to a young multiple-trauma patient and could not leave. The nurse evaluated the situation and explained to the patient that she would go to the waiting room and bring back his wife. The nurse decided to discuss the matter with the patient's wife. The wife was very concerned and talked with her husband. (Many times family members are helpful at persuading patients to accept recommended treatment.) Unfortunately, she was unable to convince him to stay.

8. *If the patient signs out A.M.A., should written discharge instructions be given?*

Generally, for "P.R." reasons, it is advisable to provide written discharge instructions even if the patient signs out A.M.A. For example, a patient has a 5-centimeter laceration of the frontal area that needs sutures. The emergency room physician also recommends admission for a possible concussion. The patient refuses all treatment. You should still write down wound care and head injury instructions according to the acceptable standard of care and protocol. The patient can also be informed that if he changes his mind he can return for the recommended treatment.

9. *Should an incident report ever be filled out for a patient who signs out A.M.A.?*

Every nurse should be familiar with her institution's policy on incident reports. Generally, an incident report is not filled out for patients who sign out A.M.A. However, if there is sensitive or additional information that is not appropriate for the E.R. record, you can complete an incident report. If an incident report is completed, you should *not* chart this fact in the E.R. report. It is generally felt that a plaintiff's attorney cannot subpoena what he or she does not know exists.

APPENDIX O

Glossary of Legal Terms

Abandonment — The unilateral termination of a professional relationship without the patient's consent and without making arrangements for appropriate follow-up care.

Abuse of process — A civil action for damages that alleges the legal process has not been used in a manner contemplated by law.

Action — A lawsuit. To begin a lawsuit someone must "bring an action" or "file suit." The "cause of action" is the legal complaint the person has against the other, like trespass, breach of a contract, or malpractice.

Administrative agency — A branch of government that administers or carries out legislation; for example, the Worker's Compensation Commission.

Admissibility of evidence — Evidence that is trustworthy and meets the legal rules of evidence so that it will be admitted into court.

Affidavit — A sworn statement that is usually written.

Affirmative defense — This is used in an answer to plead facts that do not deny the behavior but seek to excuse it. The statute of limitation and the good Samaritan statute are two examples.

Agency — A relationship between parties where one is authorized to act on the other's behalf.

Allegation — A statement made that a person expects to later prove.

Amicus curiae — A Latin word which means "friend of the court." A brief filed in a lawsuit by someone other than the parties who has a stake or interest in the suit. For example, a nurse is sued by a plaintiff for violating the Nurse Practice Act; the American Nurses' Association files a brief.

Answer — When the defendant receives a complaint, a response must be filed. This is written by an attorney and usually denies the plaintiff's allegations.

Appeal — Request to a higher court to review and change the decision of a lower court. The party who brings the appeal in a case is called the appellant.

Arbitration —A nonjudicial procedure to settle a disagreement. There are binding and nonbinding arbitrations. In binding arbitration, the parties agree in advance that the decision of the arbitrators will be final.

Assault — Placing another in well-founded fear or apprehension of immediate bodily harm.

Assignment — Transferring one's rights or property to another.

Assumption of risk — A legal doctrine which does not allow a plaintiff to win a lawsuit when a known or understood risk was ignored.

Attachment — A legal remedy to entitle one to seize defendant's property to satisfy a judgment.

Attestation — A signature by a witness that the documents required have been signed.

Battery — An unconsented touching.

Best evidence rule — The legal doctrine requiring that primary evidence (such as the original document) be introduced, or at least explained before a copy can be introduced.

Bona fide — This means in good faith, honestly, openly, and without knowledge of fraud.

Bill of Rights — Generally, this refers to the first ten amendments to the U.S. Constitution. These amendments establish a series of personal rights, such as freedom of speech and religion.

Borrowed-servant doctrine — Applied when an employee is temporarily under the control of another. This doctrine states that a person who "borrows" the use of another's employee is legally responsible for that employee's actions.

Captain-of-the-ship doctrine — Doctrine in which the physician, as "captain," is held liable for the actions of all members of the health care team. It is an expansion of the borrowed-servant doctrine. This doctrine has, for the most part, been discarded. It was once used to say that the surgeon was the captain of the operating room. As such, the surgeon was responsible for all the negligent acts of the nurses.

Charitable immunity — A legal doctrine which states that a charity organization, such as a school or hospital, cannot be sued for negligence. This doctrine thrived in the 1940's and 1950's. It has been eliminated in most states.

Civil law — The law of a state or nation regulating ordinary private matters. It is to be contrasted to criminal law.

Common law — A "judge-made" law. Common law is the legal tradition of England and the United States where part of the law is developed through court decisions.

Comparative negligence — Doctrine by which the negligence of the parties is compared and recovery permitted when the negligence of the plaintiff is less than that of the defendant. There are several slight variations of comparative negligence. See "contributory negligence."

Concurring opinion — An opinion written by a judge when the judge agrees with the result, but for different reasons.

Consent — A voluntary act in which a person agrees to allow another to do something. Consent also should be in writing.

Contribution — When two or more persons are equally liable for the plaintiff's injury. When one has paid the judgment, the payer may make a demand on the remaining persons to contribute their share.

Counterclaim — A suit filed by the defendant against the plaintiff in response to the plaintiff's suit.

Contributory negligence — A principle in which the plaintiff was unable to recover any damages if he or she contributed to the damage in any way, no matter how minute. Many states felt that contributory negligence was a harsh principle and have adopted comparative negligence.

Criminal law — The division of law dealing with crime and punishment, such as murder and larceny.

Damages — The money award granted by the court to the plaintiff. There are three types of damages. Compensatory damages are meant to reimburse the plaintiff for any losses due to the injury, including lost wages and medical expenses. Nominal damages are usually small amounts (like $5) to show that a law has been violated but that little or no harm was done. Punitive damages are awarded when the defendant has acted maliciously or in reckless disregard of the plaintiff's rights. They are meant to punish the defendant.

Decedent — A deceased person.

Defamation — A written or spoken communication that is untrue and injures the good name or reputation of another. There are two forms of defamation. Libel is the written material and slander is the spoken representation that injures a person's reputation.

Defendant — The person against whom a lawsuit is brought. When the patient sues the nurse for negligence, the nurse is called the "defendant" and the patient the "plaintiff."

Default judgment — A judgment rendered against the defendant because of the defendant's failure to answer the plaintiff's complaint. The nurse should always notify her employer, hospital risk manager, attorney, or insurance company immediately upon receiving a complaint. The nurse's attorney must then file an answer to prevent a default judgment from being rendered.

Deposition — A witness' sworn statement that is made out of court. It may later be admitted into evidence if the witness is unable to attend in person.

Directed verdict — The verdict returned by a jury when the judge directs the jury to return a verdict in favor of one party because the evidence or law is so clearly in favor of one party. It now becomes pointless for the trial to proceed any further.

Discovery — Pretrial activities of an attorney to find out information about the case. The purpose of discovery is to allow each party to learn what the other side will present in the event the case goes to trial.

Dissenting opinion — Judges who disagree with the majority may write dissenting opinions.

Dismiss — To discharge a case any time prior to trial. A judge may dismiss the case if the plaintiff cannot show in the complaint that he/she is entitled to any relief.

Due process — Requirements for an honest, fair, and orderly legal proceeding for the purpose of protecting an individual's rights. The concept of due process requires that before a person is deprived of any rights or property by the state, a notice and a hearing must be given. This allows the person an opportunity to appear and vindicate his/her rights before a fair and impartial tribunal.

Duress — The compelling of a person to do something that he/she might not otherwise do voluntarily. Consent obtained by duress or fraud is not legally valid.

Duty — An obligation created either by statute, contract, or voluntarily. This creates rights on behalf of the performing party. The nurse has a legal duty to all patients to follow the prerequisite standard of care.

Emancipation — Termination of parental control over a minor and parental duty to support the minor. Some states have a statute which allows the emancipated minor to consent for any medical and surgical treatment.

Emergency — A sudden, unexpected occurrence which can cause threat to life or limb. The Emergency Doctrine is a form of implied consent when a person's life or limb is in imminent danger and the person is unable to consent to treatment; the law implies consent to emergency treatment and assumes that the person would consent if otherwise able.

Employee — One who works for another in return for pay.

Employer — A person, firm, or corporation that selects employees, pays their wages, salaries, or commissions, retains the power of termination, and can control their acts during hours of employment.

Expert witness — One who has special training, experience, skill, and knowledge in a relevant area and who is allowed to offer an opinion, based on that training and experience, in court.

False imprisonment — The intentional and unjustified detention of a person against his/her will for any length of time and whereby the person is aware of the deprivation of his/her liberty. Locking a patient in his/her room can be false imprisonment. Not all restraint against a patient's will is false imprisonment. If a restraint is necessary to prevent the patient from injury, then the restraint is reasonable and is not considered false imprisonment.

Federal question — A legal question involving the U.S. Constitution as a statute enacted by Congress.

Federal Tort Claims Act — A statute that allows the federal government to be sued for the negligence of its employees. Before enactment, the government could not be sued because of the doctrine of governmental immunity. Nurses who are in the services can be sued only under the Federal Tort Claims Act.

Felony — A crime of serious nature which is usually punishable by death or imprisonment over one year. Murder, burglary, and arson are examples of felony offenses.

Fornication — Sexual intercourse between two unmarried persons. It is still unlawful in some states.

Fraud — Intentionally misleading another person so as to cause legal injury to the person.

Good Samaritan law — A legal doctrine designed to protect those who stop to render aid in an emergency. Every state has a good Samaritan law to encourage nurses to render emergency care.

Grand jury — A jury called to determine whether, in criminal cases, there is enough evidence to justify bringing the case to court. It is not the jury that hears the case and determines the defendant's guilt or innocence.

Guilty — A term used in criminal law where there is a finding beyond reasonable doubt. The defendant is then charged with committing the crime.

Guardian ad litem — One who is appointed by the court to manage the affairs of one who is judged incompetent. A *guardian ad litem* is sometimes appointed when a patient's life is in imminent danger and treatment is refused.

Gross negligence — The intentional failure to perform a duty in reckless disregard of the consequences.

Hearsay — A rule of evidence that restricts the admissibility of evidence that is not the personal knowledge of the witness. An out-of-court statement cannot be used to prove the truth of the matter except under certain limited exceptions.

Holographic will — A will handwritten by the testator.

Informed consent — The agreement to treatment made by the patient or patient's representative concerning medical or surgical treatment. Knowledge of the nature of the treatment, risks, and available alternatives demonstrates the consent was informed.

Immunity — In civil law, the protection given certain individuals or groups that render them free from liability. Immunity does not mean freedom from being sued. The individual can be sued. Immunity is raised as an affirmative defense.

In loco parentis — A Latin term meaning "in the place of a parent." For example, a parent may sign a form to allow school authorities to consent to the treatment of his/her children. Here the school is said to act *in loco parentis*. The court will sometimes assign a person to stand in the place of a minor's parents.

Indemnity — Legal doctrine aimed at "making someone whole." If a person has to pay a judgment due to another's negligence, that person generally possesses the right to indemnity. This means he/she can collect the amount paid from the wrongdoer.

Incompetency — The inability of a person to manage his/her own affairs because of mental or physical infirmities. Often, a guardian will be appointed to manage the person's affairs.

Independent contractor — One who agrees to undertake work without being under the direct control or direction of an employer.

Injunction — A court order requiring one to actively do something or forego from a specific activity.

Interrogatories — A written set of questions which are sent from one party to another involved in a lawsuit. The purpose of Interrogatories is to discover what is known to the other party. Interrogatories are a discovery device.

Invasion of privacy — The violation of another person's right to be left alone and free from unwarranted publicity and intrusions.

Joint and several liability — Several persons who share the liability for the plaintiff's injury. They can be found liable individually or as a group.

Judge — An officer of a court of law who hears and determines the case. The judge is responsible for guiding the court proceedings to ensure impartiality and to enforce the rules of evidence.

Judgment — The decision of the court regarding the case before it.

Jury — A certain number of people who are selected to hear the case. The jurors are sworn to hear the evidence and decide issues of fact.

Jurisprudence — The science of law upon which a particular legal system is built.

Liability — A finding in civil cases that the preponderance of the evidence shows that the defendant was responsible for the plaintiff's injuries.

Liability insurance — A contract between the nurse and the insurance company in which the insurance company (called the insurer) agrees to pay for any judgments rendered against the nurse (the insured) for any covered losses.

Libel — See "defamation."

Litigants — The parties who are involved in a lawsuit.

Loss of consortium — An element of damages sought by the spouse of an injured party for the loss of conjugal relations because of the spouse's injury.

Malpractice — Professional misconduct due to failure to meet the standard of care which results in injury to another.

Majority, age of — The age at which a child is considered to have become an adult.

Malfeasance — The performance of a wrongful or unlawful act. It is malfeasance for a nurse to perform surgery since it's outside the realm of the nurse's responsibilities.

Malicious prosecution — A suit to collect damages that have resulted from a civil suit filed maliciously and without cause.

Misdemeanor — An unlawful act that is not as serious as a felony. Usually, it is punishable by a fine or imprisonment for less than one year. Driving without a license is a misdemeanor offense.

Negligence — That conduct which falls below the acceptable standard of care that has been set in order to avoid an unreasonable risk of great harm. Negligence is carelessness.

Negligence per se — A finding of negligence that is made by showing that a statute was violated. For example, if a nurse injures someone by acting beyond the scope of his/her license, this statutory violation constitutes negligence per se.

Next of kin — Those persons who by the law of descent would be the closest blood relatives of the decedent.

Non compos mentis — A Latin term meaning the person is not of sound mind.

Nonfeasance — The failure to perform a legally required duty. For example, the nurse notes that his/her patient is attempting to commit suicide and stands by doing nothing.

Notary public — A public official who administers oaths and certifies the validity of documents.

Omission — Neglecting to fulfill a duty that one is required by law to fulfill. The nurse is required to administer medications to the patient that are prescribed by the physician. If the nurse fails to do this, he/she is guilty of a nursing omission.

Opinion — One judge will write the decision of the court, which is called the opinion.

Ordinance — A law passed by a municipal legislative body. For example Columbus, Ohio, has a number of city ordinances which are laws governing the society within their jurisdiction.

Perjury — The willful act of giving false testimony under oath.

Plaintiff — See "defendant."

Police power — The power of the state or federal government to protect the health, safety, morals, and general welfare of its citizens.

Precedent — A court will try to follow principles used in previous decisions where the facts raise similar issues. Lower courts are bound to follow the law generated by the higher court.

Privileged communication — A statement to an attorney, physician, spouse or priest. Because of the confidential nature of the information, the law protects its disclosure even in court.

Probate — The judicial proceeding that determines existence and validity of a will.

Proprietary hospital — A private hospital that is operated for profit.

Proximate — In negligence actions against the nurse, the alleged act must be the direct cause of the patient's injury.

Real evidence — Tangible evidence, such as bullets and weapons.

Rebuttal — When the other side is given an opportunity to contradict his/her evidence.

Release — A statement signed by a person relinquishing a right or claim against another.

Res ipsa loquitur — A Latin term for "the thing speaks for itself." In negligence actions, the doctrine of *res ipsa loquitur* is invoked when the plaintiff has no direct evidence, but the injury itself leads to the inference it would not have occurred in the absence of a negligent act. To invoke the doctrine of *res ipsa loquitur*, the plaintiff must show that the instrument causing the injury was under the sole control of the defendant and that the plaintiff did not contribute to the injury. By using this doctrine, the plaintiff need not prove the elements of negligence. The burden shifts to the defendant to prove there was no negligence.

Respondeat superior — A Latin term which means "let the master answer." Under this doctrine, the employer is responsible for the acts of negligence created by the employees when they are acting within the scope of their responsibilities. For example, the hospital is liable for the negligent acts of the nurse it employs.

Service of process — The delivery of the complaint to the defendant, giving the defendant notice of the suit. Service of process is usually obtained by certified mail or personal service by a sheriff.

Standard of care — An important concept that every nurse should know. Acts performed that an ordinary, prudent nurse would have performed under the same or similar circumstances.

Stare decisis — A legal principle in which courts should follow previous decisions in subsequent cases where similar facts and legal issues are present.

State statute — The legislature passed a law which is called a statute.

Settlement — An agreement made between the parties before a court judgment is made.

Slander — See "defamation."

Statute of limitation — The time period in which a lawsuit may be filed.

Subpoena — A court document requiring the person named to appear in court to give testimony.

Subpoena *duces tecum* — A court document requiring that the papers named be brought to court.

Summary Judgment — A judgment rendered by a judge when a party is entitled to judgment according to law and in which there are no material facts in dispute.

Summons — A legal document that is delivered with the answer. This requires the person named as defendant to appear in court or suffer a default judgment.

Testimony — The oral statement of a witness under oath.

Tort — A civil wrong. Torts include negligence, false imprisonment, and assault and battery.

Tortfeasor — One who commits a tort.

Vicarious liability — One who is held responsible for the liability of another.

Wrongful death statute — A statute that provides that the death of an individual can give rise to a cause of action by that individual's beneficiaries. Before these statutes were passed, suit could only be brought if the individual had survived the injury.

APPENDIX P

Case Example: Emergency Room Patient

The Plaintiff's Allegations

The plaintiff, Ima Patient, is a white female. She was 33 years old and pregnant at the time of the auto accident, January 13, 1985. While driving west on Dubay Street, she was struck from behind by another automobile. The plaintiff was wearing a seat belt at the time of collision. She experienced some abdominal pain and was transferred by squad to St. Ant's Medical Center, an affiliate of St. Ant's South.

At the time of the accident she had been returning from her family doctor's office for evaluation of vaginal discharge and to have a pregnancy test run. Her doctor did not want to treat her for the vaginal discharge unless the culture showed anything and until the pregnancy test was completed.

She was released from St. Ant's Medical Center with discharge instructions to follow up with her family doctor in five (5) days. She had appropriately called and made an appointment with her family doctor. She was also instructed to return if the pain got any worse. Since her pain remained the same, she did not return to the emergency room at St. Ant's Medical Center.

On the date in question, January 15, 1985, Ima Patient was feeling weak and dizzy. She had been experiencing heavy vaginal bleeding since the evening of her auto accident on January 13. While descending stairs in her home on January 15, the dizziness caused her to miss the last step and fall. Her sister, who was staying with her, called an ambulance squad who then took her to St. Ant's South. The squad would not take her to St. Ant's Medical Center, where she had been treated previously, because St. Ant's South was closer.

Upon arrival, the plaintiff states she was taken directly to an examination room. About 1/2 hour later, a nurse came in and checked her blood pressure and quickly asked her a few questions, stating "they were really busy" and she would be back later.

The doctor came in and conducted a full physical examination. He then ordered the following tests: abdominal series, SMA-6, CBC, urinalysis, E.K.G., and arterial blood gases.

The plaintiff is alleging negligence in her care and treatment. Plaintiff is alleging that her weakness and dizziness resulted from hypovolemia as a result of profuse vaginal bleeding. She is also alleging negligence in prescribing Septra Ds and doing X-rays, since she was pregnant. She sustained a severe allergic reaction from the Septra Ds and alleges that they were improperly prescribed since she is allergic to sulfa, which is contained in Septra Ds.

Plaintiff alleges that her fetus was stillborn because:

1. She sustained an allergic reaction as a result of incorrectly prescribed medicine.

2. The X-rays were negligently prescribed and contraindicated.

3. Her hypovolemia was not corrected or recognized, which caused damage to the fetus.

4. The physician was negligent in her care and treatment and no discharge instructions were provided.

The *nurse's defense* is that the patient would have aborted regardless of any treatment or mistreatment.

The nurse is criticized and her credibility is diminished by the plaintiff for the following:

1. Administering a dose of Septra Ds when the chart clearly indicated that the patient was allergic to sulfa.

2. Inadequate documentation of a patient with abdominal pain. The nurse failed to ask questions established as a standard of care by the National Emergency Nurses' Association and her own hospital.

3. Incorrect spelling of "aspirin."

4. Use of inappropriate abbreviations and obliteration of the charting.

5. Failure to recognize the classic sign of hypovolemia; this falls below the standard of care.

☒ EMERGENCY	INDUSTRIAL ACCIDENT	ACCIDENT DATE	☐ HOME	☐ DOA	VALUABLES	☐ WITH PATIENT	ALLERGIES:
☐ NON-EMERGENCY	☐ NEW ☐ OLD		☐ AUTO ☐ MISC.	☐ EXPIRED IN E.R.	ENV. NO.	☐ GIVEN TO FAMILY	Sulfa

BROUGHT BY	POLICE ATTENDED	NOTIFIED TIME	☐ RELATIVE ☐ POLICE ☐ CORONER	CURRENT MEDICATIONS	LAST TETANUS INJECTION
Amb				Asperin	

TRIAGE: DESCRIPTION OF INJURY OR ILLNESS

C/o's abd pain x2 days. ☒ N-V-D-V-Seen in ER 2 days ago. Skin W/D ⊕ vag bleeding

TRIAGE E.M.T./R.N. SIGNATURE   Jenny Ready, RN

PHYSICAL FINDINGS _(handwritten, illegible)_

ORDERS AND TREATMENT _(handwritten, partly illegible)_

Rx Septra DS #now

	TIME	INITIALS	B/P	TEMP.	PULSE	RESP.
	15³⁰	JR	98/60		98	30
			90/58		120	34

X-RAY ORDERS

	INT	TIME			INT	TIME			INT	TIME
☐ CHEST PA & LAT.			☐ ELECTRO LYTES				☒ URIN-ALYSIS			
☒ ABD SERIES	M	154	☒ SMA-6	MC	154		☒ EKG	JR		15¹⁸
☐			☐ CCU				☒ ABG			
☐			☒ CBC	JC	154⁸		☐			

LAB ORDERS

NO. OF SUTURES ►	LACERATION LENGTH ►

DIAGNOSIS Abd pain, unknown etiology

☐ ADMIT _____   ☒ HOME   ☐ MISC

EMERGENCY PHYSICIAN'S SIGNATURE: Dr. Jeckel   NURSE'S SIGNATURE: Jenny Ready, RN

☐ DR. _____ HAS BEEN NOTIFIED @ _____ TIME ☐ A.M. ☐ P.M.

CONDITION ON DISCHARGE

☐ FAIR   ☐ IMPROVED
☒ STABLE   ☐ GUARDED

PATIENT (LAST/FIRST/INT./MAIDEN)	SPOUSE	ADMISSION DATE	HOUR	ROOM NO.	HOSPITAL NO.
Patient Ima	Ralph	1-15-85	14⁴⁸	ER 10	

ADDRESS (STREET OR ROUTE)	PATIENT PHONE	DISCHARGE DATE	HOUR	PATIENT'S SOC. SEC. NO.
5049 Reed Rd	459-1240	1-15-85		297-54-2115

CITY	STATE	ZIP	SEX	BIRTH DATE	AGE	MARITAL STATUS	RELIGION	OCCUPATION
Columbus	Ohio	43220	F	12-17-54	33	M	Cath	

PATIENT'S EMPLOYER	ADDRESS	ZIP	PHONE
J+J			

FAMILY DOCTOR	REFERRAL DOCTOR	E.R. DOCTOR
Dr. Wm Wells		Dr. Jeckel

NEAREST RELATIVE (NOT SPOUSE)	PHONE	REG. TAKEN BY
Geraldine Patient (mother in law)	522-3446	JRC

I N S U R A N C E	F.C.	NAME OF INSURANCE CO.	POLICY/CLAIM NO.
		Blue Cross + Blue Shield	297-54-2115-32
	F.C.	NAME OF INSURANCE CO.	POLICY/CLAIM NO.
	F.C.	NAME OF INSURANCE CO.	POLICY/CLAIM NO.

REV. 5-86   299   CHART COPY

EXHIBIT 2
Emergency Department Standard of Care: Abdominal Pain

ABDOMINAL PAIN

ASSESSMENT (TRIAGE)	DETERMINE PRIORITIES OF CARE	ACTIONS
1. Initial Observation Color of skin State of Nourishment (obese, etc) Abd. swelling ? Acute distress? Nausea/vomiting? 2. Subjective (from pt., family, EMS personnel) A. History Pain–nature, duration, site, intensity, character, aggravating or relieving factors N/V–frequency, duration, description of emesis Diarrhea/constipation–frequency, color/duration aggravating or relieving factors Trauma?–nature, site, object if one Difficulty breathing or swallowing Weight gain or loss If female–LMP & pregnancy history Sexual related symptoms B. Medications C. Allergies D. Previous History E. Treatment prior to arrival 3. Objective Vital signs Level of consciousness Skin–dry, diaphoretic, etc. Color–pale, cyanotic, etc. Outer assessment of patient Total body systems assessment	1. Airway and breathing 2. Maintain circulation & cardiac status 3. Prevent further deterioration of patient 4. Total body systems assessment 5. Relief of pain and/or nausea & vomiting	1. In conjunction with M.D.: A. Obtain initial diagnostic data Laboratory CBC, Lytes, SMA–12, Amylase, Pt,Ptt If indicated–T/C, pregnancy If female–pelvic exam G/C, C/S, gram stain, etc.– if indicated Xrays Abdomen & chest EKG & ABG if indicated B. If indicated Monitor IV Oxygen Nasal/gastric tube insert Foley catheter C. Maintain adequate fluid & lyte balance D. Establish & maintain adequate blood volume E. Prevent complications Sterile technique Administer ordered antibiotics Wear gloves with fluid and body wastes F. Provide psychosocial support 2. Documentation Nursing notes if needed 3. Disposition Admission for observation Admission for surgery Referral Teaching intervention pt./family

300

INDEX

302